D0825011

Managing the Human Factor in Information Security

Managing the Human Factor in Information Security

How to win over staff and influence business managers

David Lacey

A John Wiley and Sons, Ltd., Publication

Copyright © 2009   John Wiley & Sons Ltd, The Atrium, Southern Gate, Chichester,
West Sussex PO19 8SQ, England
Telephone (+44) 1243 779777

Email (for orders and customer service enquiries): cs-books@wiley.co.uk
Visit our Home Page on www.wileyeurope.com or www.wiley.com

All Rights Reserved. No part of this publication may be reproduced, stored in a retrieval system
or transmitted in any form or by any means, electronic, mechanical, photocopying, recording,
scanning or otherwise, except under the terms of the Copyright, Designs and Patents Act 1988
or under the terms of a licence issued by the Copyright Licensing Agency Ltd, 90 Tottenham
Court Road, London W1T 4LP, UK, without the permission in writing of the Publisher.
Requests to the Publisher should be addressed to the Permissions Department, John Wiley &
Sons Ltd, The Atrium, Southern Gate, Chichester, West Sussex PO19 8SQ, England, or emailed
to permreq@wiley.co.uk, or faxed to (+44) 1243 770620.

Designations used by companies to distinguish their products are often claimed as trademarks.
All brand names and product names used in this book are trade names, service marks,
trademarks or registered trademarks of their respective owners. The Publisher is not associated
with any product or vendor mentioned in this book.

This publication is designed to provide accurate and authoritative information in regard to the
subject matter covered. It is sold on the understanding that the Publisher is not engaged in
rendering professional services. If professional advice or other expert assistance is required, the
services of a competent professional should be sought.

Other Wiley Editorial Offices

John Wiley & Sons Inc., 111 River Street, Hoboken, NJ 07030, USA

Jossey-Bass, 989 Market Street, San Francisco, CA 94103-1741, USA

Wiley-VCH Verlag GmbH, Boschstr. 12, D-69469 Weinheim, Germany

John Wiley & Sons Australia Ltd, 42 McDougall Street, Milton, Queensland 4064, Australia

John Wiley & Sons (Asia) Pte Ltd, 2 Clementi Loop #02-01, Jin Xing Distripark, Singapore 129809

John Wiley & Sons Ltd, 6045 Freemont Blvd, Mississauga, Ontario L5R 4J3, Canada

Wiley also publishes its books in a variety of electronic formats. Some content that appears
in print may not be available in electronic books.

Library of Congress Cataloging-in-Publication Data

Lacey, David.
  Managing the human factor in information security how to win over staff and influence
business managers / David Lacey.
     p. cm.
  Includes bibliographical references and index.
  ISBN 978-0-470-72199-5 (pbk. : alk. paper) 1. Information technology–Security
measures. 2. Industries–Security measures. 3. Computer crimes–Prevention. 4.
Management–Employee participation. 5. Electronic data processing departments–
Security measures. 6. Management information systems–Human factors. I. Title.
  HF5548.37.L33 2009
  658.4'78–dc22

                                  2008043719

British Library Cataloguing in Publication Data

A catalogue record for this book is available from the British Library

ISBN 978-0-470-72199-5 (pbk)

Typeset in 10/12 Palatino by Laserwords Private Limited, Chennai, India
Printed and bound in Great Britain by Bell & Bain, Glasgow
This book is printed on acid-free paper responsibly manufactured from sustainable forestry
in which at least two trees are planted for each one used for paper production.

For Gill, Musto and Cassie

Contents

Acknowledgements

I could not have written this book without the inspiration and support of my friends, professional colleagues and family. This is my opportunity to say thank you some of the people who made this book possible.

I'd like to thank John Madelin, Director of Professional Services for Verizon's EEMA Security Solutions practice, for encouraging me to write a book, and for introducing me to my publisher. John is a kindred spirit, with tremendous vision and enthusiasm for innovation and technology.

I must also thank the UK Cyber Security Knowledge Transfer Network, led by Nigel Jones of Qinetiq, for inspiring the subject of this book. Quite rightly, this Government sponsored forum has recognized the growing importance of the human factor in information security management and assigned it a high priority.

And I have to thank Professor Gene Schultz for his very encouraging comments on the original outline for the book, which helped to inspire me to go forward with the project. Gene is not only a brilliant security technologist, but also a man with fine tastes in English beer, Californian wine and Dutch cigars.

I also owe a great debt to David Evans of Link Associates for teaching me many of the more sophisticated aspects of strategic crisis management, and for reviewing the chapters "There's no such thing as an isolated incident" and "Zen and the art of Risk Management". David has a unique perspective on organizations, having spent more than twenty years coaching managing directors in the art of crisis management. He notices many small, but important, details that others do not.

I have to also thank Professor Steven Furnell, of the University of Plymouth, and Andy Smith, of the UK Home Office National Identity Card Program, and Professor Fred Piper, of Royal Holloway University of London, for reviewing the early drafts of the book. Steven is one of the brightest, hardest working academics in the industry, and highly knowledgeable about networks and human factors. Andy has the largest collection of information security books of anyone I've ever met, several hundred of them, in fact, and he's actually read them all. But I must especially thank Fred for contributing an excellent forward. I feel very fortunate and highly privileged to know Fred. He's an inspiration for my academic side, as well as a perfect role model for his students and fellow professionals. Not only does Fred exude wisdom and integrity, he's also one of the nicest people I've ever met.

There are many other experts who have contributed to the wisdom contained in this book. In particular, I'd like to thank Phil Severs, Nick Bleech, Paul Dorey and Andrew Yeomans for serving as a sounding board for many of my ideas; Debi Ashendon and Almira Ross for their observations on the human factor; Robert Coles and Phil Venables for their perspectives on risks; Howard Wright for his coaching in innovation, and J.P Rangaswami for his views on identity and technology.

I also have a great debt to my colleagues at Shell, for helping to develop and prove many of the ideas in this book, as well as my excellent, award-winning team at Royal Mail, who helped to realize many of them in practice.

And, finally, I have to thank Birgit Gruber and Colleen Goldring of John Wiley for their encouragement, patience, and advice in putting this book together. It could never have been completed without their assistance.

Foreword

Many people argue that the technology to protect our information has been available for many years. Yet we continue to hear about serious data losses, large scale identity theft and the compromise of national databases. This illustrates the 'obvious' fact that information security is not a technology problem. In reality very few people have regarded it as solely a technology issue and, ever since the start of the information age, the cliché that "Computers do not commit crimes. People do." has been quoted in numerous security presentations.

Our business information systems and data have been repeatedly undermined by design flaws, weak passwords, lost media, social engineering and numerous other bad practices. Furthermore these risks are growing with the increasing sophistication, complexity and networking of modern business systems.

People are the soft underbelly of our information security. They design, implement and operate our information systems. They use, misuse and abuse them. They manage the physical and logical access to our systems and data. In so doing they create mistakes, incidents and the weaknesses that enable criminals to steal, corrupt and manipulate our intellectual assets.

However, despite the fact that its importance has been widely recognized, the role and importance of people in information security has been consistently underestimated. This situation is slowly changing and human factor considerations are gradually beginning to enter the security management agenda.

Security is largely a game between 'bad guys', who aim to exploit other people's assets, and 'good guys' who aim to protect them. We need to understand what makes both sides tick. When we make it easier for our users and customers to gain access to systems and data, we also make it easier for hackers and fraudsters to penetrate our systems. Getting the balance right is not easy, especially in a world of continually evolving threats and technology.

Human failings have long been exploited by spies, eavesdroppers and hackers. Cryptographers, for example, have generally learned this the hard way. Flaws are regularly found in the design, implementation and operation of their systems. Even the most secure of designs can be badly implemented, introducing technical vulnerabilities to potential attackers.

Information security researchers and practitioners have been slow to address the weaknesses introduced by the human factor but it is now finally getting the recognition it deserves, largely because of a series of high-profile security breaches. Increasingly the traditional physical and organizational security mechanisms used to mediate the human interaction with information processing technology are 'disappearing' as the complexity of the human dimension to information security comes more into focus. Nevertheless there is still very little written down about how to go about improving our influence over people and their security behavior or how to introduce an effective security culture into an organization.

This book pulls together an impressive amount of theory and practice developed across many different fields and industries. The author suggests many useful, practical ideas on how to design better security awareness initiatives, and how to go about changing people's attitudes and behavior. He also suggests that the challenge of designing management systems and information systems that people can actually use should be a priority for all researchers and practitioners.

In effect, the author is arguing for an approach to information security management that is primarily focused on people and their relationships, rather than policies, procedures and processes. In addition to providing sound advice on what to do and how to do it, he also encourages the reader to think about what we are doing wrong and how to rectify the situation. The book is as much about thought provocation as about defining 'good practice'.

He is right in challenging existing assumptions. We certainly need new ideas and a new approach to information security that takes account of the new risks presented by social networking and mobile computing. This requires an increase in interdisciplinary work within both the academic and practitioner communities and this book provides an excellent platform for its launch.

Changes need catalysts (like this book) and people who are prepared to think 'out of the box' and then put their ideas forward for others to study. Not everyone will agree with all of them, indeed some may agree with none of them, but they will set the dialogue rolling and are necessary for progress to be made. The author, David Lacey, is a leading authority in the information security profession, who is renowned for his foresight and innovation and I can think of no one better suited to this role. He has an enormous amount of experience in transforming security across large organizations, and a first-class track record of success in different environments. He has also conducted considerable research into a number of aspects of human behavior so that, as well as providing practical advice on security management, he provides a number of fascinating references for further reading in a wide range of related topics.

In addition to providing a major platform for an important, emerging subject area David has also provided a highly entertaining read that will undoubtedly become essential reading for all security professionals.

Fred Piper

Introduction

Some people say that Information Security is a people problem, rather than a technical one. Others claim it's a blend of people, process and technology issues. The truth is that Information Security draws on a range of different disciplines: computer science, communications, criminology, law, marketing, mathematics and more. And like most things in life, success in all of these fields is underpinned by an ability to understand and manage the human factor.

You might ask what I mean by the "human factor". In fact, I mean the *influence of people* in information security, the unpredictable factor that causes many of our best planned systems to fail, whether because of carelessness, complacency, apathy, spite, stupidity, criminal intent or just plain bad design.

"Human factors" is also a term that is commonly used, especially in the USA, to refer to the science of ergonomic design. I use it, however, in its broadest sense to encompass the impact that people have in manipulating systems or causing accidents, as well as the challenge of harnessing their capabilities to secure our information flows, and the considerations for designing security systems, controls and campaigns that actually work.

Technology is also essential to security, of course, and increasingly so, as we learn how to apply its leverage to manage our growing business and security problems. But technology is designed, implemented and operated by people. And it's the human factor that shapes how we use or misuse information systems. People manage our physical security and grant access to our systems. They also cause, report, and manage our response to, security breaches and incidents.

The influence of human factors is, in fact, increasing as we evolve from a largely process driven business world to a more joined-up, nomadic, information society. Technology, and the networks that spring from it, are creating a new business environment, in which intellectual assets are the new engine of wealth creation, and information flows across empowered, flattened team structures, rather than in strict, vertical stove pipes between management and their staff. Individual actions are now shaped less by decrees and policies from on high, and more by the opinions of networked colleagues. As information security managers, we need to understand how to influence and harness these personal relationships if we are to be truly successful in harnessing the benefits of these new ways of working.

Security professionals have long acknowledged the importance of the human factor in safeguarding business and personal information from hackers, spies and fraudsters. But, in practice, we've rarely paid more than lip service to it. Our best practices have been little more than the publication of an occasional leaflet or an assortment of uninspiring intranet pages. That needs to change. We must all raise our game if we are to build an environment that delivers the compelling cues for good security practice.

It's now become an imperative for all enterprises to ensure that computer users really understand the security risks they face, and actually take the trouble to implement corporate security policies. It's vital also to ensure that project managers and development staff appreciate the importance of developing secure systems, based on intrinsically secure protocols and coding standards. And it's essential that we encourage good practices beyond our enterprise boundaries, extending across our supply chains, and encompassing our customers.

Human factors are climbing the business management agenda, and they will stay there for as long as we have to manage the consequences of people's failings. That problem will not go away within our lifetime. And it will become increasingly important with the growth in social networking and mobile working, and the potential for ever larger breaches of sensitive data.

More and more security professionals are acknowledging the importance of the human factor in information security. Bruce Schneier saw the light a decade ago, and has since become an evangelist, encouraging his fellow professionals to pay more attention to addressing the psychology and economics of security. A few years ago, Debi Ashenden, a senior fellow at the UK Defense College of Management & Technology, announced that the future of information security was "pink and fluffy". Debi tells me she now regrets that quote. She'll probably regret it even more, now that I've drawn your attention to it. But she's absolutely right. The fact is that security and risk managers can now learn more from psychologists than from technologists.

The UK Cyber Security Knowledge Transfer Network has correctly placed a high priority on the study of human factors, and has established a working group to help identify the problems and potential solutions. But it will take many years for the information security community to understand the nature of the problem space, identify the underlying root causes, and develop new initiatives to improve the situation on the ground.

This book aims to identify and make sense of the wide range of human and organizational challenges that we face in managing security in today's networked world. It provides helpful advice on how to manage incidents and risks, design and sell management systems, promote security awareness, change attitudes and behavior, and how to leverage the power of social networks to get the best out the organization.

- Chapter 1 sets the scene with a reflection on the impact of networks on the business landscape, and the consequences of social networking.

- Chapter 2 discusses the security roles and perspectives of people and stakeholders within an organization.

- Chapter 3 examines the human weaknesses that contribute to major incidents and our management of them.

- Chapter 4 addresses the phenomenon of risks and the difficult art of risk management.

- Chapter 5 considers the psychology of the criminal mind and the nature of individuals.

- Chapter 6 provides advice on understanding and navigating organization culture and politics.

- Chapter 7 explains how to design effective security awareness campaigns.

- Chapter 8 sets out principles and techniques for transforming attitudes and behavior.

- Chapter 9 addresses the psychological factors associated with selling your proposals to management.

- Chapter 10 shows how to design management systems and programs that are effective and long-lasting.

- Chapter 11 sets out how to harness the power and creativity of networks and groups to leverage your own capabilities.

Information security is still a relatively new subject area, a fascinating blend of art and science, which draws on many existing sciences and techniques. But it has a long way to go. Our everyday practice is primarily the result of unproven theories and self-taught skills. Donn Parker, of SRI International, used to refer to our information security practices as a "folk art", because it lacked the broader knowledge base and objective research that we expect to find in other disciplines.

We've certainly developed this art quite a bit in recent years, filling many gaps in research, knowledge and good practices. Information security today, however, remains an immature science. But that's also an exciting opportunity for all professionals. We're all party to the creation of a new field, one guaranteed to grow in importance alongside the emergence of the new, networked information age of the 21st Century.

Driving the growth of a new set of security risks are the collaborative Internet technologies that we term Web 2.0. A few years ago, Symantec hijacked the term Security 2.0 for their security product strategy. But that was largely a marketing ploy. A more appropriate use of the term Security 2.0 is, in fact, to describe the new problem space and solution space, associated with Web 2.0 developments. These challenges require a different response from the process-focused security strategies that we have been employing to address the security risks associated with traditional IT systems. In particular, we need a much stronger focus on people, their context and their relationships.

This book aims to provide a road map to help navigate the new knowledge base that underpins the new paradigm of Security 2.0. We are in the midst of a revolution to create a new form of security. It's a paradigm shift from a focus on systems and processes to a focus on people and their relationships. Whatever we call it is irrelevant. The important thing is to develop the vision, principles and the knowledge base to support it.

Creating a common body of knowledge was a key driver for the team of security professionals that developed the original British standard BS7799 in the early 1990s. We saw a business need and an opportunity to collect, document and agree commonly applied, proven practices. It was an exciting and important breakthrough. The material we assembled drew on just about everything we knew about information security at the time.

But BS7799, and its successor ISO27001, are based on a compliance-based approach to security, conceived more than fifteen years ago. They represent the practice of information security management in a process-driven business world, a world of scripted procedures based on industrial age, mass production principles. Networks are slowly dissolving the rigidity of repeatable processes. Tomorrow's information age security needs are more demanding. We need a new, complementary approach to security, one more in tune with a real-time generation operating in a nomadic, networked world.

This book is written in the same spirit as the original BS7799, aiming to fill the gaps in our security knowledge base with insights, theories and principles adapted from other academic fields, as well as from pioneering work in the information security field. I set out to pull together the most comprehensive overview of theory and practice that I could conceive of, and to present it in an entertaining style. There will no doubt be gaps, and I will aim to rectify those in future editions.

Most of the techniques described in this book are tried and tested. They're based on my personal experience of designing and implementing information security programs for large, complex organizations, such as Shell and Royal Mail. This is a book written by an information security professional for his fellow professionals, and for anyone else that might find it useful or interesting. I sincerely hope that you enjoy it and that you will learn many things that are interesting, helpful and illuminating.

David Lacey

Power to the people

The power is out there ... somewhere

What is power? And who holds its key? Many seek it. Some try to seize it. A few get to exercise it. Not all are successful. Power is an elusive goal.

Most people imagine power in terms of a kind of force or strength being exerted. That might be true for some types of power. But it's the wrong perspective for understanding power over *people*. Because in practice, such power is less about personal status, physical strength or money – though these things help – but more about how other people respond to you. Power over people is in the eye of the beholder. And you can't always buy that or gain it through status or force of arms.

It's harder to manipulate people when they're joined up through networks. And that trend is growing. That's why, these days, even prime ministers and presidents can appear powerless. And it's why captains of industry find it difficult to drive change across their organizations.

I asked a top CEO what it felt like, today, to be in charge of a big modern organization. He replied:

> *'It's like driving a big bus, except that the wheels aren't connected to the steering wheel.'*

If you work in a large enterprise, you'll already have noticed this phenomenon. It's becoming harder to make an impact on your fellow managers and staff. That's never been easy of course. But it's more challenging today. And the situation on

Managing the Human Factor in Information Security   David Lacey
© 2009 John Wiley & Sons, Ltd

the ground is much worse than you imagine. You'd be shocked if you carried out a review of how many company staff actually understand and follow your corporate policies.

I know this because I recently carried out such a survey, across dozens of organizations. The results made grim reading. The fact is that many corporate policies are not understood, communicated, implemented or enforced. Yet policy is the basis of information security. So either we've failed to get the message across, or for some reason, it's being widely ignored. But that's not just down to our own lack of competence. In fact, it's a characteristic of a modern, networked society.

An information-rich world

In today's fast-changing, information-rich world, people have many distractions. The relentless flood of e-mails is only the tip of the iceberg. A typical information worker will check his or her e-mail at least 50 times a day. But they will also look up a similar number of websites. And even more disruptive is the growing flow of real-time, instant or text messages.

Lost productivity from such distractions is estimated to be costing many hundreds of billions of dollars a year, though nobody seems to have measured the corresponding increases in efficiency that the technology brings. The jury is therefore still out on the balance of the benefits and costs presented by new network technologies.

But new technology is necessary to attract young graduates. And that provides a major edge in the growing competition to attract new talent. It's not surprising, therefore, to find that top companies that aim to attract the best staff, such as Goldman Sachs, until recently are amongst the most advanced companies in introducing the latest network technologies.

The end result is that people today have to be selective about what they pay attention to. They will concentrate on the issues that are most relevant to their immediate, personal needs.

Modern managers have little time for quiet reflection about speculative, security risks and their consequences. And, increasingly, they will prefer to consult networked colleagues or public websites for advice on new issues, rather than asking official advisers.

It's also hard to get subtle points across on complex subjects. And it's virtually impossible to communicate lengthy policies and procedures with any real degree of success. When, for example, was the last time you read an instruction manual? Yet that's what information security managers expect from company staff. And even if you can find the time to read it, how much of it would you remember? And what would prompt you to apply it?

In fact, traditional approaches to information security, such as publishing a thick manual of policies and standards, no longer work. They might be fine for enabling you, and your management, to tick your compliance boxes, to demonstrate that you're discharging your corporate responsibilities. But lengthy edicts are ineffective as a means of influencing staff. They should be consigned to the corporate dustbin.

We need to rethink and re-engineer the way we communicate and enforce our security policies. And that's no trivial feat, because the content is getting lengthier, and ever more complex. At the same time, many employers claim that literacy rates in the West are plummeting. It's becoming an enormous challenge to communicate complex security policies to a volatile organization that's constantly restructuring.

These are major challenges. We don't have all the answers. But there's quite a lot of change and improvement that needs to be applied. In particular, we need to shift from implementing security less on the basis of a 'tick-the-box' culture of defensive policy setting, and more on the basis of how people now think and behave.

We need to embrace, understand and exploit the social networks that are increasingly used by our colleagues and staff. Electronic networks are, in fact, both the source of the problem and the key to its solution.

When in doubt, phone a friend

Social networks empower managers, staff and customers. They don't operate on the same lines as traditional organization structures. They resist dominance, and they erode the traditional, hierarchical power bases in organizations. Social networks are disempowering head offices and corporate centres, weakening the influence of corporate security policy in organizations.

The nature of decision-making is changing, decisively, and for good. It's now much more a bottom-up, rather than a top-down process. Our thought leadership is no longer in the exclusive hands of a privileged group of central policy makers, and their consultants. It's out there in the peer-to-peer networks running across our enterprise infrastructures. Power is moving to the people.

Forrester Research, an independent technology and market research company, has been tracking this trend for several years. Amongst other things, they've noted that trust in institutions is progressively weakening, and that social networking is undermining traditional business models.

We can see this in many types of business. You no longer need a travel agent to sort out your holiday arrangements. You don't need to buy a copy of the *Good Food Guide* to find a decent restaurant. There are plenty of free opinions available on the Web. And they're just about good enough for most people.

The same holds true for most other sources of independent advice. Professional, independent experts are on the run. In fact, social networking might even make obsolete research analysts, such as Forrester themselves. At a Chief Information Officer Summit in Monaco a few years ago, I put this observation to Brian Kardon, their Chief Strategy Officer. 'Yes, that's a very good point. We've grasped that and are already working on the challenge,' he admitted.

In fact, the future of research is likely to be one that favors the specialist, niche operators. The broader, more general stuff can be freely accessed on the Internet.

The phrase 'The Long Tail', coined by Chris Anderson in a *Wired* magazine article, describes the tendency for business products, especially intellectual ones such as information services, to increasingly fragment in order to satisfy the individual needs of customers. The future of business is selling less of more. And the same is true of security. We need to develop a broader portfolio of tailored advice that caters more closely to people's specific needs.

Engage with the public

Smart stakeholders instinctively respond to this trend and seek to engage with their customers. Forward-looking companies increasingly seek the views of the general public on their activities.

The Royal Dutch/Shell Group, for example, tries to engage with citizens by encouraging people to pose questions to Shell executives. They learned the importance of such public dialogue many years ago, following a high-profile media campaign mounted by Greenpeace in reaction to their proposed method of disposal of the Brent Spar oil storage buoy.

Politicians are also well advanced in embracing and exploiting web technologies and other forms of social networking. Most have their own websites. Some engage in daily web chats and invite electronic petitions. Number 10 Downing Street, for example, has, for some time, run a website where e-petitions can be created by the public. And most political parties religiously consult focus groups of citizens before taking a view on any aspect of public policy.

Even the Royal Society now spends as much time engaging with the public as it does debating the finer points of scientific developments. This famous institution firmly believes that science is a wider part of our culture and cannot flourish without the support of the wider community. Their 'Science in Society' program consults with members of the public from all walks of life and all geographic regions across the UK. That's something that could not have been contemplated a hundred years ago.

The power of the blogosphere

All corporate communications managers monitor the 'blogosphere'. It's an evolving network that links huge numbers of personal web logs, enabling them to connect, interact and amplify the thoughts of popular individuals.

A few years ago, Reuters encountered the power of the blogosphere when bloggers discovered that a photograph of an Israeli F-16 firing missiles on Lebanon had been slightly doctored, in order to make the photo appear more sensational. This incident had a major impact on Reuters' reputation, forcing them to rethink their news gathering strategy and to review the way they authenticate photographic images from their agents.

But more significant is the greater challenge that news agencies, such as Reuters, face as they contemplate moving towards a future news gathering process that is increasingly based on images captured by members of the public, rather than snapped by their trusted agents.

Blogging is very different from journalism. It's more conversational and it has a greater focus on personal views than objective reporting. And, unlike newspapers, blogs are interconnected, resulting in a powerful network aggregation effect.

Karl Schneider, a former executive editor of *New Scientist* and an expert on new forms of media, sees major changes in the role of journalists. He believes they will progress from being 'creators of news', to acting in a role similar to a 'disk jockey', becoming 'curators of information' and 'sowers of seeds'. Professional news gathering is changing, and will never be the same again.

The future of news

It's interesting to speculate on the longer-term future of professional news services. Several years ago a flash movie called EPIC 2014 appeared on the Internet. It provided a fascinating glimpse of how news gathering might evolve over the next decade, shaped by competition from the progressive mergers and increasing dominance of big Internet companies.

The film also introduced a new word 'Googlezon' to the English language. As we'll see in a later chapter, it can be a useful marketing trick to invent a catchy word or phrase, if you're aiming to make a lasting impact with a memorable message.

In the film, Googlezon is a fictional company created when Google merges with Amazon. Eventually the company creates a news product called EPIC, the 'Evolving Personalized Information Construct', which automatically creates news that is tailored to individuals, without the need for journalists.

This eventually leads to the 'news wars' of 2010, in which Googlezon triumphs, triggering the downfall of the *New York Times*, which is forced to move offline, becoming 'a print newsletter for the elite and the elderly'.

Whatever your views on the conduct or capability of the media, it's clear that the death of professional news services would be a major blow to society. Whether or not professional journalists can survive, it's certain that the future of news will be based on assemblies of citizen information, of varying accuracy and reliability, increasingly personalized to meet consumer tastes, defined by their historical network activity.

Leveraging new ideas

Social networks are surprisingly powerful, perhaps more so than most people realize. They threaten to undermine any long-standing institution that fails to engage with them. Networks are a powerful leveller, with little respect for status or authority, and a potent means of leveraging individual ideas and initiatives.

Some people can single-handedly transform organizations, cultures or countries. Great men like Gandhi and Nelson Mandela seem to effortlessly change the mindset of huge numbers of people. In the field of technology Bill Gates, Tim Berners-Lee and Steve Jobs have also driven through large-scale culture change. They were exceptional individuals, of course. But how did they do it? Were they lucky, timely, charismatic, or did they discover a magic formula for persuading people to follow and support them?

Perhaps it's a combination of all or most of those things. But one thing is certain. However they approached it, their success was achieved by creating a critical mass of support across a social network. Either by chance or by design, they acted in a way that appealed to people, they created a compelling message. And at the same time, they were able to harness the power of social networks. They created a virtuous circle, a positive feedback loop that grew and grew.

In an increasingly networked society that's the key to success. Whatever you're trying to achieve, you have to find an effective means to capture people's attention, develop a compelling justification, communicate in the language they understand and exploit their support, not just on an individual, one-to-one basis, but across a networked community.

Changing the way we live

Networks are the engine of the information age, arguably the modern equivalent of the factory to the industrial age. Wherever you look, digital networks, and the flows of knowledge and ideas they convey, are transforming the balance of power across business, society and politics.

Networks are flattening organizational structures, extending supply chains beyond traditional borders, enabling the globalization of markets, businesses and beliefs. They're making billionaires out of twenty-something, Californian geeks. They're changing the way we live and work, and they're upsetting the balance of political power in the world. And there's a lot more change to come.

Where will it lead? What will be the long-term impact on our everyday life? In fact, there are numerous dimensions to the impact of networks. And many are uncertain or unknown. But we already know some of the implications.

Urban planners, for example, have long experience of studying the impact of disruptive infrastructure changes such as the introduction of roads, railways, electricity and piped water. So it's not surprising to find that leading experts in this field have already assessed the impact of the Internet on urban life.

Around 10 years ago, Professor William Mitchell, Dean of the School of Architecture and Planning at MIT, published an illuminating book called *e-topia*, setting out some of the implications of digital networks for urban planning. In particular, he spotted a number of interesting trends in US planning.

Technology companies, for example, have been progressively moving out of cities, in search of knowledge workers who prefer leafy suburbs. Millionaires prefer to migrate to upscale resorts, with good airport connections. That leaves the cities to young, single people and the businesses that need to employ them. 'Sex brings cities alive', as he puts it.

Observers in Seattle have already spotted radical, new patterns in commuting, such as the 'reverse commute' where male computer scientists, from Microsoft's suburban complex, race downtown after work each day in search of females.

I wondered how these trends might play out across in other countries, such as the UK, so I asked a logistics professor at a London university whether he expected to see the same type of changes. 'No,' he replied, 'that won't happen here, for all sorts of reasons, such as planning restrictions.' 'What might it be like then?' I asked. 'Just a lot more urban sprawl,' he replied.

But however the land lies, mobility, and the nomadic working style it enables, will have a progressive impact on our working methods, and our office and social life. Multi-tasking – checking our e-mails, sending text messages and answering telephone calls, whilst travelling, cooking a meal or attending a meeting – is here to stay.

Dilbert-style cubicles are no longer necessary for staff that can hot-desk or access everything they need while travelling. Who needs an office when there are plenty of Starbucks coffee houses and wine bars in which to meet or touch down?

William Mitchell also suggests that 21st century building design and aesthetics will probably turn out to be the exact opposite of the sci-fi chic that futurists of the past imagined. Modern architects are now thinking more in terms of light, air, trees and gardens. And future building designs will also need more nooks and crannies, in order to provide privacy for individual laptop workers.

One of the most significant impacts of the growth of the connected society is a major shift in focus, from networking with people who happen to be within physical reach, to cooperating more with on-line, distant colleagues. People are becoming more dependent on the stronger ties they develop over networks, rather than the increasingly weaker ties they make through physical encounters.

We can reach many people through networks, but, perhaps paradoxically, digital networks also encourage the growth of isolated, always-connected, virtual cliques, making it harder for outsiders to gain attention. They strengthen digital families and established communities and weaken the influence of strangers. This phenomenon introduces both threats and opportunities for security managers aiming to make an impact on a workforce that is increasingly networked and mobile.

Transforming the political landscape

Networks, and the globalization they enable, have also transformed the international political landscape. The World is now positioned at a crossroads, where political power is shifting to new regions and countries, and existing regional and international institutions are struggling to exert their traditional level of influence.

The US National Intelligence Council regularly conducts long-range research and consultation exercises, to provide their policy makers with a view of how global developments might evolve over the next 15 years. Their recent report *Mapping the Global Future*, published in 2005, considered global trends up to the Year 2020. Amongst other things, they noted that:

> *'At no time since the formation of the Western Alliance system in 1949 have the shape and nature of international alignments been in such a state of flux.'*

Futurists Alvin and Heidi Toffler were amongst the first to understand the transformational power of technology and networks. They set out their theories in a classic series of books published in the seventies and eighties. The ideas set out in these books were decades ahead of their time, so few business managers and citizens paid much attention to them.

But the Tofflers made a deep impression on governments and political stakeholders. Their book *The Third Wave* became a bestselling book in China, the second ranked bestseller of all time just behind a work by Mao Zedong, and an underground cult book in countries such as Poland. It helped transform US military doctrine, encouraging smarter tactics and weapons. And it transformed politic thinking across the globe, even though these days you'd be lucky to find a copy in a British bookshop.

I experienced a flavour of this book's influence when I visited Romania in the mid 1990s. My driver, like many locals, was naturally inquisitive about my lifestyle. He asked me what I did. I told him I worked in information technology. 'That's great,' he said, 'I'm just reading Alvin Toffler's book: The Third Wave.' I was impressed. 'It's also one of my favourite books,' I confided. Then, as he dropped me off at the airport, he leaned over and asked 'Will you ever meet Alvin Toffler?' 'I don't know,' I replied, 'it's possible. And if I do, I'll pass on your compliments.' 'No,' he said, 'please convey to him the thanks of one million Romanian citizens.'

I never did get to meet Alvin Toffler, but I did manage to close the loop. Several years later, I was having a beer in an Amsterdam Hotel with John Perry Barlow, founder of the Electronic Freedom Foundation and one-time rancher and Grateful Dead lyricist. I commented on how much his ideas aligned with Toffler's. 'That's because I admire him, and he's a good friend of mine,' he replied. So I told him the story about my experience in Romania. 'Wow, that's cool,' he said, 'I'm seeing Alvin next week. I'll tell him. He'll be knocked out.'

It's remarkable to think that a driver in Romania could be a mere three steps away from his literary hero, a person who inhabits an entirely different business and social world, in a continent many thousands of miles away. And that's just through the power of a physical, social network. Just imagine what electronic ones could do.

Network effects in business

The concept of a 'network effect', the idea that a product or service can grow in value as more and more people adopt it, is an old one, first pointed out by Theodore Vail, president of Bell Telephone, around a century ago. It's fairly obvious, of course, that the more people who have a telephone, the more calls you can make. But it took many years for the idea to be studied seriously by economists.

In fact, academics who study network effects, such as the former Stanford University Economics Professor Brian Arthur, have been both in and out of fashion in recent years, with theories of how positive feedback loops in networks might channel global wealth into the hands of a handful of first-mover, electronic commerce conglomerates.

As with many other dot-com predictions, that didn't happen as fast as many investors had hoped, so much of the excitement about network effects in business and economics has now calmed down. But there's a strong tendency for people to overestimate what will happen in the next year and underestimate what will happen in the next decade.

Many economists believe Brian Arthur got it wrong. Positive feedback loops present difficulties for economics. And there's little hard evidence to support his theory. But a lot of people didn't listen closely enough to the points he made. He differentiated *collaborative* networks, which grow more powerful with each new member, from others. There's plenty of the latter but few of the former.

For example, if we all buy a book from Amazon or a similar website, there's little collaborative value generated. In contrast, networks like e-Bay, Skype, Wikipedia and Facebook, get more useful with each new member or transaction. But there aren't enough examples of such sites, even though they are fantastically successful. The truth is that we've not been sufficiently imaginative to conceive, develop or exploit collaborative network effects. But that will, undoubtedly, come with time.

Being there

Electronic networks might be based on technology, but the resulting behaviour they generate bears more resemblance to an ecological system than a Swiss watch. Man-made, hub-and-spoke designs can create networks of surprising complexity and unpredictability. They are part of a class of networks called 'scale-free' networks, and they exhibit many unusual topological characteristics. They are, for example, more resistant to random failures than natural, organic networks, but they're also more vulnerable to deliberate attacks that target big hubs or spokes.

We are only just beginning to understand the strange properties of complex networks. Many researchers are now looking at parallels between network activity and other scientific fields. One interesting theory proposed by Ginestra Bianconi, a graduate student, is that, under certain conditions, a single node in a network can become dominant. This theory, which is based on an analogy with gaseous condensates in physics, suggests that some of the phenomena we observe in competitive networks, such as the 'first-mover advantage', the 'fit get richer' or the 'winner takes all' outcomes might actually be phases in the underlying evolution of networks.

A consequence of this theory is that the largest or fittest node, at any one time, does not always end up as the eventual, dominant participant. Networks appear to favour certain members at particular times, accelerating their influence to positions of high dominance. It's an advantage gained by being in the right place at the right time.

It might, in fact, be that large-scale success in networks is as much down to luck, as it is to skill, judgment or hard work. Networks are a great leveller. But they can also be a powerful kingmaker, under the right conditions.

Value in the digital age

Identifying value at risk is a key element of modern security and risk management. It shapes our priorities, countermeasures and enterprise programs. But where is the value in business today? It's not just in the fixed assets and bank deposits. Increasingly it's in our intellectual assets: the brands, reputation and the knowledge and skills of our employees.

For many years, technologists and economists have been studying the nature and value of intellectual capital. Much of it resides in social networks. But how do you recognize it or measure it?

At the height of the dot-com boom in May 2000, a few months after the NASDAQ hit its peak, I attended a conference in Washington DC on 'Value and Values in The New Economy'. The conference was organized by TTI Vanguard, a private technology circle advised by luminaries including Gordon Bell, Alan Kay, Nicholas Negroponte, David Reed and Peter Cochrane.

The conference was attended by technology directors, economists and academics, and it focused on the shift of economic emphasis from 'things' to 'connections between things'. Amongst other things, the speakers and attendees debated how we could measure the true value of dot-com companies.

At that time it appeared that the main reason for the huge valuations placed on Internet companies was their potential for leveraging large numbers of customer relationships. Various formulae were proposed to quantify the future potential of a start-up company. For example, by calculating the number of customers they might be able to win, the value of each relationship they control, and the capability of the company to exploit these relationships. There were some fascinating theories and algorithms put forward to help assess intellectual value. But they were largely discredited when the dot-com bubble burst.

There were also some interesting ideas on security and risk management put forward at that conference. Professor Peter Strassman, for example, suggested that security effort should be exclusively focused on employees that generate the maximum intellectual value. This might turn out to be a trader, researcher or strategist, for example.

It's an interesting view, unfortunately too far ahead of its time. I could see it being impractical during a period when most organizations were struggling to patch up the weakest links in their infrastructure, rather than harden the protection around their crown jewels. But in the future, when basic security measures become pervasive, intellectual assets become easier to identify, and security threats become increasingly targeted at our most valuable assets, Peter's ideas will certainly be worth revisiting.

Hidden value in networks

Nevertheless, there is huge theoretical value lurking in networks, at least in theory. Metcalfe's Law, named after Robert Metcalfe, co-inventor of the Ethernet and a founder of 3Com, claims that the value of a network is proportional to the square of the number of users of the system.

This assertion is based on the number of relationships between individuals, the number of pairs that you can make. It assumes of course that some form of value can actually be derived from each relationship.

The way that pairs of relationships increase with the size of a network is quite unexpected. We often experience this phenomenon when we clink champagne glasses at a celebration. When there are only three or four people, it's quite easy. Just a handful of clinks and it's done. But if you have a dozen people, it's surprisingly harder, requiring more than sixty clinks. And if you have than twenty people, it then rises to a couple of hundred clinks.

Robert Metcalfe was one of the most influential technologists of the 20th century. He's attained near legendary status in the industry. But he didn't always get his forecasts right. Amongst other things, he predicted the imminent collapse of the Internet and the death of open source software! When the Internet failed to collapse, Robert was compelled to eat his words, literally, by placing a paper copy of his forecast in a blender.

In fact Metcalfe understated the network relationship potential. Reed's Law, named after David Reed, an adjunct professor at MIT Media Lab and former Chief Scientist for Lotus Development Corporation, points out that the value of social networks scales exponentially with the number of members. That's because network relationships are not just confined to pairs. We also need to take account of larger sub-groups.

Exponential growth is a much faster rate of growth, proportional to the function's current value. For any exponentially growing quantity, the larger the quantity gets, the faster it grows. It's the sort of growth you get by progressive doubling, or even tripling. It's a sneaky form of growth, starting low and rising fast.

For example, if you place a single grain of wheat on the first square of a chessboard, then two grains on the next square, and so on, then by the time you reach the last square, you'll have reached more than a thousand times the total annual wheat production of the Earth. Early in the doubling sequence, the true power is not apparent to an observer. But after a few dozen operations the numbers become enormous.

Figure 1.1 overleaf illustrates the difference in growth between these two laws.

Theories, such Reed's Law, are purely academic if we don't know how to exploit them for real business value. But the potential prize is massive. There is huge latent value, perhaps waiting to be tapped in any large social network. This is why venture capitalists have been paying so much attention to investments in social networking technologies.

How hard can it be to exploit the power lurking in networks? That's the 64 dollar question. If we could find a way to tap just a small percentage of this power, then it would be valuable. In fact, there are some features of social networks that suggest it might be easier than we imagine.

For example, it's a rather surprising fact that the average path length between any two people in a human network is quite tiny, in comparison to the total number of network members. Most people have encountered this phenomenon as the 'six degrees of separation', which describes the counter-intuitive claim that you might be just six relationships away from anyone else on the Earth.

The idea of six degrees of separation was conceived by Stanley Milgram, a social psychologist, after experiments in which he sent out a set of packages to a random selection of people for onward transmission to a common recipient. Some observers have questioned the reliability of this claim, but a recent study of 30 billion instant messages by Microsoft researchers confirmed that the vast majority of people appear to be linked by seven or fewer acquaintances.

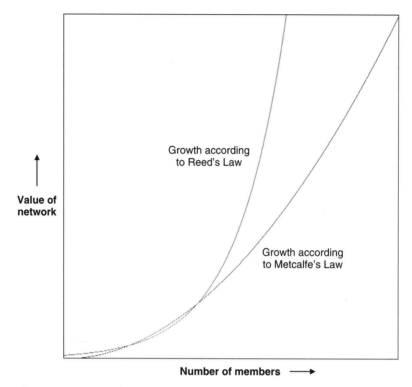

Figure 1.1   How value increases in networks with increasing membership

This surprising phenomenon explains why my Linked In account can proudly boast that I now have a staggering 27 000 professional connections just one step away from my small group of directly linked friends. Friends of friends are a powerful force that can be exploited for many purposes. It's a useful fact to know if you're seeking new employment, for example. Experienced human resources advisers will advise you that, statistically, you're far better off e-mailing your CV to friends than applying for advertised positions.

And in the security field we can use the power of social networks to cascade warning messages, or to request information about a current threat or event, or perhaps carry out a survey, or to seek assistance with a search operation. The potential of networks is only limited by our imagination. Unfortunately, in the security field, it's been the bad guys who've been first to recognize this potential. Mass mailers hijacked our address books and contact lists a decade ago, and social networks are already being exploited to distribute malware.

Network innovations create security challenges

Ever since their invention, developments in electronic networks have transformed day-to-day business life. At the same time, they've heightened security risks. It's interesting to take a step back and reflect on the impact of these changes on both

Table 1.1   The impact of network innovations on organizations and security

INNOVATION	ORGANIZATIONAL IMPACT	SECURITY IMPACT
Telegraphy and telephones	Changed the balance of power between head offices and their satellites	Heralded a new era of communications intelligence gathering
Electronic mail	Generated an explosion in person-to-person communications	Caused the collapse of traditional paper filing systems and security classification schemes
Joining up local area networks	Enabled enterprise knowledge sharing and rationalization of datacentres	Shattered the traditional security perimeters that protected many application systems
The Internet	Opened up a new world of electronic commerce	Introduced a 'Wild West' landscape of new security threats to retail systems
Secure remote access	Enabled home working and mobile access	Triggered the erosion of the barrier between personal and business lifestyles
Extranets	Enabled extended-enterprise working	Created new dependencies on the security behaviour of third party organizations
Wireless	Enabled high speed business contact from any location	Radiated company information outside the office environment
Social networking	Enables collaborative decision making and networking	Opens up new sources of information leakage and erodes authority of central security function

organizations and security, ever since William Sturgeon first laid the foundations for large-scale electronic communications.

Table 1.1 above lists the organizational impact, as well as the security impact of successive network innovations. You can see a common thread in these changes. Networks cut through barriers of all kinds, whether geographic, within organizations, between enterprises or between lifestyles.

We now call that 'de-perimeterization', a term originally coined by Jon Measham, my chief security researcher at Royal Mail Group. It's a word that is intended to encompass both the problem space and solution space, associated with managing security across boundaryless network environments. It's an inevitable and unstoppable consequence of modern technological progress.

Each advance results in a major breakthrough in business productivity. But at the same time they introduce lasting problems for the security of information, and the protection of critical infrastructure.

In practice, we never fully recover from the legacy impact of the earlier changes. Most of the effort in information security today is concerned with addressing problems created by unanticipated changes to the context of application systems and infrastructure that weren't originally designed to operate within a more hostile network environment.

You've been de-perimeterized!

In the early years of the 21st century, it seemed as though the future lay in hardening all business systems to operate across the Internet. But it was clear that the journey would be a long one, requiring new design principles and architecture.

I asked my security researchers at Royal Mail Group to develop a practical security architecture that was able to support the transition from a private network infrastructure to a public one. They delivered as promised, but the problem was that it made no sense to apply this in isolation. We would be able to operate securely outside the constraints of the enterprise. But unless other enterprises followed a similar model, we would have nobody to communicate securely with.

With this in mind, I persuaded Cisco to lend me a conference room at their executive centre near Heathrow Airport, and I invited a group of top information security managers to explore the possibility of working together to develop a common, security architecture for a de-perimeterized business world. The result was the formation of an informal, private circle of senior professionals, which helped to sow the seeds for the subsequent foundation of the Jericho Forum.

The Jericho Forum is an organization dedicated to developing solutions to meet the business demands for secure IT operations in an open, Internet-driven, networked world. Originally conceived as an invitation-only circle for large user organizations, this forum is now open to all organizations, including vendors. The aim is to get the user members to define the problem space and the vendors to fill in the solution space.

Many people misunderstand the mission of the Jericho Forum. They imagine we're advocating the removal of corporate perimeters and firewalls. That's not the case. Our perimeter defences are already leaking. We're simply stating the fact that:

> *'You've already been de-perimeterized. You'd better do something about it.'*

The Jericho Forum has published a set of 11 principles for the planning and design of systems and infrastructure for a de-perimeterized business environment. These are judged to be the quintessential design principles for moving towards a secure, collaborative extended-enterprise business model.

Many people ask why we picked 11 principles. The group set out, in fact, to produce 'Ten Commandments' for de-perimeterization. But the outcome was 11 principles. We simply felt it to be inappropriate to leave any out. Ron Condon, former editor of *SC Magazine Europe*, suggested that we must have been inspired by Spinal Tap, the spoof rock band, whose amplifier volume controls were based on a scale of one to eleven in the expectation that it would make them a touch louder.

One of the most important Jericho Forum principles is to 'assume context at your peril'. Security solutions have limitations. Technology and controls designed for one environment might not operate effectively when transferred to another. An information system developed for a private, secure network environment is unlikely to have the controls and strengths of mechanisms to be secure when operating across the Internet. And these limitations are not just technical. Changes in context create problems from a variety of sources, including geographic, legal and risk acceptance considerations.

The collapse of information management

Electronic networks have created huge challenges for all organizations. Many of our traditional information management systems, designed for a paper-based industrial age, are no longer appropriate for controlling today's horizontal information flows.

Many IT directors will privately agree that their information management has all but collapsed, and that their networks are no longer under control. But they'd probably be sacked if their Executive Board believed that.

In fact, our intellectual assets are out of control. And most of us are apathetic, or in denial. We've completely lost track of our corporate information as it's moved from the filing cabinet to the desktop. Who files minutes of meetings today? The answer, in many cases, is everyone and nobody. Plenty of copies might be flying around for a while, but can you find them when you need them?

Yet it's our intellectual assets that represent the enterprise's primary future source of revenue, profit and market capitalization. The great challenge of the next decade will be to regain control of these intellectual assets, in order to maximize their worth, and safeguard their value.

These assets include not just the valuable information resting in company databases and documents, or in its brands and reputation, but also the added value provided by the know-how, skills and relationships that are embedded in the organization's networks, both inside and outside of its corporate boundaries.

We need to develop new models for valuing, exploiting and safeguarding these increasingly important assets. But the starting point is to identify them, recognize their value, and aim to secure them. And not just for the purposes of regulatory compliance, but also because it's good for business.

The shifting focus of information security

The nature of information security changes regularly. Each decade brings a new focus through the extension of electronic networks.

The 1970s introduced the concept of risk assessment for individual information systems. New methods were developed to help determine the specific requirements of systems that were generally isolated and dedicated to a particular business application. Some worked. Others didn't. Methods based on annual loss expectancy came and went. They proved impossible to deploy because of the absence of any reliable information on incident rates and losses.

Throughout the decade the focus of attention for security controls remained on individual systems and machines. Even the most advanced military research was focused primarily on the problem of achieving better separation of users of different clearance levels sharing a common machine, or from preventing an individual terminal from radiating information to a nearby location. Most organizations managed without professional security expertise. Local computer managers looked after security.

The 1980s encouraged business units to establish secure, glasshouse datacentres in order to safeguard and showcase their growing collections of valuable hardware. The focus of security had moved, from individual machines to collections of machines. Physical security, disaster recovery and mainframe access control systems were the new priorities of the first generation of information security managers, who generally operated from the bowels of the datacentre rather than the corporate centre.

The 1990s moved the primary focus of security to the enterprise infrastructure. Local area networks were joining up at a frightening pace. Uncontrolled connectivity threatened the security of previously isolated systems. Firewalls and rules for enterprise sharing of information were the big issues for information security managers.

We developed new security standards for the whole enterprise, not just individual systems. The British standard BS7799 was created in the early nineties to support this new standardized approach to enterprise, and inter-enterprise, security.

The introduction of the World Wide Web persuaded organizations it was more important to share company information, rather than to keep it under lock and key. As one enlightened Shell business director put it to me, 'We're a big tanker, we can afford to lose a few drops.' I was inspired to develop the slogan, 'Share your knowledge with Shell, not the rest of the World.'

The early years of the 21st century introduced a much stronger external perspective. Networks stretched beyond enterprise boundaries to embrace the Internet. Security also became a business in itself. Electronic commerce was the future. Internet 'pure plays' suddenly became investments worth millions of dollars. Some businesses viewed security as a unique selling point.

For a brief moment in time, electronic security became the poster child of the marketing function. SRI International caught the mood and shocked both its clients and staff by rebranding its security research unit as 'Atomic Tangerine'. Shares in Baltimore, a UK vendor of digital certificates, rocketed and briefly entered the FTSE 100 index.

But the business fascination with electronic security dissolved with the dot-com crash, leaving a few individuals as millionaires, most investors out-of-pocket, and many employees out of a job.

The post dot-com years have been a necessary time of consolidation for information security. Most leading enterprises have used it to catch up with new processes, technology and architecture, to establish professional functions, and to adopt the more disciplined approach demanded by the regulatory compliance.

But the primary focus of most security managers remains largely an internal one, focused on the security needs within the enterprise. It's failed to keep up with a problem space that's been progressively moving outside of the corporate boundary.

The external perspective

Our network perimeters might be full of holes, but they're still needed to help protect our insecure legacy systems. In fact, for many years to come, we will need to shore up the security protection around our enterprise networks.

But an inward focus is no longer sufficient. Current technology trends, such as mobility, grid computing, and software-as-a-service, are moving the focus of corporate data flows outside of the corporate perimeter. That demands a more outward-looking security perspective. We need to shift our attention away from merely securing our own backyards, towards working together with business colleagues to build community solutions, for an emerging business environment that is based on open networks and shared services.

We also need to start paying more attention to the extramural security behaviour of users. That might seem invasive to many people. But trends such as home working, portfolio careers and social networking are removing the traditional barrier between business and personal lifestyles.

Networks have transformed our perspective of work. The view of work that we have inherited was designed to meet the needs of mass production, a legacy of the industrial age. That model required every aspect of business life to be standardized, classified and synchronized. Business was something that took place in a dedicated building, during set hours, using business equipment. What you did outside, and how you did it, was of no direct concern to your employer.

Now it's all mixed up. People instinctively grab the nearest communication channel to conduct either personal or business transactions, at any time, any place, anywhere. You can't separate business and private activities. The result is a steady drift towards a more flexible way of conducting business, using consumer devices and external services.

We are also in the midst of a steady, unstoppable march towards consumerization, a trend by vendors to develop IT products for consumer, rather than business markets. The first telephone was a functional, black device, owned by the telephone company. Progressively, consumer demand has encouraged greater and greater user choice in the styling, features and ownership of client devices.

This trend is irreversible. Vendors are now building features that appeal to consumers, not business, though some consumer devices, such as the Apple iPhone, now incorporate a range of business features, in order to appeal to both markets. And our business users now expect and demand the same functionality and personalization in their business devices as they already have in their personal ones.

Like it or not, we're going to have to take more interest in what our staff get up to outside office hours. We need to encourage them to take extra precautions when they're conducting business in insecure environments. We need to take steps to ensure that the work they carry out at home is adequately protected from security threats, and that any personal content they introduce into the office environment is free from damaging malware.

The challenge is to understand, accept and manage the consequential security risks of a business environment that's now everywhere but nowhere in particular. It's no less than a major paradigm shift for business and security.

A new world of openness

Networks enable instant communication and large-scale sharing of information and knowledge. These are powerful business capabilities. But they're also fraught with danger. Espionage and identity theft are becoming more attractive to criminals. In the past, only hostile foreign intelligence services would take the trouble to invest in stealing your information or identity. Now any criminal can make a fast buck out of it. And they have far more opportunities to get hold of it.

But organizations still need to maintain secrets. The problem is that it's becoming harder to keep them from leaking out. Employees like to share their information with colleagues, friends and acquaintances. What people do at work is no longer a secret. They advertise it in their CVs and their Linked In entries. Few people today think to keep corporate secrets to themselves.

And sharing makes perfect sense in a networked environment. It's logical that pooling your knowledge with others will gain you a bigger return. The only problem is sorting out the wheat from the chaff. Perhaps only one in a hundred items might be actually useful. The consequence is that, in practice, few staff will be bothered to search for those valuable nuggets of information in a sea of irrelevant data. But be assured that hackers, spies and fraudsters will. They think and behave in a different way from honest members of staff.

Many companies are concerned about the increasing use of social networking sites by company staff in business time. One survey carried out at the start of 2008 suggested that, in the UK alone, more than £6.5 billion a year is wasted in lost productivity. That should be balanced, of course, against the gains in productivity by enabling collaboration and knowledge sharing. The survey makes no mention of this.

But lost, or changed, productivity is just the tip of the iceberg. The use of social engineering to hijack sensitive information from companies is real and growing. Social networking sites provide a means for criminals to identify and target employees, and to connect with or impersonate them. Companies have been slow to address these new threats. Corporate policies lag far behind user behaviour, and security education and guidance in this area is generally weak or non-existent.

There are also big political and commercial issues yet to be addressed. For example, how far should we monitor employee activity? Who owns the intellectual property generated by networked relationships on social networking sites? And how can enterprises maintain the necessary control and direction across its empowered, networked groups of staff.

And it's not just cyberspace that's been affected by this new spirit of openness. During the eighties, millions of business executives were moved from the privacy and comfort of their own private offices to new, open-plan environments. It wasn't just because of economics. It was a symbolic gesture, a sign of the times, and a salute to the new culture of equality, teamwork and information sharing.

But open-plan environments have left a legacy of free access that's a dream to an insider spy or thief. Once you find an excuse to enter a building, and there are many, you can generally wander around with little challenge, grazing away at the faxes and print-outs waiting to be collected from printers, and the papers that executives are forced to leave out on their desks, because their office furniture can't accommodate the mass of paper documents that the paperless office has singularly failed to eliminate.

A new age of collaborative working

The World Wide Web has revolutionized business, but it's yet to prove itself to be a good medium for collaborative working. It might be perfectly fine for publishing, but it certainly doesn't lend itself to interaction. That wasn't the original intent of its inventor Tim Berners-Lee. As he puts it in his paper *Web Architecture from 50,000 feet*:

> *'The original idea of the Web being a creative space for people to work together in seems to be making very slow progress.'*

Many would consider that an understatement. It's clear we have a long way to go before we can tap the latent, exponential power that might be lurking in the Internet, the enormous value suggested by David Reed's law. That requires a step change, in both the skills and technologies applied to collaborative working.

Nevertheless, collaborative tools are improving. Vendors of enterprise applications are incorporating Web 2.0 features into their platforms as fast as they can. The term Enterprise 2.0 has been coined to describe the application of technologies for collaborative working in organizations. A few academic models are also slowly emerging to provide some much-needed structure to the use of what is basically a rag-bag of unconnected tools for manipulating unstructured information.

Harvard Business School Professor Andrew McAfee, for example, has coined the acronym 'SLATES' to embrace the six components of Enterprise 2.0 technology: search, links, authoring, tags, extensions and signals. Hopefully, that might be a start in the development of a basic framework and taxonomy to underpin the development and application of the necessary management controls. But we have a long way to go before we can impose an effective governance structure for these emerging technologies and services.

New business services are also emerging to encourage collaborative support for business operations. The term 'crowdsourcing' was coined by Jeff Howe, in a June 2006 *Wired* magazine article, to describe the process of outsourcing work to an undefined, large group of enthusiasts, through an open call. You can, for example, invite members of a social network to help you to design a new technology, to build or test a piece of software or to collect or analyse a large body of data.

In their book *Wikinomics: How Mass Collaboration Changes Everything*, Don Tapscott and Anthony Williams explore how companies have exploited mass collaboration and open-source technology to business advantage. It's a compelling book written with great enthusiasm. And there's no doubt that mass collaboration is an important business trend. But real collaboration success stories are, as yet, few and far between. They have yet to capture the imagination of mainstream business organizations.

The reluctance of business to take up these new ways of working is not only due to the conservative nature of most organizations. It's also because we have yet to develop and promote the new, professional business models, architectures and methodologies that are needed to underpin this approach. But the fundamental principles are clear; they are: openness, peering, sharing and acting globally. And these principles also represent major challenges in a business world that's facing up to tighter regulatory compliance, as well as a sophisticated security risk landscape.

Collaboration-oriented architecture

In fact, the real future of business is one of increasingly deeper, faster and more volatile collaboration, underpinned by secure electronic networks. It's about companies that come together more purposefully and quicker, to develop new, compelling products that the marketplace cannot deliver.

That demands a substantial degree of trust between consenting business partners, to allow or block connections between sensitive or critical information systems and infrastructure.

How will this be achieved? In the past, we largely kept our fingers crossed and hoped for the best, or relied on legal contracts to compensate us for any consequential losses, caused by a rogue third party. These options are no longer realistic, though, unfortunately, they might reflect typical practices today.

The only sensible option is to develop common architectures that enable secure, extended enterprise business operations to be established with minimal risks to either party.

Developing such solutions is a painfully slow process, but progress is being made. The Jericho Forum, for example, is developing a common 'collaboration-oriented architecture' to provide guidance for building systems that can operate securely with users sited outside of the corporate perimeter. This mode of working is already a reality for many enterprises. Many Jericho Forum members are migrating users and services to operate or connect across the Internet.

Companies such as BP, for example, have tens of thousands of users communicating securely over the Internet, rather than across a corporate network. ICI has implemented an Internet-based content monitoring and filtering system to enable mobile users to drop in and connect through any convenient access point, with full security screening of access and content. And KLM has cut its support costs substantially by giving thousands of staff special allowances, to buy and manage their own personal computers.

The long journey to a de-perimeterized, collaborative business world has begun, though the security and management models are far from mature. Organizations are naturally proceeding slowly and cautiously. In fact, few enterprises are ready to manage the degree of anarchic interaction that contemporary collaborative tools might unleash on business systems that are already struggling to meet tight regulatory compliance demands.

There are exceptions, of course. Goldman Sachs, until recently one of the more profitable and confidential investment banks, is a pioneer of Web 2.0 applications. They are managing the balance between security and innovation. But smaller, newer companies generally have the edge. They are not tied down by legacy systems and infrastructure, governance models, bureaucratic processes and restrictive enterprise licenses and procurement deals.

Nevertheless, as with any new technology, there will come a point when user power overturns corporate objection. Personal devices, aimed primarily at the consumer market, will eventually become the basis of mainstream business. We've seen it happen in the past. Security considerations and business economics initially resisted the introduction of the mobile phone, the Internet and the Blackberry. But executive power triumphed. Similarly, Web 2.0 technologies will become an essential part of business-as-usual.

Business in virtual worlds

Virtual worlds present a new and different set of challenges for security managers and corporate policy makers. I'm often asked by security managers what the acceptable use policy should be for employees who wish to experiment with sites such as Second Life, whether for research or business purposes. It's a good question, with no simple answer.

In fact, it's easy for business units to make a case for establishing a presence in virtual worlds. Customers can be reached; products can be promoted; new ideas for brands can be floated; press conferences can be held; virtual business meetings can be arranged; new extensions of IT systems can be tested. You can even make investments in virtual assets, though the business case might prove to be quite difficult for most managers.

We need limits and rules to govern the behaviour of people's avatars, the virtual representations of people in virtual worlds. Regardless of how much of a game it might seem, behaviour in any public space has security and legal implications, and an impact on corporate reputation and brand perception.

Context is especially significant in determining the appropriateness and legality of any actions. And, as we'll see later in the book, environments also help to shape people's behaviour. Staff will be compelled to act very differently in a novel environment.

We need new thinking to respond to these challenges. In the early years, the nature of the solutions will depend on what companies make of their early experiments. Will they view it as a major new marketing channel, an essential internal communications tool, or a valuable new form of collaborative working?

All of that is an unknown quantity. But one thing seems clear. It's unlikely that many companies will generate major revenue from virtual worlds, at least in the early years. Few traditional companies will view this new space as a serious basis for strategic business investment, though there might be opportunities for the niche operator.

Information security will, therefore, largely be operating in a defensive mode, aiming to keep business managers out of trouble and to safeguard corporate reputation, rather than in an enabling manner, aiming to build, develop and support a major new business channel.

Nevertheless in the longer term, virtual worlds will become a serious business environment, and we will need to adapt our traditional security governance approach to fit the new environment. How should approach this? A common theme in this book is to suggest security solutions that match the problem space. That means that we should be planning to engage with, and build solutions within, the virtual worlds themselves.

Democracy . . . but not as we know it

In February 2008, the media reported that three leading UK Internet service providers, with 9 million households between them, had signed up with Phorm, a provider of a new form of advertising service, aiming to match advertisements to customer habits, but designed to keep customer's identities anonymous to advertisers. The publicity resulted in an unprecedented backlash from privacy campaigners.

An e-petition requesting the Prime Minister to investigate the Phorm technology was launched on the 10 Downing Street website, attracting 10 000 signatures in the first two days and reaching the 'Top 10' list within two weeks. It was 'in with a bullet' as they used to say in the music industry.

At first sight, this appears to reflect a massive amount of public support. But is it really? Can 10 000 signatures really be interpreted as representing a significant slice of public opinion? It might be big in relation to other petitions doing the rounds. But it's a long way from being a majority vote of the UK population.

Civil libertarians, in particular, present a dilemma for politicians. On specific issues they often reflect a minority viewpoint. But it's a very substantial one. And they are articulate and well-organized, especially when it comes to campaigning.

Peer-to-peer collaborations sound all very healthy and democratic in theory. But they're far from perfect in practice. Minority interest groups can hijack thought leadership and collective opinion across networks. Democratic voting is an integral function of modern social networks. But not everyone wants to take part in on-line debates. And you don't need a majority of the population's voters to create a wave of change.

Social networking creates a new form of minority democracy. It's inevitable. We're just going to have to get used to it. Political activists are generally concerned about defending minority rights from the tyranny of the majority. But this time it looks like we're heading for the opposite problem, safeguarding everyone's interests from the tyranny of the minority. There are deep implications for both politics and business. Few political and business leaders, however, appreciate what's really happening.

What are the implications for politicians? I asked Lord Errol, a rare example of a peer of the Realm who actually understands technology and its implications for politicians. Lord Errol rightly pointed out that 'much of the present work of politicians is defending minority interests'. In fact, the truth is that politicians are already champions of minority concerns. The future will be business-as-usual for politicians.

But as Alvin and Heidi Toffler pointed out more than a decade ago in their 1994 book *Creating a New Civilization*, it's clear that there's a mismatch between the current political system and the emerging demands of the information age. Eventually we will need to align the two, to create a new political system that's more attuned to the structure of the Information Age.

Unfortunately, public interest in political elections in the UK appears to be waning, though there are an increasing number of attempts to mount single-issue demonstrations. In fact, many people would now prefer to select their issues and politics, in a personalized manner, just as they might select goods from a store, or order a special cappuccino from a coffee shop.

This 'Starbucks-style' politics, as the *Economist* terms it, has not so far had a major impact on mainstream politics. But it undoubtedly will. Consumer choice is an unstoppable force that's slowly penetrating politics, as well as every other aspect of modern life. It just requires campaigners to learn to exploit the power of social networks to change majority opinion.

In fact, the implications for business are more challenging. Politics has always lived with a degree of short-term anarchy generated by events and media coverage. But business needs a clearer, longer-term focus. Minority voting might be fine for local quality improvements, but it can be a dangerous distraction for an enterprise that's operating to a demanding business plan.

Corporate centre plans have rarely been popular because they aim to optimize the efforts of the whole enterprise, generally at the expense of the individual parts. In contrast, lobbyists tend to focus on single-issue arguments in support of short-term, local interests. Quiet thinkers and sensible strategists will be ignored. It will be the survival of the fastest, the loudest and the best networked.

The consequence is that, for better or worse, decision-making will become increasingly democratic, based on minority opinions. And there's nothing we can do about it, other than to get stuck in and join the debate.

The influence of top management and corporate centre directors will progressively die unless they change. In the future, the ability to craft a compelling e-mail will become more useful than a commanding physical presence. Whether people like it or not, it seems inevitable that good bloggers will eventually have the edge over traditional company men.

Don't lock down that network

Many security managers ask me whether we should be closing down risky network transactions, or learning to live with the risks the present. It's a growing dilemma for network security managers.

No long ago, I was asked to speak at a big European conference in London on the subject of 'Locking down social network vulnerabilities'. The title was chosen to attract delegates and to appeal to the media. But it's an ironic one, because locking down any feature of networks is a futile objective. And vulnerabilities also exist in real-world social networks. People have a tendency, for example, to blab to their friends and family. The differences on-line are the visibility and, more particularly, the scale.

We do, of course, need to address the security vulnerabilities presented by social networks. But constraints on network flows are rarely a sensible idea. Networks should be designed to be free-flowing, and to resist attempts to block, filter or divert traffic. In fact, resilience of flows is a primary security feature, one of growing significance. And, anyway, the best security measures to control social networking lie outside of the network.

My advice to the audience was not to lock anything down, but to pay more attention to supporting the free flow of networks. In particular, it's important to appreciate the real intellectual value that might be present in a network. Increasingly, that will be tied up in the intangible know-how and personal relationships in the information flows, rather than in the static stocks of legacy data in the connected databases.

Getting to grips with the ownership and management of personal relationships is much more important that blocking or filtering an ad hoc selection of passing data. And in most cases, educating users will be more effective than monitoring their traffic. These should be the new priorities of the modern security manager.

We need, of course, to be mindful of the risks from the insider threat. But countering such a threat requires a broader, richer set of solutions than we can achieve at the network level. To detect an inappropriate or illegal user action, we need to appreciate the full context of that behaviour, which requires much more than an inspection of data and transactions. And when it comes to deterring or detecting fraud and espionage, the most effective controls lie outside of the network environment.

That doesn't mean that network security is dead. Filtering and blocking of network traffic will continue to be a practical reality for many years to come. And monitoring of traffic will continue to provide an increasingly useful source of security intelligence, as well as delivering the essential evidence to support breach investigations.

The future of network security

So what exactly is the future of network security in a world that values information flows above security barriers? Not long ago, I was invited to contribute a thought leadership column to *Network World*, on behalf of the Jericho Forum. I chose to write about this subject. The focus of my article was the implication for network security in a de-perimeterized world, an environment in which the focus of security controls migrates from the infrastructure towards the application and data level. What will be the longer-term role of network security? Will it eventually become redundant or will it grow even more powerful?

These questions are often raised when de-perimeterization is discussed, because there is an assumption that placing security closer to the data and applications, might remove the need for controls in networks. My conclusion, however, is that there is huge potential for delivering value through security features in networks. But it will be very different from what we see today. And it will be increasingly focused on the human factor.

Networks are a convenient place to apply many types of security control. They're a good place to position controls that need to be less invasive or more transparent to users. But they also present limitations. Geography, topology, ownership boundaries and legal jurisdictions are all major constraints. It's often hard to find a convenient choke point in a network, at which you can view or control all of the traffic you might be interested in. But, on the other hand, network gateways are a great place to secure central databases. And the latest gateway platforms offer a huge range of security features. Topology can work for or against security.

Valuable security intelligence can also be derived by profiling and mining network content, traffic patterns and user behaviour. Psychological profiling offers huge potential for the future detection of fraud, espionage or terrorism. But privacy considerations are a major, growing concern. Controls will need to be designed in, from the ground up, to preserve anonymity for intercepted traffic of people who are not the subject of a security investigation.

In fact, you can monitor a user's behaviour either from within the network, or from its endpoints, such as the client and server platforms. Each option provides a very different, complementary perspective. The network view, for example, has the advantage of being able to compare or contrast an individual user's behaviour with those of a broader community. In contrast, the endpoint perspective enables comparison with historical activity. Both viewpoints are useful.

Network gateways are also a vital source of security intelligence because they can see many failed or blocked transactions, providing a greater degree of insight into near misses and attempted attacks. And as we'll see in Chapter 3, it's important to keep an eye out for near misses, because they're a potential indicator of incidents to come.

Can we trust the data?

Peer-to-peer collaboration and consultation is progressively becoming a mainstream business tool. But the integrity of knowledge to support business decision-making will be under threat if managers rely solely on the views of networked colleagues, rather than expert advisers. Networks don't always get things right. In some cases they can be positively dangerous.

'Chinese whispers', a process in which a story gets distorted as it's passed on from one person to another, can distort the true facts and figures.

I once asked a media relations director what his biggest information problem was. 'Establishing the right numbers,' he replied, 'If the correct figure is 67.5, some will round it to 67, others to 68, or perhaps even 60 or 70. And as these numbers get passed on, they get further distorted. You will end up with a range of different estimates, ranging from 50 to 100.'

The process of rumour has been studied by psychologists for many years. Early research, by Gordon Allport and Joseph Postman in 1947, examined how messages travel by word of mouth. They found that about 70% of the details of a message were lost in the first five or six exchanges, and concluded that as rumors travel, they grow shorter, more concise and easier to tell and grasp.

Allport and Postman identified three key processes that shape the development of rumours: levelling, sharpening, and assimilation. Levelling is the progressive loss of some of the details of the original message. Sharpening is the process that selects and highlights particular details. And assimilation is the unconscious (or perhaps subconscious) distortion in the details of the message.

Internet discussions, however, are quite different. They are interactive, and the original postings are also available. More recent research suggests that there is often a collective, problem-solving process at work, in which new ideas are introduced, further information is volunteered and discussed, and then a resolution is drawn, or interest tails off.

A few years ago, James Surowiecki, a columnist with the *New Yorker* magazine, published an articulate and influential book on networked behaviour, called *The Wisdom of Crowds*. The concept of the book is a hypothesis that collective group behaviour is smarter, wiser and more innovative than individual efforts. Surowiecki cites entertaining anecdotal examples from history and everyday life in order to demonstrate how this principle operates.

In fact, the title of Surowiecki's book was inspired by a 19th century book by Charles Mackay about human follies, called *Extraordinary Popular Delusions and the Madness of Crowds*. That book cites examples of the opposite phenomenon, such as witch hunts, crusades and financial bubbles.

Both these books illustrate the potential for good and bad decisions in networks. Unfortunately, you can't rely on collective voting to get it right all the time. But the more people that accept an idea, the stronger it becomes.

'Three men make a tiger' is a Chinese proverb based on the phenomenon that if three or more people mention an observation then it's likely to be believed. The proverb is reported to have come from a speech by a Chinese official called Pang Cong, in around 300 BC.

Pang Cong claimed that he'd asked the King whether he would be inclined to believe a single citizen's report that a tiger was roaming the markets in the capital city. The King replied that he wouldn't. He then asked the King what he would think if two people reported it. The King said he would begin to wonder. He then asked what he would think if three people claimed to have seen a tiger. The King replied that it must be true if three people say it.

The word of three different people might have seemed credible in an ancient society, at a time when people travelled much less on a daily basis. But it's statistically insignificant in the context of a large network such as the Internet.

Urban myths, fictional tales passed on as true stories, are an interesting feature of social networks. They have proliferated with the growth of the Internet. And it's not surprising, as it's so easy to invent a story and to spread it across a network. Someone, somewhere, is bound to believe it. And if one or more people accept it, then it will begin to gain credence. Eventually it might become accepted by a majority.

Urban myths abound in security. The wealth of hoax viruses is an example of this. They cause anxiety and waste people's time. Several years ago I received a report from a police force about a new technique that was being used by thieves to help steal laptops from cars. Using a cheap electronic scanning device, bought in the High Street, they were reportedly able to detect the presence of a laptop in the locked boot of a car. Like all good stories it sounded unlikely, but just about possible. We had to try it out. It failed, of course, to work as suggested.

The learning point is not to believe everything you read or hear over a large public network. But that's the way the world is going. And many people are surprisingly trusting of information that's generated by technology. Electronic data all looks perfectly genuine at first sight.

The art of disinformation

The real secret of disinformation, the promulgation of false information for military or propaganda purposes, is to mix a few lies with some genuine information. Such techniques have long formed a part of military strategy.

They were heavily used by MI5 during World War II to deceive German intelligence about British intentions. The Cold War turned them into an art form. At its height there were thousands of people on both sides secretly engaged in creating false trails for the other side. Today we can see a certain amount of disinformation practiced by all stakeholders in the War on Terror.

Disinformation is a complex business, a rich blend of truth, lies and opinions. Sorting out the real truth from a range of facts that have been invented, massaged, exaggerated or just selectively reported, perhaps by a multitude of players, is certainly not easy for the recipients.

In his book *Disinformation: 22 Media Myths That Undermine the War on Terror*, Richard Miniter, an experienced journalist, points to six sources of media myth: honest errors, government spin, disinformation by foreign intelligence services, historical amnesia, leaks and media failures.

The concept of 'spin', presenting facts in a distorted way to promote a particular cause, has long been a skill practiced by the media. Now it's become endemic in most government communications. And as we become accustomed to its use, it's likely to spread further. Most company communications functions also apply a small about of spin to their press releases, though much less than their government counterparts. Spin includes a range of techniques: suggestive phrasing, selective reporting and downplaying of bad news.

The potential for spin has been progressively growing with the continuing increase in analogue media to communicate news and knowledge. Images are much less precise than words for conveying information, and they can substantially alter the context and interpretation of a message. In the past, we relied primarily on factual sources, such as books and classroom lectures to gain our knowledge of a subject. Today, our knowledge is gained through a haze of sponsored images and advertising through television and the Internet.

Some spin is subtle, disguised and unconsciously absorbed. Other types of spin are less covert forms of persuasion. It can, for example, be an obvious, indirect, form of criticism, as encapsulated by Alexander Pope's famous quote in his epistle to Doctor Arbuthnot in 1733:

> *'Damn with faint praise, assent with civil leer, and, without sneering, teach the rest to sneer.'*

Fear, uncertainty and doubt, or FUD for short, is a highly effective form of deliberate, undisguised spin, used extensively in the computer industry to cast doubt on the wisdom of buying a rival product. The term was coined by Gene Amdahl after he left IBM to found his own company:

> *'FUD is the fear, uncertainty, and doubt that IBM sales people instill in the minds of potential customers who might be considering Amdahl products.'*

IBM's marketing people were certainly highly successful at planting a simple but powerful perception in their customer's minds: that nobody ever got fired for buying IBM equipment. Whether or not it was actually true did not really matter. It was enough to make purchasers think twice about the downside risks in selecting a less established product.

In fact, it's surprisingly easy to spread fear, uncertainty and doubt about any new thing that looks promising. Just float a few negative comments such as: 'But is it proven?', 'Can they deliver?', 'What's the catch?' and 'What about the hidden costs?' People will quickly begin to form doubts. Every business decision involves a degree of uncertainty. But it's not generally at the forefront of our minds. FUD is that slight nudge that reminds us to place those risks higher in our mental selection criteria.

In many financial markets, unscrupulous traders can make fast, easy money by floating damaging, false rumours about companies to encourage share prices to fall. But finding evidence of this to support a prosecution is far from easy. The problem is so serious in the financial sector that the US Securities and Exchange Commission has banned 'naked' short selling of shares (which sellers do not yet possess) in the country's major investment banks.

Countering disinformation is simple, though not always easy. The answer is, firstly, never to place your trust in unconfirmed rumours or hearsay, and, secondly to always seek a second opinion when making critical business decisions.

The future of knowledge

Wikipedia is an interesting glimpse of the potential future of many knowledge bases. It's mostly accurate, and like all good disinformation, it encourages a false sense of security. You never quite know whether that key item of information that you've decided to rely on is accurate, mistaken or deliberately distorted.

But it's astoundingly fast at gathering new information. In fact, the work 'wiki' is the Hawaiian word for 'quick'. It's proved itself to be faster than other information channels on many occasions.

On July 7th 2005, London was rocked by four explosions. Within less than twenty minutes of the first explosions, an entry had appeared on Wikipedia. By the end of the day, more than 2500 had collaborated to produce an account that was more detailed than the accounts of any single news agency. Meanwhile, the collaborative website Flickr had been breaking some of the first photographs of the bombings, taken by camera phones.

Amateurs with camera phones will always beat professional news gatherers to new, unexpected stories, simply because they happen to be there at the time. Collaborative websites, run by volunteers, are catching up with, and often overtaking, established sources of news and knowledge.

But the information is not always compiled by people that are experienced, expert, objective or trusted. As the Wikipedia site puts it:

'Visitors do not need specialized qualifications to contribute, since their primary role is to write articles that cover existing knowledge; this means that people of all ages and cultural and social backgrounds can write Wikipedia articles.'

The information on such sites doesn't carry reliability indicators, other than the fact that older information is more likely to be noticed and challenged if incorrect. As Wikipedia cautions:

'Older articles tend to be more comprehensive and balanced, while newer articles more frequently contain significant misinformation, unencyclopedic content, or vandalism. Users need to be aware of this to obtain valid information and avoid misinformation that has been recently added and not yet removed.'

In fact it's not quite that simple. Popular subjects attract faster scrutiny and correction, sometimes in minutes. Less popular entries can remain uncorrected for long periods, perhaps indefinitely. As a legal friend of mine puts it:

'Wikipedia is fine for researching your children's homework, but you wouldn't rely on it for a major business decision.'

Not everyone is that cautious however. It's a percentage game. If it's correct nine times out of ten, then few people will experience or notice a major problem. They will instinctively rely on it. Just as for deliberate disinformation, they will be caught out by the insidious lie that's carefully hidden in a sea of truth.

The next big security concern

Attempts to mislead can cause more damage than espionage. They're also highly complex to uncover and repair. The current big security concern of that nature is identity theft. Repairing the damage to a single compromised account requires an investment of days or weeks of effort.

Identity theft is the bridge between today's obsession with data confidentiality and tomorrow's broader exposure to attacks on data integrity. Integrity of business and personal data will be the most important, future concern for organizations. In fact, it's the next big challenge for all information security managers.

Confidentiality, integrity and availability are the three cornerstones of information security. The balance of significance of these factors has tended to shift over the years. In fact, there is a logical evolution in their visibility and relative significance, though it's been substantially influenced by developments such as the Cold War and the introduction of electronic networks.

Availability is the first thing you notice about information systems. When they stop, which they all tend to do from time to time, it's an obvious problem, with an immediate, but largely temporary, impact. Confidentiality of data is the next security characteristic that comes to people's attention. We rarely experience such incidents in everyday business life, but when we do it, it creates a more sinister, longer lasting impact. Integrity of data is generally the last security characteristic we notice. Few people tamper with data. We rarely experience the impact of a loss, and we don't read much about it in the newspapers. But when a breach comes to light, it's a major concern.

In the old business world of paper documents, confidentiality was a primary concern in most security managers' minds, though the reality was that misfiling of records was probably the biggest everyday problem. Early information security policies from the 1970s are quite an eye-opener, if you ever come across them. Many reflect an obsession with espionage that seems quite surprising today. That was probably due to an early military influence over the development of the subject area.

The end of the Cold War removed much of the paranoia about confidentiality. In the early days of the Internet, the biggest concern of most companies was the availability of information services. It was the most obvious and common risk, and it had a clear business impact. At that time, some security experts even suggested that confidentiality was no longer important, an unnecessary hangover from the Cold War days. But they were wrong.

A breach of customer confidentiality has always been one of the most damaging security risks to organizations. In the early days of electronic commerce, that risk was rarely acknowledged by system managers. A few high-profile breaches have served to change that perception. Today it's clear to everyone that data leakage prevention is a priority for any business process that handles personal data or confidential business information.

As we go forward into the next phase of the information age, we'll find that perhaps the most serious of the emerging risks will be the ones that threaten the integrity of our intellectual assets. This will become clear with the emergence of new threats, the increase in the value of intellectual assets and our growing appreciation of the potential business impact from such breaches.

Damage to the integrity of business information assets is rarely encountered today, but when it does occur, the impact of a breach is often substantial. Even the suggestion of a small set of unauthorized changes to a critical business database can be hugely damaging to its perceived value, and the reputation of the business services that depend on it.

Uncertainty about the extent of unauthorized changes is a disturbing concern. It's a little like walking into an airport hangar and finding evidence that an overnight intruder has had free access to a passenger jet. You wouldn't dare let it fly, without carrying out a thorough inspection of every single item that might have been affected. Conducting an integrity check of millions of records, however, is a much more challenging task.

Mistakes and bad practices can also be a threat to data integrity. Most citizens would be shocked if they knew just how bad the quality of data was that companies and government agencies held on them. And even short-term data can present major problems. Fast moving, collaborative team working can also result in errors, when team members end up working on different instances of a document.

We have to yet to experience the wake-up call to better working practices and tighter controls to safeguard data integrity. But that will emerge in the next few years. Breaches of integrity are hard to detect, and even more difficult to repair. They are the new nightmare waiting to engulf companies that places high reliance or substantial value on their intellectual assets.

Learning from networks

What have we learned in this chapter? Here's a summary of some of the key findings and conclusions.

We explored the nature of power, and the power of networks. Power and networks are inextricably linked. And both are challenging our approach to information security. Traditional approaches to security are breaking down, as networks break down corporate barriers, and their content displaces existing channels of advice. Social networks are gradually disempowering corporate centre security functions. We will need to rethink the way we communicate and enforce our policy.

Networks are a powerful leveller, with little respect for status or authority. At the same time, they're also a potent means of leveraging individual ideas and initiatives. There is huge value waiting to be tapped in social networks. Reed's Law indicates that the value of social networks might scale exponentially with the number of members. We should be aiming to understand and safeguard that value.

Ever since their invention, networks have transformed business life and increased security risks, by cutting through geographic and organizational barriers, including those between personal and business lifestyles. This is the phenomenon we call de-perimeterization.

Each decade has brought a new focus to security, through the progressive extension of networks. The 1970s introduced risk assessment. The 1980s encouraged business units to establish secure datacentres. The 1990s moved the focus of security to enterprise networks. The early years of the 21st century introduced electronic commerce.

But information security has failed to keep up with a problem space that's moved outside of the corporate boundary. Security managers need to shift their attention towards working together to build community solutions. The Jericho Forum has developed a set of principles, and is building a collaboration-oriented architecture, to enable secure business operations across extended enterprise environments.

Social networking and virtual worlds are new challenges. Lost productivity is just the tip of the iceberg. The real threat is to sensitive information. But corporate policies and security education lag far behind user practice. Social networks also present threats to democracy in politics and business. We now face the tyranny of the minority. Minority voting is fine for quality improvements, but not for an enterprise aiming to operate to a single business strategy.

The integrity of knowledge to support business decisions is also under threat. There might be some wisdom in crowds, but there is also FUD, spin and disinformation. Integrity of data will be the next big problem for security managers. Breaches of integrity are rarely encountered in everyday business but their potential impact is huge. They are hard to detect and even more difficult to repair.

The smart information security manager will aim, not to lock down our networks, but to safeguard information flows. Here are 10 principles that you might wish to consider for securing your intellectual assets in the new, networked, Web 2.0 world.

- Ensure your staff and customers are streetwise
- Understand your real intellectual assets
- Take steps to safeguard the integrity of critical data
- Focus on information flows, not static stocks of data
- Establish ownership and responsibility for valuable assets and relationships
- Engage at the same level as your staff and customers
- Respond to network problems with network solutions
- Use networks to promote awareness
- Exploit virtuous circles to leverage your efforts
- Remember that every change is an opportunity

In particular, we need to think positively. We will experience huge changes over the next decade. Everyone and everything will be affected. We should aim to keep our heads and to stay ahead, to exploit the challenges of the information age, rather than be overtaken by events that are outside our control.

CHAPTER 2

Everyone makes a difference

Where to focus your efforts

It's an old adage that everybody is responsible for security. It's certainly true. But, as much as we'd like to, we can't easily teach everyone everything about security. The real key to successful information security management is prioritization of our limited efforts. We simply can't tackle everything at once. We have to focus our efforts on conveying the most important messages to the most influential people.

This chapter aims to examine the perspective and role of each major actor or stakeholder in ensuring that our information security is as effective as we can make it across the organization, and its infrastructure.

Where should we start? Who matters most? Some people claim it's the Board that really counts. Others say it's the front-line workforce. Then again, it could be the IT function or the business unit managers who hold the key to successful security.

But the reality remains that, in practice, everybody counts. Every stakeholder makes a difference, ranging from the smallest customer to the biggest director. They all have different parts to play. And they each require a different level of knowledge and attention.

In fact, the key to harnessing the best contributions from all stakeholders is to establish an effective information security governance structure. In later chapters we'll be examining some of the options and techniques for achieving this.

In the meantime, let's start from the top, by examining the perspective of the Executive Board.

Managing the Human Factor in Information Security   David Lacey
© 2009 John Wiley & Sons, Ltd

The view from the bridge

For much of the last 30 years, most managing directors were able to happily ignore the status and operation of information security. They always took it seriously of course. It would seem careless not to. But they generally kept their distance.

After all why get involved? Unless you happened to be especially taken with the subject, it was most likely to prove to be a distraction to the real, money-making side of the business, though it has to be said that there are always a small number of business executives who take an active interest in the political leverage that security can enable.

Information security risks are complex, uncertain and hard to nail down. In the past, if you could get away with it, ignorance was always a much safer option. If things went wrong, you could always put your hands up, act innocent, and sack the IT or Security Director. But then along came the Sarbanes–Oxley Act of 2002, which heralded a wind of change through all corporate boardrooms.

Amongst other things, Sarbanes–Oxley mandated that senior executives took individual responsibility for the accuracy and completeness of corporate financial reports. Company boards were required to certify and approve the integrity of their financial reports, including the adequacy of internal controls, including security.

It also required evidence of the operation of key financial controls. And there were stiff criminal penalties for manipulation, destruction or alteration of financial records, as well as protection for any whistle-blowers. No managing director could ignore these demands. Establishing the status of risks and controls suddenly became a board level imperative.

But how far should executive boards involve themselves in the actual process of risk management? In fact, there's no easy or definitive answer to that. The best we can do is pay attention to the recommendations of respected societies and institutes.

One standard, for example, drawn by three leading UK risk organizations, the Institute of Risk Management, the Association of Insurance and Risk Managers and the National Forum for Risk Management in the Public Sector, provides a list of responsibilities for boards of directors.

Amongst other things, this standard suggests they should know about the most significant risks facing the organization, the possible effects on shareholder value of any deviations to the expected performance ranges, as well as how the organization will manage a crisis. Boards are also expected to publish a clear risk management policy, to ensure that there are appropriate levels of awareness throughout the organization, and to be assured that the risk management process is working effectively.

These are not trivial demands. And they are likely to become increasingly harder to manage, with growing business dependence on complex information systems, as well as the more challenging risks presented by emerging security threats.

The role of the executive board

There's no doubt that executive board members can add substantial value to the corporate risk management process. They can, for example, contribute their unique high-level perspective of business operations and priorities.

But managing directors should stop short of involving themselves in detailed debates about specialist risks. They're certainly not equipped to determine whether, for example, the level of anti-malware protection is adequate. It's not what they're best at doing, though that perception might not necessarily stop them from trying.

Boards should always leave specialist assessments to the experts. And if they don't have any experts on board, they should seek external advice. Board members can usefully take a leaf out of the book of certification auditors, who regularly evaluate the adequacy of control structures across large enterprises, without ever getting bogged down in the detail.

That's because good governance is about ensuring that adequate controls and processes are in place to identify the major risks, to establish key control requirements, to identify gaps, to plan remedial action and to check that it's all been carried out.

According to a global survey of board directors carried out by Ernst & Young, compliance with standards and regulations has now become the board's main risk priority. But the real challenge is to create a risk management framework that goes beyond simple compliance. Otherwise risk management will be reduced to no more than a 'tick-the-box' activity. And that means it simply won't be taken seriously.

A strong focus on risk mitigation, however, can also create tensions between board members and senior management, whose growth and performance objectives often mandate active risk taking. Life and work are full of contradictions. But delivering a business strategy requires a clear focus on direction and priorities. So it's especially important for boards to spell out the level of risk appetite that's expected of senior and middle management.

But this is a very hard thing to do realistically, without creating a potential hostage to fortune, especially given the current climate of increasing compliance and scrutiny. If you're a member of the board, you can't be too cautious because shareholders will be concerned. At the same time, you can't be seen to be too cavalier, because regulators and auditors will damn you. So, in practice, little real direction will be given by boards. And business managers will be left to decide their own limits of acceptable risk taking.

In fact, the real challenge for today's executive boards is not to get bogged down with the routine issues, the ones that the existing management systems are already well equipped to tackle, but to identify and address the bigger picture risks that ordinary business managers are less likely to address, either because the cause or the resulting impact is outside their remit, or because the probability of such a risk materializing is sufficiently remote to be ignored.

In particular, boards need to identify and consider the implications of the major residual risks, the big exposures that remain after all reasonable, practical and affordable measures have been taken. Business managers will aim to take all the precautions that they can sensibly afford to take. But the resultant, residual risk might still be unacceptable to a management team. In such circumstances, the Board might have to consider extreme options, such as withdrawing from a high-risk business, or consciously deciding to accept a large, potential risk. These are not easy decisions for risk-averse directors. They require bold judgments.

In fact, boards really need to 'think the unthinkable', to consider the big, catastrophic, unrecoverable risks – no matter how unlikely they might seem– that might occur within the horizon of their current business strategy. Things like a major run on a bank, an irrecoverable loss of a critical database or a rogue trader that bankrupts the company. And that requires bold and innovative thinking, something that's often lacking in today's risk-averse, compliance-focused governance culture. But it's the essential starting point for ensuring the long-term survival of the enterprise, in a business environment that's rapidly changing, far beyond our traditional assumptions.

A good understanding of risks to business interests can help to identify areas where more risk can be taken, though this should only be attempted with a clear appreciation of the generally accepted risk tolerance levels for a particular industry. In fact, this is precisely how information awareness can best enable business advantage: by showing how to take risks prudently with a set of eyes that are fully open.

The new threat of data leakage

Managing directors now also have a new risk to keep them awake at night. The threat of large-scale data leakage is a frightening new spectre. It's one that's largely outside most people's experience, but it's also one that's now haunting all industry and government leaders.

The unprecedented level of publicity surrounding large data breaches during 2007 was a huge shock to many organizations. Citizens were outraged. At the same time, executive boards were stunned. For the first time, it dawned on both managers and customers that a tiny, security flaw or procedural error might actually result in substantial damage to personal data, as well as business interests.

And no matter how you measure the costs of incidents, personal data breaches will remain a major, growing, serious security threat.

The private sector, for example, counts its damage in financial terms. The quintessential example of that was the TJ Maxx breach of customer credit data in 2007. The company was forced to set aside $130 million to cover the costs arising from a single data breach, including a staggering $11 million in security consultancy fees alone. That's a huge hit, enough to fund the entire security function of a large international bank.

But the full cost of the damage could have been much higher. Research of previous incidents of this type, by the Ponemon Institute, a leading US think tank, indicates that a breach of this magnitude, affecting tens of millions of customers, could easily exceed a billion dollars.

That's a staggering amount of damage. It's enough to liquidate a medium size organization. So no executive board can possibly afford not to pay serious attention to risks of this nature.

Why is this figure so high? The cost is due, in part, to the expense associated with repairing each compromised account. Unfortunately for big companies, some elements of the overall recovery costs are proportional to the number of affected customers. Big databases will cause big damage when compromised. On top of that, there are the lost future sales, and the potential reputation damage. It's a sobering thought for any custodians of large customer databases.

Centralization has always been attractive from a cost-reduction perspective. But there is a new dimension. We now have to accept the potential risk and damage from a major security breach.

Guardianship of citizen personal data is also something that no enterprise can afford to treat lightly. As Sir Colin Crosby, a former CEO of Halifax Bank of Scotland put it in his 2008 report on *Information Assurance* to the UK Treasury:

'Identity is the new currency.'

If we have personal data on employees, customers or citizens, we have to understand and meet their new expectations.

In contrast to the private sector, government agencies generally count the real costs of their incidents in political damage. We didn't see much of that in the past. But we're seeing a lot more of it today.

A single incident in 2007, involving lost computer disks sent through the post at Her Majesty's Revenue and Customs (HMRC), prompted the resignation of the chief executive, and led to a significant drop in public confidence of data guardianship, enough perhaps to swing a general election.

The incident also caused serious damage to citizen confidence for other UK Government IT projects, such as the National Identity Card Program and the National Health Service Connecting for Health system of patient records. It was a major setback for plans to transform UK Government through shared services. It also cost a staggering £11 million to send out letters to those affected by the HMRC loss. And that was the cost just of the letters, envelopes and postage.

The learning point from these incidents is that no organization that processes large numbers of citizen records can afford to be complacent about security. Citizens expected them to be proactive, to implement measures that users and customers now expect to be deployed as routine, measures such as strong encryption of personal data, at rest and in transit.

In the past, most enterprise could get away with a small percentage of incidents that compromised personal data. They rarely reflected a serious attempt to steal data and they did not attract major publicity. Both of those factors have changed. There is no longer any acceptable level of personal data loss.

The public sector, for example, processes hundreds of millions of personal citizen records, spread over thousands of databases. On this scale there is no acceptable level of loss of confidentiality or integrity. The compromise of a single percentage of national records would affect a population the size of a major city. That's a huge amount of damage and a large number of potential votes. With this in mind, it's hard to imagine that any public sector CEO could sleep soundly. They will either have to transform their information security or they will be facing a career-limiting security risk landscape.

The perspective of business management

Business managers are at the heart of risk-taking, decision-making and value creation in the organization. They have a vital role to play in identifying and managing risks. But it's difficult to get them motivated to address information security. Their mind is focused on business objectives. They have strict deadlines and tight budgets. Security is not welcome, because it will cost their projects more time, resource or money.

That's quite understandable. If you're busy, and focused on short-term challenges, then the last thing you want to do is to waste your time thinking about and planning for a set of theoretical risks, ones that might never happen. Or, even worse, reading complicated policies and standards, written by faceless bureaucrats in a remote, corporate centre.

In fact, that's a missed opportunity. Because there's so much that information security can do for a business executive. It can, for example, reduce incident levels, saving time and money. It can also leverage sales to security-conscious customers. And there are a growing number of them. Risk management can also help a manager to meet demanding deadlines and targets. And, in addition, it can help to safeguard brand value and other major intellectual assets.

Unfortunately, as we'll find out later, people rarely respond to measures that are not personal, immediate or certain. And few security messages fit this particular set of criteria. Information security is generally perceived as a long-term, impersonal and far from certain investment. Getting business managers to address information security will, therefore, always be a major challenge.

In fact, we can always find one or two motivators that are personal, immediate and certain. And they're often just enough to twist the arms of even the most hardened business managers. Take legislative requirements for example. If you tell a business manager he's likely to go to jail if he doesn't address the need for a particular control, he'll respond in an instant. It's a personal and immediate threat.

Motivations like that can give you a useful start in the race to persuade business units to eliminate major vulnerabilities before they get exploited. In the longer term, we should aim to develop a 'pull' rather than 'push' approach to information security, one that inspires managers by focusing on benefits and incentives, rather than threats. But that will take time to build, so it's worth starting out with threats, rather than promises.

The role of the business manager

What are the key things that we should expect our business managers to do? It's not enough to point out a set of security risks and compliance requirements. We also need to present them with a practical set of actions that they can take.

The first, and most important, thing that they should do is to consider, decide and agree the risk appetite for their business units. How much risk are they prepared to accept? And are they confident enough to decide and define it? Business managers need to communicate a clear, unambiguous indication of the level of risk that they are comfortable in accepting. This might sound like a simple decision, but in practice it's far from it.

Risk appetite is a subjective assessment. Individual managers tend to have different degrees of natural appetite for risks. That's why it's always best to assess risks in a group, as a management team, preferably with input from a security professional who has a good understanding of the nature of the threats to their information systems, and can help to assess the level of vulnerability of critical business systems to determined attacks.

Risk appetite can also be a tempting concept for an executive, under pressure to cut costs, to do nothing. Present any business manager with a stark choice of spending money or accepting a risk, and you can guarantee they will choose the latter. Information security risks rarely have much impact on their short-term survival and bonus. This is changing, of course. But, unfortunately, it's not changing fast enough. So it's important to challenge their assessments.

Whenever I encounter a tendency in managers to accept what appears to me to be a significant risk, I always ask the key question:

> *'Do you fully understand the nature of this risk? And, if so, can you explain it to me?'*

Often they can't, so their assessment should be firmly rejected. And the process of determining the answer to that question will encourage them to reflect more thoroughly in future on the risks to their business decisions.

As we'll see in a later chapter, self-discovery is a pre-requisite for changing attitudes. You can't force people to change their views, against their better judgment. Questions that get managers thinking differently, challenging their traditional perceptions, are amongst the most valuable influences a security manager can have on business operations.

A second important point that all business managers need to take on board is the importance of building information security into commercial requirements, specifications and contracts. Some things can be added later. But security is not one of them. That might be obvious to us, of course, but it might not necessarily be to them.

The real art of building good information security practice into business operations is to communicate and establish these essential principles. Dropping in to a business unit, and conducting a quick, detailed survey or briefing, no matter how professionally executed, will have little lasting value. Instead we should aim to embed good practice.

To make any significant impact on business managers, we will need to be smart, focused and compelling. And we will need to talk their language. We should also adjust our own expectations. Business managers will not fall into line immediately.

Changing the attitude of a single individual is hard enough. Changing the collective behaviour of a large group of managers is a much longer, ambitious process. But it's worth investing the time, effort and patience to win over even a single, hard-nosed business manager. Because, once converted, you will have an important ally to support you in your broader campaigns.

Engaging with business managers

In today's hectic business environment, time management is a pre-requisite for survival. It's the same for all managers. In fact, the key dilemma facing security managers today is deciding how much time to assign to managing relationships with business managers, and how to make the best use of opportunities to engage with them.

It's generally best to arrange brief, but regular, meetings or clinics with business managers, and to maintain a clear focus on how information security relates to their business objectives. Before each encounter, take a step back to reflect on their commercial goals, environment and issues. In particular, it's important to appreciate the pressures imposed by current business challenges, and to consider how these might be helped by the adoption of better information security measures.

The ultimate goal should be to persuade business colleagues to adopt good information security because it actually helps them manage their business, rather than to address it because it's a corporate policy or legal requirement. Threats of compliance failures might provide the initial catalyst for gaining attention. But that should be the start of a longer, more business-focused dialogue.

Good information security and risk management can help to bring in a project on time, to leverage the sales of products and services to demanding customers or to design a successful new product. That's what we can achieve, ultimately, if we apply security intelligently, and with a good understanding of the business environment. In practice, examples of this have generally been few and far between. But they can all be achieved, given sufficient belief and political will.

We need to convince business managers that information security is much more than a 'tick the box' compliance process, or a threat that they cannot afford to ignore. It needs to be accepted as good, prudent management, a practice that adds real business value. That's always an extremely difficult selling point, but it's one that's essential to engage and embrace business managers.

Business managers set the real agenda for everyday activities across the organization. They hold the key to the effectiveness of the organization's response to risks, policies and standards. Alignment with business interest is a pre-requisite for effective security. Security is a support function, not a business in itself. Its presentation and appeal will need to be tailored to meet the vision and strategy of each business unit.

But the essential, pervasive message should be that 'good security is good business'.

The role of the IT function

Whether in-house or out-sourced to professional service providers, the role of IT function is also essential to the ability of the information security function to achieve its objectives. Whether it's appropriate or not, IT managers have a significant influence on the security of systems and infrastructure.

IT professionals specify many of the detailed requirements for new information systems. They design architectures for computer platforms and network infrastructures. And they oversee the development and management of software systems, as well as the award of contracts to IT service providers.

Despite all this influence, there is a continuing power struggle between business and IT manager for control of key decisions on products, architectures and priorities. The business generally wins in the end because they have more clout, though often they will assume the wrong role to achieve this. I've seen business managers selecting technology and IT professionals developing business models. There appears to be a strange attraction for many executives to assume responsibilities far outside their competence and remit.

Persuading IT service managers to deliver the level of security that's actually needed calls for exceptional skills in relationship management. IT managers have to balance the requirements of security, with the demands of their own commercial interests, within the constraints of tight timescales and budgets. And it's especially difficult if service delivery is outsourced to managers that operate from remote locations, perhaps in different countries and time zones.

There is an old joke, in the information security community, that decisions on information systems are like a choosing a new partner. You'd ideally want someone that's rich, attractive and with a great personality. Unfortunately you're unlikely to find anyone with all three of these ideals. The most realistic option is to settle for two out of three. Which two would you choose?

Information systems are a little bit like that. In an ideal world, we'd like them to be fully secure, feature-rich and delivered both on time and within budget. But that's equally unlikely. Which two of these options should the smart IT manager pick?

The role of the security manager is to make sure it's not information security that gets ditched. It's hard to do this in any circumstances. Even if you manage to build comprehensive security into all of your service level agreements and contracts, there's no guarantee that it will be delivered.

You can try waving a paper contract at a service provider, but it will have little immediate impact, especially in an increasingly cavalier marketplace. The reality is that few service operators will actually have read your contract, and many of the clauses will be ambiguous. If you have a dispute, it might take months, perhaps years, to resolve contractual arguments. That's far too late for you to fix those immediate problems.

Two key aspects of information security that require special attention are identity management and accounting. It should always be possible to trace every action to a responsible individual who can be held accountable. If this cannot be achieved, then many other information security measures will be undermined.

Managing relationships with the IT function needs to be at the heart of the information security manager's objectives and efforts. And in today's virtual organization, it's especially important to be able to do this across the complete supply chain, which is increasingly likely to extend across many continents, cultures and enterprises.

Minding your partners

Our new capability to build secure extended-enterprise networks that span the world will herald a new wave of large-scale out-sourcing of services and support processes. Information systems and security services will increasingly move to the 'cloud' supporting new, collaborative operations across business partnerships and based on a growing portfolio of Internet-based, software services.

A new skill will be born out of this. It will be the valuable ability to manage a set of services for a constantly changing business, armed only with a contract, set in stone, a modest budget and a list of telephone contacts. It's important, of course, to get the contracts with your strategic partners right, but, at the end of the day, it's your relationship management skills that ensure that you actually get what you really need, rather than what someone decided, a long time ago, what they thought you needed.

Most IT and security managers make the mistake of focusing their attention on the in-house resources, the corporate policies and the service contracts. They're wrong. It's the management of external relationships that increasingly makes the difference.

It's not easy to get people that you don't now, who are working for a different company, in a different building, to do the things you really want, based on no more that a handful of obscure policies and contracts. You will have to try to win their cooperation and support through a more compelling approach. And that means a regular dialogue, and a diplomatic approach.

In such a situation, threats and ultimatums won't encourage the immediate fixes to those legacy systems that are flawed or broken, at least not initially.

Shooting a 'messenger of bad news' is also a very bad strategy. Your business account manager in the service organization, who will no doubt be on your side, will need to draw on your help and support, rather than your criticism, to get things fixed. In fact he will probably be already engaged in fighting an internal battle to satisfy your needs.

Threats are for the longer-term strategy, when the contract comes up for renewal. In the short term, you need to win friends and influence people in the supply company. Processes are a good starting point. Your risk management and crisis management processes need to operate seamlessly across boundaries.

In a fast-changing world, the key to gaining value from suppliers is to persuade them to deliver demands that they might not have originally signed up to. A contract dispute is a zero-sum game that can only result in a winner and a loser. And you can't afford for your supplier to go out of business. You will have to find ways of working around formal contract restrictions. That means identifying and focusing on common motivators, ones that can work for both sides.

Computer users

Computer users have long been the traditional target of security education campaigns. We tend to think of them as enterprise staff but that's no longer the case. Large companies are now finding that more than half of their IT users are actually non-company personnel.

We often think of them as being a single body of people, all using a similar desktop and all sharing the same needs. But that's far from the reality. Users are all quite different. They might be an accountant in a corporate head office, a technician in a research lab, a team of traders in a trading room, a travelling salesman, a call centre operator in an overseas country or a shift worker in a manufacturing plant. They all have very different outlooks, varying needs and they operate in quite different environments.

Local roles, environments and business objectives shape user attitudes and behavior. Another factor is their use of and interaction with IT outside of the workplace. External cues and practices can undermine the effectiveness of instructions promoted in the workplace. Most organizations have a single set of policies governing the use of IT and the expected behaviour of staff. That's simply not good enough. Each part of the organization has a very different set of needs for information, communications and security. And, increasingly, each individual needs a unique set of instruction and facilities.

We must also not forget those company staff that do not generally access corporate information systems, but who need to be part of any enterprise identity management system that involves secure access to company premises or vehicles: our drivers, security guards and couriers, for example. Increasingly they will have the same needs and access capabilities as other network users. But they might not be listed in the directories of computer users. In fact, we need a new paradigm for the future: one that appreciates the fact that users are different and that they're not all enterprise staff, or traditional PC users.

Around 15 years ago, I drew up some predictions about the future of information security. They included a change of emphasis, as we moved from a collection of isolated information systems, to a connected enterprise, and then onto a world of mobile executives operating across public infrastructure. It was as clear then, as it is today, that the real future of information security lies in equipping our users to become streetwise 'road warriors' who understand security threats and vulnerabilities, and who can establish secure communications using any convenient client device connected through any available channels.

Customers and citizens

In the past, security managers gave little thought to business customers. Their attention was firmly primarily on the organization's assets, rather than the people who consume its products.

The banks, in particular, paid little attention to the need to secure their customers' transactions. A four digit PIN, a short password or a secret word, perhaps based on your mother's maiden name, was more than sufficient. And the banks felt no need to authenticate themselves to their customers in transactions or communications.

Then along came the waves of identity theft and phishing, which transformed all of our perspectives. It dawned on banks that customers need, and expect, a stronger authentication mechanism, preferably one that works both ways. Customers also need to be educated to switch their firewalls on, to update their security patches and anti-virus protection, and to be careful about the websites they visit, and the e-mails they respond to.

But that's just the start of the paradigm shift that's changing our focus of security, from an inward to an outward one. Customers now do much more than just receiving our latest products and services. Smart organizations are encouraging them to carry out as much work as possible in designing, assembling or dispatching products and services. Electronic networks are enabling this powerful trend.

In his book *The Third Wave*, Alvin Toffler coined the term 'prosumer' to describe the future role of the customer: part producer, part consumer. Toffler anticipated a major shift from the industrial age concept of mass production, towards an information age world of mass customization, a concept that requires increasing engagement of customers in product design processes, as well as deeper access to the information systems that underpin them. In the future, most of our computer users will be customers, rather than enterprise staff.

Learning from stakeholders

So what have we learned from this chapter? We set out to examine the role that each stakeholder plays in contributing to an organization or infrastructure that can be made acceptably secure. What did we find?

Firstly, it's clear that everybody is responsible for security. But we need to prioritize our efforts. We must focus our attention on all stakeholders, but in different ways.

At the top of the organization we need to encourage our managing directors to think about the big impacts that information security incidents might cause, not just today, but perhaps over the next year or two.

Within business units, we need to persuade managers to understand the nature of the threats to their information systems, and to take appropriate action, including building security into new commercial ventures and contracts. That means we need to understand their business objectives and issues, and to convince them that information security can add real business value.

The role of the IT function is also crucial, as it's IT managers that specify new system requirements and technical architectures, and also oversee the development and operation of new systems, including the award of contracts to service providers.

Computer users and staff have always been a major target audience for our security awareness campaigns. But it's increasingly important to also look outside of the enterprise, to address the security of business partners and customers. In fact, a growing number of our users are third-party staff and customers. And they are increasingly involved in designing, assembling and delivering our products.

All of these stakeholders have different perspectives and educational needs. There is no single campaign that will satisfy all of their requirements. Focusing on the lowest common denominator across a large community will result in a diluted solution. We need rich, tailored solutions, ones that cater to people working in varying roles, in quite different environments.

Here are five key learning points from considering the views of stakeholders:

- Everybody counts, including your customers
- Different stakeholders have different needs
- Executive boards should focus on the big risks and impacts
- Business managers need to understand and manage risks
- Don't forget the contractors in your supply chain

CHAPTER 3

There's no such thing as an isolated incident

What lies beneath?

When Harold Macmillan, the former conservative prime minister, was asked by a young journalist what can most easily steer a government off course, he answered:

'Events, dear boy, events.'

Events, incidents, disasters and crises shape our lives and determine our success or failure in business, as well as life. We cannot ignore them. In fact, the whole of information security is based on the premise that we should take measures to prevent, detect or respond to events of one type or another.

No two events are the same. Some events, such as earthquakes, are unstoppable. But many others, such as computer viruses, can be avoided, given sufficient foresight. They might be out there waiting for us, but we can dodge them if we're smart. And, similarly, some, such as a potential fraud, are actually preventable. We can take preventative action to discourage them from ever happening.

Smart organizations review security incidents to determine the root causes, so that they can identify countermeasures, to prevent, avoid or help recover from future incidents. When you do this on a regular basis, you'll notice patterns emerging. And in particular, you'll find that it's people who are the underlying cause of most accidents, breaches and incidents.

But people do more than just cause incidents. They can also prevent them, report them, fix them and learn from them. In fact, whatever the nature of the

Managing the Human Factor in Information Security   David Lacey
© 2009 John Wiley & Sons, Ltd

incident, you'll find that the human factor is the major factor in both the problem and solution space.

This chapter considers what lies beneath the surface of a major incident. Accidents and breaches don't just appear out of the blue. An organization might have been unconsciously incubating a potential crisis for many months before it actually strikes.

In this chapter we'll examine the nature of events, incidents, emergencies, disasters and crises. We'll also consider the subtle and challenging art of managing a crisis to the longer-term advantage of the organization. That statement will seem quite surprising to many readers. It's hard to imagine that any organization could emerge in a better state from a major crisis. But it can and it does happen from time to time.

In fact there are two reasons for that. Firstly, major incidents create a climate for change. And that's often a good basis for driving through many overdue improvements to systems and processes. And, secondly, major incidents generate publicity. And that's also free advertising. Change and publicity are powerful factors that can be exploited to enhance future business growth or profitability.

Incidents are not all bad news. Sometimes they can serve as a much-needed wake-up call for long overdue changes. In other circumstances they can act as a learning experience to build new skills and structures. For the information security manager, they can also serve as a valuable source of justification for new budgets and resources. But the most important thing is that we should not just aim to respond to incidents. We should also learn from them.

Accidents waiting to happen

In the aftermath of an incident, there's an understandable tendency to downplay the seriousness of the situation. People in the firing line are often heard to claim, 'It's just an isolated incident,' or, 'It was a moment of madness.' But that's very rarely the case. Deeper probing of the events leading up to an incident will usually confirm that it was probably an accident just waiting to happen.

Whether you're inclined to think that most incidents are the result of cock-up or conspiracy, it's generally guaranteed that there will have been many factors at work that either combined or conspired to bring about that incident. And the human factor will have been the most significant of all.

In fact, the key to effective accident or incident prevention is a good understanding of the root causes of the incident and, in particular, an appreciation of the strengths, weaknesses and limitations of the people who are in a position to influence them.

Experience in companies such as the British Royal Mail Group shows that substantial reductions in information security incident levels can be achieved through better knowledge and analysis of security events, and targeted education of staff. Between 2003 and 2004, for example, the Royal Mail Group were able to reduce the level of laptop losses by a factor of five, by identifying the root causes of incidents, and then delivering remedial advice to users.

In Chapters 7 and 8, we'll examine a range of techniques that can help to achieve more effective communications and promote more responsible attitudes and behaviour. Using these methods, we will be able to make a big difference to the level of security incidents, though we will never be able to completely eliminate the risks presented by the human factor.

No system is foolproof

Experience has demonstrated, time and time again, that you can't rely on people to design and operate information systems perfectly. We can make significant improvements in their design, of course. But no system, no matter how carefully designed, will be completely foolproof.

Overconfidence in the human factor is a common but dangerous failing. It can cost careers, perhaps even lives. Arguably, it may have cost Germany the Second World War. Certainly the intelligence derived from the breaking of German military codes, such as those produced by the Enigma cipher machine, by Bletchley Park played a major part in the conduct of the war.

In theory, the Enigma cipher machine should have been unbreakable. The design of the encryption algorithm was secret. The number of possible internal connections for a machine of this nature was comparable to the estimated number of atoms in the observable universe. Breaking this cipher could not have been achieved by science, or by trial and error alone.

The way in which the Enigma cipher was broken provides major lessons for the designers of security systems. Enigma failed to keep its messages secret because of human weaknesses. The users weren't able to keep the design of the system secret. Valuable intelligence was obtained through bribery and theft.

And they didn't anticipate a large degree of effort and technology to be applied to the task of breaking the code. The structure and content of many messages were easy to predict. The same messages were retransmitted using different keys. Operators were allowed to build bad habits in selecting message keys. There were a multitude of human failings at every stage. But the users were unaware of these vulnerabilities.

Visibility is the key

Visibility and context are the cornerstones of security and risk management. If we can gain sight of significant events and appreciate the context in which those events have occurred, then we can make correct assessments about security threats and exposures. Otherwise we can do no more than apply intuition and guesswork.

Gaining visibility is a major problem in IT and security. Electronic events are not visible to the human eye, unless illuminated by software. And many security threats, such as espionage and fraud, are deliberately concealed. Whether they're successful or not, we're not actually meant to know about them. We often only find out about them through informers, mistakes by the perpetrators, or because the damage becomes apparent.

Understanding context is also difficult because we rarely have access to the full facts about the events surrounding an incident. Factors such as the history, motive and mind-set that lie behind a person's actions are very hard to determine. Sometimes, in the aftermath of an incident, we can reconstruct the sequence of events that led up to it. But rarely can we fully appreciate the background to the actions that led to the incident.

It would be helpful to know, for example, the significance of a particular human oversight or mistake that led to an incident. How unusual was this type of error? Was it a shortcoming in training? Have other employees made the same mistake? How many of these slips have people actually made in the past that didn't result in a major incident?

There's a shortage of independent scientific research in this area. Many surveys are carried out to measure the overall number and estimated cost of information security incidents, but few aim to identify the underlying causes. Most assumptions about the root causes of information security incidents are based on little more than subjective opinions, past experiences and educated guesswork. In most cases, we simply won't know if the root causes of a spate of incidents are down to shortcomings in culture, process, governance or just plain bad luck.

A lesson from the safety field

For many years that was also the situation with safety incidents. Then in the 1930s Herbert William Heinrich, an American industrial safety pioneer, published a book *Industrial Accident Prevention, A Scientific Approach*. This book contained groundbreaking observations on the root causes and statistics behind major safety incidents in industry. Amongst other things, Heinrich showed that as many as 95% of all workplace accidents were caused by unsafe acts, and that almost nine out of ten accidents were caused by human failure.

Heinrich looked at the statistics associated with an accidental event, such as a hammer being dropped off the roof of a tall building. He discovered that, on average, for every major incident in which someone died or was seriously injured there were 29 minor incidents (in which someone is slightly injured) and as many as 300 near misses. We can also speculate that, behind all of these incidents, there were probably thousands of bad practices that caused the hammer to be dropped from the roof.

Heinrich's findings are illustrated in Figure 3.1.

Every situation is different, of course. We cannot assume that these ratios will apply outside the environment and time in which they were developed. And we don't have an equivalent body of statistical evidence for security incidents. But it seems likely that a similar pattern would apply to many types of security incident.

In fact, there have been occasional glimpses of incident detection levels in the security which appear to support the Heinrich model. Unfortunately, they're few and far between. Back in 1996, for example, the US Defense Information Systems Agency (DISA) published an analysis of attempts to penetrate its networks. This

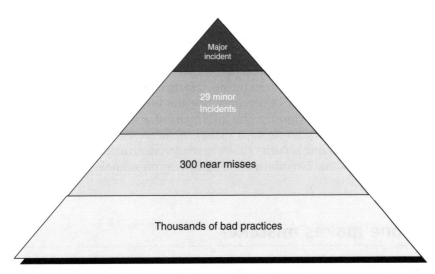

Figure 3.1 Heinrich's Safety Triangle illustrates the bad practices and near misses behind a major safety incident (adapted from H. W. Heinrich, Industrial accident prevention: A scientific approach, McGraw Hill Book Co., Inc., 1941)

study found that out of 38 000 measured attacks, 65% were successful but only 2.6% were detected and 0.7% actually reported.

The DISA example was from the early days of network security, when detection and reporting mechanisms were in their infancy. But, then again, so were the levels of attempted attacks. What it demonstrates is that if you take the trouble to look, you'll find there are orders of magnitude between the number of attempted break-ins and the number of reported breaches.

I think it would be a useful exercise for researchers, working in the field of human factors and security, to test the validity of Heinrich's ratios in the information security field. Heinrich's findings transformed traditional thinking and practice in the industrial safety field. The security community could certainly use an equivalent catalyst to help change their thinking.

One conclusion that we can draw from Heinrich's work is that we can treat the lower layers of the triangle as leading indicators of impending problems. In practice, that's what happens in the aviation safety field. As Professor James Reason, a leading expert in the safety field, once put it:

'Aviation is predicated on the assumption that people screw-up.'

The aviation industry has a robust reporting system, which captures details of near miss and minor problems. Bad practices are identified and eliminated through frequent inspections. Near misses are scrutinized to determine their root causes. The end result is that preventable accidents are minimized. Properly maintained and serviced aircraft, with trained, healthy pilots, do not fall from the sky.

The major learning point for security managers is not to wait for a major incident before taking corrective action. Unfortunately, that's typically how most organizations operate. They keep their heads firmly buried in the sand until a major incident strikes. And that then becomes a cue for an over-the-top, knee-jerk reaction, encouraging excessive posturing, debate and spending.

Overreacting to incidents is certainly not the best approach to information security. But there is an upside. The aftermath of a major incident presents a valuable opportunity to gain stronger management support that can be exploited to eliminate long-standing security flaws, to reinforce security responsibilities, and to lift security spending. No information security professional can afford to ignore that prospect.

Everyone makes mistakes

In a perfect world, we might consider the prospect of aiming for 100% error-free user behaviour. It would eliminate the need for many expensive security controls. Unfortunately that's far from attainable in real life. We cannot avoid or eliminate mistakes, no matter how hard we try.

Accidents, mistakes and breaches are caused by many human factors: ignorance, stress, fatigue, negligence, carelessness, complacency, apathy, spite, stupidity, criminal intent or just plain bad design. You can blame individuals for making mistakes. But many will be due either to a failure by management to provide adequate resources, training and oversight, or to a flaw in the design of systems and processes.

One reason we fail to spot and correct errors is because we're simply too familiar with the subject area, and not sufficiently objective to notice things that are wrong, when we usually find them to be right. We substitute our assumptions for reality, in processes where we can anticipate what's coming next.

When musicians read a piece of music they're familiar with, for example, they don't read every note. They're often playing the tune they know, rather than reading the music. For that reason, top session musicians, such as the legendary Hollywood guitarist Tommy Tedesco, practice reading music backwards as well as forwards, to sharpen up their reading skills.

That's also why it's hard to eliminate errors from large volumes of text or software. There will be numerous mistakes in the text of this book. Perhaps as much as 3–5% of the material might contain unintended flaws, despite the fact that it's been thoroughly checked, not only by me, but by Professor Fred Piper, Professor Steven Furnell, Andy Smith and my publisher. Similarly, no software is perfect. According to researchers at Carnegie Mellon University, commercial software typically has 20 to 30 bugs for every 1000 lines of code. That's a lot of mistakes.

In the 1980s many security researchers believed that the answer to secure system design lay in the use of formal, mathematical methods to verify the correctness of software. But many of the tools for achieving this were themselves flawed. And the task was impossible for large, complex, real-world systems. I recall attending an expert panel debate at the time, entitled *Small Enough to be Provable*. It was suggested that perhaps the theme should have been *Big Enough to be Significant*.

Whenever we carry out any repetitive task, there is a danger that we will fail to spot unexpected things. We often switch into 'autopilot' mode, relying on our subconscious to guide our actions. But in that state, our perception is lessened. We might not spot unusual events that we're not expecting to encounter. It's like the motorist who accidently hits a child that's run into the road. 'I didn't see him' is a common claim. And it's generally true. The motorist would not have seen the victim because he wasn't expecting to see a child in front of his car.

Robert Coles, Chief Information Security Officer for Merrill Lynch, and Professor Gerard Hodgkinson, of Leeds University Business School, recently carried out a study of information security risks in the workplace. The conclusions are unsurprising:

'Our research shows that organizations will never be able to remove all latent risks in the protection and security of data held on IT systems, because our brains are wired to work on automatic pilot in everyday life. People tend to conceptualise the world around them in a simplified way. If we considered and analyzed the risks involved in every permutation of every situation, we'd probably never get anything done.'

Much of the time, we don't notice many of the things that happen right under our noses. It's a weakness that's exploited by confidence tricksters and magicians. And that's why all systems need to be designed with a margin for human error. Human beings are far from foolproof. As Robert Coles, points out:

'We need more triggers and mechanisms in the workplace that make us stop and think before we act.'

The science of error prevention

Researchers that study the field of human error and industrial safety identify different levels of weakness that contribute to failure. Professor James Reason, a leading expert in the field, developed an approach, published in 1990, called the 'Swiss cheese' model, which has since gained widespread acceptance across industry. The model likens human systems to slices of Emmental Swiss cheese, stacked side by side. The holes in the cheese represent weaknesses in different levels of the system. In practice, they will be constantly changing in size and position. Accidents arise when a series of holes in the slices momentarily align, creating 'a trajectory of accident opportunity'.

James Reason identifies four levels of potential failure (or slices of Emmental): organizational influences, unsafe supervision, preconditions for unsafe acts, and the unsafe acts themselves. These encompass a wide range of possible failures, including active failures, such as an individual human error, or latent ones, such as inadequate resource or a lack of training. James Reason also differentiates between errors that are due to a failure to follow a plan and mistakes due to an inadequacy in the plan. Errors can be further differentiated as either a slip, an execution failure, or a lapse, a memory failure.

It might seem academic to split hairs in this way. But there are useful practical inferences from this type of research. It's helpful, for example, to determine if failures are caused by a lack of skill, a missing rule, or an absence of knowledge. By understanding the underlying causes of errors and mistakes, we will be better equipped to prevent, avoid, detect and correct them.

In fact, analysis of catastrophic accidents often indicates a long history of weaknesses across many levels of a system or process. Unsafe conditions can arise from a collective set of decisions unconsciously taken by designers, trainers or managers. In aviation maintenance, for example, research indicates that as many as 90% of quality lapses are judged to be 'blameless', impossible to attribute to the actions of a single individual. Management of such risks depends on establishing an effective awareness and reporting culture. We should aim to identify and address potential sources of incidents before they actually cause damage. But, in practice, we rarely pay sufficient attention to this objective.

When it comes to accidents, blame is not a helpful response. We're just as likely to find that our best staff are responsible for the worst incidents. And there are often recurring patterns behind incidents, things we could have spotted, if we'd actually been looking out for them. Establishing a 'no-blame' culture is an important step forward in encouraging reporting of errors, near misses and minor incidents. Creating an environment that encourages the correct behaviour at all times is also important. If you're surrounded by colleagues who routinely ignore security procedures, you'll quickly give up on them yourself.

The structures of our systems and processes can also play a part in influencing user behaviour. If a system, for example, does not respond immediately to attempts to correct its performance, its operators are likely to apply excessive degrees of correction, which might further degrade its performance. We do this all the time ourselves, for example, when information systems do not respond immediately. We press the send key over and over again. But that will only overload the system further.

We should refrain from instinctively blaming the operators of a system for failures, when the real root cause might, in fact, lie in the system design itself. A more sensible approach is to accept that people are not perfect, and that the only way to prevent accidents, mistakes and errors, is to equip our staff with the appropriate skills, resources and knowledge to execute their tasks safely and securely. And, of course, to eradicate latent weaknesses in the design of the systems and business processes that will contribute to failures.

Swiss cheese and security

James Reason's Swiss cheese model is not dissimilar from the traditional defense-in-depth approach to security controls. Great minds think alike, and often at the same time. At around the same time he was developing his approach to industrial safety, Donn Parker, at SRI International, was developing the concept of baseline controls for the information security community.

Donn had been disappointed with the effectiveness of risk assessment methods in information security. In the late 1980s it became clear to many security professionals that we didn't have sufficient reliable input data to support the calculations demanded by risk assessment methods. For many threats and vulnerabilities, it seemed that the boundaries of uncertainty were often an order of magnitude larger than the values themselves.

Donn had also noted that many organizations operated a similar portfolio of information security controls. He set out, therefore, to assemble a collection of universal controls based on his observations from numerous security reviews conducted across dozens of Fortune 100 companies. Drawing on this work, we carried out a similar exercise across Shell operating companies, and developed a set of baseline security controls for the Shell Group, based on tried and tested practices in the field. Our logic was that if we could eliminate the vast majority of bad practices, then we would greatly reduce the chances of near misses and minor incidents, and ultimately prevent major incidents.

Implementing a collection of standard, proven controls is, in fact, the fastest, most reliable and often the least expensive method of improving the level of information security across an organization. It cuts out the need for large numbers of individual risk assessments across the enterprise. It provides a common security language. And it can help reduce costs by enabling centralization of business and service functions. We'll return to this subject in Chapter 10 when we discuss options for security strategies.

The baseline approach served us well. Throughout the 1990s there were relatively few significant information security incidents encountered in Shell companies, compared to other organizations. Our work in developing baseline controls also provided the essential base material for the British Standard BS7799, the basis of the International Standard ISO27001. Each chapter of this standard can be considered to represent a slice of Emmental. They are all essential layers of controls, and each layer compensates for intrinsic weaknesses in other controls.

Managing the potential consequences of human weaknesses requires a similar, defense-in-depth approach, but a much more tailored one. ISO27001 is a fine standard, but it was designed to support an enterprise information security management system. Today we require a much greater focus on people, culture and relationships. That requires a bespoke analysis of each organization and its environment. What works for a group of accountants, for example, might not be suitable for a team of traders.

How significant was that event?

Not all incidents are the same. As we've already seen, there are major ones and minor ones. Different types of incident can have very different consequences, and they might require quite different types of response. In particular, it's useful to differentiate incidents according to their relative impact on business operations and assets.

To help distinguish different categories of incident we first need to establish a hierarchy of appropriate terms. The terms I generally use, in order of increasing degrees of impact, are: events, incidents, emergencies, disasters and crises. In fact, there is no universally agreed set of terms. But this use of terms for the various levels of event or incident, are as close as you'll find to common practice in experienced organizations.

But a word of caution: it's difficult to be precise about incidents. Good definitions are not rigid. In fact, nothing is absolute when it comes to incidents. Incidents of the same types can have major differences in impact depending on the context and circumstances at the time. And incidents are only as serious as you perceive them to be. They can have different impacts on each stakeholder. One company's minor incident might turn out to be another's crisis.

It's also important to consider, not just how bad an incident appears to be, but how bad it might have been, or might become. But levels of seriousness or business impact cannot be objectively defined in advance. An incident becomes a disaster when the response team decides to declare one. Similarly, a crisis only exists when the crisis team decides to sit. It's better to think of incidents in terms of broad descriptions rather than absolute measures. And it's also better to assume the worst possible case. 'Prudent overreaction' is the best philosophy for all crisis teams.

Events are for the record

At the lowest level in the incident hierarchy, we might experience an event. That doesn't sound too serious. It merely suggests that something out of the ordinary has happened. Something of sufficient significance that it merits the attention of local staff, or it satisfies the alerting or logging criteria of a software monitoring tool. At the very least, it warrants a note or a record of its occurrence.

Events can be good or bad. Stafford Beer once coined the term 'algedonic signals' for alerts of either good or bad performance. It's an appropriate term, as the word algedonic is derived from the Greek words $\alpha\lambda\gamma o\varsigma$ for pain, and $\eta\delta o\varsigma$ for pleasure. I won't go into some of the more colourful implications of that, other than to suggest that it's actually a useful way to think of alerts. They are not necessarily all bad. They are simply reports that are out of the ordinary, or perhaps information that gets reported through an 'out of band' channel that's outside of the normal communications channels.

Events don't generally demand or justify immediate action. Many events are consciously ignored by staff. At busy times, the logging of certain types of event might even be suspended. And the storage media used to record computer or network events will, subject to compliance requirements, often be recycled at relatively short intervals to reduce the amount of data stored, and lower the retention costs.

Things might be different, of course, if you're operating on a high state of alert, if you've just experienced a major incident, or if you need to maintain a specific record of user or system activity for regulatory compliance purposes. Then it might become essential to log and review certain categories of event. But, generally, we prefer to ignore most of the events happening across our infrastructure, which is a shame, because, as we've seen, valuable intelligence on security practices and near misses can be derived from an analysis of minor events.

Events are items of potential security or management interest. They might be transactions that meet a specific set of criteria, associated with a security event, or ones that exceed certain limits. We don't immediately react to them, unless they exhibit a recognizable, sinister quality, or if they appear to be having a measurable operational or business impact. At that point, the level of response needs to change.

When an event becomes an incident

When an event begins to register any degree of operational impact, or personal or business harm, then we tend to refer to it as an incident. An incident suggests an event of some significance, something that's memorable, reportable and has an effect of business processes or people.

Incidents generally need to be reported to local management. They might require a special procedure to be invoked. But often it's something that can be managed locally, by drawing on a standard operating practice. A serious incident might result in damage, injury, or perhaps a major breach of procedures. It's likely to be dealt with by local management, though it will need to be logged and reported to other stakeholders.

Incidents invoke procedures that are largely scripted. They might, for example, form part of a series of routine practices in an operations manual. A report of the incident might need to be produced, but it need not justify escalation to senior management, though it might perhaps form part of a routine report of interesting events for a particular day, week or month.

Incidents are significant events that happen regularly. Not every day, but certainly several times each week or month. They generally get dealt with quietly, and efficiently. They don't usually attract senior management scrutiny or media attention. And if they do, we tend to refer to them using a more serious term, such as a major incident or emergency.

The immediacy of emergencies

An emergency is a particularly serious incident. You generally know, instinctively, when you have an emergency on your hands. It's not routine, and it demands immediate attention. Normal business activities might be suspended. There will be a distinct quickening of the pace of the response. Emergency procedures might be invoked. Specialists will be consulted. And senior management might step in to take control of the situation.

An emergency response team, or crisis management team, will also be called out. And, if you have one, you might also alert your computer emergency response team, to consider a technical security response.

If it's a physical incident, there might be casualties, injuries to people or damage to property. External services, such as fire services or emergency medical units might then need to become involved. It's also possible that the seriousness of the situation will begin to generate local press interest.

Typically, there will be an emergency procedure or guideline to help shape the local or middle management response. Emergencies justify immediate attention and priority. The consequences will need to be quickly addressed and fixed, though they might not always result in major business damage, or threaten long-term business operations.

Emergencies are generally short-lived, perhaps lasting a day or even less. The organization will then resume business-as-usual. In most cases, the damage might seem to have been significant in local terms, but it will probably not be enough to make a measurable impact on the viability and profitability of the organization. If it is, then it's probably more than an emergency. It has the makings of a disaster.

When disaster strikes

You can generally recognize a disaster when it strikes. Disasters suggest a much larger level of business impact and damage. When you hear the word 'disaster', it conjures up images of hurricanes, burning buildings or severely damaged facilities. It suggests a rapid disruption of routine operations, causing serious damage to property, as well as injury to people. It's also something that might well have a significant impact on business operations and perhaps company reputation.

Disaster recovery and business continuity plans will be invoked. A 'disaster' will be declared, which means that contingency plans and fallback services will swing into action. Business continuity management teams will meet and determine how to maintain business operations in the absence of the damaged facilities. Top management will be fully briefed. Media relations, human resources and security functions might assign dedicated support staff for the duration of the incident.

There are always gaps in any business continuity plan, so a certain degree of improvisation will be required. But it's likely that the plans available will serve as the fundamental management framework for the response, setting out the key recovery processes and the checklists of actions that will be required to manage the situation.

Disasters tend to have a medium-term impact on the organization. Lost facilities might take several weeks or months to restore. Press coverage might extend for several days or weeks. But there will generally be a clear end in sight for the business response. And if the organization manages the situation well enough, it should even be able to survive the financial year with little more impact than a small dent in sales and profits.

When events spiral out of control

If things get really serious then we might find we have a crisis on our hands. A crisis is very different from other forms of incident. It's usually triggered by an incident, emergency or disaster. But, for some reason, it begins to spiral out of control, overwhelming the capabilities of both line managers and incident response teams.

The organization is likely to be seriously affected on a broad, and growing, front. There might be a serious threat to business continuity. There will be mounting press attention. And company reputation will be at risk. Top management will be compelled to intervene, quickly and decisively, to contain the growing impact of the crisis.

In fact, that's the picture for a *fast-moving* crisis. But we can also experience more insidious types of crisis, ones that slowly creep up on organizations without any warning. A company might, for example, progressively begin to lose the confidence of its staff, its customers or the press. Revenues and profits will progressively slide. Press coverage will gradually, but relentlessly, increase. And the organization will slowly begin to spin into crisis mode.

But whichever type of crisis you face, whether fast-moving or slowly engulfing, you'll generally find that scripted plans, if they exist, are largely useless. A unique, tailored response will be required, one that's based on careful analysis, smart thinking, imaginative solutions and improvised actions.

A crisis is an especially serious development for an organization, because it can threaten its ability to conduct day-to-day business. Whether based on real or perceived problems, it can significantly damage customer confidence, corporate reputation and financial standing. A crisis demands a very different response to other forms of incident, a response that is strategic, long-term and empowered.

How the response process changes

Many incidents start small and progressively escalate into more serious enterprise crises. The most interesting aspect of any such incident is how the nature of the response needed changes, as it progresses from a local, operational incident to a full-blown crisis.

Figure 3.2 shows how the nature of the response becomes increasingly sophisticated according to the severity of the impact. For the lowest level of incident, activities tend to be local, operational and scripted, with a short-term focus on physical assets, such as buildings, people and equipment.

As the business impact of the incident increases, the scope of the response activities grows, involving a broader set of managers across the enterprise and invoking a more complex, and more flexible, set of business continuity plans, with a more medium-term focus on business processes, services and customers.

At its most severe level, a crisis might begin to spiral out of control, overwhelming the organization on a broad front, and demanding a unique response from top management, with a relentless, long-term focus on the enterprise's intellectual assets, such as brand value, operational impacts, corporate reputation, media perception, market capitalization, legal liability, regulatory response, political standing and citizen concerns.

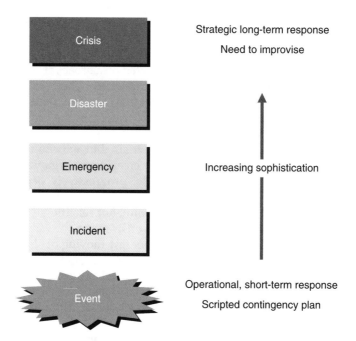

Figure 3.2 The increasing sophistication required in incident response

No two crises are the same

Mention the word crisis to any experienced group of security managers and they'll immediately begin recalling war stories about incidents they've been involved in. What's especially interesting about such anecdotes is the sheer variety in the types of incident that are classed as crises. Much depends on the nature of the business, as well as the role of the security function within the organization.

For a large international oil company, a crisis can be triggered by anything from a kidnapped business executive to an oil tanker casualty. For a telecommunications company, it might be a gas main explosion in a city centre. For the police, it might be a terrorist on the loose. For a bank, it might be a severe case of market turbulence. For an on-line gaming business it might be a denial-of-service attack. For an airliner, it might be a major computer glitch affecting customer check-in services. And, for a retailer, it might be a compromise of customer credit card data.

Different skills and knowledge are needed to cope with different types of incidents. Ideally, it would be useful to have a range of appropriate specialists on tap, possessing all the required skills, knowledge and experience. But that's not practical, for any size of organization. There would be simply too many individuals to be trained and exercised, and there would be too many teams competing to address the problem. And, of course, there's no guarantee that an expert on a particular topic, would actually turn out to be a suitable or effective crisis team member.

Crisis teams are highly empowered decision-makers, who are trusted and capable of taking charge of complex, fast-moving situations. There is a certainly a role for the expert adviser, but it does not need to be in the main crisis response team.

And as we saw earlier, the nature of the response changes as the severity of incident grows. We will need different skills at different stages in the response process.

But one thing is very clear. We cannot delegate important decision-making to a team of external specialists, no matter how experienced and capable they might appear to be. That, in fact, would be a dereliction of duty. Executive board directors are responsible for the conduct and management of company affairs. Major decisions, affecting the long-term viability of the company, will have to be taken during the crisis. The board will therefore need to establish, and maintain, sound governance and oversight of all such decisions.

One size doesn't fit all

With all of this in mind, it makes no sense to operate a single style of crisis response. The skills, membership and approach needed for a lower level operational response are very different from those demanded for the more serious levels of crisis.

In practice, experienced organizations tend to recognize this distinction, establishing a hierarchy of response teams, often termed Gold, Silver or Bronze teams, to deal with the different levels of strategic, tactical and operational responses. But, in my view, the distinction is more than a simple upgrading of the seniority of the team membership, their authority and level of empowerment. There are, in fact, quite distinct processes at work, which are illustrated in Figure 3.3

Firstly, there is the emergency response process: the set of activities needed to contain and repair damage to facilities, equipment or perhaps injuries to people. This response might have a strong health and safety focus, perhaps a significant human resources focus, and it will require the leadership of experienced engineers to repair damaged infrastructure or to establish fallback facilities. This response process should, ideally, be led by the managers who are responsible for the delivery of the affected facilities and services.

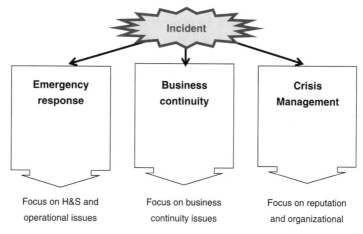

Figure 3.3   The varying focus required in incident response

Secondly, there is the business continuity management process, the collection of activities that are required to maintain business-as-usual, as far as possible, throughout a major outage of facilities or services. The skills and experience required for this are quite different from those needed for an emergency response. And the contingency plans invoked will tend to be more flexible, requiring a degree of adaptation of business processes and consultation with major customers and suppliers. This response process should, ideally, be led by the directors who are responsible for the management of the affected business processes.

Thirdly, there is the strategic crisis management process, the set of activities that are needed to stem the escalating wave of events and publicity, which might be spiralling out of control and threatening the longer-term viability of the enterprise. The skills and experience for this activity are quite hard to find, or to develop. Strategic crisis management requires decisive problem solvers and strategic thinkers, who can be trusted by senior business directors to take big decisions, and who are comfortable when dealing with the press. This response process needs to be led, ideally, by senior directors who have the full backing and empowerment of the Executive Board.

In practice, it's extremely hard to coordinate any set of complex response processes across an organization, especially when confronted with a fast-moving incident. Simplicity of organizational design is therefore essential, but the team structures will also need to be sufficiently rich to enable the correct skills and emphasis to be applied at the right level. Experimentation and regular exercises are crucial, in order to learn how best to meet this difficult challenge.

The limits of planning

One of the questions many security, risk and service managers face, when planning ahead for disasters, is determining just how much of the recovery process should be scripted in advance, and how much of it would be better left to improvisation by the response team.

Most managers are familiar with the concept of a contingency plan, the fallback arrangement needed in the event of a loss or failure of a critical business asset. In practice we need quite a few of these, perhaps one for each major facility, in order to ensure the continuity of critical business processes.

Much of the theory of modern business continuity planning is based on the concept of defining maximum tolerable periods of disruption: setting recovery time objectives, arranging fallback facilities and creating detailed manuals of step-by-step instructions. But does this, in fact, really reflect the reality of modern, or even traditional, business?

Some activities, such the processes needed to enable the smooth transfer of systems operations to a remote fallback site, will clearly require quite detailed procedures. But other activities, such as determining the precise staffing arrangements for a temporary operation, might need to be decided on the spot. Some ideas, guidance or suggestions can, of course, usefully be developed in advance, perhaps to serve as a 'straw-man' or 'Aunt Sally' proposal to speed up the development of the real thing. It's useful, for example, to have draft press releases prepared for known types of information security incident.

Time pressures during a crisis are a major consideration when planning for a crisis. Any essential information that requires a long time to gather should be captured and documented in advance, as far as possible. But there are many things that simply cannot be determined in advance. There are decisions that might require permissions from higher authorities, which cannot be guaranteed in advance. And there are facilities and assets which are simply irreplaceable, for financial or other reasons.

Some assets are irreplaceable

I once conducted a business continuity review of the oil and gas evacuation process for a developing country. At one point I enquired about the impact of an irrecoverable failure of a particular power plant. 'What happens when that fails?' I asked. 'The region will be without electricity for two years,' was the response. 'Don't you have a fallback?' I enquired. 'Do you have $50 million to enable us to build one?' was the reply.

Clearly the asset was not easily replaceable. It's an example of a facility for which we can't define an affordable recovery time objective to meet a maximum tolerable outage.

So what can you do in the absence of any realistic fallback arrangement for a major asset? In fact, there are several useful actions that can be carried out in advance to mitigate future, potential operational risks.

Firstly, we can monitor emerging risks and aim to continually adjust the protection arrangements. That might seem obvious, but it's rarely achieved in practice without a specific intervention. Action is generally prompted by major changes in circumstances. Slow, progressive changes can creep up and threaten the existence of an organization, just like a frog in boiling water that doesn't recognize the immediate danger until it's too late to respond.

Secondly, we can develop plans to streamline the rapid procurement and installation of new facilities. In particular, we can identify the key enablers and blockers for new installations or procurements, and aim to establish the guidance and prior approvals that will be needed to help cut through red tape, as well as to ensure priority attention and delivery by key vendors in the supply chain.

It's the process, not the plan

Advance planning and actions can serve to reduce the likelihood of an incident, as well as its business impact. But it's not always possible to predict future events, developments and response requirements. The underlying principle should be to aim to be smart, flexible and pragmatic about any form of disaster planning. Continuity and crisis planning is far from being a black-and-white process. In fact, the management of the recovery process is always far more important than the quality of the plans.

Plans are no more than a snapshot of the thinking and the best information that happens to be available at a particular time. In practice, all plans will quickly become out-of-date, and they will rarely be read in advance by the managers who have to implement them.

Recovery processes, in contrast, are more participative, and perhaps easier to keep fresh in the minds of managers through regular discussions and exercises. It's often better to have some smart ideas, supported by a good set of tools, rather than an out-of-date set of plans on a dusty shelf that nobody is familiar with.

One interesting observation that I've noted over the years, is that we seem to be gradually moving towards a more improvisational approach to incidents. Twenty years ago, for example, a major oil company would maintain a large collection of detailed emergency plans for many different types of incident, including events such as an airplane crash, a tank farm fire, a ruptured oil pipeline or a tanker casualty. Today it's more likely that there are fewer detailed procedures and a more generalized, flexible, response process.

There are several reasons for that. One is that our processes, systems and infrastructure are becoming increasingly complex. Another is that they're changing much faster. A third reason is that our response processes are more sophisticated, with improved communications and information sources. A fourth is that our outsourcing and supply chains now require a response that spans many different organizations. And a fifth is that our complex technological infrastructure is making the operational and business impact from a loss or failure much more unpredictable. In fact, the possibilities and consequences arising from an incident are almost endless once we link our networks across multiple systems, organizations and infrastructures.

These trends are the reasons why, when drafting the business continuity planning chapter for the original BS7799 security standard, we placed much greater emphasis on the need for a process rather than a plan. Plans are useful for ticking the compliance boxes to satisfy your auditors or regulators. And sometimes we need a proven set of procedures, specified in advance, to carry out a complex task. But it's much more important to have a well-rehearsed recovery process, where managers fully understand their roles and they are well equipped with the full range of information, services and resources they need to tackle a crisis.

People are the key to good crisis management. If a contingency plan goes well then it's almost certainly down to the skills of the people who executed it, rather than the knowledge of the person who developed it.

Why crisis management is hard

'Crisis management' means different things to different organizations. It's often used to describe local emergencies. But in the context of this book, I use the term 'strategic crisis management' to indicate the highest form of threat to the organization, something that is difficult, complex and quite subtle.

I've witnessed crisis management practiced many times by the most senior, brightest and experienced directors of top companies. And, in my experience, it's very rare to find a single practitioner who gets it mostly right. In fact, on a scale of one to ten, where ten is the best you can achieve, I'd find it hard to rate most crisis team members as higher than three, perhaps four out of ten.

So what exactly is it that's difficult about crisis management? In fact, there's quite a bit that's missing from contemporary crisis teams. Good crisis management requires a lot more than an orderly, operational response to the problem. It demands a unique blend of analysis, problem-solving, communication and organization skills. These are primarily innate, behavioural skills that are difficult to find, hard to develop, and even more challenging to apply in practice.

It's understandable, for example, that it will be hard to think clearly in the midst of a crisis. There will be emotions at play. It's a highly stressful role. Team members will feel nervous, unqualified, inadequate, or perhaps even guilty, because, for example, of the hard decisions they might have to make, perhaps in haste. And the relentless pace of the crisis means that fatigue and tiredness will progressively set in.

Fortunately, crisis management gets easier with practice. As President Richard M Nixon once put it:

> *'The ability to be cool, confident, and decisive in crisis is not an inherited characteristic, but is the direct result of how well the individual has prepared himself for the crisis.'*

That's certainly true, but, in fact, it's far from guaranteed that such practice will make perfect. Good preparation is necessary, but it's not sufficient. You also need a lot of skills to manage a crisis effectively.

Skills to manage a crisis

What are the key skills needed to manage a crisis effectively? Here are seven skills that I've found to be essential for sound crisis management. Unfortunately, you'll generally find that they're in short supply in most organizations.

Firstly, to be an effective member of a crisis team requires an objective view of the enterprise. And that's not easy to achieve if you're part of the organization. It's hard, for example, to recognize and compensate for the corporate 'madness' surrounding you, the peculiar habits to which you've gradually become acclimatized. When viewing events, you need to see through the fog of corporate spin and to strip away the bias of your own, psychological rationalization for surviving in an environment that's not completely in tune with your natural judgement and instincts.

Secondly, crisis management involves a scope that's very different from that of your day-to-day job. You have to shake off the limitations and natural assumptions associated with your normal role in the organization. Decisions will need to be made on very unfamiliar subjects, and on incomplete information. In a crisis you can't dodge, or refer, difficult issues that are well outside of your normal area of operation or expertise. And you will have very little time to consult your more informed colleagues, or to seek a second opinion.

Thirdly, crisis management requires confidence that you can solve problems across a much broader business landscape, and that other business directors will trust your judgment and follow your lead. You must not be too concerned about the possibility of colleagues subsequently ridiculing your decisions. Like it or not, you're on a rollercoaster. You will get some decisions right, and you will get many others wrong. And there's likely to be a subsequent post mortem to highlight both your successes and failures. There will be much criticism. And there might be some casualties. But all of that should not be at the forefront of your mind.

Fourthly, a crisis demands strategic thinking, rather than instinctive or tactical reactions. To manage a crisis effectively, you'll need to appreciate the bigger picture, to piece together a holistic picture, from incomplete snippets of incoming information, to determine what's really happening, and to establish the real cause of the crisis. You will need to think logically, to develop theories and, in the best possible detective tradition, to identify and ask questions to confirm or deny your hypotheses.

Fifthly, you'll also need to apply a longer-term perspective, to understand how events might begin to unfold, day-by-day, or week-by-week, or month-by-month. The aftermath of a crisis might, in fact, last for several years. Operational issues will generally be resolved quickly. But customers, business partners and shareholders will have long memories. For quite some time, they will associate your business brand with the media coverage that's generated during a crisis.

Sixthly, a crisis requires extremely good communications skills, both within and outside the organization. With little, if any, rehearsal time, you will have to be ready to brief the Executive Board, the press and other stakeholders. For the duration of the crisis, you will represent the heart, soul and public face of the organization. And you'll have to be able to develop, and contribute to, a shared picture of events with the rest of the crisis team.

Finally, a successful crisis outcome will also demand exceptionally good organizational skills. For a brief moment in time, you might have the entire resources of the organization at your disposal. Will you be up to the challenge of identifying useful ways of exploiting these resources? How will you harness this capability? And how will you engage with the workforce, to set tasks and to manage the response from a multitude of sources across the enterprise?

Many crisis teams prefer to remain locked away in their crisis rooms, focused on incoming, but incomplete, information about external events and demands. In contrast, the smart crisis team will consider how best to harness the power of the organization to help resolve the crisis. To empower, for example, smart individuals to develop their own improvised responses to events.

But be warned. It's not that easy to think proactively when you're immersed in a fast-moving chain of events. Even the best laid plans and good intentions will quickly evaporate in the heat of a crisis.

Dangerous detail

A major challenge in many types of crisis, is managing the large amounts of incoming information. It's especially hard when incoming volumes start small, but grow rapidly, which, in fact, is more often the case.

Good advance planning is crucial. Smart crisis teams will anticipate potential increases in information, and assign appropriate resources to manage the capture, assessment, assignment, tracking and filing of information and actions. No crisis team can afford, of course, to ignore the relentless stream of incoming information. But neither should they be completely overwhelmed by it.

There are many lessons to be learned from past disasters. For example, it's generally agreed by engineers that the Three Mile Island partial nuclear meltdown in 1979 was exacerbated by incorrect decisions that were made as a result of plant operators becoming overwhelmed with information, much of it irrelevant, misleading or incorrect.

Response procedures and operator training, in fact, were substantially changed following this incident, with more emphasis on actions to support the response process, rather than those to diagnose the underlying problem.

Simple checks and actions are essential to contain any fast-moving crises. But complex information feeds and procedures will work against busy crisis team members. And, with ever-growing connectivity and real-time communications, it's becoming essential that crisis team designers pay much more attention to the methods, resources and technology needed to assess and filter incoming information.

Up-to-date reference data, both on the organization and its supporting infrastructure, will also be needed in a crisis to support decision-making, as well as to answer questions from management or the media. In practice, however crisis teams will rarely have the time to phone around colleagues, to fetch copies of relevant company reports or to search corporate databases in order to establish the relevant details needed to resolve the crisis. Fast-fact sheets, or databases, should be prepared in advance, along with useful information on key assets, systems, locations, processes and people.

The missing piece of the jigsaw

Sometimes the successful resolution of a crisis hinges upon the possession of a small item of knowledge, one that the crisis team does not have. Tracking down that piece of information, or gaining the necessary know-how and understanding on how to use it, will then become a major priority. Crisis team support units need to be ready and equipped to meet such challenges.

A good example of such a situation occurred during the UK Fuel Crisis of 2000, when strikes, protests and blockades threatened to disrupt the delivery of fuel required for essential services. The methods used were also a sign of the times, as mobile phones, e-mail and the Internet were exploited to coordinate the efforts of the protesters.

The UK Civil Contingencies Committee sat to address the crisis. This committee is the highest level response team for dealing with national crises, named COBRA after the Cabinet Office Briefing Room A in which they meet. This committee had the power to intervene and control the supply of fuel across the Country. The problem was that this required a detailed understanding of the operational characteristics of the UK fuel distribution network.

The UK fuel distribution network is a hub-and-spoke network, one of a class of complex networks termed scale-free networks, which exhibit particular topological and performance characteristics. Calculating the impact of blockades on fuel distribution requires an understanding of the mathematical algorithm that underpins the structure and dynamics of this type of network.

Determining the nature of this algorithm became a major requirement for managing the crisis. The crisis team eventually established this and commemorated the achievement, at the end of the crisis, by having T-shirts printed up with the mathematical algorithm for fuel distribution on the front and 'Don't panic' on the back.

COBRA is a highly experienced crisis team with an impressive support structure, far more sophisticated than we're likely to find in an average organization. How many other crisis teams would have the initiative and resources available to develop such a response? But such challenges will grow with increasing dependence on highly complex, inter-connected infrastructures.

Crisis teams need to be ready to tackle complex problems, and to identify and apply appropriate solutions. They can't put a difficult problem to one side just because they lack the skills to tackle it. Every crisis team needs a selection of experts on tap, including a good source of technical and operational research support.

Establish the real cause

Perhaps the most important, and most difficult, challenge of any crisis team is to root out and to resolve the real cause of the crisis. At first sight, this might seem a fairly obvious task. But experience shows that it's not quite that easy in practice.

Firstly, as we've seen, it's hard for employees to be objective about major issues associated with the organization. That's generally because we're too close to the action. We simply cannot think objectively if we're already acclimatized to the corporate line and the marketing spin that we instinctively support in order to survive in today's demanding commercial environment.

Secondly, it's natural for most crisis team members to concentrate on the *trigger* of the incident, rather than the cause of the crisis. The trigger might, in practice, turn out to be a relatively harmless event or a problem that's quite straightforward to address. But the actions and behaviour that follow this trigger might bring to the surface a far more challenging, deep-seated flaw in the enterprise.

Crises can be triggered by a wide range of events, both external and internal. External triggers might include legal actions, competitor strategies, market changes, new technology or natural disasters. Internal factors might be production failures, personnel issues, safety hazards, financial losses, natural disasters, or security breaches.

But flaws are much harder to identify, especially from an internal perspective. Examples might be a business strategy that doesn't work in all environments; or perhaps a design weakness that's not previously been exposed or corrected; or it might be a contractual or staffing issue that's been brewing for a long time. Such a long-standing flaw might turn out to be the real catalyst for the crisis. But the initial response will naturally be focused on the event that triggered this flaw, rather than the flaw itself.

Are you incubating a crisis?

An organization might be incubating a potential crisis for many years before it strikes. And it will often go unnoticed or unaddressed. An outside observer might have the objectivity to spot fatal flaws in culture, communications, business strategy, risk appetite or technology. But it's generally extremely hard for insiders to notice the weaknesses that surround them. They will not stand out or appear unusual, especially if they've not presented a problem in the past.

There are, in fact, fault lines running through all organizations: cultural issues that are ready to explode, blind spots in business plans, and vulnerabilities in infrastructure. If you look hard enough you'll be able to spot major issues that are waiting to surface, serious risks that are ready to strike, and uncomfortable perceptions that are ripe to be shaped into negative publicity.

A classic example of this phenomenon was the Shell Brent Spar crisis, which was triggered by a routine business decision to dispose of an oil storage buoy in an economic, but environmentally sound, way. Shell engineers had conducted an extensive environmental analysis, which led them to believe that their disposal strategy was correct. They knew they had a sound environmental case. But Greenpeace, an environmental campaigning group, had other ideas. They mounted a sophisticated publicity campaign against the proposal. Many citizens, and customers, accepted the Greenpeace line and ceased buying Shell products in protest.

What was especially interesting about this case was that the harder Shell tried to explain the environmental case, the worse the crisis became. Why should that be? Why did customers not listen to the facts and accept their professional arguments? The reason was that the real cause of the crisis was not so much the environmental justification for the disposal of the Brent Spar. It was the public perception of Shell's communications style, and their apparent reluctance to engage with environmental groups.

The end result was that the more Shell engaged with the public, the more this weakness became apparent. The crisis was only resolved when Shell, very sensibly, decided to back down and to take steps to develop a better dialogue with citizens and environmental groups. The Shell crisis team was sufficiently experienced and sophisticated to identify and address this issue. But not many other crisis teams would have been able to respond to such a challenge so swiftly and surely.

When crisis management becomes the problem

A major learning point in crisis management is never to forget the 'first law of holes': when you're in one, stop digging. The Brent Spar incident illustrates a powerful lesson in crisis management. It demonstrates that sometimes the action you take to lessen a crisis will have the opposite effect. If a crisis team finds itself in a situation where the harder they try to resolve the situation, the worse the crisis gets, then it's possible that the response strategy might be contributing to the crisis.

In fact, every organization has potential crises waiting to happen. But it takes a highly perceptive eye and some smart analysis to spot the existing weaknesses in the organization that might trigger a crisis. We have to look inwards to spot structural flaws, as well as outwards to identify emerging trends in the business landscape that might act as a catalyst for a crisis.

Some companies take the trouble to conduct 'horizon scans' of emerging risks and issues. But few of them have the insight to recognize and address the flaws that may exist within their own organization. I've observed this phenomenon many times, when I've conducted training sessions for executive crisis teams. All crisis teams have difficulty in taking a hard, objective look at the internal politics and long-standing practices that go on within their organization.

An interesting and eye-opening exercise that you can conduct with a crisis team is to set them the task of determining the reasons why another company is currently experiencing a crisis. Select, for example, one of the companies that are currently dominating the newspaper headlines. You will find that, in no more ten minutes, the crisis team will be able to arrive at an excellent, and generally correct, analysis of the situation.

Yet set them a task involving a potential issue or crisis that might be brewing within their own business unit, and they'll generally struggle to establish and agree the real cause. They will also fail to appreciate the real risk and severity of the issue.

All organizations tend to exhibit a major blind spot when it comes to examining their own internal strategy, methods and processes. In fact, this failure to recognize the inherent flaws that exist inside an organization is the 'Achilles Heel' of executive boards and crisis teams.

Developing a crisis strategy

A key requirement of the crisis team is to develop a strategy for managing the crisis. This needs to be done quickly and at the earliest opportunity. The obvious starting point in developing the strategy is to establish an agreed set of objectives. Each crisis will be different demanding a different response and a different set of priorities. Immediate objectives might be, for example, to restore a lost service, to halt a short-time slide in sales, or to stop a hacker from mounting further damaging attacks.

But crises also demand broader and smarter thinking. There may be conflicting requirements and options. Should you, for example, accept the blame and apologize to your customers? That might help to rebuild the trust of your customers. But it will also place the liability firmly on you. Alternatively, should you aim to shift the blame onto somebody else, or perhaps to divert the media coverage onto a less damaging aspect of the incident?

A key consideration is the longer-term implications of your decisions and actions. Everything you say and do will be carefully scrutinized by the press, the authorities and your own employees. It might be tempting to stay silent, to deny everything, or even to tell a few white lies to buy yourself some time. But the truth will eventually come out. There will be subsequent investigations, enquiries and post mortems. There might also be potential whistle blowers lurking in your organization. You can't, and shouldn't, aim to cover up your mistakes.

In a crisis, the best strategy is generally to be open and honest, and to apologize sincerely to your customers. At the same time, you should stop short of admitting liability, especially if the cause of the damage is not completely certain.

Turning threats into opportunities

Many western observers believe that 'weiji', the Chinese word for crisis, is a composition of two characters that represent 'danger' and 'opportunity'. This observation has been used in political speeches by John F. Kennedy, Richard Nixon, Condoleeza Rice and Al Gore, amongst others. Some experts claim that's misleading, however. The Chinese character that's interpreted as 'opportunity' has a range of other meanings. And the most appropriate translation in this context might well be 'crucial point'.

Nevertheless, it's often suggested that it's possible to turn a security threat into a business opportunity. Can that really be true? It's certainly not something that many of us encounter in everyday business. In fact, the answer is that, as for many other things associated with crisis management, it's possible, but extremely difficult to achieve in practice.

But a crisis introduces certain factors that can potentially enable a positive outcome to be achieved. Firstly, all crises offer opportunities for business improvement, though these are often overlooked in the heat of the moment. One opportunity, for example, is the fact that it encourages a collective recognition and agreement of the need for major changes to the way we organize, manage or support our business products services.

Damage to facilities might offer an opportunity to rethink how best to optimize the provision of services. Similarly, previously unnoticed flaws may suddenly come to light in current business strategy, communications methods or organizational design. A crisis will bring such weaknesses to the attention of senior management, and it will demand immediate action and a change for the better. All major changes provide opportunities for process improvement. A crisis can serve as a useful trigger for driving through long overdue, radical changes to the organization, its processes or its infrastructure. It can also be a timely catalyst for a more objective re-thinking of business strategy.

Smart companies in a crisis will practice scenario planning, identifying the potential future consequences of key events and decisions, assessing the costs and benefits of alternative future states, and, on the basis of this, aiming to steer external perception and developments in a direction that might maximize future business opportunities.

Also significant is the fact that everything you do in a crisis will be under the intense spotlight of the media, staff and shareholders. In the heat of the crisis, you're likely to regard any media attention as a distracting intrusion. But, in reality, there's no such thing as unwelcome publicity. In effect, it's free advertising for your business products. And it's a spotlight on your own management and communications skills. It's not often that you can guarantee to hit the headlines, even if it's just in the financial pages. So it's important to plan to make the most of media attention and coverage, and aim to come out in the very best possible light.

There is also research evidence that those enterprises that manage a crisis well, and maintain a positive media response, can actually increase the long-term value of their intellectual assets.

Boosting market capitalization

One of the things that took many information security professionals by surprise was the unexpected fact that TJ Maxx somehow managed to improve their revenues and enhance their stock price, following a highly publicized breach of customer credit card data. The outcome certainly defied the projections of the doomsayers who thought the company's reputation and future finances would be permanently damaged. But TJ Maxx handled the crisis well. They launched a special three day 'customer appreciation sale' and extended offers of credit monitoring for affected individuals, as well as store vouchers for customers who could document they were harmed by the breach, effectively encouraging them to give renewed custom to the chain that had just lost their data.

The TJ Maxx recovery was unusual, but it was not a surprise to seasoned crisis management observers. There have been other similar cases in the past. In fact, there is huge potential for a good crisis management performance to lift both the business performance and the brand value. In a crisis every eye is on you, for better or worse. A bad performance will bury you. But a good one can pay real dividends, by actually boosting future sales and market capitalization.

Dr Deborah Pretty of Oxford Metrica, a research and analytics firm, has conducted research into the impact of crises on company value, which confirms this phenomenon. Like all such research, it was done several years ago when the drivers for financial markets might have been a little different. We cannot guarantee that the same results would apply in all future business environments. But there would seem to be a reasonable likelihood. Amongst other things, Deborah examined the share price performance, over one calendar year, of a selection of companies that had experienced a crisis. Deborah found that these companies tended to fall into two groups: the 'winners' who recovered well and the 'losers' who failed to recover.

Figure 3.4 shows the subsequent impact of the crises on shareholder value for the companies in question. The results demonstrate that most companies appear to experience an initial drop in (the modelled) stock price, of around 5–10%, following

Source: Oxford Metrica

Figure 3.4   Research by Oxford Metrica into the impact of crises on organizational value (reproduced with permission from Dr. Deborah J. Pretty)

a crisis. But, encouragingly, the companies that managed their crises well actually managed to boost their value by up to 15%. In contrast, the companies that failed to recover well suffered further stock market falls of a similar magnitude.

This research demonstrates the power of good crisis management to deliver a substantial financial benefit, by shaping future customer and stock market perception. The lesson to be learned is that a good crisis team performance that's effectively communicated will boost your stock market value and, in effect, pay a real dividend.

Anticipating events

Turning an incident into an opportunity is much easier if you can have some advance warning that it's actually coming your way. Smart organizations look ahead, and aim to identify and prepare for future risks, issues and problems. This might seem to be a relatively simple idea, but it's surprisingly hard to execute in practice.

Many managers, for example, are unwilling to devote time and effort to identifying and considering speculative events. It's much easier to grab their attention if we know for certain that something is going to happen. And, not surprisingly, it's even better if we know precisely when it's going to happen. That certainly helps to concentrate minds. But even then, it still requires a major facilitation effort to prepare business managers for the potential impact of the event.

One of the best examples of such an event was the Year 2000 Millennium bug. We knew the precise date of the problem well in advance. We also had evidence that some systems might crash and that production processes might need to be suspended. Given such a compelling, time-boxed date, what can realistically be done in advance to prepare the organization for such an event? It's worth reviewing some of the work that big international companies carried out prior to the Millennium, as that represents the state-of-the-art in advance planning for a potentially disruptive event.

For two years leading up to the Millennium, I worked with Y2K planning teams across the Royal Dutch/Shell Group. Remedial treatment to infrastructure ended up costing the Group hundreds of millions of dollars. But in addition, we also needed to prepare the organization for unexpected failures from the surrounding business environment. Oil and gas production, refining and distribution are critical national infrastructure.

We needed to minimize the impact of any potential outages. We were also part of a complex supply chain, with positive feedback loops as we supplied fuel to our own energy suppliers. A power failure that disrupted our own business operations might result in power failures further down the supply chain. For the first time, we had to model the impact of these failures across all of our supplier and customer value chains.

We were also aware of the potential for Y2K incidents to serve as a trigger for highlighting any perceived weaknesses in our ability to manage incidents across our complex business operations. As we've seen earlier in this chapter, it's possible for any event that attracts media attention to trigger a crisis based on the media or public perception of the organization's response to that event. Crisis teams had to be well prepared for this event.

The outcome was the need for a comprehensive, global refresh of contingency and crisis planning across all Shell companies, followed by the largest crisis exercise ever conducted by the Shell Group, involving all lines of business and a dozen or so operating companies across all geographic regions. The exercise ran for 24 hours to enable rehearsals of crisis team changeovers. The outcome was that all crisis teams were confident and well-prepared for the Millennium, and, on the day, there were no significant, unanticipated disruptions to business operations.

Anticipating opportunities

The knowledge that an event is coming your way can generate new business opportunities, though, in practice, it's far from a simple process to turn such foresight into real revenues. As part of the Y2K planning described above, we also explored possibilities for enhancing business revenue during the build up to the actual event.

For example, we were aware that customer awareness about the most severe consequences of the event would be mounting throughout 1999. There were reports of Hollywood feature films in production that would highlight the worst case impacts. We had no doubt that both businesses and citizens world-wide would be anticipating the event and might temporarily change their buying behaviour. What might they do? And what would we need to do to respond to such changes?

We ran a series of workshops with business managers to explore these possibilities. Managers were sceptical at first, but after a series of self-discovery brainstorming and analysis exercises, they quickly realized the potential for unusual changes in product supply and demand.

One possibility, for example, was that the public might buy extra supplies of essential supplies, such as bottled water. This would result in higher demand than usual for the plastic needed to manufacture the additional containers. Perhaps there were opportunities for increasing production of plastic? But anticipating short-term changes in end customer demand across supply chains is not easy. Firstly, we had to rely on retailers anticipating changes in customer demand, and, secondly, on other suppliers of components also being able to respond in time. And the further back in the supply chain you go, the longer it takes to make production changes. In practice, we would have needed to gain advance agreement across all producers in the chain, many months before the anticipated demand. The opportunity could not readily be exploited.

The learning point from this exercise is that business opportunities might be easily identified by analysis of current dependencies and future events, but it can be difficult to exploit them, because of delays in negotiating and applying changes across supply chains. Networks provide powerful new opportunities for closer information sharing and business-to-business collaboration, but the opportunities they provide will demand a much greater degree of business process agility.

Designing crisis team structures

There are many alternative options available for designing crisis or emergency response team structures. In fact, there is no single model that is guaranteed to work best across all organizations, or that will best suit a particular organization at all times and in all circumstances.

When designing a crisis team structure, the first challenge is to establish precisely how many emergency and crisis teams are appropriate for your needs. More realistically, this means how many formal teams can be officially supported. These will be in addition to the many ad hoc, local teams that are assembled to guide local departments and offices through a disruptive phase.

It's important to make this distinction because, in my view, it's good practice to encourage the leadership teams of all business units, service functions and major projects to meet and discuss the business implications of any crisis affecting the organization. You cannot have too many people responding to a major incident in an organized way. But a managed, enterprise crisis team structure cannot accommodate an unwieldy number of crisis teams. You have to place a strict limit on the number of formal teams, as well as the number of team members.

Every enterprise requires a formal, joined-up network of response teams. And that structure needs to be formally defined, recognized and supported, with appropriate budgets, resources and facilities. Each team will also need to be provided with an appropriate level of empowerment, because they will need to make decisions that impact other business units and function. That, however, shouldn't discourage local business units and offices from organizing their own teams to address their own particular needs.

As we noted earlier in this chapter, the ideal structure for managing a major enterprise crisis is to separate the response into three levels: the strategic response, the tactical response and the operational response. These are often referred to as gold, silver and bronze teams. But, in practice, there are many factors that will complicate this neat structure, such as geography, matrix management structures, outsourced operations, complex supply chains and the changing and specialist nature of many crises. In addition, we also need to manage the different types of response: emergency response, business continuity and strategic crisis management.

Crisis team structures are much more complex to design than might appear at first sight. There are many considerations affecting the choice, and the roles and relationships between individual crisis teams. No one structure will be perfect, no matter how well tailored it is to an organization. In particular, we have to aim to achieve the best possible compromise and balance between the conflicting needs for simplicity and the potential requirements for many types of specialist knowledge and skills.

How many teams?

The major consideration, underpinning the design of all crisis team structures is the organization structure itself. The logical starting point is that each business unit and service function will wish to establish its own response team. But across each major supply chain, we might also have several strategic outsourcers or business partners, each with their own response team structure.

For major projects, systems or infrastructures it would also seem prudent and appropriate to establish a dedicated response team. And the same logic will hold true for specialist functions such as IT, Security, HR and others. There might also be a need for regional, national or local response teams, especially if associated with critical facilities, sites or offices.

So how on earth can you pull all of this together into a simple structure that can be easily managed in a fast-moving, dynamic situation? The answer is through experience, delegation, and by trial and error. Managing hierarchies of response teams might sound like a hard task, but delegation of activities to specialist teams is also an essential requirement for successful crisis management.

We need to start by selecting an appropriate, initial starting structure and then conducting exercises to identify and learn from its strengths and weaknesses, experimenting, where possible, with alternative structures in order to determine the best approach. Designing effective crisis structures is an evolutionary approach, one which is repeatedly interrupted by company restructures, as well as management reviews following major incidents or cuts in budgets.

In practice we should aim to maintain the three levels of response. But we should also consider the usefulness of specialist sub-teams for particular purposes. For example, for particular incidents it's useful to employ specialist supporting teams from IT, Security, HR or Information Security, though they might not necessarily form part of the major decision-making process.

A computer emergency response team, for example, would not be expected to lead a crisis, unless it's a security incident that has a minimal impact on operational or business activities. As soon as it begins to have a major business impact, the lead should be taken away and placed in the hands of a higher-level, business-led response team.

Who takes the lead?

All response teams should be ready to accept a potential handover to a higher-level team. That means developing processes and maintaining records that do not rely on the memories of individuals, and ensuring that members are aware of the broader crisis structure that exists outside of their team.

The decision as to whether a senior-level team is invoked is for the senior team to decide. A lower-level team can make a recommendation, but it's for the senior team to make the call. In fact it's a hard decision to switch teams. It damages continuity and will sacrifice a certain amount of accumulated knowledge, but it's often necessary to introduce a higher-level perspective, and a greater degree of empowerment.

An alternative approach is to augment the original lower-level team, enhancing the team scope, membership and responsibilities, as the crisis begins to escalate. There is, in fact, no single best solution. I've concluded, through experience, that switching to a higher-level team is generally better than sticking with the original team. That's because the lower-level team tends to lack the broader perspective, authority and confidence to manage a large crisis effectively.

And confidence is vital. Not just the confidence within the team that it can deliver the best result, but also the level of confidence that the rest of the business has in the team, the belief that it's truly capable of managing the response on their behalf. As with many things in security, risk and incident management, it's trust and confidence that underpins the ability of people to identify solutions, and the willingness of the rest of the organization to support their decisions.

No response team can sit indefinitely without becoming exhausted. When members become tired, they will need to be replaced. In practice, most crisis structures are based on a single set of teams. And most of the crisis preparation is based on managing the first day of an incident. It's rare to find back-up teams, and even rarer to find examples of crisis exercises that rehearse team changeovers.

The key with such transitions is not to plan for a wholesale handover to a completely fresh team. Individual team member changes are best staggered, and carried out at convenient break points that best fit the current activities and stamina of the individuals concerned. Some people can stay alert and fully functioning for many hours. Others might become stressed very quickly and should be substituted at an early opportunity.

Ideal team dynamics

Good crisis teams require a unique blend of skills and chemistry. They need to develop the capabilities to manage large amounts of incoming information; to piece together what's really happening, generally from incomplete information; to address the immediate problems at hand; to develop imaginative strategies to guide the broader response; to communicate the latest situation to the media and to harness the full power of the resources available across the organization.

Many people assume that good teamwork needs to be based on cooperation and consensus thinking. Personally, I prefer to see argument and challenge. In the heat of a crisis, it's easy to make a mistake, to see only what you want to see, to follow the most obvious way forward or select the easy way out of the situation. Alternative scenarios and solutions also need to be considered. In a crisis, you want the best of all available solutions, not the first one that happens to spring to mind. But listening skills are often in short supply in a fast-moving crisis team environment.

Some teams follow the direction of an assigned leader. Others take their lead from the person who shouts the loudest. But it's important that at least one team member takes the time to listen, think, assess alternative approaches and intervene with a compelling counter-argument. Someone should play Devil's advocate, especially on big decisions. It's much better to have a heated debate, and perhaps a vote, on competing solutions, than to agree, by default, on a weak solution that no-one feels inclined to challenge.

Unfortunately, the nature of modern business, operating across an extended enterprise, sited across many different locations, means that it's getting much harder to establish an environment that encourages debate. It's difficult to brainstorm and argue, when you're at the end of a time-boxed conference call, rather than eyeball-to-eyeball, across the table in a conference room.

Multi-agency teams

Designing crisis team structures that can operate effectively across multiple organizations is hard. It's especially hard if there is no strong lead organization that is in a position to dictate to the other participants, for example a major customer working with a group of dependent suppliers. And, in fact, even if there is a clear lead organization that is in a position to lay down the rules and the strategy, it's often the case that the supporting enterprises are the ones that actually have the hands-on control of the necessary skills, knowledge and tools to fix the problem.

The first challenge in establishing effective, multi-agency crisis management is to ensure that each team involved has a clear understanding of the structures, roles, membership, contact details and call-out procedures of the response teams in each of the other organizations. That's not a trivial task across a fast-changing, virtual supply chain. During times of restructuring, it will be hard for external business partners to keep track of the changes.

The second challenge is to determine how best to interface with the other teams. There might be different hierarchies of teams operating across connected organizations, with varying levels of seniority or expertise. It's unlikely, in practice, that there will be a perfect match. And it will be necessary to ensure, as far as possible, that escalation processes are consistent and synchronized across the supply chain.

The third challenge is to harmonize the rules, protocols and working methods across the extended crisis team organization. Many potential issues can be resolved by good advance planning and preparation. Some might require agreements established when the crisis teams sit, such as ensuring that the timing of multi-agency conference calls will not clash with those of other scheduled, internal conference calls. Other issues, such as achieving compatible working methods, will need to be developed by trial and error, through exercises and observations.

The fourth, and most difficult, challenge is to ensure that crisis teams from external organizations are not overly secretive about events and information. It's natural, for example, for a supplier to be reluctant to disclose details to a major customer of any events that might appear to breach a service-level agreement. It's also inevitable that companies will wish to withhold details of breaches and operating practices from their competitors. But good response strategies and decisions cannot be established in the absence of the full facts surrounding an incident.

Honesty, clarity and accuracy of information are the cornerstones of effective crisis team working. Achieving that in an extended-enterprise environment is, unfortunately, far from easy. Trust will only be achieved over a period of time, as participants learn to balance the benefits of sharing against the commercial risks associated with disclosures to partners.

The perfect environment

Physical environments can have a surprising degree of influence on team behaviour. Even basic characteristics, such as the physical dimensions of the crisis room, will dictate whether the team operates as a single entity, perhaps falling over each other in the manner of a primary school football team, or whether they break up into smaller, uncoordinated groups that become distracted by particular strands of the crisis.

Such extremes sound unlikely, but it's a fundamental learning point of crisis team planning that the same people, placed in a small room, will behave very differently than when placed in a larger room. The shape of the room and the position of seating can also have a significant impact on the ability of a leader to dominate the group, and on the amount of democratic debate that is encouraged. In fact, for any size team, there is an optimum size and shape, that's not too small to prevent parallel working, not too big to prevent co-ordination of activities, yet carefully shaped to encourage equal contributions and avoid corners for quiet thinkers to hide away.

For a top-level, strategic crisis room, a round table in a calm environment is most effective. For a busier, emergency response room, a horseshoe arrangement of desks and computers, surrounding a large central white board or projection screen, can generate a strong focus for problem solving and sharing of up-to-date facts and reference information. A good supply of white boards or, better still, blank walls on which people can write, is also essential.

It's interesting to speculate on what could be achieved if money is not a major constraint. I'm particularly impressed, for example, with the layout of the US National Counter Terrorism Center, in McClean Virginia, which was designed by a theme park engineer from Walt Disney Imagineering. The operations centre has a sensible lay-out of well-spaced desks in a large, dimly lit room, with a central focus. It's a very effective layout for managing fast-moving, operational issues. The centre is also reported to have a futuristic videoconference room, featuring a table with pop-up computer consoles that can change its shape.

Digital displays are not absolutely essential. You can also achieve quite a lot with flip charts and white boards. But electronic displays do provide a certain wow factor, and they can help to convey a professional, serious environment. The most impressive electronic environment that I've come across, which is used from time to time for crisis training, is the Louisiana Immersive Technologies Enterprise (LITE) complex at the University of Lafayette. This amazing facility boasts three-dimensional immersive visualization cubes with high definition walls, floors and ceilings, supported by high-speed networks of high performance computers. The technology enables detailed maps and video images to be instantly called up and displayed in great detail.

Not to be forgotten is the need for a fallback location, in case the main crisis room becomes unavailable. That can happen for two reasons. Firstly, it might be inaccessible following a major disaster that affects the building. And, secondly, it might be hijacked by another crisis team. In many enterprises, crisis rooms are shared by more than one business unit. You certainly wouldn't want to be displaced by a more senior team when you're deep in the middle of a crisis.

One of the key challenges in handling a crisis is managing the information flow to build a picture of the event and the consequences, and then analyzing this against an uncertain future. The environment plays a major part in supporting this process. It should be a fundamental consideration in planning crisis facilities and protocols.

The challenge of the virtual environment

Unfortunately, many physical crisis rooms are becoming a luxury for modern, mobile enterprises, if not a thing of the past. The real challenge today is to manage incidents outside of a traditional crisis room, across a virtual environment of mobile staff, outsourced service providers, and remote business partners. Like it or not, the conference call is replacing the crisis room and that's a major problem for crisis management. It's hard enough to manage a crisis well in a shared room. But it's substantially harder to manage one when working with faceless people in remote buildings.

Conference calls introduce a number of characteristics that reduce the effectiveness of crisis teams. Meetings might be as regular as clockwork, but they are not continuous. Only one person can speak at a time and information is shared in a slow, serial manner. It's also hard to develop a shared, common picture of the crisis. Each team member will build their own, unique perspective of events, based on the set of information accessible through their work station and mobile phone calls.

Normal business conference calls tend to impose a set of protocols of their own. People take turns to speak, regardless of the importance of their role or contribution. Challenge is discouraged. It's rude to interrupt. Body language cannot be seen or conveyed. You're never completely sure which people are present or listening. And not everyone pays attention. Some people will be answering their e-mails, rather than listening to the speaker. And for the duration of the conference call, nobody else will be able to get through to any of the participants.

The telephone might be fine for controlling a well-scripted or rehearsed recovery process. But it's a poor tool for assessing and responding to a strategic crisis. Nevertheless, virtual team working is a feature of the modern work environment. We have to make the best of the situation. And, in fact, there are several things that can be done to improve the effectiveness of virtual crisis management. In particular, there are two main items that need to be addressed in preparing to manage a virtual team crisis. One is the team structure and the relationships between teams from different organizations. The other is the protocol for managing virtual conference calls.

Protocols for virtual team working

The most important aspect about managing a crisis through the use of conference calls is not to be constrained by the restrictions imposed by the traditional protocols used for regular, day-to-day business meetings. Different rules and protocols are needed, ones designed to prioritize information reporting, to maximize knowledge sharing, to promote debate and to enable brainstorming.

It's also important to provide team members with guidance on their roles and behaviour outside of the conference call. In particular the need to track and log individual actions and progress, and the arrangements for contacting people when their normal phone is engaged.

The number of participants taking part in conference calls can also be a potential problem. Physical crisis rooms impose a natural limit on the number of people who can crowd around the table. Conference calls don't impose such an obvious limit. They have a tendency to grow, because such calls are easy for people to join. Deputies and alternates can join in. Senior managers might also listen in. Specialists will be invited in to contribute, and might be tempted to outstay their welcome. But strict limits need to be maintained, especially when a debate is taking place.

Failure to embrace new technology can sometimes be a failing of senior team members. But the real weakness of virtual crisis management is not so much the failings or limitations of the participants. It's the failure, in fact, of current technology to enable effective, real-time information sharing and collaborative team working across remote locations. We need much better tools. Hopefully they will emerge in the not-too-distant future. In the meantime, virtual crisis management will continue to be an inefficient and frustrating process.

Exercising the crisis team

No crisis team can function effectively without training and regular exercises. The learning curve for new crisis teams is too substantial to ignore this requirement.

Team members need to become familiar with the characteristics of a crisis, which are very different from their day-to-day business. They will also need to develop and understand their own role in the crisis team. And they will have to understand how the crisis team operates: how it processes incoming information, makes decisions, gets things done and with whom it interfaces, as well as when, how and to whom it needs to deliver briefings on progress.

Training and exercises are essential to ensure that a crisis team is fit for purpose. And there is no substitute for professional guidance from experts or experienced practitioners when it comes to planning a training and exercise program.

Exercises can range from simple unannounced call-outs (to test escalation processes), to full-blown, multi-agency exercises, with live teams, professional scripts, actors, mocked-up information systems and perhaps the participation of emergency services and press representatives. The costs can vary from next-to-nothing to hundreds of thousands of dollars. That might seem expensive, but it's comparable with the effort that's generally expended when preparing for a major leadership team event. And the need to prepare the organization for a major crisis is every bit as important.

Exercises need to practice what Michael Charlton-Weedy, a seasoned crisis training expert, calls "variable geometry". That means they should be designed to meet a range of objectives, including the need for both personal team development and evaluation of the team's capability. Michael sees the basic principles of exercises as being clarity, honesty, coherence and integration of lessons learned. The same principles apply to live crisis management.

Each level or type of response team will require a different focus for training and exercises. An exercise for a top-level, strategic crisis team, for example, should focus on the major vulnerabilities of the enterprise, especially those that might have a major impact on corporate reputation and on the enterprise's longer-term survival. An exercise for a business continuity team should focus on more immediate disruption to critical processes and supply chains, perhaps bringing out the difficulties in detecting, reporting and responding to events and failures.

Good exercises need to be credible and realistic, yet surprising and unexpected. It's useful to challenge and stretch decision-making, management and communication processes, as far as possible. Good scenarios will raise uncertainties, for example about the ownership of issues, decisions or problems. It's also useful to include ambiguous scenarios that might suggest alternative strategies or solutions.

A good exercise should compel the crisis team to accept or reject major risks in arriving at decisions, and force them to prioritize their actions. It should also aim to test and highlight weaknesses in reporting and escalation processes. Independent formulation of exercises is important. Otherwise we will only test what we already know. And high quality observation, by people with knowledge of other systems, can provide valuable feedback to enable improvements.

Exercises are opportunities for team members to improve their skills and confidence, as well as to come to terms with their own limitations. And that's important, because no team will achieve perfection. But the team does need to reach a level of capability that's good enough to enable it to take big decisions, without constant checks and consultation with the business managers that normally run business operations. And it's essential that the rest of the corporate leadership team and middle management can gain sufficient confidence to trust the crisis team's judgments and to follow its lead.

Learning from incidents

So what have we learned in this chapter? We set out to explore what might lie beneath the surface of a major incident: the near misses and bad practices that shape the events, incidents, emergencies, disasters and crises that we experience. We also examined the complex art of managing a crisis well, and perhaps even to the longer-term advantage of the enterprise. Here's a summary of some of the key findings and conclusions.

Firstly, we established that incidents don't just appear out of the blue. Behind every major incident, there are likely to be dozens of minor incidents, hundreds of near misses and perhaps thousands of bad practices. A certain percentage of human mistakes and accidents should always be expected, which is why all systems should be designed with a margin of human error in mind.

Not all incidents are the same, and the terminology changes as the impact becomes more severe. In general, events are mainly for the record; incidents demand a response; emergencies justify immediate management attention; disasters require contingency plans to be invoked and crises need top-level management intervention. And as we move up the scale of severity, we find that the nature of the response changes from a short-term, operational focus on physical assets, to a long-term, strategic focus on intellectual assets.

In the most serious incidents, there will generally be three distinct recovery processes at work: emergency response to repair the damage to assets or services; business continuity management to maintain business-as-usual throughout the incident; and strategic crisis management to stem the escalating events and publicity that might threaten the long-term viability of the enterprise. The skills needed to execute these processes are quite different.

In many cases, especially for the higher levels of incident management, the response process is more important than the plan. Incidents today are becoming increasingly complex, which requires a more improvisational approach. But strategic crisis management is hard to execute well, because it demands objective thinking, and a unique blend of analysis, problem-solving, communication and organization skills. It also requires competent people, who are decisive and able to operate without guidance, rapidly assessing and appreciating the significance of new issues in a fast-changing business environment.

A crisis can also bring to the surface a more serious, deep-seated flaw in the organization. It's important when developing the crisis response strategy to recognize this possibility and to focus on the underlying causes of the crisis, not just the events that might have triggered it. The best strategy in any crisis is generally to be open and honest, and to apologize sincerely to your customers. The truth will always come out in the end.

Any major incident presents opportunities for business improvement, which are often overlooked. In the aftermath of an incident, you can drive through major changes to the organization, infrastructure or services. You can also aim to exploit the publicity from media coverage to present the management in a good light. Smart companies will also practice scenario planning to help steer developments in a direction that might maximize their future business opportunities. And research shows that enterprises that manage a crisis well can boost their market capitalization.

Advance planning is crucial to ensure that the appropriate skills, information sources and facilities are readily available to the crisis team. Team organization requires careful thought, because there are many different skills required and many options available for organizing them. Response processes today often have to operate across multiple organizations, demanding honesty, trust and harmonization of rules, protocols and working methods.

Some advance thought should also be given to the design of the crisis room, as the physical dimensions and layout can have a significant influence on team behaviour. But virtual team working is becoming the norm, and that presents a new set of problems. Crisis team conference calls require different protocols from traditional weekly business calls. Strict rules are needed to prioritize reporting of information, to maximize knowledge sharing, and to encourage creative debate.

Training and exercises are essential for all crisis teams. Team members need to understand the nature of crises, their role in managing them, and how it relates to the rest of the crisis team organization. Good exercises should stretch the decision, management and communication processes as far as possible. Exercises are opportunities for team members to improve their skills and confidence, as well as to come to terms with their inevitable limitations.

Here are six key points to learn from incidents

- Don't wait for a major incident before taking preventative action
- Identify and address the root causes behind minor incidents and near misses
- Employ different skills and processes to recover damaged facilities, maintain business continuity and manage strategic crises
- Crisis management is difficult; practice helps but it doesn't guarantee success
- Advance planning is crucial; it can be the difference between survival and failure
- Crisis conference calls need special conference protocols – different from your regular Monday morning calls

Zen and the art of risk management

East meets West

The title of this chapter might, at first sight, sound just a little bit zany or pretentious. But there is a point to it. The subject of risk management has quite a few parallels with Robert Pirsig's cult book *Zen and the Art of Motorcycle Maintenance*. Pirsig's book explores the contrast between Eastern and Western philosophical traditions. In particular, he argues for a perception of the world that encompasses both rational, logical deduction and creative, intuitive insight. In fact, that's the same type of perspective we need for risk management.

The motto of Pirsig's book is taken from a conversation between Socrates and Phaedrus on the art of speechwriting:

> *'And what is good, Phaedrus, and what is not good . . . Need we ask anyone to tell us these things?'*

In practice, risk management is often like that. There might be numerous complex factors and consequences associated with a risk or an event. But we usually know, instinctively, what's good and what's not so good. So why do risk managers try to put numbers on these risks?

The judgments underpinning risk management are, in fact, a blend of cold logic and gut feeling, with the latter always dominating the former. Gut feeling is invariably the deciding factor in any risk assessment, whether for personal,

Managing the Human Factor in Information Security   David Lacey
© 2009 John Wiley & Sons, Ltd

commercial and political reasons, or because of the simple fact that we don't have enough hard, objective data to calculate risks precisely.

Two conflicting trends will continue to maintain this situation. The first is the increased amount of data that we can assemble and mine, to help calculate our risks with more precision. The second is the increasing volatility, complexity and sophistication of business, technology and security environments. The former trend encourages us to build systems to help model historical risks. But the latter makes it difficult to be precise about emerging new risks.

Technology might be precise and predictable. But networks are changing our information systems from strictly deterministic processes, such as applying a software algorithm to calculate a useful output from a given input, into more probabilistic ones, such as coordinating the outcome of a series of interactions between people, software and data in remote locations.

A further problem is that everyone has their own unique perspective on risks. A nuclear scientist doesn't view the world in quite the same way as a Zen Buddhist. A statistician will carefully weigh the significance of events and outcomes. But a superstitious footballer will leap to conclusions, imagining cause and effect patterns between unconnected events. People are also naturally biased. They make errors of judgment because of inherent factors such as experience, loyalty or their personal interests.

And we all have misconceptions about risks. Many of us feel concerned about providing our credit card details on-line, but few of us hesitate to do so over the phone, or become concerned when a waiter disappears with our card in a restaurant.

History continues to demonstrate that organizations are bad at risk management. The 2007 sub-prime crisis, for example, was a predictable risk, but it caught out many leading banks, all of which employed sophisticated risk management systems. These systems helped some banks to lessen their exposure, when they detected early warning signs in 2006, but they failed to prevent massive losses. As we practice it today, risk management is an immature, flawed process.

But, regardless of its shortcomings, risk management is here to stay. Over the past three decades, it has grown from being an obscure engineering technique or insurance practice, into an everyday, mainstream, business tool. Modern business needs to navigate a maze of growing hazards and compliance demands. We have no choice but to put in place a system of checks and balances to safeguard our assets.

This chapter sets out to explore and explain the nature of risks. It examines the reasons why it's hard for people to assess them and considers how we can best go about identifying and managing them. It also looks at lessons from more experienced sectors that practice risk management, such as the process industries and financial sectors. Finally, it considers some of the arguments against the use of risk assessment in the information security field.

The nature of risks

What is a risk? That's a good question and one that's not quite as elementary as you might at first think, because, in practice, many managers misunderstand the nature of risks. And even more of them find it surprisingly hard to measure and manage them.

If you take any group of business managers and ask them to name some big risks that are of current concern, they'll quickly come up with a list of important issues, requirements and problems. But many of the items they suggest won't, in fact, be risks. They might be very relevant business pressures, but unless they're expressed as an *event*, they are not risks.

Risks are possible events, and they're generally bad ones, though in a small number of cases you might, if you're lucky, encounter a few pleasant ones. They are occurrences, ones for which you can calculate a potential business impact, and for which you can estimate a probability, over a given time period. Issues, requirements and problems are ongoing items that are generally handled differently. They are less volatile than risks, which can change on a daily basis.

In the finance world things are different, as investments present the possibility of upside or downside risks. But when managing security, technology or information, upside risks are rarely encountered, so it's fairly safe to begin by focusing primarily on the bad events that cause business harm, rather than aiming to identify good ones that can deliver benefits.

The term risk is sometimes used interchangeably with the word 'chance', especially in conversations, to convey a degree of uncertainty associated with an event, such as in: 'What's the risk of that happening?' But there are subtle differences between these terms. A risk can be assessed and quantified based on knowledge. Chance can be calculated using statistics. But uncertainty represents an absence of knowledge and confidence.

Who invented risk management?

Risk management is a discipline that grew out of the insurance industry. You can trace its origins back thousands of years. Communities have long recognized the benefits of sharing the cost or effort of repairs arising from damaging events. The Greeks and Romans operated early forms of insurance, and these early ideas were subsequently developed into a finer art by institutions such as Lloyds of London, drawing on lessons from major disasters such as the Great Fire of London and the hazardous world of marine insurance.

Experience from major events and disasters, has since helped to refine the techniques and expand their scope. In fact, the compulsion to apply risk management has been primarily driven by catastrophic events, such as Titanic, Three Mile Island, Bhopal, Chernobyl, Challenger, Exxon Valdez, Enron and 9/11.

Published standards and guidelines for risk management first began to appear in the 1990s. One of the first guidelines was developed in Canada. That was followed by an Australian and New Zealand standard.

During the 1990s, risk management was increasingly adopted and exploited across the financial sector, prompted by the rapidly growing derivatives market, and by big losses at banks such as Barings. Much of the early focus of financial regulators and banks was on the management of market and credit risk, but increasingly the scope has widened to include operational business risks.

Over the last decade, risk management has also become an essential component of corporate governance. In the 1990s, it was a recommended good practice. Today it's mandated by regulatory compliance. The large bankruptcies of companies such as Enron, at the turn of the century, led to the passage of the Sarbanes–Oxley Act of 2002, which tightened up the need for internal controls associated with financial reporting. Risk management is an integral part of that process. Emerging legislation seems likely to further extend the scope of risk management across the enterprise.

The end result has been that risk management has broadened its focus from being an obscure tool, for mitigating catastrophic incidents or unaffordable insurance claims, to being a widely applied business tool.

But risk management has still to win the hearts and minds of business executives. It's still perceived by managers as primarily a compliance requirement, something that's necessary to satisfy auditors and regulators. It has a long way to go to becoming accepted as a beneficial tool, one that, for example, can ensure that stretch targets are met, that projects deliver on time and that critical business processes don't fail.

We could be so lucky

Risk management aims to reduce the impact of the uncertainty surrounding potential bad events. It's a more reliable alternative to blind faith or just plain luck. As Peter Bernstein, author of the 1960s classic book *Against the Gods: The Remarkable Story of Risk*, once put it:

> *'If everything is a matter of luck, risk management is a meaningless exercise. Invoking luck obscures truth, because it separates an event from its cause.'*

But faith can also work wonders by encouraging positive thinking, and by helping to overcome many of the risks to achieving goals. And there's also much more to luck than meets the eye. Napoleon, for example, expected his generals to be lucky. This might have been more than just wishful thinking.

As Frank Knight pointed out in his famous 1929 book *Risk, Uncertainty and Profit*, it's essentially luck that generates profits for entrepreneurs. In reality, they can only hazard a guess at the number of products they're likely to sell at a particular price. The risks that give rise to their profits are, in fact, largely errors of judgment.

Some people like to gamble. They should be entrepreneurs. Unfortunately, they sometimes emerge as development managers. I once came across a development team that believed they could navigate through product acceptance tests without removing all of the bugs. 'Rolling three sixes' they called it. It's an unprofessional approach and it's rarely successful. But it's a fact of life that some people will get lucky from time to time.

Research by psychologists has demonstrated that certain people are consistently luckier than others. Statistically, of course, some are bound to be. But there are also sound reasons for this. Richard Wiseman, a professor of psychology and a former magician, has extensively studied the nature of luck. He found several characteristics that distinguished lucky people from their unlucky counterparts.

Unlucky people are more anxious than lucky people. That prevents them from exploiting unexpected opportunities. They miss out on many of these because they are focused on particular things. Unlucky people, for example, go to parties looking for a perfect partner and miss opportunities to make other friends. They look through newspapers searching for a certain type of job advertisement, overlooking other openings.

In contrast, lucky people are more relaxed and open. They see what is really there, rather than what they are looking for. They create and notice opportunities, make decisions based on intuition and create self-fulfilling prophesies through positive expectations, and a resilient attitude.

Luck appears to be partly attitude, partly effort and partly calculated risk. Thomas Jefferson, famously, stated:

'I am a great believer in luck, and I find the harder I work, the more I have of it.'

Hard work helps. But so does a positive attitude. As Tennessee Williams said:

'Luck is believing you're lucky.'

In fact, there is no reason why we should not all be a lot luckier.

Components of risk

For most business purposes, risk is expressed as a function of the likelihood of an event taking place, combined with its impact on business performance. In the information security field, it's often expressed as a triple: the function of an identified threat, the associated level of vulnerability, and its business impact.

In practice, risks are generally measured and compared in terms of the probability of the risk occurring, multiplied by a measure that represents the relative size of the business impact. All of this might sound quite straightforward in theory, but it's considerably less so in practice.

A threat is something that threatens your business. It's an indication of an impending event or action: an expression of intention to inflict evil, injury or damage. It might be a technical threat, such as a computer virus, worm or Trojan. It could be a human one, such as a hacker, spy or fraudster. And it can also be an accident or disaster, such as a fire, flood or hurricane. But threats are not so easy to assess. A small number might be visible, regular and measurable. But most are unknown, unpredictable or random.

In the absence of any security countermeasures, our businesses would be vulnerable to any of the above threats. In practice, however, we apply a range of controls to prevent or reduce the potential business damage. But assessing the vulnerability of information systems to particular threats is far from easy. An average business manager will have no idea about how to go about this. A security professional will be slightly better placed. Some exposures can be measured with special techniques such as vulnerability scanning software. But not everything is as knowable or measurable.

The concept of business impact is a much easier one to understand and to estimate. But business impacts have many dimensions that are less tangible, perhaps uncertain or immeasurable. Consequential losses such as reputation damage or loss of future sales, for example, are impossible to predict with any certainty.

But managing risk is something we all have to get to grips with. And it's now part of everyday business practice. The components might be difficult, if not impossible, to establish precisely. But the theory is compelling and it's been well marketed to executive boards, auditors, regulators, governments and consultants. It's well embedded, and it's certainly not something that's going to go away within our lifetime.

Gross or net risk?

If you talk to business managers about risks, they'll generally assume that you're referring to 'net risks'. That means the risks that remain after all the current controls and countermeasures have been applied. It's important to make that distinction, because professional risk managers also consider 'gross risks', the risks that would exist if there were no countermeasures in place.

Gross risks are difficult for the business managers to get their heads around. But they do have their uses. Risk managers like them because they complete the picture. They're useful, for example, for demonstrating good corporate governance by showing that the organization has understood the nature of its fundamental risks and addressed them by implementing an appropriate portfolio of business or security controls.

Identifying gross risks is also useful for gaining a better insight of the business controls that exist in the organization, and for assessing their effectiveness, as well as their value. Gross risks provide a glimpse into the potential consequences if the business controls either failed to operate, or were downgraded or removed. Understanding what might happen if business controls fail is useful for appreciating the exposure to a rogue trader or fraudster, who might perhaps be in a position to ignore or bypass these controls. In fact, the whole basis of risk management is essentially the transformation of gross risks into net risks, through the application of controls. It makes sense, therefore, to have some visibility of gross risks.

But, unfortunately, there are two major problems associated with this concept. The first problem is that there are an awful lot of gross risks, perhaps only limited by our imagination. Take the prospect of a building collapsing, a vehicle crashing or a personal computer electrocuting a user. These are all everyday risks that we rarely consider because we assume that we have standard, universally applied measures in place to mitigate these risks. If we remove these controls, then a potential risk emerges. But once we begin to speculate on that basis, we'll end up wasting a lot of our time considering many theoretic risks that simply don't warrant any exceptional treatment.

The second problem is that the very concept of gross risks creates confusion in the minds of many managers. Risk management might appear, at first sight, to be a simple and straightforward process, but in practice its execution is fiendishly hard. To be effective, it requires a substantial degree of simplification in order to make it palatable to busy business managers.

Simplicity, in fact, is the key to successful risk management. Advanced concepts are fine for the risk management professionals, but they should be kept well hidden from ordinary staff as far as possible.

Don't lose sight of business

Risk management is the science of identifying significant events, assessing their likelihood, and their consequences, and then taking appropriate steps to either avoid them, reduce their impact or, perhaps, to turn them to advantage, *while still meeting business goals*.

The latter rider is extremely important. We can't realistically respond to risks by closing down projects or business units. Occasionally, of course, that will need to be contemplated. But a decision that clearly goes against local business goals should only be proposed if it clearly contributes to the higher, overriding business interests of the organization.

In fact, that's the major difference in perspective between a security consultant carrying out a risk assessment, and a chief information security officer assessing the results. Senior security executives are a part of the corporate leadership team and have to deliver a business contribution, rather than just follow a corporate process. They need to contribute to the broader, longer term interests of the enterprise.

Risk assessments need to be considered in the context of the current business strategy, and within the constraints or limitations of local politics and culture. There is no easy formula for achieving this. It requires good perception, sound judgment and a willingness to accept the wrath of the business, for an over-cautious assessment, the consequences of a damaging incident or for one that underestimates the risk.

Attempting to convert a downside risk to a business advantage is always a possible option. But it's a very hard one to achieve in practice. And it can also be a dangerous strategy for the inexperienced practitioner. As we saw in Chapter 3, it can work well in some circumstances, such as during a crisis. But, it's generally one to be avoided by security and risk management professionals. The important point to note, however, is that business risks are the prerogative of business managers, though it's the independent security or risk manager that serves as their conscience.

How big is your appetite?

Risk appetite is the amount of risk that an organization is prepared to accept or tolerate at any particular time. And, just like our physical appetite for food, it's a subjective, changing feeling, not an absolute, objective or static measure. Not everyone is equally hungry. One person's calculated gamble is likely to be another's unacceptable risk.

Risk appetite is a relatively new concept for most organizations. It's an inevitable development, given that the risk management process has now moved across and down the enterprise. A degree of consistency is needed. Managers need to understand what precisely constitutes an acceptable risk. And directors need to demonstrate that they have delivered appropriate guidance to enable risk decisions to be made in a safe, secure and consistent manner.

Defining clear guidance on risk appetite for an organization is a much better approach than allowing individual managers to decide their own level of acceptable risk, or requiring them to refer low-level risk assessments upwards for approval. Debating the level of risk appetite also provides an opportunity for the views of external stakeholders, such as business partners, advisers or auditors to be captured and factored into future business decision-making.

But calculating risk appetite for an organization, or even a local business unit, can be a difficult exercise. People have widely varying attitudes to risk. Their personal risk appetite will be influenced by factors such as age, gender, personality, lifestyle, religion, culture and logical capacity. In addition, there will be differences in perspective arising from their role, responsibilities and accountabilities within the organization, as well as from the nature of their employment contract, their bonus targets, and the perceived consequences of their decisions.

Different stakeholders within an organization will always have varying perceptions of risks, and different motivations for accepting or rejecting them. Commercial pressures and bonus-related targets have a major influence on the willingness of managers to accept risk. And at senior management level, the potential impact on market capitalization and corporate reputation will be a more significant factor.

Some organizations are more conservative than others, even within the same industry sector. It's often, in fact, the case that companies with very opposite views on risk appetite might both dominate an industry. BP and Shell for example are both highly successful energy companies, but with very different appetites for risk and how it might shape business strategy.

Risk appetite should also be clearly linked to the risk capacity of the organization, the overriding constraint set by the maximum amount of money that the enterprise can afford to lose. But it has to be admitted that even that hasn't stopped rogue traders from bankrupting their employers or managing directors from gambling away the corporate assets.

Enthusiasm for taking risks is also shaped by the local business environment. Risk appetite can be choked by stifling bureaucracy. It's interesting, for example, to compare business risk appetites across different countries.

A recent study, backed by the International Finance Corporation, showed that Brazilian entrepreneurs have a much lower appetite for business risk. That might come as a surprise, given the dynamic outlook one tends to associate with Brazilian nationals. But this risk aversion is shaped by the fact that starting a business in Brazil can take 152 days, require 18 different processes and 2600 hours a year, on average, to keep up with the taxes, which can be as much as 69% of the second year profits. As an observer quoted in The Economist put it:

> *'If Bill Gates had started Microsoft in a garage in Brazil, it would still be in the garage.'*

It's an emotional thing

Following a major train crash at London Paddington in 1999, John Prescott, Transport and Environment Minister, immediately undertook to install a £1 billion rail safety system, suggesting that 'money is no object'. Yet previous safety risk assessments had rejected expenditure on such an expensive system.

In January 2008, after a long flight over the Arctic, a British Airways jetliner crash-landed just short of London's Heathrow Airport. All 152 passengers on board survived. The cause of the crash was an unknown failure. But no jetliners were grounded. Yet several years before, BA had been forced to ground its entire Concorde fleet following an accident in Paris during take-off, in which many people died.

Why is it that our response to incidents can vary so much? Clearly the circumstances are very different, including the political climate, the technical analysis of the failure and the economic pressures at the time of the incidents. But an overriding consideration is often the fact that when many people die, there is a need for a more radical response. Regardless of the real cause of any incident, the citizen perception of a real or anticipated incident can trigger strong emotions and reactions. And we have to respond to these reactions as much as the facts of the incident.

Bruce Schneier has coined the term 'security theatre' to describe countermeasures that are intended to provide a perception of improved security, whilst doing very little to actually reduce the real security risks. Security theatre always comes to the fore in the aftermath of a major incident. But it's also a natural, intrinsic consideration for everyday industrial and national security, which needs to take full account of the need to reassure the public as much as the need to deter real threats. And there's nothing wrong with that. Reassuring the public is a major objective of security.

'Never under-estimate people's misconceptions and outrage about risk,' says Phil Venables, the highly experienced Chief Information Security Officer of Goldman Sachs. He's absolutely correct. And his view is backed up by Dr Peter Sandman, a long-standing expert on risk communications and creator of the insightful and attention-grabbing formula:

$$Risk = Hazard + Outrage$$

Big risks trigger powerful emotions in people, including feelings such as fear, guilt, shame, anger, anxiety and depression. In some cases the public outrage from an incident will be much bigger than the hazard itself, sometimes resulting in the need for an entirely different strategy for risk mitigation. In fact, as we saw in Chapter 3, the underlying causes of some crises might, in some cases, not be the hazards themselves, but the nature of the crisis responses.

As Peter Sandman puts it:

'The engine of risk response is outrage. Sometimes the problem is too little outrage; people are apathetic and I help my client arouse more outrage so they protect themselves. Other times the problem is too much outrage; people are excessively angry or frightened – usually because of things my client has done wrong – and I help find ways to calm the situation. Still other times the outrage is rightly high about a risk that is genuinely serious, and the job is to help people bear it and sustain it and act on it.'

Some risk factors lessen or increase the potential for outrage. People are less outraged by risks they elected to accept, rather than ones that are forced on them. Fairness also matters. A risk that affects some people more than others can encourage outrage. The level of public confidence in an organization's ethics also plays a part. Frightening risks are also more likely to generate strong emotions. And the nature of the response to the risk can have a major effect. In particular, it matters to people whether the organization deemed responsible says 'sorry'. That clearly helped TJ Maxx recover from their breach, as we saw in the last chapter.

Companies can develop surprisingly deep relationships with their customers. They can be as temperamental as a marriage. And the response to a major incident or risk has to be handled in a personal, caring manner. Just like a marriage, sometimes you can smooth things over with counseling. But, at other times, you will have to prepare yourself for the rough and tumble of the divorce courts.

In the eye of the beholder

People have widely varying levels of perception and appetite for risk. No two people will perceive, assess and manage a risk in precisely the same way. Their personality will make a difference. Optimists will be less cautious than pessimists. Confident people will take more chances than shy, nervous types. At one end of the spectrum, we might find people who are dare-devils, who enjoy sailing close to the wind. Some might even become addicted to risk-taking. But at the other extreme, we will encounter cautious, sensible people, ones who are reluctant to dive into the deep end or rock the boat, and who are inclined to avoid big risks or decisions.

There are many dimensions to personality, each with an impact on risk perception. The well-known Myers–Briggs personality type indicator, for example, uses Carl Jung's theory to assess people against four criteria, which measure whether a person is extrovert or introvert, sensing or intuitive, thinking or feeling, judging or perceiving. Each of the 16 Myers–Briggs personality types will have a different take on the nature of a risk and its appropriate response.

Age, gender and lifestyle are also important factors. Research shows that a young, single male will accept a much higher level of risk than an elderly, married woman. Females are more risk averse than males. And young executives will have less to lose than a middle-aged manager with a family, a mortgage and, if he's lucky, a final salary pension.

Pressure to achieve short-term bonus targets can also override common sense. And the higher the stakes, the greater the levels of greed, fear and risk appetite. Rogue traders are extreme examples of this. They are prepared to gamble incredible sums to recover from an underperforming trading position. Nick Leeson, for example, ran up losses of $1.3 billion at Barings Bank.

But reckless risk-taking can, in fact, be encountered at all levels in an organization, including executive boards, many of whom have demonstrated an astounding capacity for high-risk investments. One such example was the hugely extravagant set of bids by top phone companies for British 3G mobile licenses at the turn of the century. The rush for control of the spectrum encouraged all boards to play Russian roulette with their assets. Each paid billions of pounds for the right to operate an unproven technology in an uncertain new market. Three years later, one mobile phone company was forced to write off a massive £10.2 billion of assets.

Not long after that, we witnessed a similar madness in the financial sector as leading banks piled into highly leveraged investments in sub-prime loans. 'What were they smoking?' screamed the headline of the November 2007 edition of Fortune magazine along with pictures of the CEOs of four leading banks with combined losses of more than $20 billion. Clearly, in the pursuit of higher profits they threw caution to the wind.

Religion and belief can also play a part in risk perception and appetite. 'Pascal's wager', which argues that in the absence of any firm evidence it's a safer bet to believe in God, suggests that religious people might be more risk averse than non-religious people. Religion itself is a form of risk management.

Individual religions can also influence thinking and behaviour. A fatalist might be more inclined to accept, rather than fight, the consequences of a run of bad luck. A Zen Buddhist might prefer to focus on the spontaneity of the present moment, rather than engage in speculation about longer-term events. Everybody has deep-seated beliefs of one sort or another, and they are impossible to ignore no matter how objective you might try to be.

Alcohol can also play a part. Research at the US National Institute on Alcohol Abuse and Alcoholism has also shown that people are less able to distinguish threatening situations from safe ones after they've consumed a few drinks. The research team discovered that when people drink, neural circuits in the visual system and the parts of the brain involved in assessing threats are not as active as they are when the person is sober. The brain's reward system also becomes active under this influence. That's a fatal combination, which encourages people to take rash actions. It's what some people refer to as 'Dutch courage'.

In the field of criminology, a preference for risk-taking is linked with a willingness to commit a range of crimes, especially ones that offer short-term gratification. That doesn't, however, mean that people who take risks are likely to be criminals. But people who commit crimes are clearly greater risk-takers. And, as we'll see in the next chapter, every sizable organization is likely to harbour its fair share of latent criminals.

What risk was that?

Risk assessments are personal judgments, and not everyone is equally good at making them. There are many reasons for this. An obvious one is that not everyone has the same level of knowledge and experience. The average manager, for example, cannot be expected to understand the level of the threat from hackers. Most people will be aware that a threat exists, but we cannot expect them to appreciate their likely targets, techniques and modus operandi.

Risk assessment is even harder when it comes to the more sophisticated threats presented by hostile intelligence services or illegal information brokers. These types of threat are well outside of the day-to-day experience of the average business manager. They are likely to be perceived as something out of a James Bond fantasy. Yet the risk of espionage is very real. Research into intellectual property theft indicates that it's a large and growing problem for companies.

According to a series of annual surveys carried out during the 1990s by ASIS, the international society for industrial security, US companies collectively lose tens of billions of dollars each year. And the levels of loss are growing significantly.

Within an organization, there will be huge differences in the perception of information security risks. An end user will not be able to identify technical vulnerabilities as well as an IT professional. A business manager will not be able to judge threats as well as a security manager. And a director will not be able to spot weaknesses in governance processes as well as an auditor.

The logical and sensible conclusion is that specialist risks, such as information security risks, are best assessed by a partnership formed of a knowledgeable expert, who understands the nature of the threats and vulnerabilities, and an experienced business manager, who can best judge the business impact of the risk. And this partnership should as far as possible, draw on the experiences, or data, of people who have experienced similar risks in the past.

Living in the past

One way to gain a better understanding of the future likelihood of risks is by studying past performance, near misses and incidents. As the Spanish philosopher, George Santayana, put it:

> *'Those who cannot remember the past, are condemned to repeat it.'*

It certainly makes sense to examine past events objectively, rather than making assumptions based on selective experience and perception. We can also learn a lot from past mistakes. In fact, no prudent risk manager can afford to ignore the past. To repeat a mistake would appear careless to an independent observer, such as a person carrying out a security review or compliance audit.

But there are also dangers in placing too much reliance on historical performance. Many enterprises today operate in a volatile business and security environment, where new forms of risk emerge each month, and many forms of risk appear to be growing, often in unexpected step changes.

Some industries also operate in cyclical markets, where long periods of rising demand can be suddenly interrupted by steep falls. Financial markets are like that. Recent past performance can be highly misleading, though analysis of longer periods of market performance can provide an insight into leading indicators of impending changes.

When it comes to making any judgments about the unknown, however, the truth is that we have few options available other than an analysis of the past. As the author Robert Pirsig commented, a decade after his 'Zen' book was published:

> 'Who really can face the future? All you can do is project from the past, even when the past shows that such projections are often wrong. And who really can forget the past? What else is there to know?'

Something is clearly better than nothing. But as we'll see in Chapter 11, when we examine techniques to predict the future, there's plenty more that can be done to help identify and assess future trends and their potential business impact.

Who created that risk?

All businesses are surrounded by risks. No commercial transaction is completely free of them. Some can be avoided, but many others can't. Risks can be man-made or natural. And they can be the result of conspiracy, cock-up or just plain bad luck. In fact, it's worth reflecting on how different types of risk are introduced into an organization, because, through this type of analysis, we can better understand how to avoid or eliminate risks at their source.

Not all risks are inevitable. There are some risks that we willingly decide to accept. They are the risks that result from business decisions taken by executives who are fully conscious of their implications. An example of that might be the decision to establish a business operation in a high-risk environment. A bank might, for instance, decide to open a branch in Iraq or Afghanistan. Any company that takes such a decision will almost certainly have considered the operational risks, as well as the likely cost of the necessary countermeasures. They will be major factors in the business decision.

Other types of risk, however, are a natural part of day-to-day business life. We have no choice but to live with them. We cannot, for example, prevent risks such as a global pandemic or an economic downturn. We can, of course, take steps to mitigate their impact. But we do not consciously choose to accept them. They are simply part of the contemporary costs of being in business.

And then there are the risks that people introduce into organizations, perhaps through bad practice or ignorance. Risks such as a computer virus, introduced through a USB storage device, or a laptop with confidential data that's stolen from the back seat of a car. Some risks might be introduced deliberately, perhaps for financial gain, revenge or mischief. But most risks created by people are introduced unconsciously. Many of them can be avoided through simple, low cost awareness initiatives. They can be considered low hanging fruit for security and risk managers.

But it's not always that simple, in practice, to pin down and eliminate the real source of a risk. Fear, greed and politics will often mask the real sources of a risk. How can it be, for example, that an investment bank, managed by experienced directors, and employing sophisticated risk management systems, can lose tens of billions of dollars from a simple credit risk?

The likely answer is that, in spite of all their business controls and risk management systems, they simply gambled it away. When you're on a winning streak, it's hard to stop betting, especially with the market egging you on. At the end of the day it's greed and fear, rather than cool, clear logic that drives most big decisions.

It's not my problem

A further problem with many types of risk, especially security ones, is that the party that's responsible for creating or managing the risk, might not be the party that actually suffers the damage from a resulting incident.

It happens all the time. If a manufacturer or service provider makes a mistake or a bad judgment, it's the customer or a member of the public that suffers. Innocent people can end up suffering physical injury, financial losses or personal embarrassment, through no fault of their own. The cause might be an oversight such as a keying error, a mix-up of records or a flawed product design. But the party responsible for creating the risk does not experience the pain, unless, of course, a successful legal claim is made.

There's nothing new about this. It's a common problem in many fields. Air pollution is a good example. The offender might not even be in the same country as the people affected. In economics, an impact on a party that's not involved in the transaction is termed an 'externality'. Moral hazard' is the term given to the phenomenon that a party which is insulated from the consequences of a risk might be persuaded to act less prudently than it should.

A manufacturer, for example, might decide to cut corners to reduce the cost of a design, perhaps introducing a security or safety hazard. Similarly, an insured party might be inclined to take greater risks, in the knowledge that the insurer will take the hit for any consequential incidents. This concept of moral hazard is very old, originating in the insurance industry many centuries ago. In recent years, it's been increasingly applied to a wider range of risks in the financial sector.

But responding to a moral hazard is not easy. The obvious response is for government or industry to provide some assured protection for the injured party.

But that can sometimes make the situation worse. If a bank knows, for example that its investors will be bailed out by the authorities, it might encourage greater risk-taking, the opposite, in fact, of what was intended.

Over time, society will increasingly demand that incentives are introduced to compel parties that create risks to be more responsible. In the absence of such incentives, however, the best that we can do is to encourage greater foresight and better working practices, and, of course, to ensure that we all have a good lawyer at hand.

Size matters

Interestingly, the size of an organization can also make a difference to its ability to manage risks effectively. For example, Warren Buffett, the world's most successful investor, claimed that the size of the big banks was a major contributor to the 2007 meltdown in financial markets. In particular, he observes that:

'There are firms that, in terms of risk, are conducting themselves in a way that makes them too big to manage.'

'We have clearly seen situations where, if the chief executive knew what was going on, he didn't let on.'

Size matters because the bigger the business, the larger the stakes, and the more powerful the stakeholders. It becomes a much bigger deal to intervene. When you're making huge amounts of money, it's very hard to apply the brakes. Nobody will want to kill the goose that lays the golden eggs. There will be many vested interests that resist any change.

Big transactions can intimidate cautious people. I've always been impressed by the awe that surrounds very large transactions or money transfers. Slight delays can incur large penalties, as well as the wrath of senior managers and business directors. You need nerves of steel to present any challenges.

Big companies are also less agile, and less easy to adapt to new forms of risk. Smart companies should, ideally, plan for hard times when they are at their strongest point. But that's easier said than done. It's difficult to persuade people to cut costs when they're making money. And it's equally hard to get them to address downside risks when everything appears to be going well.

Getting your sums right

Assessing a risk requires the ability to judge probabilities. Unfortunately, not everyone is equal when it comes to this task. Some people enjoy mathematics and logic. They can't start the day without completing a Times crossword or Sudoku puzzle. Others have a deep loathing for mathematics, preferring to rely on their intuition.

Some people are superstitious, imagining that there is some relevance in a statistically insignificant connection between an action and an outcome. Many footballers, for example, are like that. They have lucky charms or rituals that they believe help them to score goals. The theatre is also full of superstition, such as avoiding whistling in the wings. What causes this?

A major factor in our ability to judge probability seems to be the degree of dominance exerted by the left-hand side of the brain. The brain is divided symmetrically into two halves: the left and right hemispheres. These two halves look similar, but have different functions. The left-hand side is the more technical side, dealing with linear mathematical problems and language. The right hemisphere is more holistic, dealing with spatial geometry, emotional expression and visual aspects.

The inference is that people with a strong, left-hemisphere dominance are likely to be much better at logic and probability. Some observers also suggest that men and right-handed people might perhaps have an edge in this area. But the key implication is that not everyone is naturally good at assessing probability. In other words, it's not generally wise to rely on the judgment of a single individual, unless you know that he or she has a reasonable grasp of logic.

It helps to understand statistics. Most of us appreciate that the probability of random events is not necessarily influenced by the outcome of preceding events. If you've just thrown three heads in a row it does not mean that tails is more likely on the next throw. Unfortunately not everyone grasps that. Some people instinctively feel that events should average out over a period of time and that 'overdue' events will therefore be more likely. But that's incorrect.

Many people also expect that random events will be evenly spaced or distributed. If there is an average of one event of a particular type occurring each year, then surely we should expect to experience one event in a typical year? Wrong again. In fact, there's only a one in three chance, approximately, of that happening. The most likely outcome in any one year is for no events to occur.

In fact, this suggests a smart way to ensure you hit your bonus targets. If there are only a small number of occurrences of a particular type of incident per year, then you should propose bonus targets based on bettering this average rate. In most years you can expect to beat the average, though once in a while you'll fail badly.

These sums get much harder when networks are involved, especially if they're hub and spoke networks. But even simple networks can create misunderstandings. For example, I've encountered many business managers who fail to understand why it's so hard to achieve end-to-end network performance targets. The reason for this is that they assume that if an overall end-to-end performance target is, say, 95%, then each link in the chain needs to meet this level of performance. Unfortunately, that's not true. If there are five or six links in the chain, then you need to achieve around 99% across each link. That's considerably tougher.

Some facts are counterintuitive

But even those people who enjoy mathematics and logic, and are fairly good at it, will fail in their calculations from time to time. Many things that are logically sound can also be counterintuitive.

One well-known gambling trick, for example, involves betting on the outcome of a throw of two dice. Suggest to your opponent that he will win if the total of the dice is between 2 and 4 or 10 and 12, but that you will win if it's between 5 and 9. That means he will win on six of the possible numbers, and you win on only five. At first sight, it sounds a fairly even gamble, with a slight edge to your opponent. But if you calculate the real odds, you'll find that they're actually 2 to 1 in your favour.

Even harder for many mathematicians to grasp, is the 'Monty Hall' problem, based on the American game show 'Let's Make a Deal' and named after the show's host. The scenario is that you're on a game show, and given the choice of three doors to open. Behind one door is a car, and behind each of the other two is a goat.

You pick a door. Let's say you choose door number 1. The host, who knows what's behind each door (which is important), will then open one of the other doors, say door number 3, and show you a goat. In fact it's always a goat (which is important). He will then invite you to either switch to door number 2, or to stay with your original door number 1. What would you do? Is it to your advantage to stick or switch?

Most people, including many mathematicians, imagine that the odds are even between the car being behind each of the two remaining doors. They generally elect to stick with the door they had previously chosen. In fact, one study of 228 subjects showed that 87% chose not to switch. But they would be quite wrong. The probability of winning the car is, in fact, doubled by switching.

That fact seems counterintuitive to most people, but it's true. The probability of success is two-thirds if you switch, compared to one-third if you stick. That's because you started off with a one third chance, and the remaining doors combined had a two-thirds chance. If you switch you're effectively switching to that two-thirds chance. The source of confusion to most people is the fact that they are assuming that non-random information (the host's choice of door) is actually random.

It takes a long time for most people to come to terms with that fact. Some people never accept it. They continue to argue the point. But the learning point to note is that even good mathematicians can sometimes get their sums wrong. Never underestimate the capacity for misconception, especially when it comes to calculating probabilities.

The loaded dice

Many mathematicians believe that they take a perfect, objective view of events that might even give them an edge in business. That might be the case most of the time but, it's not all that difficult to fool a professional statistician.

Nassim Nicholas Taleb, a trader who made tens of millions of dollars out of the stock market crash of 1987, and went on to write the book *The Black Swan: The Impact of the Highly Improbable* presents a very simple challenge:

> *'You toss a coin 40 times and it comes up heads every time. What is the chance of it coming up heads the 41st time?'*

Most mathematicians will immediately shout 'evens'. It's the obvious, logical response, reflecting the assumptions of professional statistician. But that demonstrates a major weakness in the way they've been trained to think. As Nassim Taleb points out, you would be a real sucker to believe that the odds are evens, because, quite clearly, that coin is loaded. The chances of a coin coming up heads-up forty times are vanishingly small, less than one in a trillion. When you observe such an unusual pattern, it's likely that either someone is cheating, or that there's another factor at play that we haven't yet identified.

Many clever investment and risk management models fail, either because the practitioners are not sufficiently streetwise, or because our minds are not open to new or unknown developments. No risk management methodology is perfect. They simply represent the best approach that we can currently apply, based on the very limited information we have available. There are always many factors, dimensions and details that we fail to see or appreciate.

Interestingly, one of the secrets of Nassim Taleb's financial success is to challenge the orthodox thinking of the bankers and economists who rely on risk management models that are largely built on sand. He uses the metaphor of a 'black swan', to describe the impact of a rare, unpredictable events that takes everybody by surprise. The metaphor is based on the old belief that all swans were white until black swans were discovered in Australia. Unexpected events or discoveries regularly drive a coach and horses through our traditional assumptions.

Major, unexpected events of this nature cannot be easily accommodated in traditional models of prediction. As a result we tend to place too much weight on the likelihood that past events will repeat. But that's a flawed assumption. As Nassim puts it:

> *'History does not crawl, it jumps.'*

Few people are prepared for major unexpected events. But they happen regularly, and they have huge influence on everyday business. Events such as 9/11 and Enron have dramatically shaped the way we perceive and manage information security. They were not anticipated, but they were possible and predictable.

The lesson is that, occasionally, we should take some time out to think the unthinkable, to devote a small percentage of our time to preparing for highly unlikely, but quite possible, events. That's, in fact, how Nassim made his fortune, by investing a small amount of his money on unlikely, but feasible, future events. We'll consider the impact of black swans in more detail later in this chapter.

The answer is 42

In Douglas Adams' highly entertaining book *The Hitchhikers Guide to the Galaxy*, the answer to life, the universe and everything, turns out to be '42'. Unfortunately, the question that prompted this answer was not clear at all. There's a lesson here.

Many security managers and academic researchers spend a good deal of their time searching for numbers to answer their problems. They believe that the ultimate goal is to establish a set of numbers that indicate and justify the true value of security. It's a misconception. Numerical answers should never be accepted at face value.

Coincidentally, '42' is also the number of days proposed by the UK Government for the detention of terrorist suspects. Some observers suggested a link with the Douglas Adams book. But it's actually a logical, round number, representing an even number of weeks, and a 50% increase on the previous limit.

Donn Parker always used to quote an imaginary figure when asked for an assessment. Interestingly, the less rounded it is, and the more decimal places there are, the more convincing it sounds. In fact, a major shortcoming of most numeric answers is that they rarely convey the accuracy or context of the input data. With security, that's a particular problem, as many of the accepted figures are based on hearsay, speculation or spin. The margin of error can often turn out to be larger than the number itself.

For many years there was a generally accepted statistic that 80% of companies without a disaster recovery plan who experienced a major disaster, went bust. I went to some lengths to find the source of that statistic, without any real success. I eventually concluded that it probably came from a very old survey, carried out by a physical security company, but in a context quite removed from the ones in which it was being applied.

That particular figure might have been influenced by the 'Pareto principle', otherwise known as the 80/20 rule. It's based on the idea that, for many things in life, 80% of the impact comes from 20% of the cases. The principle is named after an Italian economist, Vilfredo Pareto, who observed that 80% of the income in Italy went to 20% of the population.

Now that's a very specific context. But, ever since, it's been widely and often inaccurately applied to just about every walk of life. It's become so established that you can quote it for just about any subject to an executive board and they'll accept it as a reasonable ratio. Yet there is no universal law of this kind. It's simply an illusion.

It's just an illusion

When it comes to observing events, it's not just our lack of mathematical ability that lets us down. Our eyes can also play many tricks on us.

Optical illusions are an entertaining way of demonstrating that you can't always believe what you see. I especially like Adelson's Illusion, illustrated in Figure 4.1, because it demonstrates how the context of an image, in this case the pattern and background lighting, can be the cause of a deception. The illusion is that the

Edward H. Adelson

Figure 4.1   Adelson's Illusion – squares A and B are the same shade of grey (reproduced from http://web.mit.edu/persci/people/adelson/checkershadow_illusion.html, ©1995, Edward H. Adelson)

squares labelled A and B in the sketch, though seemingly opposite colours, are, in fact, exactly the same shade. It's quite a striking demonstration of the fact that you can't always trust your eyes and perception to get things right every time.

As with many optical illusions, the effect is actually caused by the success, rather than the failure, of our visual system. The visual system is not designed to operate as a light meter. It aims to perceive the nature of the objects in view. And it does this correctly despite variations in light and shade.

The learning point for information security management is that, like our visual system, security systems that are designed for a particular purpose will often ignore details that are not needed for the task. Every viewpoint takes a selective view of reality. In practice, we only take in a part of the picture, even when the whole is within our sights.

Context is king

Our perception of risks is often coloured by a failure to appreciate the true context of an event. The significance of many types of risk can vary widely according to their context. Not all events of a similar type, for example, are equally damaging. Yet we regularly identify, assess and convey risks with minimal appreciation of their context.

The loss of a laptop is not a major problem, for example, if it did not contain sensitive data, or if the data was encrypted, or if it becomes irreparably damaged. A door left unlocked might not be a problem if there is a security guard stationed outside. And security vulnerabilities in a platform might not be a significant risk, if the platform is attached to a secure private network.

The legality of an action can also depend on location, time of day, preceding events and other circumstances. In fact, assessing the nature of an action without the full facts can lead to misleading conclusions. Ed Gibson, a Microsoft security expert and former FBI special agent, once put the following questions to me during a debate we were having on the subject of the legal and moral aspects of so-called ethical hacking.

Question: A person is found inside a bank 'tinkering' with the bank vault combination. Is he a bank robber?
Answer: If the bank was closed and he was not hired by the bank to check the vault, then he's a criminal.
Question: A person is found rattling door knobs on people's homes and, when a knob turns, he walks in. Is he a burglar?
Answer: If the person rattling door knobs walks into a home without the permission of the homeowner, then he's a burglar.
Question: A person rapidly approaches the driver of an automobile stopped at a traffic light, shows a knife and tells the driver to get out. Is he a carjacker?
Answer: If the person with the knife and driver are not actors for a movie, then he's a carjacker.
Question: A person trained in software technology spends his livelihood trying to find vulnerabilities in code. Is he a hacker?
Answer: If the person does nothing with the information, then he's a 'security researcher'.
Question: A person who exploits software coding errors posts vulnerabilities on the Internet, rather than providing the information to the software manufacturer. Is he a criminal?
Answer: If the person posts the vulnerabilities on the Internet, he's a criminal.

The key differentiating factor in all these cases is: 'Was the person engaging in legal activity?' But that's not always clear from observation alone. You need more information about the circumstances surrounding the event to draw the correct conclusion.

We also need to appreciate the expectations in the minds of the people involved. Take privacy considerations for example. Bugging a telephone call is illegal, yet overhearing the same call on a train is not. The intelligence gleaned might be same, but the privacy expectations of the person making the call are quite different.

The lesson to absorb is that we can't generalize about a threat, vulnerability or business impact, without an appreciation of the surrounding context. Move the goalposts just slightly, and an innocent event can become a serious crime. And a minor incident can become a major risk. In fact, a major weakness of many risk assessments is that they don't capture, define and convey the associated assumptions or context.

Perception and reality

In his book *Beyond Fear*, Bruce Schneier emphasizes the difference between the perception and the reality of security. In particular, Bruce correctly points out that people exaggerate spectacular, but rare, risks, yet downplay common ones; that they have trouble estimating risks for anything outside their normal situation; that they judge personified risks to be greater than anonymous ones; that they underestimate risks they take willingly, yet overestimate ones outside their control and that they overestimate risks that have a high media profile.

In fact, there are numerous examples of risks that have been either exaggerated or downplayed in people's imagination, ranging from mosquito-borne infections to terrorist attacks. I won't bother to list them all. Instead I'll refer you to David Ropeik and George Gray's book *Risk: A Practical Guide for Deciding What's Really Safe and What's Really Dangerous in the World Around You.*

But none of this should come as a surprise. They are all very natural, human reactions. We don't view the world objectively. We perceive events and risks in a heavily filtered way. We become acclimatized to living with day-to-day risks, so we tend to ignore them. That's why most car accidents are likely to happen within half a mile of home. We also tend to worry more about risks that are at the forefront of our minds, ones that are easy to recall or frequently pointed out.

Many people will be particularly obsessive about the last incident that happened to them. Dr Paul Dorey, a highly experienced Chief Information Security Officer for Barclays Bank and BP, calls this the 'stolen wallet syndrome'. At any risk assessment session, someone will always be obsessed about a recent personal loss.

And we can't help being influenced by the media. If they're excited about a risk, we'll pick up on that. Personified risks, in particular, will seem much more real and immediate. An image of Osama bin Laden is much more frightening than a general description of a terrorist. People pay a lot more attention to things that are personal, immediate and certain. And, as we'll see in Chapter 8, these are factors that we can exploit to influence people's behaviour.

We're also, understandably, more concerned about risks that we don't control. Airplanes are scarier than cars, even though they're less dangerous. And most of us are very wary of the unknown, and that includes regular risk-takers, such as stock market investors, who often demonstrate a strong aversion to uncertainty.

Steve Greenham, an information security manager at GlaxoSmithKline, puts it another way. He makes the point that:

> *'People overestimate everyone else's risks and underestimate their own.'*

I've christened that maxim 'Greenham's Law'. My experience suggests that he's absolutely right. It's a natural reaction. The reason is our inescapable lack of objectivity when it comes to assessing risks and issues that are close to home. We simply cannot see through the layers of routine and culture that surround our day-to-day business life. All employees have to acclimatize their thinking to the artificial culture and often illogical corporate decisions that are part and parcel of modern business.

People are also naturally biased when they come to make judgments. 'Cognitive bias' is the name given by psychologists to the tendency of people to make errors of judgment owing to inherent factors, such as their experience, loyalties or perhaps their personal ego. We often do this unconsciously.

Psychologists have been examining the subject of risk perception for many years, though some findings are inconsistent and many are little more than common sense. One interesting finding is that people tend to be more risk-averse when it comes to gains than losses. When it comes to winning, they prefer safer bets to more rewarding gambles. Yet when it comes to losing, they prefer to gamble rather than accept a certain loss.

Another interesting research finding is that when it comes to gambling, experts tend to be more confident about their assessments, though they generally perform no better than anyone else. In fact, that's something we've all noticed, especially when it comes to financial investments.

It's a relative thing

Perception of risk is a relative, rather than an absolute assessment. It's shaped by our personal experiences, especially the most recent ones. In fact, there's an interesting phenomenon that some researchers call the 'contrast principle', which causes us to judge things by reference to existing experiences.

This principle is easily demonstrated by placing one of your hands in hot water, and the other in cold. If you then place both of them in lukewarm water, one will feel cold, the other hot. That's fairly obvious really. But we're not always conscious of such relative comparisons when we make judgments in everyday life.

When we make a choice, we do it by comparing similar offers that we're already familiar with. That's how we decide, for example, if a product has the right features, quality and price. And that phenomenon can, in fact, be used as a marketing trick. If a vendor offers us something that beats an existing offer, it appears to be good value. We might not be able to judge its true value, but we can be tempted by an apparent reduction in price or an increase in product features for the same outlay.

Some politicians have latched onto this concept. That's perhaps one of the reasons why the choice today between political parties is so bland. It's a much bigger risk for a political party to offer a set of policies or a direction that is completely different from the existing party in power. It's safer to offer a slight variation, which is easier for voters to grasp.

When it comes to risks, we tend to judge them by comparing their relative probability or impact against things with which we're familiar. New types of risk are particularly hard to judge. We need to find something familiar against which we can compare them. It's easier to be relative than absolute when making a judgment. For that reason it's much better to ask managers to rank, rather than quantify risks.

Risk, what risk?

A major difficulty with some of the largest risks that we face is a lack of concrete information. In the absence of hard facts, we can draw few reliable conclusions.

In such situations, when risks are down to guesswork, it's likely that business managers will play them down, and security professionals will play them up.

In fact, few people have a good grasp of the likelihood of everyday events. We know that, statistically, we're more likely to die in a road crash than in an airplane. But how much greater is the risk? In fact, it's more than a thousand times. And if the average person struggles with such well-established risks, it's not surprising to find that business managers are less inclined to accept many of the less familiar risks associated with information security.

Unprecedented risks are especially hard to manage. Past experience and current perspective are major factors in judging risks. We all have a tendency to ignore potential problems that have yet to materialize. Managers who've never experienced a major failure or disaster will be less conscious of downside risks, and will pay less attention to impending warning signs. And, of course, the desire to meet business goals will influence management opinions on whether a risk is worth addressing.

All of this tends to make managers over-optimistic about risks. Richard Feynman discovered this when he was investigating the cause of the Space Shuttle Challenger disaster. Amongst other things he noted an enormous difference of opinion across professionals of the probability of such a failure, with estimates ranging from roughly 1 in 100 to 1 in 100,000. The higher figures came from the working engineers, and the very low figures from management. In fact, senior management will rarely overestimate a business risk, and their risk appetite will generally be higher. Security managers will often need to serve as their conscience.

Something wicked this way comes

In the mid-1990s, with the help of my colleagues, I drafted a forecast of the long-term outlook for emerging security threats of relevance to a global business. It was disturbing to say the least. My research identified terrorists with nuclear, chemical or biological capabilities, organized crime with sophisticated technology and the emergence of cyber warfare. It was quite clear that we would continue to face an increasing set of serious security risks.

But the problem was not in convincing ourselves that the threats were real, but in convincing others, who were at that time expecting to see a safer, more secure world, having witnessed the end of the cold war. Longer-term scenarios always need to be treated with caution. They're fine for stretching people's thinking, but they don't have the same immediacy and credibility as familiar, day-to-day hazards.

Today, if I conducted the same exercise, I'd find some equally disturbing results. It's no exaggeration to say that we face a set of real, large, but uncertain threats. Many are hard to contemplate, and even harder to plan for. There are devastating risks to human life, such as the prospect of a biological terrorist attack or a global influenza pandemic. And these threats could strike tomorrow, or perhaps not for a decade or more.

Responding to such threats by investing money and resource is a major leap of faith for any business manager. Establishing facts about such threats is difficult, if not impossible. There will be conflicting views, and widely varying claims.

Take the prospect of an influenza pandemic. Government authorities have been warning us for many years that a global pandemic presents devastating consequences for our critical national infrastructure. It will dramatically reduce the number of available workers in all sectors, threatening essential services. The Department of Homeland Security has stated that, 'The avian flu bears the potential for societal disruption of unprecedented proportion.'

We certainly know that something big is coming. But just how big might the impact be? That's hard to predict precisely. One reason is the very large difference in severity of the three pandemics that occurred in the last century. Rates of serious illness, hospitalization and deaths depend on the virulence of the pandemic virus, and can differ by an order of magnitude between more and less severe scenarios. That's a very large degree of uncertainty.

And when is it coming? We simply don't know. I've yet to find an expert who is prepared to even hazard a guess on the most likely year. In fact, the best advice we have so far is that it's likely to happen anytime in the next ten years.

How can you put numbers on a potential risk of that nature, one that can happen anytime within the next decade and with an order of magnitude of difference in the degree of impact? We certainly can't use a simple, standardized, risk-ranking formula. We need to treat such risks on an individual basis.

The black swan

As mentioned earlier in this chapter, Nassim Nicholas Taleb has suggested the analogy of the 'black swan' to highlight the type of rare, high-impact and hard-to-predict event that occurs from time to time and takes everyone by surprise. The concept is based on the original Western assumption that all swans were white, until black swans were discovered in Australia in the 17th century.

A black swan is an event that meets three criteria. Firstly, it's outside the realm of normal expectations. Secondly, it carries an extreme impact. And, thirdly, despite the fact that it wasn't expected, people will concoct explanations after the event, making it appear more predictable than it really was.

Black swans can be used to explain many trends in life, including the success of ideas and religions, and the dynamics of history. Their effects may also be increasing. Examples of black swans include the rise of Hitler, the demise of the Soviet bloc, the rise of Islamic fundamentalism, and the spread of the Internet. These were all unanticipated events of major impact.

Take the 9/11 terrorist attack, for example. We did not imagine that such a scale of attack was possible. And that's a contributing reason. If we had anticipated the possibility, we might have demanded greater action to prevent it. We are often surprisingly blind to large, random events or changes. Yet many contemporary trends are the cumulative effect of just a handful of significant shocks. But we don't tend to cater for black swans in our risk assessments.

Exploiting this logic has made Nassim a very rich man. He gambles on unexpected events that provide huge returns on investment. He also claims that such events are on the increase. So it's worth investing at least a small percentage of your time to ensure that your risk posture takes account of the potential impact of those very large, but low probability impacts.

And there are certainly some very big shocks waiting in the wings. Over the next decade or two, we are likely to see a major pandemic, a cyber war and, potentially, the collapse of secure electronic commerce through the emergence of a quantum computer that undermines contemporary public key cryptography.

Double jeopardy

There's an old security joke about a dumb terrorist who tries to take a bomb on a plane. When challenged, he claims he did it because he'd heard that the chances of two bombs going off on the same plane were extremely remote. Now that might seem quite ridiculous, but business and personal logic often operates on similar lines.

Several years ago when reviewing business continuity planning requirements for the oil and gas evacuation processes, I encountered a planning assumption called 'no double jeopardy'. This rule was based on the fact that two highly improbable events are not likely to strike at the same time, so contingency plans need not be extended to cover situations where more than one low-probability risk might coincide.

It's a reasonable planning assumption. Lightning rarely strikes twice in the same place. So why bother to draw up expensive plans to cater for a very remote prospect? The answer is that it depends on the nature of the threat.

You might, for example, think that it's a good idea to have a combination of gas and electricity power in your home because they provide mutual back-up. And they do most of the time. But there are events that can cause both to fail. In the past it might have been a general strike for example. Today it might be an earthquake or flood. In the future, it might be a cyber-war that takes out critical infrastructure.

I first encountered examples of potential double jeopardy risks when reviewing contingency plans for the millennium bug. It was a time when multiple simultaneous failures were possible, perhaps even likely, during a very short window in time. We therefore had to ensure that no vital planning arrangements were invalidated by such an unusual event.

Multiple simultaneous failures are very unlikely events. But they're certainly worth considering. The learning point is not to focus just on the individual risks, such as power or supply failures, presented by a major hazard, such as a fire or flood, but to consider the total, overall impact of a damaging event.

What type of risk?

No two risks are the same. And they don't readily lend themselves to easy comparison. How, for example, do you equate a financial risk with one to human life? You can, of course, do it by placing a financial figure on a person's life. Money tends, in fact, to be the main common denominator to enable risks of completely different types to be compared.

But the jury is still out on whether it really helps to bring together quite different types of risk under a unified approach. Some organizations, such as the Royal Mail Group, do, in fact, operate a joined-up approach to managing all categories of business risk, whether financial, commercial or related to technology, projects, safety and security. But many other organizations choose to apply quite separate processes and techniques, especially when it comes to financial risks.

The process industries, companies that process raw or refined materials, have relatively mature processes for assessing industrial hazards. These have been driven primarily by health, safety and environmental requirements. In the financial sector, banks differentiate three categories of risk: credit, market and operational risk, with the latter often acting as an umbrella that covers anything that does not fit the first two categories.

Operational risk is a relatively new concept that has only emerged in the last decade or two. Regulatory compliance is the primary driver, especially the demands of the Basel 2 international standard, which offers major financial benefits for banks that can demonstrate that they meet the necessary risk management requirements.

Large engineering projects also demand attention to risks that might threaten their overall cost, timing or success. Estimating how much contingency to build into project activities is an important and difficult problem. Dependencies between activities create wide and complex variances in the overall impact of delays of individual activities. It's a similar problem to that of assessing the impact of security breaches on critical infrastructure components.

Business continuity management requires a business impact assessment to be carried out at an early stage in the planning process. In contrast, that demands a top-down, rather than bottom-up, approach to risk identification and mitigation. Business continuity management focuses on the impact of residual risks, i.e. those remaining after other countermeasures have been implemented. And the emphasis is primarily on the recovery from, rather than the prevention of, damaging events.

Over the last three decades information security management has developed its own, individual approach to risk management. Most competing methodologies have progressively merged into a universally agreed approach. The approach is not dissimilar to the techniques used to manage other forms of operational risk, such as industrial hazards. But the level of maturity of information security risk management processes is much lower. In fact we can learn quite a few things from a study of other areas, in which risk management has been established and exploited for a much longer period.

Lessons from the process industries

Examples of process industries are those that process oil and gas, petro-chemicals, water, sewage, food and pharmaceuticals. They have a long experience of managing operational risks and industrial hazards. Management processes include risk mitigation techniques such as safety cases, major accident risk assessments, quantitative risk assessment and hazards analysis.

Over the years these organizations have learned to consider risk analysis and mitigation activities much earlier in the lifecycle for the development of a new facility or a planned merger or acquisition. Techniques have also been developed to enable the assessment of an overall risk profile for a large, complex plant, or to identify risks in a potential new design or layout for a facility. The identified risks might, in fact, extend well beyond the facility perimeter, including the surrounding structures, population or environment. The scope, consistency and holistic nature of these assessments are far more advanced than in the field of information security risk management, and so are the standards, accreditation processes and the degree of integration of risk management with business operations and management.

I have found in practice that methods from the process industries, such as 'hazard and operability analysis', can be successfully adapted for business continuity and information security risk management purposes. This is an especially useful approach in environments that are already familiar with the technique. One advantage of the hazard and operability analysis approach, for example, is that it's performed by a multi-disciplinary team of operators, engineers and managers. This makes it a powerful tool for pooling knowledge and raising awareness of risks, as well as for achieving collective buy-in to a risk assessment.

The concept and structure of a 'safety case' is also a sound idea that can be adapted for information security purposes. Such cases are much more comprehensive than a conventional security risk assessment or requirements analysis. A safety case sets out claims, arguments and evidence. A variant of this for security purposes would merit a useful place in the systems development cycle for critical systems and infrastructure.

Hazard safety culture is also more institutionalized in the process industries than information security culture. In many safety-aware environments, for example, you will not be allowed to walk down a staircase without being reminded to grip the handrail. Yet in the same organizations, you can leave confidential papers and sensitive media out on your desk without the blink of an eyelid. Security lags far behind safety in these environments.

The real lesson from the process industries is that with persistence and time, the management of risks and hazards can be fully integrated into development and operational business processes. There is, in fact, no reason why the same cannot be done for information security. But at present we are a long, long way from achieving this.

Lessons from cost engineering

The need to manage risks for large engineering projects has encouraged the development of a wide range of methods, to quantify the impact of delays to individual activities. Various techniques, such as Monte Carlo methods and parametric modelling, have been applied for many years, though there is, in fact, little evidence to suggest that our ability to estimate contingency values using these methods is actually getting any better.

Monte Carlo techniques are also used in financial risk management, to help value investments. They were originally developed in Los Alamos during World War II by the Manhattan Project team, and were named after the famous French casino. Essentially, they use simulation algorithms and random numbers to help improve the accuracy of estimates, based on multiple dimensions, each of which involves a degree of uncertainty.

A parametric model is a set of related mathematical equations, in which alternative scenarios are defined by changing the assumed values of a set of fixed parameters. This approach is simple in concept. You first collect quantitative historical data about project cost growth and associated practices. Then you look for correlations between these two aspects. Because this approach relies on the availability of historical data for analysis, it is less easy to apply to information security risk modelling.

A more recent technique is reference class forecasting, which aims to predict the outcome of a planned action based on actual outcomes in a reference class of similar actions to that being forecast. This technique is based on prospect theory, a theory developed by Daniel Kahneman, a Nobel Prize winner, and Amos Tversky. One interesting aspect of their research was that they found that people tend to underestimate the costs, completion times and risks of planned actions, whereas they tend to overestimate the benefits of those same actions. But you don't need to be a Nobel Prize winner to arrive at that conclusion. Forecasts based on reference class forecasting, however, have been found to produce more accurate results. They are more objective, relying less on the natural human bias in people's estimates.

The major learning point from risk management in the engineering world is that the answer does not lie in mathematical methods, but in techniques that enable a more objective perspective. Reliance on human estimates tends to result in an excessively optimistic view of risks.

Lessons from the financial sector

The financial sector has witnessed rapid growth in the development and application of risk management techniques. Most financial risks are managed through traded financial instruments. Although not directly relevant to information security, there are some interesting concepts and techniques that are worth examining.

Many techniques have been developed to help assess and manage credit risk. Credit scorecards, for example, draw on historical data to manage the risk. A database can be populated with observations on the characteristics of former clients. A mathematical model can then be developed to generate a credit score, which ranks the probability of default for new clients, based on these characteristics. Various mathematical techniques have been developed over the years to enable these scores to be calculated, though no single technique appears to have been found superior to others in all circumstances.

Many security managers have considered the usefulness of applying these techniques to information security risks. But there are a number of significant problems. Firstly, we don't have enough reliable historical data to enable such calculations to be performed. And, secondly, the volatility of incident rates and the uncertainty of business impacts would invalidate most conclusions.

Numerous techniques have also been developed to manage market risk, the risk that the value of an investment might decrease due to market factors such as changes in stock prices, interest rates, foreign exchange rates or commodity prices. Market risk is generally managed through a value-at-risk methodology, a measure of risk developed by JP Morgan in the 1980s.

Value-at-risk (VAR) is the maximum loss over a given period of time, such as ten days, for a particular confidence level, such as 95%. It's commonly used to measure the market risk of asset portfolios. But it doesn't provide any indication of the severity of loss above the specified confidence level. And it's often the outlying 5% that causes the real losses. VAR estimates are also based on the data from preceding years, so they get more optimistic, the longer things go well. Unfortunately, we all know that the longer the markets continue to go up, the more likely they are to crash.

Market risk is very different from specific risk, which measures the risk of a loss due to a change in a specific industry or sector, as opposed to a market-wide move. Specific risks can be managed through diversification of investments. But there will always remain a degree of systemic risk, a risk that cannot be diversified away, as it relates to the movements of the whole economy. The impact of a systematic risk, however, might not be the same across all portfolios.

Diversification, hedging and insurance are the key techniques for managing financial risks. The concept of derivatives underpins most forms of financial risk management. Derivatives are financial instruments designed to reduce the risks associated with a particular investment or transaction, by taking an opposite position or hedge in the futures market.

Over the last decade the use of hedging methods increased enormously. The original concept of hedge funds was to offset potential losses for investors, by hedging them against loss-making market movements using techniques such as short-selling. But, ironically, hedge funds have since developed into funds with high risk appetites that aim to leverage their returns by accepting a much higher degree of risk. Such leverage increases short-term gains, but it also amplifies potential losses. As we have seen, a tiny ripple in the marketplace can quickly turn into a tsunami that overwhelms investors.

Financial risks are often managed by transferring the risk elsewhere, or by exchanging a series of low-impact risks for a high impact risk of lower probability.

The classic example of how this approach can go badly wrong was the 2007 sub-prime lending meltdown. Sub-prime loans to customers with allegedly poor credit ratings carry a much higher risk, which is offset by greater returns from higher interest rates, personal mortgage insurance, annual fees and late payment fees. This approach, however, introduces a vicious cycle, a positive feedback loop that progressively increases the fees as default-prone borrowers begin to experience problems, leading to an inevitable meltdown in the market.

The major lesson from the financial sector is that risks need to be managed at several levels, many of which extend outside of individuals to embrace communities and markets. Risks can be transformed in many ways through derivatives and other financial instruments, and accepting a higher level of risk can generate short-term business benefits. But there's no such thing as a free lunch. There's always a potential downside risk associated with any way of making easy money. We all discovered that during 2008.

Lessons from the insurance field

The insurance industry invented risk management many centuries ago, and they've been refining their methods ever since. In fact, the field of actuarial science has been a formal mathematical discipline since the 17th century with the growing demand for life, health, home, credit and mortgage insurance. This field is a pragmatic blend of mathematics, economics and risk management.

Calculating insurance premiums is an interesting process. It draws on estimates of future events and trends, such as mortality rates, inflation rates and interest rates, in order to arrive at a realistic net present value for a future sum. It also involves a wide range of tools for data collection, measurement, estimating, forecasting and valuation.

Concepts such as life-tables, excess damages, self-insurance and re-insurance, have long been used to spread risks and smooth cash flows. And techniques such as stochastic modelling (using random numbers) have increasingly been exploited. But the field has yet to embrace many of the more recent developments from the rest of the financial sector.

Nevertheless there is much that information security can learn from this field, including the ability to exploit external reference data and historical data to help predict future trends, and the ability to calculate a quantified value for a wide-ranging portfolio of risks across a large, complex enterprise.

There are also some interesting practices to consider from the insurance user's perspective. The concept of deductible or excess charges, for example, helps motivate customers to avoid making claims. Many organizations adopt a tiered approach that exploits a combination of self-insurance and third party insurance. A large organization might require each business unit to pick up, say, the first million dollars for a major loss. Then the corporate centre might pick up the next ten or so million dollars, with the rest being externally insured. This tiered approach serves to reduce premiums, as well as encouraging business units to mitigate risks. It's a powerful combination of motivators.

The limits of percentage play

In theory, risks that are manifested on a regular basis, such as credit card fraud, can be closely monitored, and the level of security adjusted to contain losses if they threaten to exceed a target threshold. The objective then becomes, not to eliminate fraud, but to contain it at an acceptable level, a point where the cost of the damage is less than the price of security.

This works fine if three conditions hold. Firstly, that you expect to experience relatively steady levels of crime. Secondly, that you are able to monitor and measure the level of financial damage. And, thirdly, that you are able to adjust the security level to match current incident levels.

But this is a demanding set of conditions. It requires up-to-date information on actual fraud levels. It demands a capability for real-time adjustment of preventative security measures. And it assumes that levels of incidents will remain relatively constant, not subject to unexpected large swings. Furthermore, it also assumes that incidents will not result in unanticipated, consequential damages, such as lost sales, financial penalties, legal claims or reputation damage.

The level of outrage associated with incidents involving customer data is also growing. In today's privacy-conscious climate, even relatively small incidents can generate sensational media headlines. Customer databases have been steadily growing in size, as a result of relentless centralization, globalization and consolidation. Small percentage loss rates now involve very large numbers of records. As we saw earlier, a 1% compromise of citizen records on a national government database represents a population the size of a major city.

And the volatility in incident levels is becoming greater. We now experience unpredictable jumps, peaks and troughs at frequent intervals. Clearly, the risks associated with such percentage play are becoming higher, making this rather optimistic approach unsustainable.

Operational risk

One of the more recent developments in the financial sector is the steady growth of operational risk. Essentially, this is as an umbrella term to cover a broad range of risks that are neither credit nor market related. It covers the full spectrum of risks arising from a company's business operations, including information security, business continuity, physical, fraud and environmental risks. It's also an essential component of Basel 2 compliance.

The Basel Committee defines operational risk as:

> 'The risk of loss resulting from inadequate or failed internal processes, people and systems or from external events.'

In practice, operational risk requires data. Lots of it, in fact, including historical data on losses, errors, failures, frauds and lawsuits, as well as data on risk indicators, such as staffing levels, transaction volumes, turnover rates and failure rates, Almost anything, in fact, that might signal an increasing level of operational risk.

The concept of operational risk has been around for a decade or two, but it's still a relatively immature practice. Companies that practice it have yet to demonstrate that the demanding and expensive approach of collecting and analyzing incident data, coupled with the ambitious idea of overseeing such a wide spectrum of risks, can be made to work efficiently, and add real business value.

It's one thing to implement a process because it's a necessary regulatory requirement, with financial incentives. But it's a much greater ambition to exploit it for business benefits that are more than just a reward for meeting compliance demands.

Joining up risk management

Joining up risk management across the organization might sound like a sensible, straightforward process to implement, at least in theory. But, in practice, it's far from easy to join up the view from the bridge with the reality down in the engine room. Many types of risk, especially technical ones, are simply not sufficiently visible or understood at the higher levels of the organization. They tend to be addressed well before they reach the radar of top management.

Major breaches of customer data regularly demonstrate that phenomenon. Board directors often express surprise when discovering the true impact of a technology failure. 'We never knew that was possible' is a common reaction. Executive boards are frequently caught off guard by risks they had neither understood nor considered. On the other hand, many IT managers are often equally surprised by the lack of major business impact from failures in systems that they had anticipated might bring down the enterprise.

In fact, the outcome of risk assessments of individual systems is often illuminating and surprising. I've sponsored many such assessments and am always surprised at the outcomes. Typically, many systems that IT and security staff instinctively assume to be essential to business operations, will turn out to be less critical than others that had escaped the radar of security and risk managers. Assumptions about the business criticality of systems can be misleading when made without consultation with the business managers responsible.

In fact, there are many differences that become apparent in risk perception, appetite, scope and priority as we move vertically through an organization. Employees are heavily influenced by the immediate interests of their day jobs and careers. Documenting risks associated with a person's work might, at first sight seem like an admission of a personal failure, though they can also be perceived as underlining the importance of their work. Personal politics will play a part. Some employees will talk up risks in the hope of achieving greater recognition and resources. Others might be wary of highlighting hard-to-mitigate risks to senior management. The end result will be a range of inconsistencies in the assessment of risks across the organization.

Visibility of compensating controls will also vary widely across the enterprise. Risks in one part of the organization are often mitigated by actions taken in other parts. Measures addressed centrally, such as insurance, or the filtering and monitoring of incoming network content, might not be visible to many parts of the enterprise, resulting in incorrect local assumptions about vulnerabilities or potential business impacts. Incidents in one part of the organization might also cause business damage elsewhere, which might not be immediately obvious. A call centre manager, for example, might not appreciate the full impact of a local failure on future sales or brand value.

One of the interesting strategic decisions to be made when joining up risk management is whether to take a top-down driven approach to risk management or whether to aim for one that's driven from below. Over the years, I've worked with risk management processes that operated both ways. In practice, neither approach was superior to the other, nor did they work as smoothly or effectively as anticipated.

But a top-down approach to risk assessment seems the logical starting point for joining up risk management. After all, it's the board perspective that should set the tone, direction and priorities for addressing risk across the enterprise. It's not, however, without its hazards.

To initiate a top-down approach, executive board members sit down, with appropriate experts at hand, and attempt to identify and rank the big-ticket risks, mapping the likelihood of risks against their impact. It's a useful, therapeutic learning exercise for all participants. And the output is insightful and illuminating. It's also highly confidential, as it encapsulates the leadership team's perspective of the organization's priorities, weaknesses and threats.

The result of this output can be cascaded down the organization for endorsement and action. In an ideal world, this will set the agenda for risk management across the enterprise. The problem, however, is that in practice many of the conclusions are likely to be privately criticized by the lower-level managers, who understand the real issues much better.

Executive boards might have a unique, helicopter view of the enterprise. But they're not experts on the detail, nor can they be expected to understand the more specialist processes and issues. Directors with insight and experience of business systems might also be out-of-date about key issues, relying too heavily on prior experience, perhaps gained during an earlier part of their career. I've often heard directors claim that 'I know this system, I used to manage it'. But that might have been several years before, when the business and compliance environment was very different.

It's also hard for an executive board to admit that they might have got the assessment wrong, especially after it's been documented. It requires a brave manager to stand up and challenge a Board paper. And it requires a very enlightened Board to come clean and admit they don't fully understand their own organization.

Enterprise-wide risk identification and assessment requires a more objective perspective and a well-equipped, multi-disciplinary team. Knowledge sharing, challenge, plus a willingness to research uncertain assumptions and to correct misconceptions are essential for arriving at a balanced overall assessment. A degree of political independence is crucial to ensure greater objectivity and help overcome personal or political bias.

An alternative approach is to identify and assess risks in a bottom-up fashion. Using this approach, assessments from across the enterprise are collected, ranked and merged to form an overall Top 20 or Top 50 list of leading risks. It's a time-consuming exercise, but a straightforward one.

In this case the tables are reversed. It's generally the executive board members that will challenge the findings. 'These aren't the real risks' is a typical reaction. In fact, many of the risks might have been simplified and massaged, for political or presentational reasons, before they reach the board.

The real source of the problem is that, for all the reasons cited earlier in this chapter, risk assessments are subjective and open to misinterpretation, and political manipulation. One manager's minor issue might be another's crisis. And the scope, context and interpretation of risks varies enormously across the enterprise.

Risks need to be quantified to enable comparison and ranking. This is usually done by attaching probabilities and financial impacts. Various instructions, scales and weightings can be applied to match the ranking process to the organization's risk appetite. But many of the numbers entered will be based on little more than educated guesswork, rather than hard, objective evidence. Some will simply be plucked out of the air.

Risks are also difficult to appreciate, compare, rank or combine, on the basis of short, one or two sentence descriptions. Such definitions cannot convey the full implications, context, degree of uncertainty or reasoning behind each assessment.

A further, major problem, when identifying and comparing a large number of risks across an enterprise, is that people have different preferences in their choice of risk descriptions. Some people, for example, like to work with very general headings and descriptions of risks. But others prefer more specific ones.

General or specific?

If you ask a group of managers to identify a set of risks, you'll get a mixture of general and specific risks. It's a personal preference thing.

Some people prefer to employ a general description such as 'a loss of confidential information', though it's not clear how such a risk could be calculated? A risk as general as that will encompass physical risks, personnel threats and technical exposures. It might include the theft or loss of a disc containing personal data, a leak of personal information though social engineering or espionage, or a hacker gaining access to a database containing sensitive data. A general risk description covers a multitude of different types of incident.

How can a manager be expected to calculate a precise probability for such a broad range of incidents? It cannot be done. It represents the sum of numerous smaller risks, most of which will not be obvious, without carrying out a comprehensive, end-to-end review of all systems and processes that handle the data. Assessing the business impact will be a little easier, but, then again, there are many possibilities. There might be, for example, as few as a dozen records compromised, or perhaps as many as several million.

On the other hand, many managers will be more comfortable operating with specific risk descriptions, such as 'a compromise by a hacker of the customer credit card database in the e-commerce portal' or 'the theft of a laptop containing customer names and contact details from the sales department'. In these cases, the probability and impact will be easier to estimate, but there will be a substantially greater number of individual risks to be assessed.

In practice, risk descriptions will be more specific at the lower levels of an organization, but will become progressively combined and generalized as they are referred upwards. There is no easy, consistent way of doing this. And it will create much debate and argument. In fact, I've yet to find a single group of managers who are all able to agree on the level of generality that's appropriate for entering a risk on a risk register.

In practice, most risk managers take a pragmatic approach, and will accept a mixture of both generic and specific risks. That's a sensible approach to begin with, because the most important thing is to get managers thinking about risks, and identifying and managing the ones they are most concerned about. Getting them to present them in a consistent, structured way is something that might come with increasing maturity. But, given our current level of evolution, it has to be regarded as icing on the cake.

Identifying and ranking risks

For any exercise involving risk assessment, it's important to be able to identify, assess and rank individual risks. Checklists of common risks facing organizations can be a useful starting point for this purpose. They can help prompt ideas, or act as a check for any obvious omissions. But to ensure the maximum contribution from the managers responsible for the risks, it's generally a better idea to start with a blank sheet of paper, or whiteboard, and encourage some creative brainstorming.

In Chapter 11, we'll discuss approaches that encourage creativity. But for the purposes of identifying risks assessment, the most effective technique is quite easy and straightforward. In fact, all that's needed to capture and rank the most obvious risks is a simple, two-dimensional, physical chart. Here are some general tips on how to go about this process.

Firstly, risk identification and assessment is best done as a group exercise by the responsible managers together with a range of stakeholders and knowledgeable specialists. Useful people to attend such a session might be IT portfolio managers, risk managers, security managers, auditors, compliance managers and anyone else that might contribute value.

This type of process is more objective, eliminating cognitive bias and enabling greater sharing of knowledge amongst stakeholders, as well as helping to build a collective agreement on the relative size and rankings of risks. Such buy-in is also valuable for ensuring future support for investments in new security measures.

In order to generate the conceptual space for identifying and comparing risks, it's best to plot the risks on a scatter graph, such as the 2 × 2 grid illustrated in Figure 4.2. This is a classic design, one that's been used for many years in risk assessments. I've been using such a grid since the early 1990s. The design is, in fact, based on the classic Boston Consulting Group matrix, originally developed in the 1970s for the purpose of assessing business growth and market share.

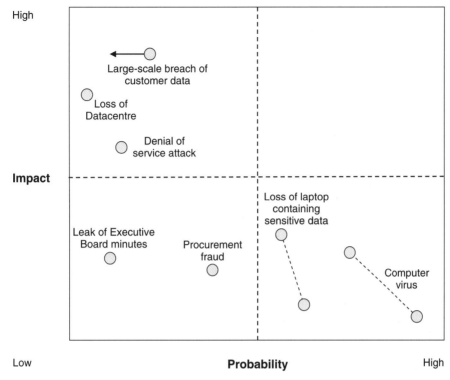

Figure 4.2 Illustration of a common technique for ranking relative size of risks

This style of chart offers many advantages for an initial identification of risks. It forces decisions on both the probability and impact of risks. It also provides an analogue measure, which is richer than can be obtained using alternative techniques such as classifications based on broad categories such as high, medium and low.

Diagrams of this kind also enable ranges of values, or future movement in the ranking of risks, to be captured, by, for example, attaching lines, areas or arrows to particular nodes. They also enable other additional dimensions of choice to be depicted by, for example, varying the shape, size or colour of each plot. Uncertainty or ranges of probabilities and impact can also be indicated by extending the area of a plot. But there are no hard and fast rules on how to plot your risks. It's a matter of taste. You can use as many columns or rows, and as many shapes and symbols as you like. The goal is to capture and document the richest, most accurate, picture you can possibly achieve of the current and emerging risk landscape.

A major advantage of this technique is that it does not demand precise, quantified assessments of individual risks. That would be a much harder exercise, requiring a larger degree of off-line research and consultation. But this type of exercise provides a valuable starting point, because it enables a relative ranking of risks to be achieved in a short space of time. And you can always refine the output of the exercise at a later stage.

Ranking of risks is a more natural approach to risk assessment than attempting to quantify individual risks in isolation. It enables managers to draw on their previous experience and the opinions of their colleagues. It's also consistent with the 'contrast principle' that we considered earlier in this chapter: the theory that people instinctively draw comparisons of new proposals or ideas with previous experiences.

Relative importance is much easier to agree in practice, and it provides a higher-level picture of the overall risk landscape, as well as a context for considering a particular risk. Subsequent research will, of course, be needed to fill in the detail. But that can then be done in a selective way, allowing you to devote more of your valuable time and effort to the research and assessment of the bigger risks.

Using checklists

Pre-defined questionnaire and checklists of information security risks can be a helpful source of prompts for brainstorming, as well as a useful check on the completeness of a risk identification exercise. But such lists can also be as much of a hindrance as a help, especially when it comes to pin-pointing the really important risks.

In fact, long checklists can be a distraction to clear thinking, and a barrier to creative brainstorming. A large selection of very small risks can also mask or dilute the significance of more relevant, important risks. It's better to first identify and assess the risks that spring to mind, and then to apply the checklists towards the end of a risk assessment exercise to help fill in gaps.

Questionnaires can be used in several ways, either to help gather input or to serve as a prompt for broader discussion. They also help generate ideas ahead of a risk assessment exercise, and capture views from remote participants who cannot attend a face-to-face meeting. They can serve as a starting point for discussions on risks, or as a means to inject ideas into a brainstorming session.

Open discussions are better for identifying the most relevant risks. It's usually more illuminating to ask business managers open questions about risks, in order to generate a wide-ranging debate, rather than simply firing closed questions that require no more than a 'yes' or 'no' response, and therefore limit the focus of the discussion.

The most effective questions are often simple, general ones, such as 'What's your biggest nightmare?' or 'Which assets do you regard as your crown jewels, and what's the biggest threat to them?' Open questions such as these can help to identify risks that would not be spotted using prepared checklists. An approach based on open questions, however, demands an interviewer with suitable expertise and experience. In contrast, the prepared checklist approach can deliver better results in cases where such expertise cannot be obtained.

Categories of risks

Another approach to help identify risks is to consider 'categories' of risks. In fact, most organizations prefer to categorize their risks in order, to encourage consistent reporting and presentation of risks, as well as to enable an easier comparison across business units. There are, however, no universally agreed checklists. In practice, each sector or line of business will tend to develop its own variation, though they will often follow common patterns and categories.

At the very highest level, you might, for example, decide to split risks into internal and external ones, though some risks will possess both of these attributes. Beyond that there are no limits. The Institute of Risk Management, for example, suggests a breakdown of business risks into: strategic, hazard, operational and financial. But this is just one example, though it can serve as a useful starting point for developing your own choice of categories.

A more detailed breakdown of business risk categories might include further headings such as management, operational, financial, reputational, project, procurement, supply chain, technology, information management, security, or health and safety. However, again, these are only examples.

The Basel Committee on banking supervision breaks down operational risk into seven categories: internal fraud; external fraud; employment practices and workplace safety; clients, products and business practice; damage to physical assets; business disruption and systems failures; execution, delivery and process management.

Another approach is to adopt the 'PESTLE' analysis headings that are widely used by business managers to analyse the business landscape in planning exercises. The PESTLE headings are: political, economic, socio-cultural, technological, legal and environmental. Some people add an extra 'E' for Ethics, and call it 'STEEPLE'. The advantage of these headings is that they're already familiar to many managers.

Information security risks can also be categorized using the traditional headings of confidentiality, integrity and availability. Some authorities have suggested broadening these three pillars to include authentication and non-repudiation. But these last two are less useful as risk categories. Such an approach might seem a little abstract but it can help to identify risks, such as those to data integrity, which many managers might not otherwise spot.

A more natural approach to identifying security threats is to apply categories based on potential sources of threats, such as hackers, criminals, failures, floods, earthquakes, hurricanes, malware and so on. Sometimes a change or combination of approaches can help to provide a fresh perspective. It might be appropriate, for example, for injecting some variety to monthly or quarterly risk management meetings.

But whichever approach you decide to adopt, your goal should always be to keep the ideas flowing, and the business discussion focused on the most significant risks. Risk management is a means to end, not an end in itself. And that end is a potentially powerful tool that might enable a better, selective treatment of hazards. In practice, simplicity and focus are more important than completeness.

It's a moving target

One of the difficulties presented by information security risks is that many of them are growing in both likelihood and business impact, and not always in a smooth or predictable manner. There are, in fact, several reasons for this phenomenon.

Firstly, threats such as espionage, identity theft and extortion will become more extensive and sophisticated, as offensive organizations, such as intelligence services and organized crime, increasingly find that many of their objectives can be met using relatively low-cost techniques such as hacking, phishing or network attacks.

Secondly, vulnerabilities in platforms and networks will continue to grow despite our best efforts to patch them up. We all have a strong desire to develop more secure methods for building new systems and applications. But the challenge is one that is currently beyond the combined efforts of the security community. We are making progress at a slower rate than the steady growth in vulnerabilities.

One reason for this growth in vulnerabilities is the escalating complexity of the infrastructure, with increasing interfaces, applications and attack points. Another is the relentless growth in the functionality and size of software applications and platforms. And a further factor is the growth in determined efforts to identify security flaws in products. It's not that the vulnerabilities themselves are new, but that they are newly discovered. Development practices have actually improved over recent years, with increasing awareness of the risks, but there remains a rich seam of vulnerabilities buried in legacy code that's still waiting to be mined. There is now an established commercial market for buying and selling new security vulnerabilities. Over time, it will become a lucrative trade.

Thirdly, the business impact of information security risks is steadily rising. There are two reasons for that growth. Firstly, the value of information assets is increasing, as organizations recognize their true potential, and learn how to exploit them for profit. And secondly, there is increasing operational and commercial dependence on information systems and networks, resulting in bigger impacts from major incidents.

On top of all that, there is growing external visibility of business failures and breaches, and increasing concerns and demands from customers, business partners and regulators. Visible risks and incidents can have an impact on future business and will attract regulatory demands. All of these factors are combining to drive the growth of information security risks. Existing risk assessments should be regarded as temporary, uncertain and understated. They will need to be revisited on a regular basis.

Comparing and ranking risks

Once an initial set of risks has been identified and ranked, it will be necessary to quantify, as realistically as possible, the likelihood and business impact of each of the major risks. This process is needed to enable a register of risks to be established, setting out the nature and implications of each risk, as well as the mitigating actions to address them.

Risk registers help to build a bigger picture of risks across an organization, enabling immediate comparisons and ranking of risks with assessments carried out by other business units or disciplines. Risk registers generally follow a common, simple format. They're essentially a league table of risks ranked by a combination

Risk No.	Risk Description	Business Impact	Impact Value	Likelihood Rating	Overall Score	Risk Owner	Mitigating Actions	Control Status	Comments
01	Customer credit card data breach	Multiple impacts, e.g. fines, recovery costs,	$1 m	Unlikely	6	David Lacey	Compliance with PCI Security Standard	Amber +	Audit scheduled 1st Qtr 2009
02	Distributed Denial-of-Service attack								

Figure 4.3   Example of a Risk Register

of probability and business impact. Figure 4.3 shows a typical extract from a risk register.

Key items to consider when designing a risk register are: the name, scope and nature of the risk; the stakeholders affected; the relative size of the risk; the risk appetite (such as 'tolerate' or 'fix'); the compensating controls in place; the risk treatment measures, action plan, responsibilities and review dates; and, ideally, the measured value at risk.

In practice, it takes time to build up a complete set of reliable information about each risk. Organizations might aspire to implement an enterprise-wide framework in a short space of time. But this is unrealistic. Risk management is an evolutionary process, with frequent adjustment and refining of both the techniques used and the risks themselves.

One of the greatest challenges for information security risk management is estimating the likely probability and impact of future incidents. It's far from easy, for all the reasons previously stated. But, no matter how flawed the process and the end result, it has to be done. Regulatory compliance, for example, increasingly demands it.

A good starting point is to begin by collecting current and historical incident data. This is essential for banks that aim to meet Basel 2 compliance requirements. But any organization will benefit from greater visibility of their incidents. And, as we'll see in a later chapter when we consider the benefits of incident reporting and awareness campaigns, there are substantial benefits from understanding the source and patterns of security incidents. Such information will help to reduce future incident levels, as well as contributing to more accurate risk assessments.

External sources of incident levels are also valuable in assessing security risks. Regular security breach surveys are carried out by the UK Government, ISSA and vendors such as Symantec. These surveys are generally based on estimated incident levels and impacts. More accurate, but also more specific, is the research carried out by the Ponemon Institute on the costs of data breaches, which is based on studies of real incidents.

Risk management strategies

In risk management literature, you will often see references to four generally accepted strategies for addressing risks: risk avoidance, severity reduction, risk acceptance and risk transfer. In practice you will probably exploit a combination of all of these. But you don't have to use, or address all of those alternatives. The list is no more than an easy-to-remember checklist of options.

Risk avoidance is the basis of most security countermeasures. Anything that can be done to enable this, especially if the measures are cheap and have no significant impact on business, will be an attractive option. And there are many options available besides technical measures, including enhancing physical protection, improving the level of supervision or stepping up monitoring for particular activities or transactions.

If the risk and the cost of countermeasures are both unacceptably high, however, then it might be necessary to consider more radical options. The ultimate preventative measures are abandoning a project, closing down a system or withdrawing a product or service. But that will require substantial confidence, authority and management support.

Severity reduction is also a straightforward, commonsense approach. Contingency plans, fallback arrangements and incident response processes will help to minimize the business impact of an incident. More sophisticated measures might include attempting to reduce the sensitivity of information, by, for example, advising executives to be more cautious about the content of their e-mails, in order to minimize the impact of a potential compromise.

Risk acceptance is more than a 'do nothing' option. It implies a documented acceptance of responsibility. It's not, therefore, quite as passive or defeatist as it might first appear. Self-insurance of risks by large organizations, in cases where the costs of premiums are higher than the anticipated losses, is the classic example of risk acceptance.

Risk transfer through hedging or insurance is also widely used to mitigate financial risks, as discussed earlier in this chapter. Securitization is a good example of risk transfer. It involves pooling and repackaging financial assets that generate cash-flow into securities which can be sold on to investors. For other high-risk ventures, it might be sensible to consider sharing a risk with one or more business partners. This is commonly done by venture capitalists, for example, many of whom prefer to spread the risk of a high-risk investment with several other investors.

Communicating risk appetite

Risk appetite, as discussed earlier, is something that should ideally be set by the executive board. The problem is how best to communicate it to the rest of the organization.

One way of expressing and communicating risk appetite is by using a similar two-dimensional matrix to the one we used for risk identification and assessment. An example is illustrated in Figure 4.4 overleaf, which maps a scale of increasing risk probability against increasing categories of business impact. The top right hand corner of the matrix indicates the highest levels of risk, and the bottom left hand corner represents the lowest levels. The objective should be to communicate clear dividing lines to indicate the limits of acceptable risk, as well as an indication of the appropriate courses of action to mitigate them.

	Low	**Probability**	High
High	Develop a contingency plan	Implement controls to reduce the risk	Avoid – take immediate preventative action
Impact	Monitor the level of risk	Consider measures to reduce the risk	Implement controls to reduce the risk
Low	Tolerate – if more efficient to do so	Monitor the level of risk	Consider measures to reduce the risk

Figure 4.4 Illustration of technique for communicating risk appetite

When cascading down guidance of this nature, it's essential to be as objective as possible. Terms such as 'high impact' can be interpreted in widely varying ways by different business managers across the organization. It helps to be as specific as possible. Each boundary of the chart, therefore, should have clearly expressed limits, based, for example, on quantified probability levels and financial impacts.

Risk management maturity

Several years ago, when tasked with establishing a business risk management process across several functions of the Royal Mail Group, I decided to seek the advice of an experienced practitioner. Phil Severs, Head of Information Risk at HBOS plc, was my first port of call. Phil is a seasoned practitioner of operational risk. In fact, he's one of the most experienced in the field, having been an early pioneer at Barclays Bank in the early 1990s.

I asked him how to go about introducing risk management across a new function. Phil drew up a sophisticated diagram of the full components of a modern, information risk management architecture. Then he proceeded to convince me not to go off and implement it. At least not all in one go.

One of the most common mistakes made by risk managers is to design a complex risk management framework and then expect managers to be immediately able to fill in the content. Experience has shown that it's simply not possible to obtain quality information using that approach. If managers are forced to enter rich descriptions of risks to which they've given little prior consideration, the quality of the data will be poor, and the enthusiasm of managers for the exercise will be considerably reduced.

A fast track approach to risk management does not exist. If you take that approach, you will lose your audience before they've even begun to identify a risk. Risk management is a subtle art. It takes time to coach business and IT managers into the process of identifying, assessing and managing risks. Managers need time to absorb the concept and to think about the risks. If you present them with a complex framework or a set of electronic forms with lots of data items to be filled in, they will be irritated and confused. And the risks will be poorly assessed and documented. It's better to consider an approach based on increasing levels of 'capability maturity'.

Capability maturity is a concept developed around 20 years ago at the Carnegie Mellon Software Engineering Institute. At the time it was a breakthrough development for measuring the effectiveness of software development, using principles from quality management. We'll examine this concept in more detail in a later chapter. But the major learning point is to recognize that many processes, including risk management, require time and experience to develop into a best practice.

Risk management should be introduced one a step at a time. Start with a simple list of risks. Then add some meaningful descriptions. Next estimate probabilities and impacts. Then identify risk appetite. Next define mitigating actions and responsibilities. Carry on refining the list, each time adding new dimensions such as stakeholders, progress and review dates. Then consider merging sets of risks across business units and service functions. Over time, you will progressively build a high-quality enterprise risk management framework.

Two things are needed to make this work. Firstly, you will need an overarching framework that defines all of the items and processes that will generate an enterprise-wide risk register. And, secondly, you will need a set of forward and backward compatible forms or spreadsheets to capture the evolving information.

There's more to security than risk

Many information security professionals operate on the basis that all information security controls are driven exclusively by risks. That's simply not true. Any organization that aims to operate on this basis will not achieve a necessary and sufficient set of information security measures.

In fact, risk management is far from being the sole source of requirements for information security. There are several other drivers for information security, besides risk management. Examples of these include functional requirements, commercial considerations, corporate policy and legal requirements.

Functional requirements include security features such as identity management and access control. The strategy for implementing such features is more likely to be based on technology strategy and the economics of service provision, rather than information security risks. Risks can be mitigated by local solutions and will generally encourage a tailored, rather than standardized, approach to identity management across an organization.

Commercial considerations might include the need for security features to be added to products and services, or development and operational environments, in order to leverage sales in markets that place a high value on security. In such cases, the appropriate level of security might exceed the actual level of risk encountered in the organization. Instead it will be selected and targeted to help deliver a competitive edge in the external marketplace.

Corporate policy might include political considerations and requirements, such as a decision to restrict the circulation of minutes of meetings. This will often reflect corporate culture, in addition to historical or projected levels of security risk.

Legal requirements for security will also include ongoing considerations such as the need to comply with data protection and copyright legislation. Although these should be consistent with local security risk assessments, they will also be influenced by accepted levels of practice across organizations.

You can, in fact, establish all of these requirements without even speculating on potential future events. Risk is just one factor in establishing information security countermeasures.

It's a decision support tool

In 1983 I attended a US Government Conference on computer security, hosted by NIST. It was a time when risk management methods were in their infancy in the information security world. But, at the time, they were seen as a major, emerging solution to the challenging task of determining the most appropriate level of security to be applied for a particular system in a particular situation. Security countermeasures were relatively expensive in those days, especially in the government field, so determining the optimum level of security was an important consideration.

Amongst many high-profile speakers at the conference was a professor of risk management, with extensive experience in applying risk management techniques in many high-risk sectors, such as the nuclear industry. The professor outlined a range of well-established techniques that might be adapted to the new field of computer security. Some of these involved complex calculations based on scores, weights and averages. At the end of his presentation, he proceeded to answer questions from the audience. I was particularly struck by one question and answer.

The question from the floor was a simple one:

'How do you stop a manager from manipulating these figures to get the decision he wants to get?'

The answer was a real eye-opener:

> *'But that's exactly how this process works. You wouldn't make a decision on these figures alone. That would be madness. You make your decisions on a much richer set of information and then use these techniques to support your judgment.'*

Risk assessment is a decision support tool, not a decision-making device. The techniques employed operate on a vast oversimplification of the richness of the problem space. We reduce complex uncertain problems to simple one-line descriptions. We adopt crude categories, such as high, medium and low to compare the likelihood or impact of a risk. We filter out important detail such as the knowledge and skills of the person who assessed the risk and the level of uncertainty or volatility of a measure. No sane person would make important decisions on such a narrow set of data. The results need to be chewed over and consumed in moderation, as a nutritionist might suggest.

The perils of risk assessment

Risk management has become one of the fastest growing and heavily marketed disciplines in the business and security fields. However, it's not without flaws or critics. The latter might include me, to some extent. I've rarely seen much real business value achieved by the contemporary methods that we observe in practice. But my views are relatively mild compared to the hostility towards risk assessment demonstrated by Donn Parker, of SRI International.

Donn is a highly experienced security researcher, author and consultant. Amongst many achievements, he's responsible for developing the concept of baseline controls and founding the International Information Integrity Institute, the first major international club of senior information security professionals. This club is known as 'I-4', which, ironically, is better known as the Interstate route to Disney World. In his book *Fighting Computer Crime*, Donn sums up his objections to the use of risk assessment for information security:

> *'The concept of risk of loss should never have been introduced into information security. Many years ago at SRI, we naively attempted to perform a quantified risk assessment for a bank that insisted that we do so. (All too often, clients know what they want, but not necessarily what they need.) Competent, experienced consultants performed the assessment; the costs were enormous and the quantitative results of annual loss expectancy were so ludicrous that we had to reject them. Fortunately, the qualitative findings and recommendations made sense, and the project was a painful success, but we learned an important lesson about the folly of risk assessment.'*

That's a fair point. The method used didn't deliver the results. But was it the method, the practitioners or the circumstances surrounding the project that failed to deliver as anticipated? The answer is probably a mixture of all of those factors.

In the early days of information security there was a lack of solid incident data, as well as a proliferation of unproven methodologies, and a shortage of experienced practitioners. The smart way to assess risks in the 1980s was to use the sharp eyes of a seasoned professional. In fact, at that time, commercial risk assessment methods were not permitted to be employed in the national security area.

It's dangerous to expect a realistic breakdown of security risks and recommended controls to be determined by any unproven method that's processing incomplete data. Annual loss expectancy calculations, in particular, can only be calculated on the basis of reliable estimates and stable incident levels. Any methods that use simplified data inputs will produce uncertain outputs. Yet many risk management methods treat all inputs as being equally reliable. Some assessments might be based on accurate measures, but others on no more than a wild guess.

Risk assessment methods take elaborate views of threats and exposures and shoe-horn them into a simplified set of categories, losing the richness of the original assessment. The end result is an imperfect assessment that turns a complex set of problems into a crude set of indicators for a binary set of control decisions.

Learning from risk management

So what have we learned in this chapter? We set out to explore and explain the nature of risks, why it's surprisingly hard for people to assess them, and how we might best go about identifying them, assessing them and managing them. Here's a summary of the key findings and conclusions.

Risks are events, generally bad ones. In the security field they're generally expressed as a triple, a function of a threat, the associated level of vulnerability and its impact. Risk management is a blend of logic and feeling, with the latter dominating the former. Everyone has a different perspective on risks, and most people are bad at assessing them. Many managers also misunderstand the nature of risk, and they will struggle to measure and manage it. Meeting business goals is an important underlying consideration. But calculating risk appetite is a difficult exercise.

People have widely varying attitudes to risk, influenced by factors such as age, gender, personality, lifestyle, religion, culture, logical capacity and pressure to achieve bonus targets. Risks can trigger strong emotions and reactions in people, frequently overriding common sense. They are best assessed by a combination of a business manager and a security expert, preferably in a wider group of stakeholders.

Many financial services organizations have sophisticated risk management systems, but that will not necessarily stop them from gambling their assets away. The size of an organization can also make a difference. Large profits and returns and big transactions will create vested interests and intimidate cautious people.

Assessing a risk requires the ability to judge probability, but not everyone is good at that. Our perception of risk is often coloured by a failure to appreciate the context of an event. People will also tend to exaggerate spectacular, but rare, risks, yet downplay common ones. Unprecedented risks are especially hard to manage, as past experience and current perspective are major factors for assessing them. Sometimes, also, the party responsible for creating a risk is not the party that suffers damage.

We can learn from other industries. The process industries teach us that security, like safety, can be embedded into development and operational business processes. The engineering world demonstrates that the answer does not lie in clever mathematical methods, but in techniques that enable a more objective perspective. The financial sector teaches us that risks can be managed at several levels, many of which extend outside the organization. And the insurance field demonstrates the importance of external reference data in helping to analyse the past and predict the future.

Risk assessment requires an objective perspective and a multi-disciplinary team. But it takes time to coach managers to identify, assess and manage risks. Complex frameworks are off-putting. It's better to start simple and progressively increase the level of sophistication.

External sources of incident levels are valuable in assessing security risks. They need to be quantified to enable comparison and ranking. But risk assessments are neither definitive nor lasting, needing to be revisited regularly. And many information security risks are growing in both likelihood and business impact.

Risk management is not the sole source of requirements for information security. There are other drivers such as functional requirements, commercial considerations, corporate policy and legal requirements. But risk management is here to stay, though it must be seen as a decision support tool, rather than a decision-making device. Risk management techniques oversimplify the richness of the problem space. It will always be an imperfect process. Important business decisions should not be based solely on the outputs from such a narrow set of data. Many observers believe that the credit crunch demonstrated a failure of risk management. They're wrong. In fact, it reflects a spectacular success in creating a convincing illusion of control that satisfied the regulators. That's the real power of risk management.

Here are seven key points to learn from risk management:

- Risk management is a measuring stick, not a decision-making process
- Risks assessments should never be regarded as absolute judgments
- It's best to rank risks before attempting to quantify them
- People will assess risks very differently; they are best assessed by a group of experts
- Risk management should be introduced progressively, in simple stages to keep business managers on board
- Use sophisticated methods with caution; they can give misleading results
- Risk management won't stop your managers and directors from gambling away the organization's assets

Who can you trust?

An asset or a liability?

Managing directors are often heard to claim that 'people are our greatest asset'. They are, in fact, largely correct. But the other side of the coin, and the warning that is rarely expressed, is that people are also our greatest liability. Most of us are in the dark about the insider threat. That's not surprising, as the average manager rarely uncovers any crimes committed by his employees. Espionage, fraud and insider dealing are secret activities. They're intended to be invisible and to go undetected, at least until the business impact strikes.

Even after the damage has been done, it's often the case that the resulting impact will go unnoticed, hidden amongst other losses or failures. And when an incident does come to light, the ensuing security investigation will often draw a blank, and the case will be quietly shelved. If the offender is actually identified, there might not be sufficient evidence or motivation to prosecute. Often they will, instead, be persuaded to quietly resign.

The result is that many insider threats are overlooked, ignored or deliberately downplayed. In practice, nobody really knows for sure what's going on inside an organization. On the one hand, the overcautious security manager might be concerned about all manner of theoretical threats that do not exist. On the other, there will be many business managers that are sceptical or complacent about serious threats that really do exist. That's the dilemma presented by the insider threat. We don't know how real it might be. We cannot easily demonstrate whether espionage is an ever present danger to our business, or just some form of James Bond style fantasy.

Managing the Human Factor in Information Security   David Lacey
© 2009 John Wiley & Sons, Ltd

Yet there are many factors that suggest that the insider threat might be growing. Information is becoming more valuable, and much easier to steal and sell. Staff turnover continues to increase, potentially triggering a progressive decline in employee loyalty. And social networking is enabling external criminals to more easily target company staff and their secrets. To counter these threats we need to understand the nature of the insider threat, to be alert to the warning signs that might indicate the presence of a fraud, and to be able to recognize a spy or fraudster when they're inside our organization. But none of this is particularly easy.

This chapter examines what we know about the type of people who engage in crime: what they're really like, what motivates them, and how they might go about their activities. In particular, it explores the insidious, but fascinating, nature of the inside security threat. And it provides some suggestions on how we might go about recognizing and investigating their activities.

The chapter concludes with a brief discussion on the fashionable subjects of trust and identity. In fact, we can't really get to grips with people and networks without also examining the nature of the relationships between them. Trust is fundamental to risk acceptance between individuals. And it's identity that underpins transactions between trusted partners. Risk and trust are two sides of the same coin. And identity is the glue that joins them.

People are different

The first thing to appreciate about people is that we they're all very different. That might seem obvious. Yet, in practice, it can take a while for managers to accept the full implications of this fact, especially when they join an organization that is associated with a stereotype image for its employees.

It's natural, for example, to expect that investment bank traders will behave in an extrovert, competitive manner, that nurses will be caring and compassionate, that doctors will be wise and authoritative and that civil servants will be conservative and dour. It's also quite normal to assume that all company staff will be loyal, ambitious and upwardly mobile. But, in fact, this might not be the case. People might look and act the same on the outside, but they can be very different on the inside. Not all will fit the stereotype associated with their work.

That's why it always comes as a major shock to managers and staff to discover that one of their colleagues has been dishonest. Ideally, we should be able to identify all the potential spies and fraudsters before they cause any business damage. Some organizations go to some effort to try to achieve that. Our security and intelligence services, for example, have been attempting to root out potential spies for decades. Unfortunately, it's much harder to do this in practice, than we might imagine in theory.

Even organizations with considerable experience of espionage and fraud have difficulty detecting criminal activities by insiders. The Central Intelligence Agency, for example, was unable to spot Aldrich Ames because he looked like everyone else, even though he exhibited many of the classic personality traits and behaviour associated with a person who might betray his country. Similarly, many police forces have been found to be riddled with corruption, even though the crimes took place under the noses of professional fraud investigators.

These examples are not just cases of 'the cobbler's children being the worse shod'. They reflect the disturbing fact that internal threats often go unnoticed, even where there is a high awareness of the threat, substantial internal expertise in combating crime, and a regime of strict vetting for staff. There are reasons for that. In theory, we can identify warning signs in people's character, attitude and behaviour that are closely correlated with a propensity for espionage and fraud. But, unfortunately, in practice, we'll find that many of our most loyal, effective and highly regarded staff also exhibit the same personality traits and behaviour.

The rule of four

Back in the 1970s I recall asking a friend in the British Security Service about his views of the level of trustworthiness of staff. 'Surely,' I suggested, 'the vast majority of staff are loyal and can be trusted?' 'Not necessarily,' he replied. He then proceeded to pass on a rare gem of unsubstantiated hearsay, which I now refer to as the 'rule of four':

'In every four people, one is an out-and-out crook, another is honest to the point of stupidity, and the other two will take a risk assessment to see what they can get away with.'

Since then, I've kept an eye out for indications or evidence to support this theoretical statistic. I've yet to find any conclusive proof that it's correct. And I'm not even sure if my friend invented it, or based it on research, experience or perception. But, for many security professionals, there is a ring of truth about it. And, in the absence of any evidence to the contrary, it's not a bad rule of thumb to apply, as a starting-point for your assumptions.

I find it fascinating to note other people's reactions when I tell them about this theory. At first they will all smile and agree. Then they will look slightly concerned, as the uncomfortable implications begin to dawn on them. None of these options are flattering. Think about it yourself. Which one might *you* be? Are you stupid, crooked or scheming?

The rule of four might, in fact, prove to be one of those interesting ratios, like the 80/20 rule, that fit many situations we encounter. It's interesting to note, for example, that surveys of people's attitude to privacy, for example, follow a similar pattern. One in every four people appears to highly concerned, another won't care a jot and the remaining two will tend to apply a risk assessment.

Robina Chatham, a visiting fellow at Cranfield School of Management, who studies organizational politics, uses a 2 × 2 matrix, based on the dimensions of integrity and political awareness, to illustrate four distinct types of employee. She uses the analogy of animals, suggesting that staff fall into four categories: innocent sheep, cunning foxes, smart dolphins or dumb baboons. It's an interesting variant of the rule of four.

Many psychology researchers have studied honesty in children. The results indicate that cheating starts when you're young. In fact, all children are tempted to cheat, lie or steal, every once in a while, especially when under pressure to perform well at school, or to impress their peers, or perhaps avoid hurting the feelings of a parent or teacher. Most children resist the temptation to cheat, at least most of the time. Some get caught, or feel guilty and resolve never to do it again. A small minority discover they enjoy it, and will carry on cheating. They might turn out to be the crooks of the future. But, in fact, the vast majority of children are neither completely honest, nor blatantly dishonest. They simply adjust their behaviour to suit the circumstances. They represent the 50% of the rule of four.

But, whatever the correct percentages might be, there are certainly many people inside our organizations who are generally honest, but might be tempted or talked into doing something they know to be wrong. In fact, there is research evidence to indicate that people can be persuaded to do surprisingly bad things, when placed in particular environments, roles or circumstances. The desire to mimic the actions of our peers, or to obey authority, can be much more powerful than we might imagine.

The need to conform

Experiments carried out by Solomon Asch, a social psychologist, in the 1950s first demonstrated the power of conformity within groups. Participants were found to be heavily influenced by the judgments of other people in their group, to the extent that they would willingly report clearly incorrect observations. The experiments showed that the level of influence varied according to the degree of unanimity of the other group members. But even a small group of dissenters can have a significant influence.

A decade later, following the Nuremberg trials of war criminals, psychologists tried to understand the nature of the human behaviour that might have made such atrocities possible. Stanley Milgram conducted a number of experiments on people's obedience to authority, and found that, regardless of sex, education or values, people tended to obey others that they perceived to be in charge, despite knowing that the resultant actions might, at least in theory, hurt or kill another person.

In the early 1970s, Philip Zimbardo, a professor of psychology at Stanford University, conducted a famous piece of research in which two dozen college students were randomly assigned to be prisoners or guards in a mock prison. They quickly became acclimatised to their roles. The guards become sadistic, and the prisoners became depressed, potentially creating a degree of psychological damage. One third of the 'guards' were judged to have exhibited sadistic tendencies, while many of the 'prisoners' were reported to be emotionally traumatised.

These disturbing experiments demonstrate the powerful influence of groups, situations and roles on human behaviour, and our surprising willingness to adapt to them. In later chapters, we'll explore how this phenomenon, and others, might be used to enhance the security behaviour of employees.

Understand your enemies

Understanding your enemies should be an integral part of any professional security risk management. It's essential, for example, to appreciate their capabilities in order to design a set of security defences that can withstand their attacks. All good risk assessments should take account of the motives and modus operandi of potential enemies.

Every organization will face a range of external and inside security threats. In order to better confront such risks, we need to form a good picture of what type of people they might be, why they do it, what they're after, how they go about it, and how we might best deter them. Criminals, spies and terrorists tend to have preferred methods and channels of attack. Some of them might be trade secrets, and others might change over time. But any that we can find out about should be taken into consideration when designing security countermeasures.

It's also worth considering the impact on criminals of new or changed counter-measures. Professional criminals react quickly to new security measures. They'll switch to another target, or perhaps employ another method. Closing down one form of fraud will tend to encourage the establishment of another. Crime can sometimes be compared to an inflated balloon. Squeeze any part of it slightly and another part will immediately expand. But squeeze it hard enough overall and it will collapse.

Motivation is also an important factor. Many forms of extortion, sabotage and network attack are prompted by personal motives. Such crimes can present the most dangerous forms of attack, because they're driven by determination to attack you, rather than a preference to select the softest target. And they're hard to stop. If, for example, you're experiencing a determined denial-of-service attack by an individual with a grudge, simply adding extra security measures to deter the attacker will not be enough. To close down such an attack, you might actually have to locate and catch the attacker.

The face of the enemy

I'm always fascinated by the appearance of real criminals, spies and terrorists. They're often quite different from what we might expect. One or two might actually look like thugs. But most of them would not stand out in a crowd. They look just like everybody else.

In his famous 1980s book *The Hacker's Handbook*, Peter Sommer, writing under the pseudonym of Hugo Cornwall, quotes Bob Courtney, the former Director of Security at IBM:

'There are three categories of insider who commit crime. Single woman under 35, ladies over 50 who want to give the money to charity, and older men who feel their careers have left them neglected.'

It's a delightful description, but I'm not sure I believe this statement. Cases like this probably do exist. But the profiles described are certainly not the most common ones encountered. One thing is true, however. And it's something that should be of concern to every security manager. The fact is that the profiles of fraudsters are often very typical of many managers and staff in key positions of trust, the people who are generally above suspicion.

Of course that doesn't mean that people with a particular profile that happens to correspond to a typical fraudster, are likely to commit a crime. But what it does mean is that you cannot assume that a seemingly normal person in a position of trust, will not be persuaded to commit a crime. Often it's the most unlikely people that are found cheating.

In fact, there are common profiles for fraudsters. In the oil and gas industry the typical profile of an illegal information broker, a person that sells inside information and influence on large procurement contracts, is an experienced, middle-aged, industry professional. The sort of person you would employee yourself. They will have a good CV, as well as a powerful network of high-level management contacts across the industry, which, of course, they will exploit to the full.

Run silent, run deep

In the late 1980s the oil and gas industry were confronted with the unpleasant fact that, for many years, their procurement processes had been thoroughly infiltrated by networks of illegal information brokers. What made it especially shocking was that nobody had the slightest idea that it had been going on. It was only uncovered as the result of a determined and sustained undercover investigation by the Norwegian police authorities. They uncovered a substantial network of several dozen professional brokers, operating across several companies and countries in the North Sea area.

But catching them in an illegal act was not so straightforward. Stealing and selling information, other than trade secrets, is not a crime in many countries. And the activities are largely invisible, perhaps no more than a whisper between professionals, or a glance at a confidential document. It's far from easy to establish evidence on the criminal activities of a person who doesn't want to be discovered, and actively takes steps to avoid detection.

The major oil companies have since undertaken numerous initiatives to pool their knowledge on the subject, but they can do little more than prevent the employment of potential perpetrators. Some have been prosecuted, but many others evaded prosecution. Yet the proceeds of their efforts were huge, often a small percentage of the value of a large procurement contract. A smart broker operating in this field can make as much as a million dollars in a month.

The perpetrators of these crimes, like many other insider criminals, are often individuals who are de-motivated by lack of progression up the corporate ladder. Their skills and assets are a combination of background research, inside information, networking, outrageous bluff, name-dropping, bribery and coercion. They will seek to capture potential clients such as contractors bidding for large contracts by offers to help secure contracts in exchange for a percentage of the contract value. To demonstrate their capability they will present a copy of the contractor's own bid. If that fails they might resort to threats. But the most disturbing characteristic is the lack of reporting by staff of such approaches. Large-scale fraud can exist in a mature industry for decades without detection. One therefore has to assume that undiscovered corruption probably exists in most industries.

In fact, the invisible hand of espionage reaches across both the private and public sectors. Government sponsored espionage threatens any organization that might have any information of value to a foreign power. Huge amounts of confidential data are routinely stolen from corporate databases without the knowledge of company directors or their security advisers. In recent years, US and European government security agencies have been compelled to issue warnings to their industries about the mounting threats from cyber espionage. US intelligence authorities have suggested that as many as 140 foreign intelligence organizations have tried to hack into US computer networks.

This is only to be expected. Hacking is cheap, fast and can be carried out remotely. And the necessary skills are becoming widespread. Perhaps the only item in doubt is the actual number of countries in the world, which, interestingly, can range anywhere from 189 to 266 depending on how you go about counting them. But whatever the precise number, it represents a lot of competing national interests.

These threats run silent and deep. By the time an organization discovers it has a problem, it might have been thoroughly penetrated, and its confidential data fully compromised. Whether your concern is an information broker manipulating your contracts or a foreign intelligence service stealing your trade secrets, it's clear that, unless you take steps to educate your staff, you might be a sitting target for your enemies.

Dreamers and charmers

Discovering a spy or fraudster within the organization is a shocking and unsettling experience. It creates a feeling of betrayal and uncertainty, especially if there is no clear indication of the full extent of compromise, or the possibility that inside information might be further exploited on a future occasion. Damaging insider acts can include fraud, insider dealing, theft of intellectual property, disclosure of trade secrets, product contamination, sabotage of services or modification to data. Sometimes the damage will be readily apparent. But in many cases it will not.

It's not just current employees that carry out such deeds. According to surveys carried out by ASIS, the international society for industrial security, US companies lose many tens of billions of dollars each year from theft of intellectual property, and two of the largest sources of risk are former employees and on-site contractors.

The motivation for most acts of disloyalty is generally personal gain or vengeance. But there are other motivators. Excitement or attention seeking are potential triggers for some. Others can be tricked or persuaded to carry out an act by a much stronger personality. Some people will also commit crimes out of loyalty or love, for a person or a cause.

Spies are surprisingly difficult to spot. Agents are selected for their ability to avoid suspicion as much as their access to information. They can come in any shape or size, and have varying motives. Some might be volunteers, keen to support a cause, impress a person, or simply make some money. Others might be seduced or blackmailed into passing secrets. And one or two might even be unaware that they are leaking information.

A smart security manager will keep up to date with current trends in the motivations of agents and fraudsters. Fashions and motives change over the years. A hundred years ago, Mata Hari, an exotic dancer and prostitute, epitomized the classic agent, able to exploit her feminine charms to entice people to betray secrets. Fifty years later, political idealism was the motivation for the Cambridge spy ring of Burgess, Maclean, Philby and Blunt. They were part of the British establishment, and completely above suspicion.

Fast forward a few decades later, and we find a different form of agent, the vulnerable secretary seduced by a handsome agent runner, a technique masterminded by Markus Wolf, the East German spymaster. The Tom Clancy book *Clear and Present Danger*, written in 1989, includes a similar sub-plot in which the widowed personal aide of the FBI Director is targeted for a romantic relationship. Romance was also a motive behind a major fraud at a leading UK bank at that time. The security investigators coined the term the 'romancer' to describe this new style of criminal.

In recent decades, money has been the primary motivator for persuading internal staff to betray their employers. That trend will no doubt continue for some time. But coercion, through violent threats to friends or family members, is a technique increasingly used by criminals to gain the cooperation of hackers. Political idealism is much less likely following the end of the Cold War. But religion is a growing motivator for idealistic betrayal.

Fantasy is also a possible factor, and one likely to grow, given the disinhibiting effects encouraged by cyberspace. A 'Walter Mitty' complex has been a factor in many cases of espionage. Increasingly, we'll also find that social networking will serve as a powerful vehicle for unconscious compromises of secrets, through social engineering of targeted victims.

The unfashionable hacker

From the very early days of computing, there have always been a small percentage of programmers who could not resist breaking into systems. These are perhaps the types of people that Bruce Schneier regards as having a 'security mindset', one that instinctively thinks about clever ways around security controls.

The word hacker, in this context, has nothing to do with being a bad golfer. It's used to describe someone who breaks into systems. The word was, in fact, hijacked from an earlier description of a skilled programmer, someone who cuts code and patches systems in a fast, clever and elegant way. Some security experts still prefer to use the term 'cracker' to distinguish those with criminal intent from smart coders. But this word has not caught on with the broader security community or the media.

Hackers are generally obsessive individuals, the sort of people who read computer manuals, study operating systems and take things apart. As Steven Levy, a writer on the subject, puts it, they are 'possessed not merely by curiosity, but by a positive lust to know'. Hackers are often addicted to computers and cyberspace.

They are not necessarily natural criminals. Many simply have an obsession that coincides with a criminal act. But some have darker personality traits, such as anti-social behaviour, or perhaps a craving for power, recognition or revenge. Such personality problems can stem from a lack of love or respect, encouraging them to retreat into a secret inner world, and, at the same time, making them vulnerable to exploitation by others.

There is no stereotype appearance for a hacker. They can be emaciated, overweight or even handsome. They can come across as the perfect boy-next-door, or an upwardly mobile young executive. But what they all have in common is an addictive, compulsive nature and an unusually high degree of software skills.

Fortunately, hacking is not especially fashionable, at least not in the same way as drugs, alcohol or smoking. Hackers tend to be perceived as nerds or geeks. They are not popular role models, so their actions are not widely copied. And that's just as well. Young people are heavily influenced by their peers, particularly ones who are perceived to be 'cool'. Take smoking, for example. Children don't smoke because smoking is cool. They do it because they perceive other smokers as being cool. Fortunately hackers aren't cool. Otherwise we might have more of an epidemic on our hands.

John Maxfield, a former computer hacker, phone fraudster and FBI informant, once suggested that hackers fall into several categories. They can be pioneers or explorers, fascinated by exploring the limits of new technology. They can be scamps or game players, with a sense of fun. They can also be vandals, who cause damage for no apparent gain. And they can simply be addicts, who cannot control their urge to penetrate systems.

And people can change. John Maxfield is now a computer security consultant. Kevin Mitnick, at one time regarded as the most dangerous hacker in the world, is now a respectable security consultant, with a business card in the shape of a skeleton key. An old sidekick of his, Susan Thunder, a former groupie and prostitute, reported to have slept with military personnel to steal passwords, is now an elected public official. And Steve Jobs and Steve Wozniak, who started their careers making 'blue boxes' to enable telephone hacking, went on to found Apple.

But hacking has been increasingly criminalized. It's a dangerous pursuit for young people. Organized crime now take an interest in them, and that's a frightening experience. They might start by asking for something quite innocuous. But their demands will grow. And it's not easy to refuse their demands, when there might be threats of violence to friends and family.

Hackers, like many other criminals, are not easy to identity. In fact, when it comes to identifying any of your enemies, outside appearances can be deceptive. The defining characteristics of criminals, spies and hackers are generally on the inside, rather than the outside of the person. They could be the person sitting next to you on a train, or a colleague across the desk from you.

The psychology of scams

I'm often compelled to challenge my fellow professionals' views about the level of sophistication we should expect to encounter in criminals. I often hear claims such as: 'These guys are smart'. But I don't accept that. One or two might be cunning. But if criminals were really smart, they'd be running legitimate businesses. In fact, many criminals are not especially clever, but they do possess street-smart know-how. And even confidence tricksters are smart enough to apply basic psychology to their scams.

Take phishing, for example, which aims to trick people into revealing sensitive information such as banking details, by sending an official-looking e-mail. You'd think that most people would see through such an obvious ploy. But when it comes to designing these e-mails, there's generally some clever psychology at work.

Suggest to anyone that they might be cut off from their money, and you'll grab their attention. Pretend to be someone in authority, and people will be tempted to obey. Similar psychology lies behind Nigerian-style advance fee frauds, which aim to persuade people that they might gain a big money reward through some process that involves an initial down-payment to cover expenses. These scams work because they appeal to people's greed. Information brokers often persuade customers to pay them, and agents to accept bribes, through a combination of a threat and a promise. They'll promise a big reward if you go along with their demands. If not, they'll use their influence to ruin your business or career.

People are also surprisingly cooperative towards fraudsters who masquerade as officials. Authority has a major influence on behaviour, and a uniform will help reinforce this. If you dress up and pose as a policeman or security guard, most people will freely allow you search through their handbags or wallets without any question.

As with many things in life, fear and greed are classic motivators for people to trust fraudsters. Vanity and compassion are also psychological factors in many frauds. Few people can resist praise. It builds trust and helps to set the scene for an imminent scam. Many victims are also taken in by hard luck stories. It's hard, for example, to resist a woman who breaks down and burst into tears. Seduction and entrapment are further age-old methods for persuading a victim to cooperate. Extortion is most effective when it starts with modest favours and progressively escalates the demands.

Blackmail and extortion present a high risk to the perpetrator that the victim might call the police. Smart criminals will aim to ensure that it's not worth the hassle, by setting the initial price at a level that's easy for the victim to meet, without involving other people or escalating the demand to a higher level. A modest amount is easier to cover up than a large sum that breaks the budget, requires authorization or is likely to attract attention.

Visitors are welcome

The term 'social engineering' is used to describe the process of manipulating people into divulging information or carrying out a particular act that's to the benefit of an attacker. The same exposure applies to both the physical and cyberspace environments.

Given the growing attraction of social engineering to criminals, as a quick, safe and easy method of obtaining increasingly valuable data or identity credentials, it's clearly important to ensure that all staff are alert to the potential dangers presented by unaccompanied visitors and unsolicited phone calls and e-mails. Professional thieves aim to catch people off-guard. They will have convincing, prepared stories to explain their presence and actions, and they will aim to exploit employees who wish to provide the best possible experience to a senior manager or an important customer.

It's best not to leave decisions on granting access to sensitive facilities or data to each individual's personal judgment. Most employees are simply too trusting. They naturally welcome strangers and provide help if asked. They do not wish to come across as unnecessarily intrusive and rude. Strict rules and protocols should therefore be established.

'Pretexting' is a useful device to enable social engineering. It's the art of creating a story or scenario, the pretext, in order to persuade a person to release information or perform an action. Pretexting has also been widely used by private investigators to obtain information to support their investigations. But it's a bad investigative practice that gives security a bad name.

I've observed several security investigations where thieves have been caught inside sensitive buildings. The first thing that caught my attention was the nature of the pretext they deployed to enter the building. Many impersonate a regular visitor that's likely to arrive unannounced, such as a telecommunications engineer. The second thing I noted was the locations they chose to operate from. They're generally the ones that enable the fastest exit. Criminals don't want to be caught. And that factor can help you to identify and locate them, though few building security managers bother to exploit such insights.

Several years ago, I was involved in a series of interviews of applicants for security manager positions in sensitive buildings. The first question I would ask is what they would do if the chief executive arrived at the reception point without an office pass. Should they be allowed in? Or should they be turned away? Both answers are clearly unsatisfactory, one from a security point of view and the other from a business perspective. Virtually everyone I interviewed got the question wrong. I only ever heard one good answer to the question. It was a refreshing, pragmatic compromise:

> *'Sir, I recognize you. This time I will let you in. But next time you forget your pass I'll turn you away.'*

In practice, we rarely encounter such common sense. It's an area greatly in need of improvement. These days, it's far too easy to enter sensitive buildings, and that's primarily because we're failing to educate and empower our security staff. Over the last 20 years, we have switched from unhelpful security guards towards welcoming receptionists. The ideal balance, from a security perspective, lies somewhere in between.

Social engineering can be much safer and easier when the attacker is operating across a network. That's because it's not as easy for victims to detect the nervous gestures of criminals, their fear and their guilt. But there's a downside for the ruthless, sophisticated attacker. It's less easy to influence and manipulate people's emotions over a network. In fact, electronic channels can work both for and against a fraudster.

Where loyalties lie

It's easy to imagine that the first loyalties of all staff should be to the organization. But, in fact, that's not necessarily a good thing in all cases. The real world does not operate like that. People have many different types of loyalty, at very different levels: loyalties to their families, their friends, their communities, their associations, their countries, their beliefs and their ideals. Loyalty towards the organization has to be balanced against all of these considerations.

And loyalty is a double-edged sword. It can encourage a person to be hardworking and upright. It can also make a person commit a security breach to protect the interests of a colleague or a cause. And it can also protect the organization from the bad behaviour of managers by acting as a brake on unethical operations. Every organization will, unfortunately, from time to time turn a blind eye to unacceptable activities. They're often easier to ignore than to confront. It's generally better for the long-term interests of an enterprise if employees draw on their loyalty to society by speaking up against unethical behaviour.

Honesty and openness are the best policy in today's highly transparent, connected world. That's because it's becoming virtually impossible for organizations to maintain long-term secrets about their activities. Information is becoming increasingly public, activities more transparent and whistle blowing is becoming easier and more common.

Signs of disloyalty

How can you spot a person who's likely to betray your trust? Are there warning signs, typical personality traits or common patterns in behaviour? The answer is yes. There are common characteristics in spies and fraudsters.

People who betray trust are likely to be immature individuals who enjoy violating rules and regulations. They probably have an inflated view of their abilities and they may feel bitter, perhaps even vindictive because their talents have not been fully appreciated. They might be impulsive risk-takers, more concerned about their immediate wants than the longer-term consequences. Some might even be closet psychopaths who take pleasure in manipulating other people and enjoy beating the system.

Unfortunately it's not that easy to apply this knowledge, as many honest, trusted employees also share these traits. In fact, it's the impulsive risk takers that often provide the essential competitive edge that's needed in today's challenging business environment. The business world is full of greedy, arrogant, vindictive, impulsive, power-seeking executives. Many of them end up in positions of power, because they are ruthless, scheming and manipulative.

There are warning signs of impending trouble, though they are rarely heeded. For example, we should be alert to potential problems from employees who tell lies, break rules, fiddle expenses, pick fights, bully staff or who appear to enjoy punishing others. We should be concerned about anti-social loners who show little interest in developing healthy relationships, as well as those that constantly over-estimate their abilities, or who clearly like to take risks without regard to the implications.

And we should also look out for obvious behavioural changes that might reflect an underlying personal problem, as this could trigger a disloyal act. Excessive alcohol intake, drug use, mood swings, poor personal hygiene or unexplained absences from work might reflect a major, concerning change in personal lifestyle or circumstances.

Now I'm not suggesting that people who act a little strangely should immediately be interrogated or removed from a position of trust. But it's clearly a good thing for a manager to be alert to potential anti-social behaviour or personal problems, and to offer help, or to at least be alert to other warning signs that might indicate an impending fraud. There are, for example, changes that might suggest advance preparations for a criminal act. Actions such as attempts to remove or ignore management controls, requests for a higher level of system access, refusal to take holidays or perhaps volunteering to work alone over a weekend.

Simple, traditional control measures, such as segregation of duties and periodic rotation of duties, can help to reduce the opportunity for fraud. But it's essential to harness the eyes and ears of the organization to look out for, and to challenge, any inappropriate or highly suspicious activity they might encounter in their staff, colleagues or managers.

The whistleblower

Several years ago I came across a case of an executive assigned to a new job in an Eastern country. On his first day he was handed a briefcase containing money, as a welcome present by a business partner. He handed it back immediately and made a critical, formal complaint. Shortly afterwards he was transferred back home, and informed that he lacked the necessary skills to manage the local culture. He was a little upset to say the least.

What went wrong and who was to blame? Clearly the executive was right to reject the money and report the incident. But he went about it in a clumsy way, which caused offence, distress and damage to local relations. In some cultures, the way you handle a sensitive incident can often be more important than the business impact of the incident itself. A managing director in a developing country once told me, for example, that in his country, a single insult could cause more business damage than a multi-million pound loss.

Regardless of how much you might be outraged by the fraudulent activities of a colleague, it's important to be sensitive to local culture when handling complaints, criticisms and accusations. Causing a loss of face can have significant consequences in many cultures. Such incidents need to be managed with sensitivity. Whenever you make an accusation, it will cause offence and outrage. Incidents need to be handled professionally, fairly and diplomatically.

Some cultures are, of course, more sensitive than others. But the learning point is that, in an increasingly litigious society, presenting an accusation can be a little like walking on eggshells. An accusation can upset or irritate your colleagues, your boss and your staff, as well as the person you are accusing. And the consequences can be as serious to the accuser as the person who is in the wrong. The 1999 film *The Insider* is a classic example of both the potential power and the perils of whistle blowing. It tells a tale of a tobacco executive who sets out to publicize serious accusations about his company. Not surprisingly, his career quickly goes into free-fall.

Whistle blowing is essential to both deter and catch fraud. But implementing a whistle blowing process requires much more than an appropriate policy and reporting point. Employers and staff need to be fully educated and aware of the gravity and consequences of making accusations. Mistakes can have serious consequences. They can cause personal distress and cause question marks to be placed against an innocent person's career. The accusing person might also end up in court as a potential witness. Employees need to be reassured that they will be given the full support of management and colleagues, and that they will be protected from potential recriminations or reprisals. In some countries, such as the UK, there is legislation to protect employees who raise genuine concerns.

And people who receive complaints and suspicions need to be trusted, trained and experienced in dealing with such cases. The design of the process needs to consider the sensitivities of all stakeholders, as well as the need to be highly discrete about investigations, not only to protect staff, but to avoid tipping off fraudsters. Security, human resources or internal audit functions are generally the most appropriate places to receive such complaints. In a large organization, you might even need to establish a specialist helpdesk or enquiry point to handle such reports.

But whistle blowing is no longer confined to the organization. Internet sites are springing up to capture anonymous reports. Wikileaks, for example, is a website that publishes anonymous submissions and leaks of sensitive corporate and government documents. In the first year of its launch, its database had grown to over a million documents.

Anonymous reporting, like loyalty, is a double-edged sword. On the one hand it gets all kinds of facts of public interest out into the open. On the other hand it's also a potential vehicle for unfounded gossip and rumour. But, like or not, it's part of the rich tapestry of business life in the new connected, information age.

Stemming the leaks

Encouraging employees to report inappropriate behaviour is clearly a good thing. But unhelpful, unnecessary disclosures that damage business interests can be a nightmare to companies. Unauthorized leaks of confidential corporate information to the press or public are not always helpful to society or business. They can be motivated by personal, political or mischievous reasons. And when it comes to politics, for example, not everyone will agree on what's right and what's wrong.

Leaks are often hard to investigate, and even harder to stop. But we can expect to see a lot more of them, because they are a natural phenomenon of a society that is less hierarchical, better networked and more spontaneous. In any healthy society, where individuals prize their feelings, beliefs and ethics as much as their job security, there will be leaks.

A further factor is that job security continues to decline, eroding the traditional motivator for many staff to bite their tongue and support the company line. In addition, we now have powerful tools at our fingertips, enough to send an entire database of confidential information to any person or location we choose. Such power can be seductive for any impulsive employee out to cause mischief.

Dealing with a leak is a thorny problem. If it's personally motivated then it's likely that the leak will be calculated to maximize damage. If it is politically inspired, then there's a good chance that a proportion of your staff will be sympathetic. I once became involved in the aftermath of a political leak to a leading newspaper. Not surprisingly, I found that the views of my colleagues were polarized. Half were sympathetic and suggested that the culprit should be exonerated. The other half supported a strong punishment.

The only effective means of minimizing leaks is to develop a culture of corporate loyalty. This is getting harder to achieve, but you can start by appealing to those staff who are seeking a long-term career, and who can be made to feel they are part of the organization. Staff who have served in expatriate positions, for example, often feel a deeper bond with the organization. They are likely to have been given a trusted and empowered role, and will have formed close relationships with colleagues and their families. Their personal and business lifestyles have become a lot more entwined.

It's also prudent to sacrifice a small loss in flexibility and avoid appointing new entrants to highly trusted positions in the organization, which might handle big secrets or large amounts of sensitive information. As with many things associated with achieving good security, convenience will be one of the first casualties.

Stamping out corruption

Many people in the West are surprisingly naïve when it comes to recognizing the potential for corruption inside their organizations. Most would never think of taking a bribe themselves. And a surprisingly high proportion of them will assume that public officials and company directors are likely to be honest. But, in fact, most employees refrain from crime and corruption because they have too much to lose. The security of a good salary and perhaps a pension generally outweighs the risk of being caught trying to defraud the company. Managers and staff who enjoy high status, high living standards and high income are less inclined to take a bribe than less affluent employees with lower job security. But a workforce of low status staff, with low living standards, on low salaries can create an environment that breeds widespread corruption. They have less to lose.

If left unchecked, corruption will become institutionalized, perceived as a perk of the job. Individual concerns about illegal actions will be balanced by a feeling of safety in numbers. The more widespread it becomes, the less inclined people will be to challenge or report it. In such cases radical action will need to be taken. And there are, in fact, many things that can be done to improve the situation.

New management should be brought in. Clear business principles and codes of conduct should be introduced. Investigations and prosecutions of offenders should be carried out, and they should be done consistently and visibly. Objective, independent selection processes should be introduced for filling senior positions. Promotions should be based primarily on merit and achievements, rather than personal recommendations. Greater transparency and segregation of duties should also be designed into systems. Audit trails should be regularly inspected. And conflicts of interest should be avoided, both in the design of jobs, and the selection of individuals for them. Higher wages, and better career development, should also be considered, especially for key jobs in security or finance. To many managers, that might seem to be an unjustified leap of faith, potentially throwing good money after bad. But it can help to reduce losses in environments with high theft and fraud rates.

All of these measures will, of course, increase costs in the short term, but they are also likely to deliver much greater savings and benefits in the longer term. And not only will they help reduce losses, but they will also ensure that the company is far less exposed to legal or regulatory challenges.

Know your staff

Pre-employment security checks are also a useful tool for preventing spies and fraudsters from entering the organization. They will never be completely foolproof, but all organizations should carefully consider the benefits of such checks. The downside is that all checks take time and cost money. And the more thorough the check, the higher will be the cost. The costs themselves, however, are relatively small in comparison to other costs associated with hiring an individual. But the delays in carrying them out can sometimes be a major nuisance for projects and essential business operations.

Conducting a security check requires no special skills, except at the very highest levels of vetting, but it's becoming an increasingly convoluted process, especially for an international workforce. The first thing to check is the identity of the person, to ensure that they really are who they say they are and not someone else. It's irresponsible not to do so. There are varying degrees of identity check that can be made, and a range of external services that can be employed.

Individuals might adopt a false identity for many reasons. It might be because they are illegal immigrants, criminals, terrorists or have a poor credit history. Or it could be because they are planning to commit an internal crime. I've even encountered cases where one person arrives for a job interview, but a completely different person turns up for work. That's a potential problem for any organization that routinely recruits staff through a central, recruitment office and then assigns them to report elsewhere for work. But there are simple practical solutions to prevent such substitutions from being carried out, such as taking a photograph of the applicant at the interview stage.

There are many elements to a person's identity. For the purposes of pre-employment vetting, the first key element is 'what you are': your biological attributes, such as your appearance, fingerprints, voice or even your DNA. Then there is your 'attributed identity': the things you inherit such as your name, date and place of birth, and your parents' names and addresses. Thirdly, there is your 'biographical identity': your personal history, including your original birth registration, electoral register information, tax records and employment history.

Identity can be established by interview, document inspection, references and database checks. There are many different types of check that can be performed, including verifying the person's identity, their right to work in the country, confirming their employment history and qualifications, performing a financial credit check, and, in exceptional cases, checking criminal or intelligence records.

Statistics from security companies such as Kroll indicate that around one in ten candidates will fail a criminal records check. If a criminal records check is not feasible, then it's worth insisting on a self-declaration that the person does not have a criminal record. Character and professional references should also be taken up, though the impartiality of referees can never be guaranteed. And, of course, you should ensure that all of these processes are legally compliant.

It's also important to check that the person applying for a job has not previously been rejected for work by the organization, or been dismissed because of fraudulent activities. For this reason it's essential to maintain databases of previous applicants and cases of terminated employment. Surprisingly, not all organizations take the trouble to do this.

Checking employment history is also important. A long gap might, for example, mask a prison sentence. A more thorough approach is to interview previous employers and line managers. You can, in fact, go on to conduct as many in-depth interviews as you like, but the cost and time required will escalate and you will get diminishing returns.

At the end of the day, none of these processes of identity verification and background checking are foolproof. They can help eliminate a few potential bad apples. But at best, they can only reassure you that the person has not been caught doing anything wrong. And in the deceitful worlds of espionage and fraud, this will never be sufficient to provide a cast iron guarantee. As one of my security colleagues, who led a team of security vetting investigators, used to point out: 'We can't read people's minds.'

We know what you did

We might not be able to know what people are thinking or planning. But we can observe what they are doing at their desk or across networks. Communications monitoring might seem highly intrusive to many people, but it's becoming commonplace in many organizations. And it's growing in both scope and sophistication.

During 2007 I managed a research project on behalf of Chronicle Solutions, a security vendor, and the University of Plymouth, to study the requirements and potential for monitoring human behaviour in digital networks. The findings indicated that nine out of ten organizations carry out some form of monitoring of employee and customer communications. But it's generally tightly controlled, subject to considerations such as legal advice, Board approval and staff agreements, not to mention the need for a convincing business case to justify the resources to carry it out.

Privacy is a major issue, of course, but many of the concerns can be overcome by preserving the anonymity of the subjects of the monitoring, at least until there is sufficient indication of a possible security breach to launch a formal security investigation. Using technology to automate the monitoring process enables the content of transactions to be kept from the eyes of IT and security staff, until something of concern is detected.

Automated fraud detection methods are also improving all the time. You can detect potential crimes by, for example, highlighting transactions that exceed staff authorization levels, products incorrectly priced, sales that occur outside business hours, or suspicious values that are just below authorization limits.

Researchers at the University of New Mexico have looked to nature for inspiration for automated methods of managing information security. It's a good place to look. The human immune system, for example, is an impressive, reliable system for deciding what is benign and should be safeguarded, and what is foreign and needs to be confronted and closed down. There are many other parallels with nature. For greater survivability we might consider, for example, aiming to emulate key survival mechanisms from nature, such as sex and death. Take death the latter, for example. The potential for security compromises and failures increases with time. It's better to kill processes on a regular basis and generate fresh, uncorrupted ones.

Several years ago, inspired by research emerging from the University of New Mexico, I directed a research project, sponsored by the UK Government, to develop an automated fraud detection system, based on the design of the human immune system. It was a fascinating learning experience. Working with Kings College, University of London, we built a fraud detection system based on digital 'antibodies' that could detect and report potential fraudulent transactions. It worked, though it was not an effective operational system. The project, however, was intended as a learning experience, rather than a fraud detection exercise. And the results demonstrated that the concept was a viable, real-time solution to the challenge of fraud detection, though it required a much greater amount of research to convert into an operational business system. But this is a field worth watching for the future.

Data mining technologies are also powerful tools for sifting through large databases and identifying items of interest to security. Data fusion, combining information from multiple sources, can provide unique, fresh perspectives. The major challenge with this approach is satisfying citizen privacy expectations. Several initiatives to combine citizen data for counterterrorism purposes have been abandoned because of privacy concerns. The more information that is combined, the larger will be the threat of personal intrusion and the possibility of mistaken identity.

Neural networks, technology inspired by the human brain, can be trained to recognize and report anomalies in data that warrant closer inspection. The self-organizing map or 'Kohonen map' is a popular form of neural network model, which offers the potential to simplify the presentation of a multi-dimensional analysis in the form of a two-dimensional map, which is useful for human analysis of the results.

Data visualization techniques are also a powerful tool to help a human observer to spot suspicious transactions that might be submerged in a sea of legitimate data. These techniques enable operators to monitor multiple streams of complex results simultaneously. They have great potential for wider use, in both business and security.

Monitoring can also detect undesirable user behaviour, such as visits to illegal, inappropriate or dangerous web sites, or the use of prohibited protocols or services. Increasingly, many security managers monitor outbound communications for signs of information leakage, such as the sudden export of a large amount of confidential data. Security vendors are developing solutions as fast as they can to meet the growing demand for data leakage prevention.

The possibility of detecting a potential criminal or crime before it occurs is a particularly fascinating challenge. Academic researchers at the University of Plymouth, for example, have already developed a theoretical insider threat prediction model that can measure attributes such as user role, access privileges and level of IT sophistication, and then map them against identified threats and on-line actions. These models are relatively new and unproven in practice, but they will certainly improve with time.

The real problem is deciding what to do if you uncover convincing evidence that a member of staff is likely to commit a fraud. Should you confront them, at the risk of tipping them off, or should you place them under surveillance? In fact, neither solution is satisfactory. And they both present a threat to civil liberties. From a business perspective, the primary aim should always be to deter a potential criminal, rather than to hope to catch them in the act.

Reading between the lines

E-mail, messaging, chats and blogs are rich in social and linguistic information that can provide valuable intelligence to help detect suspicious activity. Inferences can be drawn about the profile of the sender as well as the nature of the message. A surprising number of techniques exist to assess the psychological profile of people from their network traffic. We've all heard of lie detectors being used by the intelligence services. Similar techniques, and more, exist to draw inferences about people from their electronic communications.

It's long been known that people become nervous when attempting to deceive. There is an old story that persons suspected of a crime in West Africa were asked to handle a bird's egg. If they broke it they were considered guilty. Interestingly, there is a similar tale from ancient China that suspects were considered guilty if they could manage to keep a mouthful of rice dry for a short period, the logic being that saliva tends to decrease during emotional stress.

The polygraph lie detector operates in a similar way, measuring physiological responses such as blood pressure, pulse, respiration and skin conductivity. It's surprising to note that, although such devices have been around for the best part of a century, there is little solid scientific evidence to indicate how reliable they are. They are certainly far from perfect, having failed to catch spies such as Aldrich Ames, who passed two polygraph tests while spying for the Soviet Union. But they can serve as a deterrent. The spy John Walker, for example, was advised by his handlers not to accept any position that required a polygraph test.

Technology that analyses voice changes in telephone conversations is now widely used by insurance companies to detect fraudulent claims. It enables trained operators to assess the risk level of a claim by monitoring changes that suggest emotional stress. These systems are a useful deterrent to potential fraudsters. Attempts to knowingly deceive another person can also be detected from unconscious cues and activities in messages. Liars have to create convincing stories and present them in a sincere style. Stories based on imagined experiences are qualitatively different from those based on real-life experiences. By analyzing the content and sequence of messages it's possible to differentiate a true story from a false one.

The linguistic profile of liars is also different from that of people who tell the truth. The choice of words used by people and the way they're used conveys useful psychological information that is independent of the context of the message, and hard for a person to imitate or disguise. Linguistic profiling can be used to identify and authenticate a person, as well as to indicate sudden changes of personality. Research studies have shown that many people change their choice of words following a large-scale trauma, such as the death of a popular figure, or a major terrorist incident. They will, for example, increase their use of the collective 'we', relative to their use of 'I' in their speech.

Software is also now available to sift through large amounts of textual data and extract meaning, such as significant themes, concepts and ideas. It's already being used for analyzing customer feedback, in order to identify issues and trends.

We can also draw inferences about message senders, from the volume and pattern of their connections within their social networks. Inter-personal relationships can be classified as, 'strong ties', such as those between close friends and colleagues, or 'weak ties', the friend-of-a-friend type. Surprisingly it's the weak ties that are the most useful ones in gaining business, finding a job or detecting crime. Close friends and colleagues tend to work in the same physical and social space, so they offer little that's new. But acquaintances operate across different networks, so they are more useful in providing new information and introductions.

When analyzing network traffic patterns, suspicious connections are also more likely to appear as weak ties, because they tend to be covert, intermittent and selective. Terrorist networks, for example, operate in cells that are weakly inter-connected. Criminals groups will also tend to employ a friend-of-a-friend specialist for a particular job.

Whatever your views of civil liberties, the fact remains that the possibility of a Big Brother style surveillance society is looming larger. We can discover a lot about people by analyzing the content, style, sequence and recipients of their messages. Psychological profiling of people from their network traffic is a powerful, though not a completely reliable, tool for intelligence and crime prevention, detection and investigation. And it's only in its infancy. The privacy debate is set to grow.

Liberty or death

As Patrick Henry famously put it, in a speech to the Virginia House of Burgesses:

> *'Give me Liberty, or give me Death!'*

Many people agree with him. They would sacrifice their security for their freedom. But not everyone thinks that way. Society has always been divided on this issue. And it's always likely to be.

It's impossible to write about the human factor in information security without mentioning the important subject of civil liberties: the rights of individuals to be free from government interference. The rights to freedom of association, assembly, religion and speech, as well as the right to privacy, are fundamental civil liberties.

Civil liberties have been enshrined in constitutions, charters, covenants and bills of rights ever since 1215 when the rights of the King's subjects were written down, with a pigeon feather, on a piece of vellum. Notable examples of declarations of rights include the US Constitution, the European Convention on Human Rights and the International Covenant on Civil and Political Rights.

Information security technologies should pay close attention to this field, as their actions will increasingly have an impact on civil liberties. Identity management systems and security monitoring technologies can block or intercept information flows and detect inappropriate behaviour. They can also help to enable the protection of personal data.

There's always been tension between privacy and security. It's an inevitable confrontation. In an interview in the New Yorker magazine, Mike McConnell, US Director of National Intelligence, quotes one of his advisers, Ed Giorgio, as saying:

> *'We have a saying in this business: 'Privacy and security are a zero-sum game.'*

There's certainly a lot of truth in that. Ideally, we should be aiming to achieve both objectives. But, in practice, security and privacy often work against each other. We need to find and strike the right balance between the rights of users to privacy, and the needs of security and intelligence agencies to identify criminal, espionage and terrorist threats. In practice, we'll generally find that the most appropriate compromise will depend on which of these conflicting issues happens to be the most burning one at the time.

Every security manager will naturally have their own personal views and political leanings. But these should not be allowed to determine policy and actions on issues that concern user and customer rights, at least not in isolation. In most organizations, policies regarding people will be ones for human resources functions to determine in consultation with staff representatives. Legal judgments will need to be based on advice from corporate lawyers. And security and intelligence considerations will have to be decided in the light of current and emerging threats. If we don't agree with a judgment, we should present a strong argument. But the final decision should not be left in the hands of the security manager.

So what are the implications for an information security practitioner? Firstly, it's important for every security professional to understand the laws regarding interception, privacy and human rights. Unfortunately, they're not consistent across different jurisdictions. Some countries, for example, might require a company to scan employee e-mails, but other countries might ban such an activity. And others might allow it as long as due cause can be established.

Secondly, it's vital to take the broadest possible view. The subject of civil liberties attracts single-issue campaigners from both ends of the political spectrum. Security practitioners cannot afford to be aligned with either extreme in their actions. In our professional judgments and recommendations, we should aim to reflect the broader interests of business and society.

And, thirdly, it's important to be alert to future trends and developments. The world is changing. Large-scale surveillance is becoming easier, cheaper and more pervasive. Many of the tools are in the hands of citizens and business, as well as governments. We can secure a proportion of our own personal data using encryption, but many other traces of our physical presence and behaviour will be increasingly available, through e-commerce transactions, video cameras, citizen photographs and mobile phone and GPS tracking.

Terrorist threats will also become more sophisticated and dangerous, as advances in knowledge and technology enable easier development of weapons of mass disruption or destruction. The balance between privacy and security will become harder, and more emotional, as the stakes become higher. The information security manager of the future will need to be a diplomat in the struggle between privacy advocates and homeland security champions. No one view is likely to triumph. And the optimum balance will depend on the particular time, place, circumstances and context.

Personality types

It would be useful if we could identify potential criminals from the results of standard personality tests. There are clear dangers in such an approach, of course. The results are most likely to be both offensive and inconclusive. But personality tests are a measure that's increasingly used in recruitment assessments, so we should at least examine the potential that they might offer from a security perspective.

The market for personality and psychometric tests has grown enormously over the past decade. In a modern, de-layered, team-oriented and customer-focused enterprise, personality is an important asset for employees. Personality tests can also help to build a more robust selection process that can withstand legal challenges. They can serve as a defensive strategy, in response to increasing regulation and legislation. The techniques employed are crude, but they're relatively cheap, quick and easy to apply.

The idea that we might be able to categorize people according to their personality goes back to Carl Gustav Jung, who first developed this theory in the early part of the 20th Century. Having been born to an introvert father and an extrovert mother, Jung noticed a difference between these two types of personality. He went on to suggest that personality is characterized by a number of dimensions, in which people tend to lean towards one extreme or another, in the same way that most of them are left-handed or right-handed.

Jung's theory forms the basis of the Myers–Briggs personality type indicator, which assesses people against four criteria, measuring whether a person is extrovert or introvert in their outlook; sensing or intuitive in their information gathering; thinking or feeling when making decisions; and judging or perceiving in their outward lifestyle. The first three dimensions were postulated by Jung, and the fourth added by Katharine Briggs and her daughter Isabel Myers. The end result is a matrix of 16 possible personality types that suggest the defining characteristics of an individual.

The Myers–Briggs-type indicator is crude, but it's easy to measure and apply. Dividing a population into 16 types is a useful starting point for many purposes, including matching between people and careers, identifying leadership styles, understanding compatibilities in relationships, building teams, managing conflicts or helping to counsel victims. In a simpler form, these concepts are also useful for marketing, advertising and determining the general style and design of communications that might appeal to particular groups of people.

No measure is perfect. Not all of us are right or left handed, for example. Some of us are ambidextrous. People can be equally comfortable at both extremes of the measurement spectrum. Others might be found in the centre of the scale. And many of us will try to adapt our attitudes and behaviour to the environment we find ourselves in. If teamwork, for example, is a major job requirement, then we're all going to strive to be great team players, regardless of our natural instincts.

There are also fundamental weaknesses in any system that only takes a tiny, selected snapshot of people's characteristics, attitudes and behaviour, and then attempts to summarize the findings as four binary decisions. A Myers–Briggs rating captures and conveys very limited information. It provides no indication of values or motivations, which are equally important factors in any personal assessment. And it doesn't indicate whether people are actually any good at a task.

A further weakness is that the questions behind Myers–Briggs assessments are closed ones, forced-choice questions which fail to capture richer responses such as 'it depends', and under what circumstances the answer might vary. And the assessment can change significantly with people's evolving knowledge or motives regarding the purpose of the test.

We should also take account of the 'Barnum effect', covered later in this chapter, which suggests that many people are inclined to believe just about any generalized description of themselves, given by an authoritative source. That's why, for example, horoscopes work so well.

Jung himself was well aware of the limitations of reducing the almost infinite number of human psychological traits into a narrow set of arbitrarily imposed categories. As he put it himself:

> *'One can never give a description of a type, no matter how complete, that would apply to more than one individual, despite the fact that in some ways it aptly characterises thousands of others. Conformity is one side of a man, uniqueness the other.'*

There are other models that can be used to obtain a richer perspective of an individual's personality. The Five Factor Model, for example, which is based on the personality traits of openness, conscientiousness, extraversion, agreeableness and neuroticism, but uses a continuous range for each factor, rather than a choice of two extremes. However, for most business purposes, accuracy in a method is less important than ease of use. The Myers–Briggs ratings are easy to measure, well understood and simple to apply. That's what makes methods popular with managers. It's a rating that more and more organizations will be inclined to apply and exploit.

Personalities and crime

It's fairly obvious that an extravert personality type would be a good match for a good sales person. The more uncomfortable question is which of the many personality types makes a good criminal?

I have to emphasis that I'm not for one moment suggesting that it's a sensible move to apply ratings such as Myers–Briggs indicators, either as a selection criterion for trusted jobs or as a means to assess people's inclination for crime, fraud, espionage or terrorism. These ratings give no indication at all of a person's values, motivations, ethics, history or behaviour. But, as a common language for categorizing personality types, it's worth exploring whether they might provide us with a better insight into the criminal mind.

Each of the 16 Myers–Briggs indicators are defined by four capital letters, each representing one of the four dimensions: 'E' for extravert or 'I' for introvert; 'S' for sensing or 'N' for intuitive; 'T' for thinking or 'F' for feeling; and 'J' for judging or 'P' for perceiving.

We all have a good idea of the meaning of these terms. But they are used in Myers–Briggs assessments in a specific context. Extroverts are more outwardly focused, whereas introverts are more inclined to thought and refection. Sensing people prefer to rely on tangible, concrete facts, whereas intuitive types are more comfortable with abstract, theoretical ideas. Thinking people prefer to apply logic to decisions, whereas feeling people tend to act on empathy and intuition. And judging types are more decisive whereas perceiving types prefer to keep their decisions open.

The ideal profile for a criminal mastermind, for example would be 'INTJ', a highly organized planner and capable leader. It's quite rare in the general population, but found in quite a few IT directors. In contrast, the ideal profile for a lone fraudster might be an 'INTP': a shy, analytic loner, though one in good company, as Carl Jung himself was deemed to be one. But the main point to note is that personality tests such as Myers–Briggs cannot tell you who will commit a fraud. They can, however, indicate who is likely to be most suited to carrying one out.

The dark triad

Anti-social personality disorder results in what is commonly known as a sociopath, or what used to be called a psychopath, a deceitful and manipulative person who exhibits a strong disregard for the rights of others.

Surveys indicate that more than 1 in 20 males show signs that they might develop an anti-social personality disorder during their lifetime. And it's diagnosed in more than 1 in 30 males and 1% of all females. It's obviously higher in certain populations, such as prisons, where surveys have indicated it can be as high as three out of four inmates. But there is also some evidence that many of the identifying traits can be found in CEOs of major corporations.

An even more disturbing set of personality traits is what psychologists now refer to as the 'dark triad'. It combines the self-obsession of narcissism, the impulsive, thrill-seeking and callous behaviour of the psychopath and the deceitful and exploitative nature of Machiavellianism, a tendency to manipulate others for personal gain, named after the Renaissance writer Machiavelli, who wrote extensively on the subtle, cunning art of politics.

These traits are often found in fraudsters and spies. They can also make men attractive to women. Such men are perceived as 'bad boys'. They are the 'lady killers' who steal other men's partners for brief affairs. Many women are drawn to them, perhaps because they are exciting or masculine. Dark triads have more partners and prefer short-term relationships. James Bond is regarded as the epitome of the dark triad: disagreeable, extrovert, womanizing and a cold-blooded killer.

Some psychologists believe that these characteristics might perhaps represent an evolutionary survival strategy, though it's clearly not one that is widely adopted by the population. The reason for that might be because it's less effective when practiced by too many people. But dark triads are very real, dangerous people. They are not commonplace but, from time to time, you might find one lurking in your own organization.

Cyberspace is less risky

One of the attractions of hacking is that it's seemingly less risky than other forms of espionage or crime. You can even do it from the comfort of your home or office. You're distant from the victim. He can't look you in the eyes, hit you or chase you. As Donn Parker once put it:

'Remote computing freed criminals from the historic requirement of proximity to their crimes. Anonymity and freedom from personal victim confrontation increased the emotional ease of crime, i.e., the victim was only an inanimate computer, not a real person or enterprise. Timid people could become criminals. The proliferation of identical systems and means of use and the automation of business made possible and improved the economics of automating crimes and constructing powerful criminal tools and scripts with great leverage.'

Hacking is a much easier, safer and more acceptable criminal act than physical theft or extortion. It doesn't suit all criminals. Direct face-to-face deception of an individual involves a degree of ruthlessness, often associated with an anti-social behavioural trait. And some individuals enjoy the pleasure of manipulating others, even if it means conning a widow out of her life savings.

The term 'confidence trickster' was inspired by a 19th century crook called William Thompson, who would chat with strangers and ask them if they had the confidence to lend him their watch, at which point he'd walk off with the watch. That requires a lot of brass neck. Not many people will have the confidence themselves to carry out such a brazen fraud.

But even normal people can be tempted to carry out much more extreme acts in cyberspace than they would contemplate in everyday, face-to-face life. It's a phenomenon that John Suler, a researcher and writer on the psychology of cyberspace, calls the 'on-line disinhibition effect'. On the Internet, we tend to relax more, open up and feel less inhibition. We can be unusually hostile, rude and angry. We can explore dark subjects such as pornography, which are normally regarded as unacceptable. We might also commit acts, or reveal information, that we would never contemplate in the physical world.

John Suler points to several factors that contribute to this disinhibition effect. There is 'dissociation', the feeling of anonymity that cyberspace encourages. We imagine that nobody really knows who we are, so we can dissociate our acts from our true self. There is also a feeling of invisibility, that other people can't actually see or hear us. We are concealed, just like a peeping Tom. We can dress as we please. There are no rules for our physical behaviour. And we don't have to look other people in the eye.

Then there is the 'asynchronous' nature of our interactions, the delayed response of our actions. They don't register immediately. It encourages a feeling that we can suspend time before other people discover our actions. We can say or plant something bad, then escape before it's discovered. We can carry out an 'emotional hit-and-run'.

Another factor is a phenomenon termed 'solipsistic introjection', which causes us to feel that our mind has merged with our on-line companions. We hear or imagine their responses as voices within our heads. We create our own visual images for their appearance. It's just like an episode in an imaginary play or a novel. We feel we are talking to ourselves, rather than other people. All of these things blur the boundaries between reality and the more daring fantasies that we might choose to act out within the safety of our imagination.

Combining this with the 'escapability' of cyberspace, results in the phenomenon of 'dissociative imagination', where we begin to believe that the imaginary characters we've created might exist, in a new space, a make-believe world that does not demand the same responsibilities as the real world. A place where rules and norms are different. We become imaginary people carrying out acts with no real consequence in the physical world.

The dilution of authority over the Internet is also a contributory factor. The real world has little influence in cyberspace. We will be less intimidated by authority, and more inclined to speak our minds, or perhaps to misbehave.

An interesting, and important, question to consider is whether these effects actually lead to the creation of a new, false on-line persona, or whether it unleashes the true self, one that might have been lurking beneath a 'surface personality' constrained by real-world cultural norms and expectations. Unfortunately, this is a big subject and too complex an area to be discussed in this book. And the answer is far from clear cut.

There are many factors and layers that lie behind a person's identity and personality. People are complex and different. But it's clear that we can develop on-line identities and personalities that are markedly different from our physical, face-to-face ones. And the behaviour associated with these on-line identities is more open, less inhibited and increasingly daring.

Set a thief

There is an old saying 'Set a Thief to catch a Thief'. The suggestion is that if you really want to catch crooks, you should consider employing someone who has been one himself. Will this help you? It might if you have absolutely no idea how thieves operate. But if that's the case, then you shouldn't be in the business of security, or you should at least be aiming to find out from a more experienced policeman, criminologist or security investigator.

Professional security people need to keep abreast of the current techniques used by thieves. That doesn't mean employing a former thief. Some techniques remain the same and are therefore well known to experienced security practitioners. Others continue to emerge, but we should seek up-to-date intelligence rather than retired criminals to keep abreast of them.

But the mind set of a crook is different from the average person. They see opportunities that we can't. It's their business. In the next chapter, we'll explore the usefulness of a 'security mindset', one that's alert to weaknesses in systems and products. That's a rare skill, not something that everyone can readily develop. But it's not beyond the average person's capabilities to consider security controls from the perspective of an attacker. And that's something that every security professional should aim to do.

It's a glamour profession

One unfortunate tendency of our typical reaction to cyber incidents is that we have a habit of making computer crimes seem quite respectable, perhaps even a little glamorous. If a thief physically steals a small amount of money we call him a cheap crook. But if an executive embezzles millions of dollars we call him a 'white-collar' fraudster. Some people might even take that as a compliment. And it's even worse if he uses a computer. We call that 'high-tech' crime. It almost sounds attractive. It might, in fact, inspire children, rather than deter them.

These actions need to be discouraged, not glamorized. Yet most of these labels are created by law enforcement authorities, rather than the media. Perhaps some detectives prefer the added prestige of dealing with upscale, white-collar, high-tech crime. It's understandable, but wrong.

In fact, it's the security community that is the worst of all for glamorizing computer crime. I often hear security professionals use terms like 'cool' to describe a sophisticated hack. And we're happy to treat famous hackers and fraudsters as celebrities. Kevin Mitnick, a famous ex-hacker, and Frank Abagnale Jr, a famous fraudster, for example, are now successful consultants and popular keynote speakers.

It's good, of course, to encourage reformed criminals to take up a respectable day job. And former fraudsters can also provide a valuable service by explaining the mindset and techniques of criminals. But there is always an associated danger that by celebrating their achievements, we might also be sending a dangerous message to future generations of hackers and fraudsters that crime might actually pay.

There are easier ways

There are, in fact, easier ways than crime to make a fast buck or even a regular income. As the left-wing German playwright Bertolt Brecht once put it:

> *'It is easier to rob by setting up a bank than by holding up a bank clerk.'*

This is certainly true. A serial entrepreneur once told me that he'd always aspired to run a bank, so he bought one. You don't actually need any money to buy a bank. If you're a good deal maker, then the financing can easily be arranged. And it's useful to have one, because they open up all sorts of doors.

Many years ago, when I was attempting to understand the nature of the insider threat, I asked John Austen, founder of New Scotland Yard's Computer Crime Unit, what sort of person tends to commit fraud. Without any hesitation he replied:

> *'It's bank managers that rob banks and computer directors that rob companies.'*

That statement is supported by research surveys of fraud and fraudsters. KPMG's *Profile of a Fraudster Survey*, for example, looked at 360 profiles of fraudsters across Europe, the Middle East and Africa. Amongst other things, it revealed that nine out of ten frauds are carried out largely by male members of top management, with more than six years employment. Greed and opportunity were the motives in three out of four cases.

This presents a dilemma for any security investigator and his management. Every now and then, when investigating incidents, you will have to suspect and investigate your own boss. That can be a career-limiting action. But it should never be forgotten that the typical profile of a fraudster is a hard-working, competitive, ambitious, arrogant, risk-taking, male. And that's exactly the sort of person that ends up at the top of an organization.

I just don't believe it

It's often claimed that fraud and computer crime are understated because managing directors are reluctant to pursue a prosecution for insider crimes. It's certainly true that it's much easier to quietly retire executives who've been caught in the act, rather than prosecute them. That will save money as well as avoiding negative press coverage and potential reputation damage.

But, in most cases, I've found that the main barrier to any lack of enthusiasm to prosecute is, in fact, the emotional reaction to such incidents. Prosecutions are time consuming and expensive to pursue. And they don't tend to result in any positive impact on brands or reputation. But investigations and prosecutions are absolutely necessary. They serve as a deterrent, and they're often mandated by corporate policy. Disclosure of an incident might also be mandated by law or industry regulations.

Given enough time, most directors will, in fact, be prepared to bite the bullet and do the right thing. As events unfold, many managers tend to take an increasingly harder line, as the facts and implications begin to sink in. The fact is that it takes people a little time to come to terms with major events. Good communication and timing are therefore essential in explaining incidents to top management.

It's important to anticipate the reactions of business managers on discovering a shocking truth about the behaviour of an employee. There's a distinct pattern to them. The psychological reaction has similarities to those triggered by a bereavement of a colleague, though it's clearly not as emotional. The first reaction, for example, is to deny that the event has happened. The typical response is:

'I don't believe it. I know that man. He's not like that.'

Eventually, after studying all the facts and evidence, it will dawn on the management team that this person really did commit the crime. Then the distancing will begin to emerge:

> *'It was nothing to do with me. He must have been acting on his own. And I didn't hire him.'*

These are all natural reactions. And, finally, when the incident has sunk in and impact has been assessed, the outrage and anger will begin to set in:

> *'I think we should prosecute. He's a bad sort. We need to set an example.'*

The timing of the decision to prosecute is important. If you are too quick in forcing a management team to decide, especially when you have very limited evidence, then you will get a weak, defensive response. Management might initially be more inclined to sack the individual, pay him off and drop the accusations. But, the longer you can wait to confirm your initial suspicions, establish solid evidence, and allow your management to come to terms with the facts, the more likely you are to achieve the right decision.

Don't lose that evidence

Delays in confirming initial suspicions about a fraud or breach, however, can be dangerous. Evidence can be lost, trails will grow cold, and suspects will try to cover their tracks. For all of these reasons, it's important to be quick, decisive and discreet about preserving audit trails.

At the outset of any investigation, there will be uncertainty about the facts of the incident and the possible suspects. Questions will need to be answered about who might have done it, how it was achieved, when and where it all happened, and what the full scale of the damage might be. Inspector Clouseau was not far off the mark in *A Shot in the Dark* when he remarked:

> *'I believe everything and I believe nothing. I suspect everyone and I suspect no one.'*

Real investigations are, unfortunately, a bit like that. We can only act on the known facts. But we also have to assume the worst case. Unless we know better, we have to assume, for example, that the perpetrator might have breached sufficient controls to bypass normal limits of authorization. We have to assume that, as is often the case, there might be previous cases of fraud by the same person, or that the fraud might have been going on for many years.

For these reasons evidence should be preserved across the widest possible scope, and for the longest time period, until the facts indicate otherwise. Speed is important, because audit logs and records might otherwise be lost. Computer memory can be overwritten. Paper records can get discarded. Files might be deleted. Back-up media will be recycled. And we should also look beyond the enterprise for evidence. Suppliers, customers, partners, couriers, communications providers and banks might also possess relevant records.

But investigations also need to be discreet and low profile, to avoid tipping off suspects and triggering speculation or leaks of information. In such cases, we cannot exploit the full power of our investigative networks without the risk of unintended exposures. Delays can also be caused by requests for search orders and assistance. And in practice, many pieces of evidence will be lost in the first few hours or days following the incident.

In many respects, we might be sleepwalking into a surveillance society. But we have a very long way to go before we achieve a situation in which forensic quality evidence is continuously available when needed.

They had it coming

It's not just management that might be in denial following a major incident. Criminals themselves are also unlikely to accept the real facts of a crime they've committed. Rationalization of actions is a classic, essential element for all crime and anti-social behaviour. Criminals rely on this process of denial to reduce their inhibitions and to justify their actions.

Whether the crime is against an individual or an organization, the perpetrator will seek to explain away their crime by adopting an argument such as:

'They can afford it. They had it coming. It's no more than they deserve.'

Through this type of rationalization, it becomes possible to imagine that the crime hasn't really harmed anyone, that it was the victim's fault or that it was something that needed to be done.

Rationalization works at any level, even for serial killers. In his classic book *How to Win Friends and Influence People* published in 1937, Dale Carnegie recounts the story of 'Two Gun' Crowley, one of the most dangerous criminals in the history of New York, someone who would kill 'at the drop of a feather'. When finally cornered and under fierce gunfire from the surrounding police he wrote a letter saying:

'Under my coat is a weary heart, but a kind one – one that would do nobody any harm.'

He was sentenced to the electric chair. When arriving at the death house, he said:

'This is what I get for defending myself?'

The point that Dale Carnegie was making with this story, is that criticism is futile, because it only puts people on the defensive and causes them to justify their behaviour. Criticism is an ineffective motivator and it provokes an unhelpful reaction. But the key learning point for security managers is that we should not tolerate excuses for justifying criminal or undesirable behaviour. Good security is more than just the application of controls to prevent or detect actions. It's also about creating a climate that discourages bad behaviour and, equally importantly, the excuses that go with it.

The science of investigation

There's a striking contrast between real-life criminal investigations and those portrayed in literature or on television. Forget the *Crime Scene Investigation* TV images that show a bullet flying through the air depositing a shower of fine particles on the gunman. It doesn't happen like that. It takes up to ten minutes, in fact, for particles to deposit themselves, by which time the gunman will most likely have left the scene.

Forget also the portrayal of MI5 security operatives in the British TV series *Spooks*, which prompted Dame Eliza Manningham-Buller, a former Chief of MI5, to say:

> *'I wish life were like Spooks where everything is, (a) knowable, and, (b) solvable by six people.'*

When it comes to investigations, reality and fiction are quite different. Not every investigator is a Sherlock Holmes. Investigation is a very difficult skill requiring a unique blend of observation, pattern recognition, logic and psychological skills. And even if detectives had these all of these skills, few would be permitted the time necessary to carry out an extensive investigation.

Investigative science is a relatively young and immature field that's been slowly evolving. Some criminologists consider its historical evolution as comprising three 'waves' of development. The first wave was characterized by the study of clues, pioneered by Scotland Yard in the 19th century. The second wave was concerned with the analysis of crime patterns. And the third wave is focused more on the human factor. It's the study of the criminal psyche, the fascinating world of criminal profiling.

Criminal profiling helps investigators to understand the nature of unknown criminals, based on an analysis of the manner of the crime. The key assumption is that their behaviour reflects their personality. It might not work perfectly every time, but it can deliver striking results in many cases.

Geographic profiling of the locations of crimes is also highly effective in pinpointing the residence of serial criminals or the most likely areas in which they might next strike. There are parallels with nature. Researchers from Queen Mary College, University of London, have studied the foraging patterns of animals and insects, such as bumblebees, to understand how serial criminals might choose their targets. They both tend to target particular areas, neither too close nor too far from their residence, creating a 'buffer zone' around their neighbourhood, in order to avoid attracting attention to themselves.

We can apply this type of thinking to other security situations. As I mentioned earlier in this chapter, it's instructive to study how thieves operate in large office complexes. Some masquerade as telecommunications engineers to gain access to the building. And once inside, they look for targets on specific floors, near lifts and staircases that offered a fast getaway. They also have prepared stories to explain their presence and behaviour, in case they are challenged. Understanding their modus operandi and logic helps to catch them by anticipating their targets. It also demonstrates the weakness of security tests to break into buildings. If you have a 'get out of jail' card up your sleeve you simply won't be forced to operate in such a restrictive manner.

Lessons from the field of criminal and geographic profiling are likely to be of increasing value to information security managers, given the growth of cyber crime, and, in particular, the potential for a single individual to hold an organization to ransom by threatening to disrupt, damage or destroy essential business data and services. Such an attack might turn out to be a cat and mouse game of observation, logic and deception, with the attacker aiming to exploit the desire of the business to avoid any damaging publicity.

So far, cases of cyber extortion have been confined to a small number of industries. But it's set to grow with increasing business dependency on data and technology, coupled with the growing risk profiles associated with today's highly networked IT infrastructures. Smart security managers should equip themselves with the tools and contacts for quickly investigating and tracing potential attackers, because, increasingly, if a person is really determined, we will need to do more than just deter him. We will have to pinpoint and arrest him.

The art of interrogation

Identifying a suspect is only the start in solving the crime. You also have to establish compelling evidence or persuade the suspect to confess. The art of interrogation is easy to describe, but very hard to put into practice. It demands a patient, calm, logical approach. Yet, at the same time, you have to think quickly to stay one step ahead of your suspect.

The starting point is to begin by looking for short cuts. Have we got any damning evidence? Can we find an informer? Does the suspect have any previous form? If these lines of enquiry draw a blank, however, then it's all down to the art of interrogation. We will first have to decide whether we believe that the suspect might be guilty, from his behaviour, appearance and answers to questions. Then we will have to extract a confession, or perhaps try to identify inconsistencies in his version of events.

Interrogation is a classic confrontation between two human beings. It's a fascinating blend of logic and instinct. There are psychological tricks that can be deployed. But the real key is to think logically and objectively, yet at the same time, keep an open mind. Unfortunately, it's hard to be objective, when you're relying on your instincts.

The starting point is to consider the modus operandi, motive and likely characteristics of the perpetrator, and consider how they might fit the suspect. There's a lot you can tell, for example, from a person's dress, style, views and body language. Attitudes and views can suggest motives. Nervous gestures can indicate they have something to hide.

In any interview process, you also need to ask the right questions. In the case of an interrogation, they should be largely open ones that encourage more than a 'yes' or 'no' response, prompting the suspect to elaborate as much as possible. Closed questions can also be useful from time to time, to confirm or deny specific theories, for example.

The experienced interrogator will look for possible signs of deception, such as unusually brief or excessively detailed answers, hesitations in responding, sudden memory lapses, signs of irritability or anger, and inconsistencies. Surprise questions are also useful, as they might catch the suspect off guard. And, of course, like any good fact-finding interview, the questioning should continue for as long as possible.

Guilty people will tend to become increasingly stressed throughout an interview. It will be difficult for them to keep up a consistent stream of lies under persistent questioning. Eventually, they will make a mistake, or perhaps feel tempted to relieve the stress through an admission of guilt.

It can also help for the interrogator to form a bond with the suspect, as this might encourage him to drop his guard. Flattery can help. We could, for example, compliment the suspect on his skills and knowledge. We might also try to play the 'nice guy' to a colleague's 'nasty guy'. This technique is well known to most criminals, but it encourages suspects to talk. Casual conversation establishes an impression of the suspect's normal behaviour, which will help to spot changes that might indicate the suspect is covering something up.

Guilty people are likely to be more nervous than innocent ones when confronted with the details of a crime. And there are some simple tests that can help indicate whether a person is guilty or not. We might, for example, ask the suspect whether they think we should call the police, or speculate on disciplinary options. A guilty person is unlikely to support a hard line. We might also consider putting out items of evidence on the interview desk. A guilty person will, understandably, tend to look more closely at them than an innocent one.

The directions of the suspect's eye movements are also another possible test. There is a theory that when people recall events, their eyes look in a particular direction, and when they are inventing a story, their eyes look the opposite way. There are, of course, dangers in interpreting the outcome. The suspect might be recalling a false account he has learned. He might also be aware of the technique, and exploit it to mislead the interviewer.

In practice, interrogation is more of an art than a science. It's a fascinating field and, like crisis management, it's one that's rarely mastered to its full potential. But it's an essential part of the security manager's toolbox. And it also provides us with a richer insight into the criminal mind.

Secure by design

Thinking like your enemies can help to encourage the development of systems that resist attack. In fact, there are several approaches that can be taken to achieve this. We can, for example, design products that resist attack. We can also design measures that reduce the value of stolen or lost assets. Then again, we can reduce the opportunity for, or damage from, a breach, by, for example, implementing 'least privilege' access rights to systems and data. We can also deter attackers by deploying visible audit trails and employing a tough, consistent policy on investigating and punishing perpetrators of breaches.

The art of designing systems that are intrinsically secure, because they contain built-in deterrents to attackers and thieves, is one of the most underdeveloped areas of security. Occasionally, we encounter interesting examples of this, such as digital rights management (DRM) which aims to prevent illegal users from obtaining value from intellectual property. Another example that springs to mind is the special type of cash container used by some banks and couriers, which will spray banknotes with a special dye when forced open. The design of US Postal Service vans is also an interesting example. Such vehicles are rarely stolen because of their unique shape, which reduces their black market value. Nicholas Negroponte applied this principle to the design of his $100 'One Laptop per Child' computer, intended for free distribution to children in developing countries. The design is deliberately unique and garish, to act as a deterrent to theft.

Designing systems and intellectual products that can resist theft should be a fundamental area of information security research. Several years ago, Jon Measham, a security researcher in the Royal Mail Group, wrote a discussion paper on the merits of this approach. He called it 'value-less security'.

There is also a thriving research centre in London that applies this principle to the design of physical goods that might be targets for theft. The Design Against Crime Centre, at London fashion college Central Saint Martins, devises innovative gadgets and adapts everyday items to make theft as difficult as possible. Amongst other things, they have developed a slash-proof backpack, an alarmed laptop case and a pub chair with sufficient space to hide a handbag inside. Professor Lorraine Gamman, the Centre's Director, has a delightful ambition:

> *'I personally would like to design a phone that blows up when someone steals it. That would be one way to stop thieves using it.'*

It certainly would, though I imagine that the health and safety issues would be a slight barrier, to say the least.

Science and snake oil

Most people can be persuaded or tricked, from time to time, into doing something or believing a point of view. We can even manipulate our own thinking. The way criminals rationalize their actions is a good example of that. Can such a concept be converted into a science?

The field of neuro-linguistic programming (NLP) is an interesting one to study from that perspective. Its methods and techniques lack a reliable scientific basis, but they have been slowly infiltrating many respectable professions. In recent years, it's also crept into the information security field. It's used, for example, by some security practitioners to help carry out more effective social-engineering tests, as part of a security penetration testing exercise.

NLP is an alternative approach to psychotherapy that was developed by Richard Bandler and John Grinder in the 1970s. It's an unusual mixture of science, ancient religion and new age thinking. NLP aims to enhance personal communications and influence. It's widely used in counselling, though there appears to be no solid, empirical basis to support its claims.

NLP operates by analyzing the structure of verbal patterns of communication, as well as non-verbal cues such as eye movements. Amongst other things, it aims to enhance the state of mind by a process called 'anchoring', which associates a gesture, voice tone or touch with a particular state of mind.

NLP offers techniques to read people's subconscious signals and manipulating their behaviour, perhaps reinforcing particular states of mind, or even hypnotizing people into carrying out our suggestions. For a non-practitioner, it's impossible to tell how effective these techniques might be in practice. But there is a possibility that a security manager, a trainer or a criminal, might employ them to advantage.

In fact, there is likely to be something in this approach, as experience generally shows that the way we approach people, talk to them and interact with them, can have quite an influence on their response. But many psychologists appear to be divided about the effectiveness of NLP techniques. For every one that swears by them, it's easy to find another that believes they're bogus.

The truth is that we don't really know enough about this field to judge its effectiveness. Perhaps it only works for certain practitioners or subjects. Perhaps we can be misled by someone sending out false signals. Would an NLP practitioner have an edge in a game of poker? And what would be the outcome of two or more NLP experts competing in such a game of bluff?

The art of persuasion is not a completely reliable one. As Abraham Lincoln was once attributed to say:

> *'You can fool some of the people all of the time, and all of the people some of the time, but you can not fool all of the people all of the time.'*

But even if such techniques work for only a few subjects, in only a few circumstances, they should not be dismissed. An attacker only has to get lucky once. A security manager has to be lucky all the time.

The art of hypnosis

In 2007, a New Hampshire convenience store clerk reported that he was robbed by thieves who used hypnosis and mind control techniques to persuade the clerk to ignore the fact that they were taking more than $1000. It started with a game. 'Think of a wild animal,' the thieves said, 'and we'll write down what's in your mind'. Then it escalated to personal questions about a former girlfriend, then finally to a form of mind control. It sounds quite amazing to the average person. Can this type of crime really be possible?

Certainly there have been many other reported examples of this technique being practiced in Europe and the Far East. One possibility is that the victim is cooperating. Another is that the victim has been carefully selected and prepared over a long period of time. Experts will point out that you can't get subjects to do things that they don't want to do, things that might, for example, violate their basic sense of right or wrong. But then again, it's perfectly possible that the victim was tricked into believing that the act was not a crime, or, perhaps, was for a good cause.

Hypnosis is a respectable profession, often used for medical purposes, and there's plenty of evidence to suggest that it works, to relieve pain, for example, though not everyone is equally susceptible. But this type of medical hypnosis is generally carried out as a slow, calm process, with a willing subject closing his eyes and relaxing. The interesting question, from a security perspective, is whether an alert person can be instantly and unexpectedly tricked into carrying out an act to support a crime.

That's the type of trick a stage hypnotist demonstrates at every performance. How do they do it? The tricks of the trade of stage magicians and hypnotists are closely guarded secrets. But there is one well-known technique that's reportedly used by stage hypnotists. This trick is called the 'handshake interrupt'. It relies on catching a person by surprise, when his subconscious mind is in control. We're all familiar with that mindset, the autopilot state that we seem to enter when, for example, we're driving a car. The practitioners of the handshake interrupt claim that we enter this state whenever we begin to shake hands with someone.

The stage hypnotist sets off to shake hands with his subject, but interrupts the handshake before it's complete. The hypnotist will grab the subject's wrist and bring the subject's hand up towards their face. The hypnotist will ask the subject to look at their hand and then instruct them close their eyes. The result is claimed to be instant hypnosis, or so we are led to believe. But stage hypnotists also select their subject with care. And there are, in fact, plenty of tests that have been designed to assess people's susceptibility of people to hypnosis. Sleep walkers are reported to be the ideal types. About one in ten people might fall into this category.

In the absence of any scientific evidence to support this phenomenon, we can't be sure if instant hypnosis is actually science, snake oil or simply an urban myth. But if it really does work, then it's something that all security managers should be alert to.

The power of suggestion

'What a fool believes, he sees,' sang Michael McDonald. It's very true. And we don't have to be trained hypnotists to persuade people to see something that they are wanting or expecting to see. Horoscope writers do it all the time. Many people are also open to suggestion, either in response to leading questions, which encourage a particular response, or through devices such as charm, sympathy flattery or seduction.

The 'Barnum effect', named after the famous 19th century circus master, is an interesting phenomenon. It's based on his remarks that his shows provided 'a little something for everybody'. It describes the effect that a generalized character assessment can be readily accepted by most people as a personalized one. It explains, for example, why highly generalized horoscopes in newspapers are commonly perceived as being accurate personal predictions. And why people are impressed with the very general descriptions presented by mind readers and mediums.

The Barnum effect was first highlighted in 1948 by Bertram Forer, a psychologist, who carried out a classic experiment to demonstrate the effect, by carrying out a personality test on a group of undergraduate students, and then providing them with an assessment of their personality. The students were led to believe that the description was uniquely generated, when in fact the text was a general one taken at random from an astrology book. Amazingly, the students rated the description as 4.3 out of 5 for the accuracy of the text. Below is the text that Forer used. Judge for yourself how well it works for you:

> *'You have a great need for other people to like and admire you. You have a tendency to be critical of yourself. You have a great deal of unused capacity which you have not turned to your advantage. While you have some personality weaknesses, you are generally able to compensate for them. Your sexual adjustment has presented some problems for you. Disciplined and self-controlled outside, you tend to be worrisome and insecure inside. At times you have serious doubts as to whether you have made the right decision or done the right thing. You prefer a certain amount of change and variety and become dissatisfied when hemmed in by restrictions and limitations. You pride yourself as an independent thinker and do not accept others' statements without satisfactory proof. You have found it unwise to be too frank in revealing yourself to others. At times you are extroverted, affable, sociable, while at other times you are introverted, wary, reserved. Some of your aspirations tend to be pretty unrealistic. Security is one of your major goals in life.'*

Research has shown that there are two major aspects of such descriptions that influence the degree of acceptance. The first is the perceived authority of the source of the description, which helps to give it credibility. And the second is the nature of the content, and, in particular, whether it is flattering to the subject. Obviously, people prefer to believe good things about themselves.

It's just an illusion

There are different forms of magic, ranging from the ancient rituals of the Middle East to Arthur C. Clarke's third law prediction which states that:

'Any sufficiently advanced technology is indistinguishable from magic.'

Then again, there is the art of illusion. A colleague of mine is an amateur magician and a member of the Magic Circle. He once informed me that he regularly meets up in London with his magic friends, and they take turns to entertain each other, generally starting with the prompt:

'Whose turn is it to cheat?'

Amongst other tricks, magicians and fortune tellers use the Barnum effect extensively. They call it cold reading. But whereas fortune tellers aim to persuade their audience that they really do possess paranormal powers, most professional magicians and illusionists are refreshingly honest about their skills. They generally admit it's an illusion, not magic.

Mind-reading tricks are actually much easier to perform than most people realize. The secret is in the audience's perception rather than the skill of the performer. The Barnum effect shows how easy it is to create an account of events that everybody can relate to. We might be unique but we all have many things in common. Typical devices used by psychics, for example, are to mention the loss of someone close, an illness, a bad accident or a financial gain, perhaps through a property changing hands. These are things that happen to most people.

It's even easier in the case of a nightclub act that selects people from the audience. With knowledge of the Barnum effect and the ability to select an individual, they can narrow down the general script and make it even more specific. A young lady for example will be interested to hear things about travel and romance. A young man will be more focused on his career and ambitions. Occasional failures will occur, of course, but they're only apparent to one person in the audience. The act works because people are eager to hear interesting things about themselves, described by someone who appears to possess a mystical authority. It's not external magic, but internal self interest that makes the illusion.

Professional illusionists operate quite differently. They prefer to use real science. I once met a semi-professional practitioner who claimed he could create absolutely any illusion I might suggest, given enough budget. MIT Media Lab even got in on the act once, by creating a new magic trick, based on invisible electric beams that the magician could interrupt with his hands, to operate lights, sounds or equipment. Such tricks are often simple in concept, but highly impressive to see in action.

One of the most important tricks employed by magicians is the technique of 'misdirection'. It's a trick of the mind, which enables them to deceive their audience by encouraging them to focus on one particular thing, leaving them blind to other events. This trick works because of the limitations of the human mind, which prefers to concentrate on one thing at a time. The magician first builds a picture for his audience of what they can expect to see. That means they might not actually notice other things that happen before their eyes. He will draw attention to the things he wants the audience to concentrate on and deliberately ignore the things he wants them not to notice. He will exploit his body language to direct the audience's vision, which will tend to focus on where the magician looks. He will use phrases such as 'there's nothing up my sleeve' to direct the audience's attention to his arms, enabling him to produce an object from somewhere else.

Misdirection is a surprisingly effective technique. It's also used by confidence tricksters to fool their victims. The learning point for security managers is that people are easily tricked. Even our smartest staff can be deceived by a knowledge-able and skilful practitioner. And these tricks are much easier to perform than we might expect. They demonstrate that you can't even trust your own eyes, never mind other people.

It pays to cooperate

Trust, or even its absence, is the basis of all relationships between people. It's a personal, subjective thing. Trust is based on experience. It takes account of factors such as competence, honesty, security and dependability. But there are no absolute, objective or permanent measures of trust. People will each have a unique perspec-tive, a different opinion and a varying level of propensity to trust other people.

Trust is also a social contract with social implications. People might start by giving you the benefit of the doubt. Sometimes they might have no option but to trust you. But real trust is built over time. It has to be earned. If you let someone down, it will damage your reputation, and the amount of trust that people will place in you in the future.

We can, if we wish, design useful measures to assess levels of trust by, for example, averaging a range of individual personal ratings. But these measures are no more than a means to an end. Trust means nothing in the absence of an objective. You're generally trusted only to do something specific in a particular context.

Trust is an essential pre-condition for any collaboration between parties. No matter how selfish a person might be, it's often better to cooperate, rather than compete, with other people. Knowing which strategy to apply is essential to survival. This is demonstrated by a classic contest from game theory called the Prisoner's Dilemma, which illustrates how trust between two parties operates in practice. The game is a non-zero-sum game, which means it's one in which both sides can end up winning or losing. The scenario is as follows.

Two prisoners are being interrogated and each given the option of betraying the other prisoner, in exchange for a reduced sentence, though this is known to extend the other prisoner's sentence substantially. Naturally, each will want to receive the lowest possible sentence. If both stay silent, both will serve short sentences. If both spill the beans, both will serve medium sentences. If only one stays silent, he will get the highest sentence, while his colleague will get off quite lightly.

The natural reaction is to betray the other person. But things change when the game is played repeatedly. Cooperation will begin to surface, because of fear of subsequent revenge by the other player.

The learning point from this game is that long-term cooperation is the result of cumulative, short-term experiences. Robert Axelrod, a professor of political science, has studied the conditions necessary for a strategy to be successful. Amongst other things, he found that, interestingly, the best strategy is to be 'nice' to begin with, but prepared to retaliate, to avoid being exploited. Successful strategies are also forgiving, to avoid long runs of revenge and counter-revenge. And they should not strive to score more than the opponent. In fact, even the most selfish individuals should, if they wish to be successful, learn to be nice, forgiving and non-envious.

Artificial trust

There are less conventional ways of encouraging people to place their trust in us. Similar to the science fiction fantasy of truth serums to compel people to tell the truth, we now have the prospect of drugs to persuade people to place more trust in others. The drug oxytocin, a hormone also know as the 'cuddle chemical', has been tested at Zurich University and found to encourage higher degrees of trust. It's believed to be released during hugging, touching and orgasm, in both sexes, and seems to be associated with bonding and social recognition.

There is some research evidence that this drug increases trust and reduces fear. It might also have a significant impact on risk perception. Perhaps, in years to come, this type of drug will be exploited by criminals or intelligence services to create a false sense of security in their victims. The real implication, however, is that trust is not only subjective, it can also be manipulated.

Researchers at Stanford University's Persuasive Technology Lab have been studying the psychology of Facebook, especially what they term 'high-contextualized trust'. Key factors in establishing such trust might include things such as the degree of accountability for actions, lifestyle profiles, environment factors, the strength and number of connections, the social pressure to participate, the level of understanding of potential problems and the predictability of the environment.

On-line trust is, in fact, a rich, complex area. We are only beginning to scratch the surface of the factors behind it, and the possible means of measuring or communicating them. But it's very clear that trust is far from being a black and white issue, though it might force a simple binary decision on whether or not to enter into a transaction or relationship. And at the heart of trust are the very uncertain areas of identity and risk.

Who are you?

Cogito ergo sum, as Descartes would put it, which translates as 'I think, therefore I am'. His logic was that if you can think, then you must exist. You must also have an identity. But identity operates at many levels. It's an image in your own mind. It's something that you recognize about your physical presence. And it's also something that is conveyed when you're on-line in cyberspace.

Identity is a rich, complex device with many dimensions. We can use it in many different contexts to assert particular characteristics about yourself or others. 'Are you a man or a mouse?' 'Trust me, I'm a security professional.' 'I work for J.P.' 'My name is Bond, James Bond. I have a license to kill.'

And, just like risk and trust, identity is a means to an end. There is no universal absolute identity for a person or thing. Identity makes no sense without a context and a clear objective. Identity can also be an emotional, highly personal issue. Some people are very proud of their identity. Others prefer anonymity. And a few will spend their lives in search of an identity. Not everyone has the same perspective on identity. There are many different contexts, uses and objectives for personal identification information, so it's not surprising to find that there are numerous variants in everyday use.

In an earlier part of this chapter, when we looked at identity checking as a component of pre-employment security screening, we considered biological, attributed and biographical information. But that's only part of the identity spectrum. Consider the following list, for example. Any combination of these can be used to identify people for a useful purpose:

- **Inheritance:**   Your name, race, nationality, age and family
- **Location:**   Where you are and where you've been or plan to go
- **Contact details:**   Your home address, e-mail address, phone numbers
- **Employment:**   What you do, your CV and aspirations
- **Publications:**   Books, papers, stories, postings and Google entries
- **Class:**   Your social or demographic class
- **Networks:**   Friends, acquaintances, clubs, social networks and interest groups
- **Opinions:**   What you stand for, what you like and dislike
- **Skills:**   Your psychometric profile, languages, competencies
- **Qualifications:**   Academic achievements, accreditations
- **Assessments:**   What people think of you, your potential, work appraisal, credit rating
- **Credentials:**   The cash you carry, your credit cards, passport, identity cards

We can structure such a list in as many ways as we like. The entries can go on as long as we wish, though we'll quickly hit diminishing returns. The point I'm trying to make, is that identity is a growing and open-ended set of characteristics. We'll never arrive at a definitive view of a person's identity. There will always be new, emerging dimensions.

For practical business purposes, it's more useful to limit these characteristics to a more manageable set. J.P. Rangaswami, the imaginative managing director of BT Design, suggests that identity can be defined using just four main categories: what you stand for; what you belong to; what you like and dislike and what you've done or would like to do. That's an interesting, commercial perspective. The logic behind his choice is that other attributes have become less relevant. They only mattered when socio-economic groupings actually meant something, when marketing people might aim to predict your propensity to buy something based on the categories they decided put you in. Today that no longer works. The marketing perspective is much richer. We live in a world of 'long tails' where many small interests count for many small sales.

The attributes of identity are, in fact, all in the eye of the beholder. They're about utility rather than value. And they're constantly changing. What works well today for a particular business objective might not work tomorrow. Many personal characteristics evolve over time. Some are fixed, but others variable. Some are objective, but others subjective. And some are personal choices, whilst others are the assessments of others. Identity is a dynamic, personal characteristic. Nobody should ever claim to be able to control it.

How many identities?

And identity is not a single attribute. Everyone has multiple identities, many different roles and persona. You might be an employee, a computer user, a system administrator, a bank customer, a frequent flyer, a passport-carrying national, a taxpayer, a member of a library or a card-carrying member of a political party. The only limit is the size of your wallet for carrying all those identification cards.

Just a decade ago, many people rather simplistically believed that we might all gravitate towards adopting a single, universal electronic identity, perhaps based on a unique digital certificate that would prove absolutely who we are and what we might be entitled to. A credential that could be used to gain access to whatever information we needed, either for work or pleasure. For many years, people actually strived to develop such a universal authentication process, perhaps based on a multi-function, smart card system.

But they were wrong, and it's not hard to see why. They focused on the technology, what could be built and how it might be implemented and used, rather than how people actually went about their business, and the legal and commercial considerations behind everyday decisions on trust and assurance.

It's impossible to imagine a world in which we would trust a bank, for example, to issue or control an identity credential that also controlled our right to vote. Or, in fact, to rely on a government identity card that was needed to gain everyday access to our money and financial transactions. We simply don't have a universally trusted, supreme authority to manage our credentials, one that we would all be comfortable in allowing to see and monitor our transactions, and to decide when our access rights should be withdrawn.

In the absence of any central, trusted authority, the management of identity credentials will remain a highly devolved, fragmented process, though it will always be possible, of course, to adapt common authentication or credential management systems for multiple uses.

But we should never rule out the usefulness of a hierarchical method of managing identity credentials. Often, in practice, it can prove to be a pragmatic solution to many of our requirements. National identity cards, for example, can be useful for providing much of the evidence required to be accepted by an employer for a job, or to open a bank account. A further consideration is the long term impact of emerging, disruptive technologies, such as electronic money or quantum computing.

The latter, for example, might, amongst other things, trigger the breakdown of existing public key cryptographic processes underpinning electronic commerce. Such an event would result in major changes to the way we manage electronic identities. In particular, it might lead to the need for a more hierarchical approach to the management of identity credentials, in order to support alternative, secure solutions.

But one thing is for certain. The future of secure electronic commerce will not look like it does today. The cryptographic systems we use today will not be effective in 20 years. What will replace them? And what are the implications for security? Might we expect the emergence of a new, supreme authority that is able to see, monitor and control all secure transactions? Or, alternatively, will business and citizen concerns press for a solution that further devolves the control of identity credentials into the hands of individual users?

Laws of identity

There is an old axiom of logic called the 'law of identity'. It states that an object is 'the same as itself'. That might seem fairly obvious, but mathematicians and philosophers like to be rigorous about the inferences they draw. In fact, it's such a strange concept that it actually prompted Jonathon Keats, a conceptual artist, to campaign for this law to be made a statutory law in Berkeley, California. His proposed law stated that every entity 'shall be identical to itself' and any entity caught being 'unidentical to itself' was to be subject to a fine of up to one tenth of a cent. It was an amusing example of art imitating life. But the law was not passed.

In fact, in designing identity systems, we've been much less rigorous than our philosophical colleagues. Vendors and service providers have built products and designed grand, global schemes without adequately thinking about the essential rules and principles that are needed to achieve long-lasting solutions that meet real business and consumer needs. The state-of-the-art of both the identity and access management systems is highly immature. In fact, there's a lot wrong with both the products and the way we use them. Too often they offer a poor compromise of real business, security or user needs against what's cheap and easy to develop. We haven't put enough effort into the specification and management of these systems.

In fact, there are many failings in identity management today. In practice, we don't identify people adequately, and we don't restrict their access rights sufficiently. Management of third party users is rarely satisfactory. Many of our identity systems don't scale properly; they become out of control as they evolve. And we rarely manage exceptions adequately. Also, we don't de-register our users promptly, when they no longer require access. And we don't safeguard personal identity information as well as we should. Yet, at the same time, our requirements for extended-enterprise working are becoming richer, more immediate and more complex. Clearly, we urgently need to develop a much better basis for the future.

In fact, it requires a major leap in both vision and capability to deliver the solutions we require. Some vendors are trying. Microsoft, for example, can't resist grand schemes. They've also had their fingers burned in the past, when attempting to build an all-encompassing, global identity scheme, without full consideration of the issues. At the turn of the century, they launched an initiative called Hailstorm, an ambitious attempt to establish Microsoft at the centre of the market in digital information provision.

Hailstorm demanded a high degree of trust, security and confidence by business and citizens. But it was far too ambitious for the time, both in vision and security. And they also misjudged the market. Customer expectations and reactions were very different from what Microsoft had originally envisaged. Hailstorm was quickly abandoned, leaving a still unfilled, major gap in the market for a global, secure identity management system. But every cloud has a silver lining. The consequence of Hailstorm was that some Microsoft engineers began to examine why it might have failed. And one of them, Kit Cameron, believed that, in the process, he had stumbled on some fundamental truths about on-line identity. He decided to publish his version of a set of universal 'Laws of Identity'.

Kit Cameron's work is an interesting mixture of useful ideas, common sense and motherhood. There are, of course, no real, absolute laws of identity. But a set of design principles are a good start. And these laws provide a much-needed, user-centric emphasis, which should help to encourage a more responsible approach to privacy. Kit's work has also achieved a surprising degree of attention from developers, in a field that has been hitherto characterized by a singular lack of imagination and business interest. Kit's laws of identity are as follows:

1. **User Control and Consent:**   Technical identity systems must only reveal information identifying a user with the user's consent

2. **Minimal Disclosure for a Constrained Use:**   The solution which discloses the least amount of identifying information and best limits its use is the most stable long-term solution

3. **Justifiable Parties:**   Digital identity systems must be designed so the disclosure of identifying information is limited to parties having a necessary and justifiable place in a given identity relationship

4. **Directed Identity:**   A universal identity system must support both 'omnidirectional' identifiers for use by public entities and 'unidirectional' identifiers for use by private entities, thus facilitating discovery while preventing unnecessary release of correlation handles

5. **Pluralism of Operators and Technologies:**   A universal identity system must channel and enable the inter-working of multiple identity technologies run by multiple identity providers

6. **Human Integration:**   The universal identity metasystem must define the human user to be a component of the distributed system integrated through unambiguous human–machine communication mechanisms offering protection against identity attacks

7. **Consistent Experience Across Contexts:** The unifying identity metasystem must guarantee its users a simple, consistent experience while enabling separation of contexts through multiple operators and technologies.

Do they work? Are they all sufficient and necessary? I have some doubts. Personally I'm not sure that it's practical to develop a system that prevents governments and employers from accessing user activity without the user's permission. Real life doesn't tend to work like that.

But these laws are a useful selection of good practice design principles, based on many well-established security and data protection practices. They are a good start for any professional designing an identity management system, though, in practice, we'll actually need a much richer set of design principles, to meet the increasingly complex requirements of business, citizens and security managers, operating in an extended enterprise environment, and to overcome the large number of weaknesses in contemporary identity management systems.

Learning from people

So what have we learned from this chapter? We set out to examine the nature of the people who engage in crime and how we might recognize and investigate them. What conclusions have we drawn?

We noted that not everyone is honest, and that many will adjust their behaviour according to the risks of getting caught. It's also clear that everyone is different. But many people who commit fraud and espionage will tend to fit a particular profile. Unfortunately, it's also one that coincides with the profiles of many effective managers inside our organizations.

A basic understanding of psychology helps to understand the criminal mind and the threats and scams they promote. With careful observation of our staff, we could detect many of the warning signs. But it's not that easy, in practice, to catch spies and fraudsters. Even the CIA with all of their security awareness and personnel scrutiny, were unable to detect spies operating within their agency.

In today's empowered business world, countering the insider threat is an increasing challenge. Spies and fraudsters can cause enormous business and political damage, but they're extremely difficult to detect. They might look no different from any upwardly-mobile executive. But new techniques are emerging all the time to draw conclusions about people's behaviour by monitoring their communications. These are promising techniques, which need to be explored. But respecting people's privacy will, of course, be a major and potentially overriding consideration.

Catching crooks in the act is not the only answer. There are other counter-measures that can be deployed to prevent or deter criminal activity. We can, for example, aim to design systems that are intrinsically more secure. We can also vet new staff, and stamp out corruption by tighter organizational controls, and by ensuring that our key staff have more to lose than to gain by taking a bribe. We can also encourage whistle blowing, though that might, in practice, be at the expense of encouraging greater leaks of confidential corporate information. But, whether we like it or not, the business world is becoming more open, transparent and leakier. We have to adapt to that trend.

The human factor will always remain the soft underbelly of our business operations. People are far from perfect. They make mistakes and can be easily fooled or persuaded. And we need to equip them with better tools to enable on-line trust to be more effectively established. But trust is a means to an end. And, as long as there are multiple ends, there will be many different ways of establishing trust and the identities that underpin it. There is no easy route to building a simple, standardized, secure identity system. We can postulate laws of identity, but translating them into action will always be a major challenge.

Here are six learning points to help in managing the insider threat:

- Treat your data like hard cash – it's a valuable asset
- Accept that a proportion of staff will steal from you
- Don't expect to be able to recognize crooks by their appearance; they might be your colleagues or management
- Aim to build systems and office environments that deter theft and fraud
- Be consistent in investigating and prosecuting fraud to act as a deterrent
- Don't leave any scope for staff to justify their illegal or inappropriate actions

---

Managing organization culture and politics

When worlds collide

What is 'organization culture'? What do we mean by this rather abstract and all-embracing expression? And why is it so important to understand and manage it? Getting to grips with organization culture is essential for all information security professionals. We need to understand and be able to influence organization culture if we are to achieve any significant improvement in user security behaviour. In particular, we need to develop and embed a healthy culture of secure information management.

But what do we mean by a healthy security culture? Is it about encouraging fear and paranoia in your staff, or is it more about trust and empowerment of people? The answer is, in fact, all of those things and more. Fear can work, to some extent, in most environments. But trust and education will work better in all of them.

Business objectives and security cultures also need to be aligned, as far as we possibly can. Sometimes they're incompatible. That can be frustrating, but it's nothing unusual. Business is full of contradictions. It's just one of the realities that modern managers have to live with. In such cases, we simply have to learn to focus on the most important factor of the day, whilst at the same time ensuring that we do the least damage to any other conflicting interests. And often that means, not just striking a balance, but developing a more sophisticated solution that can cope with a broader spectrum of demands.

We might, for example, have a business that handles confidential information, but needs to foster a greater degree of openness and sharing to better meet its business objectives. Encouraging a state of security paranoia will not be productive for that environment. But promoting a culture of openness will also

Managing the Human Factor in Information Security   David Lacey
© 2009 John Wiley & Sons, Ltd

present dangers. Instead, we will need to foster a smarter style of security culture, one that is trusting and empowered, but, at the same time, can recognize the associated risks, and is able to discriminate between different requirements for information sharing. That might sound easy, but it's very difficult to achieve in practice. It can, however, be done, with sufficient, smart effort.

And no two organizations are the same. They might share common challenges, of course, but each enterprise will have its own, unique perspective on business and security. Understanding common issues and solutions, while at the same time respecting individual, local needs, is the key to a successful enterprise change program.

This chapter examines many of the characteristics of organization culture and office politics that we can expect to encounter, across the global landscape of enterprises, countries and communities. And it sets out some universal principles that can provide the essential foundation for building an effective information security organization, as well as a successful, enterprise-wide change program.

What is organization culture?

I've always been fascinated by organization culture. It's a surprisingly powerful influence on employee perception, attitude and behaviour. Yet it's not an easily defined or static characteristic of any enterprise. It's more of an elusive, evolving phenomenon. Not everyone sees it, appreciates it or automatically becomes part of it. And new aspects of culture continually emerge and evolve, often combining in quite unpredictable ways, creating varying influences across different groups of employees.

One reason for this volatility is the accelerating rate of restructuring and staff turnover, which generates successive vintages of attitude and experience. Many banks, for example, have cultures shaped by progressive waves of intake of teams from outside companies, brought in, for example, whenever a new line of products is needed. For a brief period, these newcomers might trigger a new fashion in thinking and behaviour. But it never stands still.

Globalization has also had a major impact on organization culture. Many years ago, each country tended to run its own business operations in its own distinct style, even within international organizations. Centralization of operations, supported by digital networks, have since enabled global lines of business to be supported, introducing a massive change in working attitudes, relationships and methods.

A new factor that is now beginning to shape contemporary organization culture is the increasing influence of the external interactions of staff, through private clubs and social networks. These invite a fresh perspective on thinking, and, at the same time they replace local interactions with nearby colleagues. People have less time today to mix with colleagues in the next room, or even those across the desk. The office is becoming more anonymous. Responses to new issues are now often shaped more by external conversations, than by internal debate.

No organization culture is likely to maintain its dominance over the longer term. But they can certainly last long enough to remain as an important factor, a blocker or an enabler for the successful execution of any security program. It's essential, therefore, to understand the nature of this phenomenon.

Many different descriptions have been put forward to define what exactly we mean by organization culture. Each tends to have a different viewpoint. We can, for example, choose to define it in terms of what it encompasses:

> *'The attitudes, values, beliefs, norms and customs of the organization.'*

That certainly nails down its scope. But it tells us little about what it might look like, or how it came to be.

Another way of looking at organization culture is to think of it in terms of how it might have evolved, where it came from. One definition suggests, for example, that it might be:

> *'The result of conversations and negotiations between members.'*

or

> *'A pattern of basic assumptions that has worked well enough to be considered valid.'*

These statements provide a more useful perspective, because they suggest where we might look, in order to understand how we might go about influencing it, for example, by aiming to shape discussions across social networks.

Another approach, which is useful if we wish to capture, define or communicate the key characteristics of corporate culture, is to consider a comparison with everyday things that we already understand, by, for example, asking a question such as:

> *'If the organization was an animal which one might it be?'*

This is a simple but powerful vehicle for conveying the agreed, preferred perception of the organization culture to a newcomer or outsider. It's not difficult to grasp, for example, the arrogant style of a lion, the innocent nature of a lamb or perhaps the cunning behaviour of a fox.

Out of all the numerous descriptions of organizational culture, the one that I like best is:

> *'Organization culture is what people do when you're not watching them.'*

And there's a lot of truth to this. It reflects how people will tend to behave in the absence of corporate oversight, the true, natural, subconscious culture that's evolved from the environment, instincts and circumstances of staff. If we can understand this, we will have a better idea of what people would do if we were to remove management controls, and how they might aspire to behave if we were to truly empower and trust them.

But a large part of organization culture will always remain hidden from the management and staff themselves. We're often blind to the views and habits we've acquired over the years working for an organization. A colleague of mine once summed up this phenomenon as:

'Organization culture is the insanity you can't see around you.'

And that's much truer than we all realize. A major strand of the real culture that differentiates any organization is the sum of the local practices that people have absorbed, often against their initial, better judgment.

Organization culture is often an insidious, corrupting influence. We can try to resist it, but it will slowly creep into our thinking and lifestyle, shaping us into a different person, a corporate animal that adopts thoughts and behaviour that we'd never have otherwise embraced.

You can see a classic example of this process in 2006 film *The Devil Wears Prada*, the story of an intelligent girl who changes into a star-struck, fashion victim, as a result of psychological bullying, coupled with glamorous rewards for conformance. Geraint Anderson's 2008 book *Cityboy: Beer and Loathing in the Square Mile* illustrates a similar story of how a bright young graduate, the son of a Labour peer and a missionary can be sucked into an unsavoury, hedonistic culture, against his natural instincts. As he puts it:

'I always had this nagging doubt at the back of my mind that what I was doing was somehow wrong, and that I was part of a system that was making things worse.'

The real organization culture is shaped by this madness that we can no longer see, because we've rationalized it away in order to survive or succeed in an environment that rewards a different set of qualities from the ones we would choose ourselves. Authority and peer pressure are powerful factors. Perceived rewards are even stronger. And the combination of both is impossible to resist.

Organizations are different

John Meakin, Group Head of Information Security for Standard Chartered Bank, has lengthy experience of managing security across diverse communities. I asked him for his views on security culture and how it changes across communities:

> *'There are two aspects of information security and culture. The first is the very desirable 'security culture' that we all aspire to inculcate in our organization, whereby staff and customers take systems security seriously, follow instructions, adhere to controls, and look out for breaches. It's a great ideal and very difficult to achieve, but it's possible by alignment of security mechanisms and goals with business goals, and continuing, persistent communications and education. Then there is human cultural variety, between nations and geographies, and the way in which it makes life difficult. I have seen two different cultural groups within security teams take exactly the same policy, technology and processes, and one succeed in making systems more secure, while the other succeeds in making them less secure, because different cultural norms have led people to misinterpret and mis-implement the security. Maybe a one-size-fits-all approach to security technology and process isn't right.'*

Every organization is characterized by its own unique blend of culture, risk profile and governance processes. Differences can also often be found within the same organization, between remote offices, sites or business units. Things that we might take for granted, such as humour, style, decision-making and perception of risks can vary greatly across enterprises, as well across countries, cultures and communities.

To be effective in managing people and relationships, we need to be able to adapt our presentation style, our marketing techniques and our methods of governance. For maximum impact, they will need to be tailored to suit each enterprise or local environment. Some themes might be universally successful. Though it's rare to find a single approach that works best in every organization or circumstance. Be suspicious of consultants that tell you otherwise.

But there are universal solutions. Standards can be made adaptable, for example. That might sound contradictory, but it's true. Codes of practice, such as the international standard ISO27001, are designed to work well in many circumstances. They're deliberately designed that way. Codes of practice are very different from conformance standards, as they allow flexibility in the interpretation of the content. Regulatory compliance is also becoming increasingly standardized and globalized, though specific legislation can vary widely from state to state.

Psychological principles for behaviour change are also universally applicable, though specific solutions will need to be adapted to the local environment. And the needs of people for security education and awareness are similar, though the content and the most effective communication style will be quite different across different cultures. In fact, the aspirations and targets for information security will also be quite common across most organizations, but they will all have varying levels of maturity in their information security practices, and quite different priorities for their security programs.

Organizations might be very different, even between departments and sites, but many of the fundamental principles and methods we need to apply are quite similar. They just need to be adapted appropriately to the local environment. The smart, experienced security professional will take proven methods and best practices developed outside the organization, and then adapt them to an internal, long-range information security program, that's tailored to the local risk profile, the level of security maturity, the local culture, its governance style and, of course, the size of the budget and resources available.

Organizing for security

When it comes to organization structures, it's also very clear that one size does not fit all. Few organizations share the same legacy, objectives, context or degree of information security maturity. We might have common standards, technology and compliance demands. But it's a different matter when it comes to organization structures.

I've helped to design many organization structures for IT and security functions and I can assure you that there is no universal structure that is right for all organizations, or even a single structure that will work for one enterprise in all circumstances or occasions.

All modern organizations structures are temporary ones to satisfy current objective and budget limits. They are not designed to last indefinitely, or be duplicated across enterprises. The optimum shape will depend on many factors, including the nature of the business challenges, the structure of the enterprise, the maturity of the security function, the experience of the staff, the nature of its business relationships and the organization of other business and supporting functions.

The most important starting point is to consider the current position and direction of the continuing 'pendulum swing' between centralization and decentralization of business and support functions. This is an inevitable feature of every organization, which, at any point in time, will tend to favour one of these options more than the other, as the perceived advantages and drawbacks fade or grow in a complementary fashion.

Centralized functions are much more efficient. They have lower costs, they're generally better structured and they're more able to exploit the sharing of specialist skills. But over time, they become out-of-touch with local business problems, resulting in increasingly strained business relationships and detached policy-making. There's a tendency for centralized functions to become progressively arrogant, out-of-touch and disliked by business units.

In contrast, devolved functions are more expensive, generally several times the cost of a central function, but they are closer to the heart of each business unit, and they can maintain better relationships and stronger influence with local business managers. Over time, however, they will tend to become more detached from the centre, less cooperative with corporate initiatives and there might be growing political in-fighting and diversity of standards.

Tackling 'localitis'

Most security managers assigned to a remote business unit will progressively 'go native', and become more accommodating towards immediate, local business interests, sometimes to the detriment of the longer-term interests of the enterprise.

This phenomenon is well understood in the diplomatic world. It's been termed 'localitis'.

It's always been the case that when diplomats are assigned to a particular country, they tend to become supportive of the local interest. Regular postings to the same location reinforce this influence. That's why it's a good idea to occasionally rearrange your diplomats. Henry Kissenger did this to good effect in the State Department in the early 1970s, assigning arabists to Israel, and vice versa. It's a useful trick to help eliminate bias and broaden people's perspectives.

A further factor in designing an organization is the balance of needs between long-term, global objectives and short-term local business pressures. Which is most important for addressing the organization's current priorities? Is it the need to build a solid corporate strategy and join up individual business unit practices? Or is the need for better security outreach and business relationships?

Many organizations aim to get the best of both worlds by establishing a central corporate policy unit, as well as a strategic steering committee of representatives from business units, to oversee enterprise initiatives. This might seem a neat solution. But the reality is less tidy.

Major rifts will quickly open up between the dictatorial approach of the central policy unit and the selfish interests of business unit representatives. In practice, the latter will often collaborate privately to agree and decide the outcome of future debates. They always have this power, as there are generally more of them: they can outvote the central unit.

The central unit, however, can seek the support of the CEO on big ticket issues. It's a card they need to play selectively, one to keep firmly up their sleeves until a major enterprise objective is under threat. In practice, the outcome is often a paralysis of strategic decision-making. Sometimes an impasse is reached. Independent consultants might need to be brought in to referee. If nothing else, they will have the unintended side effect of uniting the in-house executives against a common, external adversary.

Devolved security functions will always present a management challenge for any organization bent on driving through major changes, such as a common architecture, infrastructure or set of central services. But, on the positive side, devolved teams are smaller. And size often matters. In fact, the number of people in an organizational unit can make a surprising amount of difference to its effectiveness.

Small is beautiful

In the words of the British economist, E.F. Schumacher, who worked with the legendary J.M Keynes:

> *'Man is small, and, therefore, small is beautiful.'*

Schumacher's point was that workplaces should be dignified and meaningful rather than merely efficient. But it's not just efficiency that appears to grow with size. Complexity will also increase. And, as we saw in Chapter 1, the total number of relationships in a network grows exponentially, just like the champagne glass clinks at celebrations that quickly get out of hand when a large group is present. This makes large functions unwieldy to manage without a strict hierarchy of control.

In fact, it's interesting to note how the complexity presented by relationships grows with increasing team size. When you operate by yourself, you can be surprisingly efficient. If you decide to team up with a few others, the level of productivity can actually fall significantly, as communications overheads grow and responsibilities overlap. It's often a case of one and one equalling much less than two.

As teams grow and the work becomes more structured, they will become more efficient, as the benefits of structure and specialization begin to take effect. But at a certain point the group will become too large and complex to manage effectively. In fact, there appears to be a natural limit at around 150 people. Up to this point, relationships are reasonably manageable. People know each other's names. The unit can be comfortable, aligned and productive. Above this limit, things start to break down. People become divided. Management loses control, and an anonymous culture begins to set in.

Some companies, such as Gore Associates, a private company that prizes its culture and ways of working, and has been profitable for several decades, maintains a strict limit on the size of its plants: no more than the magic limit of 150. Start-up companies also experience the effects of growth, as they grow quickly from a small partnership to an extended family, then to a tribe, and then a faceless community. At each stage there is a substantial change in the culture of the organization, the structure of the enterprise and the complexity of the relationships.

The same considerations exist when a large organization decides to outsource its operations. Staff numbers for a particular function, such as IT, can drop from several thousand to a few hundred. The culture changes significantly. Suddenly, all knowledge at the strategic management level becomes available to everyone, but deeper knowledge of front-line business operations ceases. In effect, the traditional, vertical information flows have been replaced by horizontal ones.

Outsourcing provides a timely wake-up call to the new, networked business environment that's progressively coming everyone's way, as electronic business moves into shared services in 'the cloud'. In the future we will have much less hands-on control and knowledge of our business operations, relying more on the intelligence we can gather from networks, and from friends of our friends, rather than from subordinates. We will need to change the direction of our attention, from downwards and inwards, to sideways and outwards.

In search of professionalism

We discussed earlier that organization structures are short-term decisions. In practice, they rarely survive more than 18 months. That's because of the constant business restructuring that modern business generates, for one reason or another.

Many security managers regard restructuring as an irritating distraction. And that's certainly true. But there is a positive side. It enables us to make regular adjustments to the 'pendulum swing'. And, perhaps more significantly, it also opens up opportunities for career development.

Professional development of staff should, in fact, be a major, longer-term goal and consideration. There simply aren't enough existing or emerging security experts in the field. And the subject is getting progressively more complex. If we don't take action to develop our staff, we're all heading for a major crisis.

In fact, I can't stress enough the importance of professional development for information security practitioners. I use the word practitioners, rather than professionals, because not every practitioner is a professional, and it's not just security managers that need training and development. It's equally important to arrange for the education of all managers with responsibility for information security activities.

You can't leave it to chance or 'serendipity'. As the late George van Eps, a legendary jazz guitarist, put it:

> *'Luck won't do it, and ignorance can't.'*

Education and practice are the keys to success in any field that requires specialist knowledge and skills. But, unfortunately, we have nowhere near enough professional information security training available to meet current demands, never mind future requirements. The capacity of university courses in the subject is very limited. We can anticipate a growing skills shortage.

And the standards required to deliver professional information security services are not entirely clear. It's still very much an emerging subject. Most of the leading professionals in the field are self-taught. I'm one of them myself, as Fred Piper regularly points out: totally unqualified, though regarded by some as an expert. Am I a consummate professional or a charlatan? It's your choice.

And that's because in the past there was no established body of knowledge or professional training. Yet, today, the scope of the subject is huge, encompassing many niche areas, each worthy of an individual course in themselves. There are many schemes to award certificates to people, by applying various criteria, such as multiple-choice examinations or interviews. Personally, I'm not a great fan of qualifications, though I was a founding director of the UK Institute of Information Security Professionals. To me, it's the training and the experience, rather than the qualifications, that really counts.

I believe we need to put more people on Master of Science or post-graduate Diploma courses in information security, or arrange an equivalent level of professional training. In fact, that's the first thing I did after joining the Royal Mail Group. I arranged for all staff with full-time or part-time responsibility for information security to be professionally trained by experienced Royal Holloway University of London (RHUL) lecturers. In my view, RHUL were the best source of professional education at that time, and they remain the very best today.

Such programs of training are expensive, upfront investments, but they deliver tremendous value by enhancing the quality, effectiveness and productivity of the information security function. They also deliver substantial cost reductions by removing the company's dependency on expensive external consultants. Within two years, my team had been able to achieve a large-scale accredited certification, and had reduced security incident levels significantly. Five years later, the team collected the *SC Magazine* European Award for 'Best Security Team'.

There is no substitute for training. Certificates, qualifications and mentoring schemes are little more than the icing on the cake. None of them can make a real difference without the underpinning professional education.

Developing careers

Despite our best efforts, there will continue to be a growing shortage of skilled, experienced information security professionals. That's very easy to predict, because there is simply not enough investment in training, and the numbers of experts demanded by organizations, including vendors, consultants and small and medium enterprises, is continuing to grow.

Two decades ago, only a handful of large or specialist enterprises bothered to employ a specialist. Today, almost every medium and large organization needs one or more full-time professionals.

Now, if you happen to be a wealthy investment bank that's prepared to pay top-dollar salaries to attract the best talent, then you can easily look to the market to recruit the specialists you need, at any time, to meet your current or emerging requirements for information security expertise. But if you're an average organization that's likely to lag behind the leaders in the emerging talent wars, then you should seriously think about investing in the development of your existing staff.

The shape of your organization design needs to take account of the skills and experience you have available. Not only will that shape the quality of the services you are able to deliver, it will also have a major impact on the development of your professional staff.

In the early years of my time at Royal Mail Group, for example, we initially structured the information security function into multiple specialist central units. This enabled the business to make the very best use of the scarce skills available. I didn't, for example, want to waste valuable technical expertise on generalist activities. And at the same time, I didn't wish to assign well-rounded, generalist staff to technical duties that were outside their experience.

That approach enabled a body of specialist knowledge and methods to be developed by each individual unit, as well as delivering the best possible portfolio of professional services to the business.

At a later stage, when my staff were better trained and had a more substantial base of standards and methods to support them, it made sense to develop the specialist practitioners into broader security roles, enabling the organization to reap more from their growing capabilities, as well as encouraging each individual to develop a broader set of skills.

Information security roles today are a mixture of generalist skills and specialist knowledge. I believe it's useful to develop what I'd term a 'job family', a collection of consistent job descriptions underpinned by standards for skills at varying levels, in order to provide a clear development path for practitioners, and to serve as both a benchmark for their capabilities and a measure of their progress.

Skills for information security

Identifying skills for selecting new recruits is always a major challenge. The range of information security requirements, short term and longer term, is becoming numerous and varied. Which set of skills should we actually look for?

The first instinct is to focus on the skills needed for immediate tasks. But it can be dangerous to place too much reliance on, say, the technical skills that are needed to support a current technology or architecture. Demands for technical skills will come and go. Applied skills, such as project management skills, are much longer lasting.

Technical and applied competencies are generally learned through short training courses. It's not very difficult for people to acquire them. It's far better, in fact, to focus on the skills that we can't easily develop in our staff through normal development options.

Take behavioural competencies, for example, such as relationship management, which are generally learned through life experiences. And these are often more useful to possess in the longer term, as they dictate how well people can actually apply their acquired technical skills.

Cognitive skills, such as problem solving, are even harder to acquire, perhaps impossible, in fact, for some individuals. These competencies are much more of an innate ability, the skills that our parents tell us we were born with, or have acquired over a long period of time. Unfortunately, the behavioural and cognitive skills that we need to carry out many information security roles have yet to be generally recognized or agreed.

But there are many such skills that are clearly desirable. For example, it's likely that the ideal information security practitioner would, for example:

- Pay attention to detail: because security is only as good as the weakest link in the chain, so a good eye for detail can help spot potential exposures

- Be convincing: to ensure that their recommendations are accepted by managers and colleagues

- Be solution-oriented: by focusing on practical solutions, rather than get bogged down by specific problems

- Demonstrate integrity: in order to gain and retain the trust and confidence of managers and colleagues

- Be challenging: to encourage change to existing working practices that might present potential security exposures

- Be realistic: by not setting unrealistic targets or expectations that are unlikely to be met

- Be curious: to investigate beneath the surface of a problem, especially when investigating an incident

- Have good pattern recognition: in order to spot trends and anomalies that might indicate a potential security breach

- Apply systems thinking: to understand and develop the architectural solutions needed for complex, networked infrastructures

When we look at such a demanding list, it might seem unlikely that an information security practitioner would possess, or even be able to develop all of these skills. But an ambitious wish-list can provide the starting point and serve as a potential yardstick for assessing the suitability of staff for a longer-term career in information security.

Information skills

One thing that's always fascinated me is the large difference in what I'd call 'information skills' that clearly exists between different business communities, even though they might have recruited their members from a similar educational background.

I first noticed this when I left the British Foreign and Commonwealth Office to work for the Royal Dutch/Shell Group. At the FCO, the standard of reading, writing and information management was extremely high. Each day, hundreds of incoming telegrams from overseas posts would be examined, copied and distributed across the office to desk officers, who would scan them, research their background, draft a response, clear them across Whitehall and then dispatch them, often with copies sent out to hundreds of recipients for information.

Not only were the documents concise, accurate and agreed. They were also well-crafted, with an appropriate degree of negotiated Whitehall spin skilfully applied. All of this took place within hours of the incoming telegrams being received. The Foreign Office desk officers were also hungry for background information, whether in the form of dispatches, speeches, intelligence, press cuttings, news wire services or just copies of other people's telegrams. Information overload was not a major issue for them, because they had mastered the art of scanning and speed-reading documents.

In contrast, the executives at Shell were much more selective about their reading material. They were slower to draft and agree formal responses, generally preferring the phone to the keyboard. They complained about having their in-trays filled with background information that did not demand immediate actions. They paid less attention to the management of their personal correspondence, and were reluctant to share knowledge with their colleagues. But they cut great commercial deals.

During the 1990s, when knowledge management became a business priority at Shell, I invited the Head of Library and Records from the Foreign and Commonwealth Office to brief a group of Shell executives, who were interested in improving the Group's knowledge management capabilities. The Shell executives were impressed and surprised by the Foreign Office skills and achievements. The key question they asked was how the FCO had achieved such a high standard of information handling? What was the motivation for staff to behave that way? Both sets of staff were equally bright and educated: graduates of equal calibre from similar universities. And there were no financial incentives or other obvious rewards.

The answer was that the secret was in the FCO culture. People take many cues for their everyday behaviour from their peers, as well as their environment. The Diplomatic Service has evolved to be a well-oiled, information machine, operating in a fast-moving political world. A week can be a long time in politics. But a day is a long time for the Foreign Office.

In contrast, the Shell Group is an engineering and production company, investing in long-term ventures that might not deliver a return on investment for several decades. Each perspective reinforces a particular set of attitudes and behaviour towards information. The skills developed by their staff flow from this.

The legendary IBM president Tom Watson Senior used the slogan 'THINK' to encourage his staff to focus their minds on solving the big issues. Every office had a sign on the desk. It was also reproduced in the lobby of IBM headquarters and spelled out in flowers, fifteen feet long, in the company grounds at Endicott. That might sound a little extreme, but there's a lot to be said for such a philosophy. If you're making long-term business decisions, such as where to build a new manufacturing plant, it certainly helps to focus your executives' minds and free them from unnecessary distractions.

Today, our information skills and communications channels have moved on quite a bit. Text-messaging and an ability to multi–task provide the answer to the increasing demands for faster, remote collaboration. In fact, I'm highly impressed with the rapid communications skills of young, 'Generation Y' people. We can learn a lot from their attitude and their style. They are already much better equipped to cope with a faster moving environment, characterized by high volumes of shorter messages.

Young people think and behave differently. They are more comfortable with multi-tasking and multi-media. They can manage dozens of user accounts. And they think differently about security. If they forget their password, they create another account. If they lose their address book, they ask their friends to help them recreate it. They look outwards, more than inwards for direction. They absorb analogue media immediately, rather than slowly grasping the intricacies of prose. It's a different, not necessarily a better, way of working. And it can create bad habits. You can't, for example, keep creating new accounts for a major business system. But the mindset is more in keeping with the dynamic, networked environment of the future.

The down side, however, is that this way of working is not necessarily any more productive. In fact, in many ways, it's probably a lot less efficient. Multi-tasking is not simultaneous processing. It's a rapid switch of attention between multiple activities. That can slow you down in carrying out any task. Interruptions and distractions now take up a major part of a knowledge worker's time. E-mails, texts and phone calls can hinder the completion of longer, more important tasks.

Young people might also be losing their ability to concentrate. We don't yet know the longer-term effects from a lifestyle of continual interruptions. But it's certainly more stressful. And it's getting harder to find a young person with the patience and concentration to read a novel such as *War and Peace*.

We need to ensure our team members are equipped with the skills required to surf, sift, speed-read, send and spin information. These are all essential capabilities for a contemporary information security practitioner. But such skills are more a matter of training, attitude and practice, rather than innate capabilities. And that means cultivating an environment and a culture that encourages the development of these skills. But it's important also to retain an ability to concentrate attention on the single, hard security problems that we are increasingly likely to face in the future. And that means regular planning sessions away from the everyday distractions of the modern office environment.

Survival skills

You might believe that you possess all of the key technical and cognitive skills needed to be the perfect information security professional. But you'll never make a chief information security officer unless you also have the necessary political survival skills.

As people progress through an organization, they will generally go through several distinct stages, each of which challenges them in new, very different ways that often surprise them. Previous jobs, in fact, rarely prepare people for the challenges that lie ahead.

When we first start out in a job, for example, we're given simple, though perhaps challenging, tasks to do. And if we turn out to be good at doing them, then we might be selected for a promotion, or headhunted for a new job. At that point, the job will change dramatically. We will no longer be required to carry out the tasks we were originally trained to do. We'll be given the completely different role of supervising other people.

And not everyone is comfortable with the role of managing other people. It can be a shock at first. But if we manage to crack it, and, at the same time, impress our management, we might even gain a further promotion. This time, however, we'll enter the more surreal realm of middle management. And no matter how effective a supervisor we might have been, to survive middle management requires an entirely different set of skills. We need the ability to recognize and navigate successfully through the maze and the hazards of local office politics, where budgets are fought over, and where back-stabbing, ingratiation and empire building are commonplace tactics.

The secret of surviving this stage, and moving up to higher things, is to develop a good political antenna, the ability to understand what motivates other managers, where they're coming from, where they want to go and how they intend to get there. Only then can we gain an insight into their likely tactics and actions, and to form an idea of how likely they are to succeed.

And, if we can navigate successfully through this labyrinth of politics, then we might rise to an even headier level, one where everything is different yet again. At this more senior level, it's not so much our ability to survive the political infighting that counts. It's our ability to breeze into a boardroom, and convince the managing directors to support our proposals. And that demands a different set of skills: to be a convincing, compelling and likeable communicator, a smooth operator rather than a streetwise, backstreet fighter.

Navigating the political minefield

They say it gets easy when you get to the top. That's probably true. But getting there can be a rough, tough process. Navigating through the political minefield is a hazard most of us would prefer to avoid. But it's an inevitable part of corporate life. And it can't be eliminated, at least, not from the top. I've encountered many managing directors who've declared war on office politics. Their efforts made absolutely no difference.

I was interested to read a recent *Computer Weekly* survey which asked readers to vote on 'How do you get a well paid job in IT?' The answers were: Promote yourself: 30%; Suck up to the boss: 45%; Nose to the grindstone: 25%. Now this was clearly designed and treated as a joke. But there is a large element of truth in the results.

It's important for any security professional aiming to change an organization to understand, accept and navigate its politics. Each year, I give a lecture to post-graduates at Royal Holloway University of London. The most common question I'm asked by the students is:

> *'What is it that makes a successful chief information security officer?'*

My answer is very simple, though it often comes as a surprise to many students:

> *'It's not technical ability, performance or track record. It's presentation and political skills.'*

The fact is that you can only get the very top jobs if you have an ability to impress managing directors, CIOs, HR advisers and headhunters. But getting the job is only the beginning. You will also need a range of political skills to survive the corporate jungle. Engaging in corporate politics is about developing your own personal agenda, forming alliances, cutting deals and scoring points over colleagues. Unfortunately, that's largely what's known as a 'zero-sum' game: you will either win or lose. But the prize is worth fighting for, as it's likely to be a much bigger budget, headcount, salary or bonus.

You can, of course, choose not to play the political game. And that option might seem, at first sight, to be a sensible one. But other managers will not see it that way. They'll assume that you're engaged in politics. If you're not playing the usual games, they're likely to assume that you have a hidden agenda behind your innocent actions. They will interpret instinctive reactions as carefully planned tactics. Whether you like it or not, when you're in a middle or senior management role, you're automatically playing a competitive, zero-sum game.

Interestingly, research into the economics of happiness, an increasingly significant area of economics, indicates that we'd all be much happier if we stopped playing these political games. We'd all be much happier if we worked fewer hours, travelled less and carried out more acts of kindness. But such a change in perception is unlikely to transpire. It's a sad fact of life that, unfortunately, virtually all individuals have a fierce, competitive instinct to keep up with, or do better than, their peers. It's hard to resist. I admire anyone who can rise above it.

To succeed, we have no choice but to accept office politics as the natural backdrop to corporate life. We might elect to join in, or to stay apart, but either way, we have to get to grips with it. We have to understand and manage this phenomenon. And we have to adapt our strategies to take account of it. Playing the political game is not like a game of chess. It's much less predictable. There are more players, and they generally tend to base their moves on gut feelings, rather than logic.

Robina Chatham has been researching organizational politics at Cranfield School of Management. She believes that integrity and political awareness are the primary dimensions of interest. If, for example, you construct a 2 × 2 matrix based on these dimensions, you will get four quadrants, representing four different personality types, in the classic Jung tradition. As mentioned in the last chapter, Robina uses the analogy of animals to illustrate four different political animals, based on each quadrant of this matrix. The 'sheep' is the executive with high integrity but low awareness: behaving correctly but not really having a clue about what's really going on. The 'fox' represents the opposite quadrant, characterized by low integrity and high political awareness: selfish, charming and manipulative. The 'baboon' is the quadrant that's low on both counts: emotionally illiterate and powerless. And the 'dolphin' is the one we should all aspire to be, at the top right corner of the matrix: politically astute and always acting with integrity.

Personally, I've always found that a thick skin and a good sense of humour are the most important requirements to ensure long-term survival in a contemporary, large business organization. Logic, commonsense and hard work are not the critical success factors for a successful career. We might not like it that way. But that's the way it turns out and, unfortunately, always will be.

Square pegs and round holes

As we saw in the last chapter, many organizations like to employ the Myers–Briggs indicators as a convenient measure of people's preferred inclinations. Regardless of their theoretical shortcomings, they can also serve as a useful starting point for determining the most appropriate choice of roles within an information security function.

The key concept of the Myers–Briggs rating system is to assess people according to four dimensions, or scales, measuring whether a person is extrovert or introvert, sensing or intuitive, thinking or feeling, judging or perceiving. That gives 16 different personality types, which suggest the defining characteristics of an individual.

As we saw in the last chapter, each Myers–Briggs indicator is referred to by a combination of four initials representing the dominant trait, for example E or I in the first initial position would represent extrovert or introvert. And each of the 16 personality types has a well-established description that we can try to match to a particular role in an organization.

For example, we might consider the following matches:

- INTJ for a strategist
- ENTJ for a security project director
- ENTP for a security researcher
- INFJ for a security policy developer
- ISTP, ISFP or INTP for security architects
- ESTP or ENFP for security 'evangelists'
- ENFJ for a security awareness trainer
- INFP, ESFP or ESFJ for security relationship managers
- ISFJ and ESTJ for general security managers
- ISTJ for an auditor.

These indicators will, of course, tell you absolutely nothing about whether people will actually be any good at, or even want to carry out these roles. They also say nothing about personal preferences, experience and, most importantly, track record. But, in the absence of anything better, they can provide a helpful starting point for matching the people you have available to the roles you need to fill.

What's in a name?

As Shakespeare put it:

> 'Tis but thy name that is my enemy.'

And the same often applies to many professionals operating in the information security field. Job titles, and the overlapping responsibilities they encompass, have been evolving in a convoluted fashion, driven by frequent corporate restructures. It's now got to point where it's not clear to the rest of the organization just who does what in the information security function, and where they should be directing their enquiries.

These days, you can choose from a broad selection of possible labels, such as 'information security', 'information risk' or 'information assurance', to describe a similar set of activities. You can also adopt labels that cover related business subjects, such as 'privacy' or 'compliance'. And you can even attempt to combine them as 'governance, risk and compliance' or GRC for short. The key questions are what you choose, and why you might select them.

Behind the scenes, these job titles or department names have become an umbrella for quite similar activities. But the labels convey very different meanings to other people. To most ordinary business managers, the word 'security' conjures up an image of a security guard stopping you from doing something. The word 'privacy', on the other hand, sounds as though it's connected with protecting the civil rights of individuals. The word 'risk' generally comes across as something to do with the protection of investments, perhaps a form of insurance. The word 'compliance' evokes an image of someone with a clipboard, who comes around once a year and points out things that you've forgotten to do. And the word 'assurance' sounds like it's something to do with quality management.

In the mid 1990s, Shell decided to be forward looking and briefly rebranded it's information security committee as 'Shell Trust'. It was highly confusing for business people. They thought we were responsible for managing the pension fund or some other investments. We quickly reverted back to using the word security.

And, of course, none of these terms sound remotely technical, unless we add a prefix such as 'electronic' or 'digital' which can transform an otherwise dull sounding function into one that might seem cutting-edge and glamorous. 'Electronic security', for example, is an exciting sounding description that invokes images of spies and eavesdroppers, equipped with the latest electronic gadgets. 'Digital risk' comes across as a fashionable new management function.

We also tend to adopt misleading qualifiers. We call people 'managers' when they control no staff or resources, and 'advisers' when we'd really like them to take the decisions. 'Architect' is also becoming more commonplace, though it's hard to imagine what a business manager would make of it, as there is nothing in information security that remotely resembles a physical building design. 'Evangelist' sounds like someone to be avoided, perhaps a salesperson or a fanatic.

'Chief information security officer' or CISO seems to be the top job title to which most professionals aspire, though it will mean very little to a business manager or member of staff. There is also a growing number of related titles such as 'chief privacy officer', which generally suggests a lawyer rather than technologist, or 'chief risk officer' which, in many industries, might come across as a health and safety specialist.

Job titles should be selected with great care, because they help outsiders understand the function that a professional is there to perform. 'Security' has always worked reasonably well because it's largely self-explanatory. We all know what to expect. I'm much less impressed with the growing fashion in the public sector for the US term 'information assurance'. Its scope is not obvious to a lay person. And it suggests additional skills, not usually found in the security function, such as information management. When did you last meet a security professional who was proficient in taxonomies? The word 'assurance' also lacks the authority of 'security'. If I tell a manager he'd better do something because it's necessary for security, he'll take it seriously. If I say it's for assurance, it sounds less compelling.

Job titles are also important for enhancing people's self-esteem, and demon-strating their level of professional development. Important sounding titles are useful for enhancing staff CVs. At first sight, it might appear to cost nothing to allow somebody to adopt a grand-sounding title. But it will influence future benchmarking exercises and can leverage staff claims for promotions to higher salaries. Job titles should never be plucked out of the blue because they convey authority and competence, and they drive expectations for career development and salaries.

Managing relationships

We might possess the highest level of technical expertise in the world. But it does not matter a jot if good relationships with business managers and other key stakeholders cannot be created and maintained.

In theory, security managers should be good at this. After all, to survive in the security world, we have always needed to network with other security managers to gain privileged knowledge about recent incidents and emerging security threats. But in the business world, we also need to connect with business managers, customers and colleagues to ensure they fully understand and will respond to our initiatives.

Relationship management is, in fact, a well-understood, long-practiced art. Diplomats and salesmen have been doing it for thousands of years. There are long-established principles for building good relationships. Every information security manager should study them.

The fundamental learning point in managing any relationship is to recognize that other people are less interested in you than they are in themselves. Telling them about our own achievements does not create a great impression. But asking them about their own interests, issues and achievements will make you very popular. And finding out about what business managers and IT managers are getting up to is very useful intelligence for any information security manager.

It's helpful to ask a business manager, for example, to explain how his business works, what problems he faces, and what he hopes to achieve. That's exactly the sort of information you will need to do your own job. And if you can also show some interest in their extra mural interests, then there's a good chance that you will form a useful bond with them, instantly raising your chances of obtaining their future cooperation.

Your style and presentation will also make a difference. Most people respond very well to simple things, such as a pleasant, polite introduction and a smile. Threats and criticism are not an effective basis for influencing people. They will cause the other person to become defensive and less cooperative.

But humour can help to win friends, if used tactfully. According to a recent study by Gil Greengross, a researcher in anthropology at the University of New Mexico, self-depreciation is a highly effective means of seducing members of the opposite sex. He suggests that the style of humour used by the actor Hugh Grant in his popular films is the most effective technique for attracting women.

Background research on other people can work wonders. Knowing how to pronounce a person's name correctly and being aware of their achievements will get you off to a good start. And remembering their personal details will work wonders for future encounters. It makes them feel important. Listening to other people will also help you to better understand their motivations, priorities and management style.

I'm always impressed by professional diplomats. They will breeze into a room, recognize a face from the past, and then instantly recall their name, family details and personal interests. A typical encounter with a diplomat you haven't seen for several years might go like this:

> *'How are you David and how is Gill? It must be five years since we last met. Are you still living in Wimbledon? And are you still driving that Morgan car?'*

How do they do it? It might seem impressive, but the technique is simple. They have a good database of personal information on their contacts. And they will check this information against the guest list prior to any event. The results are highly effective. As Dale Carnegie once put it:

> *'Remember that a person's name is to that person the sweetest and most important sound in any language.'*

Everyone today has access to a contacts database and calendar, in their Microsoft Outlook system, for example. They're valuable business tools, but rarely fully exploited. A key consideration, of course, is to ensure that data protection, privacy and security considerations are respected. Nobody will like it if their personal address or date of birth, for example, is published or compromised.

You can even maintain an excellent database using nothing more than ordinary business cards. I recall visiting Arish Turle, an ex-SAS officer and founder of Control Risks, several years ago. On shaking hands with him, I commented, 'It must be fifteen years since we last met.' He immediately took me to a large cupboard full of thousands of carefully filed business cards in alphabetical order of names. He fished out my business card from 1989, with the date and notes from the meeting on the back.

Whether in business or at a personal gathering, remembering people's names and interests, asking them about themselves, rather than telling them about you, making them feel important and being generally pleasant, are the real secrets for fostering good relationships. And if you can, make notes of what they say and review these notes before your next meeting. That will help you to be much more effective in managing your relationships.

Exceeding expectations

One of the most common failings in delivering services to people is to disappoint them by failing to deliver on your promises. It needn't be that way. It's not difficult to exceed their expectations. It just requires a bit more forward thinking. The trick is not to promise too much. Even politicians get that. As Michael Howard said in his first public statement, after being elected the leader of Britain's Conservative party:

> '*My approach is a simple one: Promise less, deliver more.*'

I wish airline pilots would learn this trick. I'm often sitting on a delayed flight when the pilot announces:

> '*Ladies and gentlemen, we apologize for the delay in getting you off the ground, but we hope to make up the time and we anticipate that we will still get you there on time.*'

It's nice to hear that at the time, but I can guarantee that every passenger will be disappointed when the flight finally arrives 15 minutes late.

It didn't have to be that way. The pilot could have said:

> '*We apologize for the delay in taking off. That means we will be a little late in arriving, but hopefully no more than half an hour.*'

When the flight finally arrives 15 minutes ahead of this estimate, I can guarantee that people will go away much happier and be more impressed with the airline.

It's a trick, an illusion, of course. And it works well, though it's not without hazards. Excessively low expectations, for example can be dangerous. People might begin to expect less of you, and they will not take you seriously. But it's generally much worse to make unnecessary promises, especially if they're optimistic.

It's far better to delight customers by under-promising and over-delivering. And, from an information security management perspective, it's also best to persuade business managers to expect and prepare for the worst possible outcome. The side benefit of this is that you will also help them to exceed their own expectations.

Nasty or nice

As Douglas Macgregor, a famous MIT social psychologist, pointed out in his classic 1960 book, there are two fundamentally different approaches adopted by managers to managing people. It's a matter of taste. Some managers favour an authoritarian management style. Others prefer a more participative approach. In practice, you can achieve effective security either by instilling fear, paranoia or suspicion into your staff, or by building on positive motivators such responsibility, trust and empowerment.

Great minds do not think alike on this subject. Galileo, for example clearly favoured a softer, educational approach, declaring that:

> '*You cannot teach a man anything. You can only help him discover it within himself.*'

In contrast, Joseph Stalin preferred a much harder line. As he succinctly but disturbingly put it:

'Trust is good, but control is better.'

Information security managers can be either nasty or nice. Which one is best? Personally, I've always favoured the latter, and for good reason. Fear and criticism will not get the best out of people. They will become defensive. They will not like you. They will only do as you say when you're watching them. And that's not appropriate in a modern, empowered organization, where trust is paramount.

A recent research paper by Debi Ashenden, of Cranfield University, and Professor Angela Sasse, of University College London, on the role of the chief information security officer, argues that a new paradigm is needed that transforms the identity of CISOs from 'corporate bullies' to 'security cheerleaders' if they are to be more effective. That's a move in the right direction.

But it might not be entirely your call. Many Board directors, for example, prefer to take a harder line on security. They are less patient and perhaps more inclined to expect their security directors to wield a stick rather than dangle a carrot. Unfortunately, few managers and staff, including CISOs themselves, respond well to that approach. Most staff will naturally prefer to be trusted, empowered and free to form their own decisions about what information security really means for them.

But all managers are different. Some will be nasty and others will be nice. And you, yourself, might be a Galileo. But your managing director might be a Stalin. So what will be the nature of the security culture that you eventually decide to implement?

In search of a healthy security culture

When information security managers tell me they're aiming to introduce a better security culture into their organizations, I often wonder what they really envisage.

The term 'security culture' means very different things to different people. It all depends on their experience and their outlook. What exactly might they envisage? Do they imagine a style of organization where people take an obsessive interest in security, perhaps challenging strangers and colleagues at every opportunity? Or could it be one where everyone is drilled to follow the rules, no matter how inappropriate they might appear? Might it be one where people are rarely found to make mistakes, because, for example, of excessive checks and balances around critical processes, or, more disturbingly, because they are frightened to do so?

In fact, very different words and images come to mind when we hear the term 'security culture'. Some are negative ones, such as fear, paranoia and suspicion. Others are more positive ones, such as trust, empowerment and openness. Some practical objectives also come to mind, such as the need to ensure that employees are educated and capable of securing their data, especially in hostile environments, or perhaps the ambitious goal of creating a new climate of responsibility and ownership.

In the past, some organizations developed impressively high levels of paranoid thinking and defensive behaviour. At the height of the cold war, for example, many of my colleagues in the Foreign and Commonwealth Office acted on the assumption that they were constantly bugged, followed or photographed. One or two of them might have been, from time to time. Top secret material was afforded extremely high levels of protection. Procedures were followed to the letter, and often beyond. Standards were sometimes excessive. We worried, quite unnecessarily as it turned out, about leaks of radiation from PCs in offices. And it was not unusual for people handling sensitive material to check, more than once, that their cupboards and doors were closed before leaving the building, and even sometimes to come back and check them once again.

All of that was achieved through a combination of factors. There was a high awareness of the risk, a well-established culture of secrecy in handling information and a strong fear of being caught committing a breach, which might have limited an otherwise promising career.

But things have changed significantly since then. The risks are very different today. Civil servants do not feel threatened by foreign powers. The impact of disclosure of documents is less than it used to be. People today are encouraged to share information. And they're often less interested than we might expect in having a long-term career in public service.

These changes have acted as powerful environmental cues to shape the attitudes and behaviour of staff. That's largely why we are seeing increasing security breaches reported in the press. To correct this, we need to introduce a new set of rules, cues and motivators to shape perception. Security culture can be shaped or changed. But it's primarily through visible events, actions and rewards, not by policy, diktat or wishful thinking.

The state of the local environment and the actions of nearby staff can have a highly contagious effect on security practices. If you work in an office where security cupboards are left open, confidential papers left out on desks overnight, and strangers allowed to roam unchallenged, even the best-behaved staff will quickly give up on security.

We have to prompt people to take a broader security responsibility. And it's nothing to do with role or seniority. A few years ago, for example, I visited the office of a managing director, who was a champion of security. I ended up leaving his office with him late in the evening. We were the last to leave the building. As we descended down the stairs, I noticed a large window had been left open. 'Should that window be open at this time?' I asked him. 'I don't know,' he replied, 'I've never thought about it before. But now you mention it, I don't think it's sensible to leave it like that.' 'Why don't we close it?' I suggested. 'Yes, that's a good idea,' he said, 'You're absolutely right.'

It's that sort of instinctive behaviour that we have to encourage. But it's not easy. We need to persuade people to take the initiative themselves rather than waiting for a prompt, suggestion or command to do something. Fixing security weaknesses is not obvious, even to experienced directors and managers who take security very seriously.

In my view, a healthy security culture is one where people are fully aware of the risks, fully conscious of their responsibilities, and take sensible, appropriate precautions to avoid incidents.

Understanding the factors that underpin a healthy security culture is fundamental to effective information security management. Security means different things to different individuals. The starting point, therefore, is to establish a common vision of what the desired security culture is, and an indication of how we might recognize it when we finally achieve it.

How do we get our employees to become more observant, more pro-active, and to go that extra mile for security? The answer is to focus on the motivators that reward the right behaviour and to create the right climate for security. We'll be covering that in more detail in later chapters.

In search of a security mindset

There is an interesting phenomenon that goes well beyond security culture. It's sometimes referred to as a 'security mindset'. As Bruce Schneier puts it:

> 'Security requires a particular mindset. Security professionals – at least the good ones – see the world differently. They can't walk into a store without noticing how they might shoplift. They can't use a computer without wondering about the security vulnerabilities. They can't vote without trying to figure out how to vote twice. They just can't help it.'

Bruce's remarks about the security mindset are very true. There is a quite rare state of mind that appears to view things very differently from that of a normal person. In fact, it's the ideal type of thinking that we need to design effective security countermeasures, the mindset that challenges existing perceptions and thinks like an attacker.

It does seem that some people naturally think this way. They like to play Devil's advocate. They search for flaws. These are the people who are invaluable when we're designing security measures or managing a crisis, but we rarely try to seek out or employ people with this capability.

It's also a capability that's extremely difficult to teach. People who believe in the concept of 'natural talent' would probably claim that it's something you're born with. It's certainly a cognitive skill, but I'm not convinced it cannot be acquired. As with many things in life, determination, patience and practice are key factors in acquiring skills that seem quite rare.

We certainly need these skills when it comes to evaluating cryptographic algorithms. That's a very special and demanding talent. It's easy for a normal practitioner to overlook potential flaws in algorithms. They're extremely hard to identify. It takes a special mindset to absorb a complex piece of mathematics, and to assess and highlight the weaknesses.

I've experienced this myself. I once hired the late, great Donald Davies, the inventor of packet switching, to review a cryptographic algorithm. 'How long will it take?' I asked. 'It'll take three weeks,' he replied. 'Just give it to me in any computer language. I can read them all. And I'll put it in my head. Three weeks should be enough thinking time.'

I've mentioned this story to a few leading cryptographers. The general reply is, 'Yes, that's how I do it'. But they also acknowledge that Donald had a special, unique ability to quickly absorb a complex algorithm submitted in any form.

These are rare skills that we can't buy on the streets. They are exceptional people. And we don't generally appreciate them or search them out, except perhaps in times of war. To a large extent, that's down to our ignorance. But it's also something we don't need for everyday business.

In fact, few organizations could justify employing such people on a full-time basis. But when we need them, they're absolutely invaluable. It's important, therefore, to learn to appreciate their value, to recognize when we need them and, more importantly, to know where to find such skills on the rare occasions that we need them.

Who influences decisions?

Organizations can be very different when it comes to identifying sources of influence. They respond to very different sources of influence. Hierarchical organizations, for example, respond well to senior champions, ultimately the CEO. Democratic ones respond much better to peer-level discussions and suggestions. More sophisticated organizations respond best to respected thought leaders. Understanding these differences can have a major impact on the design of your behaviour change program

I first discovered this when we were planning a major security awareness campaign for Shell UK. We initially planned to establish a network of champions across the business, and then to encourage them to spread the word across the enterprise. To help do this, we enlisted a professional behavioural psychologist to interview a selected set of potential champions. The psychologist came back and informed us that the strategy would fail.

He had identified from his interviews that in this community, business managers tended to arrive at firm decisions on new issues only after discussions with their peers. We might be able to temporarily convince a selected group of managers to back our campaign, but there was no way they would continue to support it, if colleagues did not back the idea. We needed an alternative strategy. Instead of relying on selected champions, we decided to issue an education pack simultaneously to every senior manager in the company. That did the trick. The results and feedback were highly encouraging.

In many US companies, it's less common to encounter such democracy. The CEO generally has an enormous influence on thinking, and many opinions flow downwards. But digital networks are now challenging these vertical information flows, progressively replacing them with horizontal ones. We are, in fact, witnessing the last gasps of a hierarchical command and control organization.

Working in the Foreign and Commonwealth Office demonstrated a very different form of decision making. It took me a while to understand the protocol of meetings. Most people would talk around the subject, initially. Then they would magically migrate towards a common view. It was an impressive show of democracy, though hard to spot the catalyst. Eventually I figured it out. Essentially, they waited for, and responded to, the most heavyweight thought leader within the room.

But the business world continues to change. European companies, for example, are being increasingly influenced by hierarchical US company practices. On the other hand, there is also a relentless background trend towards the more sophisticated, thought leader approach.

Dealing with diversity

Increasingly, all businesses are becoming more international, either through expansion, globalization, new business partnerships or offshore outsourcing. Managing security across an international community is very different from supervising a local team or business unit. In fact, the starting point in learning to manage any security program that spans diverse cultures and nationalities is to understand the key characteristics of the different nations, cultures and religions.

Foreign cultures and communities often have very different priorities and values. Confusion can easily arise because of differences in language, manners, formality, loyalty, openness, empowerment and methods of social networking. Eastern business generally operates through extensive business networks, for example, whereas Western culture prefers to encourage more reclusive entrepreneurs. And some cultures promote obedience, whereas others breed absolute arrogance. Religion can also play a major part in shaping attitudes towards networking, acceptance of authority and risk perception.

In the Far East, the concept of 'face' has a substantial impact. It will influence people's perception of your own behaviour, whether, for example, you praise or criticize others. And it will also discourage people from admitting the actual existence of problems and failures.

I first encountered this when I ran a workshop in Thailand for security managers from Far Eastern countries. I started off by asking the attendees to tell me about their local problems. Not surprisingly, there were none of those, as to admit a problem is to lose face. It then dawned on me that the sensible way to go about this was to challenge each manager to identify recommendations of actions for improvements. That turned the session around. To fail to find an improvement was now a failure that affected people's face.

When dealing with a range of cultures and nationalities, it's important to identify the real factors that shape peoples' motivation and decisions, both individually and collectively. Questions and instructions can then be appropriately framed, to generate maximum impact.

Taking the trouble to understand other cultures, interests and their politics and geography, will also create a surprisingly good impression. It can be embarrassing if you appear to be ignorant of important, local facts. A good vocabulary and friendliness are key attributes in most countries for helping to gain respect. Many of us also wrongly assume the others are likely to be more similar to us than they actually are. It's a very dangerous assumption. In fact, it's much better to assume that people from other cultures will be different. Not only are you likely to be right, but, more importantly, you're less likely to make an error.

Hierarchy can be important in many cultures. The concept of 'face' will discourage subordinates from correcting their boss. Attitude is also important. Many Asians love to negotiate, for example, but will be offended by arrogance and conceit. It's much wiser to be humble. People's sense of humour can also vary enormously. Jokes are best avoided, unless at your own expense. In particular, it's best to avoid sarcasm and irony.

Patience is always a virtue. Few Asians, for example, will make quick decisions. They attach less importance to time. And excessive importance can be attached to bureaucracy and paperwork. Many Asian executives also prefer to focus on longer-term relations, rather than immediate deals. They might even accept short-term losses if they are likely to lead to future gains. And their negotiation strategy is more likely to be based on a win–lose approach, rather than the generally preferred European strategy of win–win.

Don't take yes for an answer

Language differences between cultures can easily result in misunderstandings. It's absolutely essential, following a meeting, to confirm that all requests or instructions have been completely understood.

Even simple, everyday words can present major problems. Some English words don't exist in other languages. For example, the word 'no' does not exist in Thai vocabulary. Other words might be translated with an entirely different meaning, such as the Japanese word 'hai' which translates as 'yes', but does not always signify agreement. For example, if you ask 'Don't you...' it will mean 'no'.

And then there are the words that cannot be translated into English. For example the word 'sisu' is a unique Finnish concept that represents the philosophy that, if something has to be done, it will definitely be done, regardless of what it takes. It's a concept that goes beyond normal agreement or determination. And the word 'integrity' is a cornerstone of information security management, but it doesn't translate to an equivalent word in some languages.

Gestures can also be misleading. Asian people often shake their heads to indicate their interest, in a manner that can be interpreted by Western observers as a sign of disagreement. Italians use hand gestures in a way that can completely transform the meaning of their words. They might say they agree with you, but their hands might indicate the opposite.

The context or tone of a meeting can also be significant. In some cultures there might be several levels of formality, which are important to recognize and respect. Politeness can also be a major barrier, as it might sometimes discourage any use of the word 'no'.

But the most common problems are caused by the word 'yes' which can mean many things other than 'I agree'. When someone says 'yes' they might actually mean 'I don't understand' or even 'over my dead body'. To an Indian, 'yes' is one of the most awkward words in the dictionary. It's often used to fob off a child or an outsider. And when a Japanese executive says 'yes', it might be the outcome of meticulous testing of various shades of meaning, which might have led him to conclude something quite different from what you actually said.

Even people who share a common language can encounter problems. British and American executives often misinterpret conclusions because of differences in meaning between simple phrases such as 'let's bin that idea' which means 'let's trash it' in the UK but 'let's file it' in the USA. I've experienced that one myself, when dealing with executives in Houston.

Learning from organization culture and politics

So what have we learned in this chapter? We set out to examine key differences and similarities in organization culture and office politics, and to establish some universal principles for developing effective information security organizations and change programs. How did we get on?

Firstly, we established that understanding culture is a must for security professionals. But it's not something that's static or easily defined. There's a strong trend towards an outward-looking perspective for staff. But most organization culture is based on 'the insanity you can't see around you', the madness you can't grasp when you're actually part of it.

Security culture can be based on fear, or it can be based on inspiration. But trust and empowerment are more effective, and go much further. Business and security cultures are often incompatible. But many aspects of business today are full of contradictions. It's just something we have to accept and work around. Organizations are also very different, though many of the underpinning principles, techniques and standards are similar. To be effective in managing relationships, we need to adapt our communications and governance style to the local environment.

When it comes to designing an organization structure, the important thing to grasp is that both the requirements and the solutions can vary widely, both across and within enterprises. But an important starting point is to establish the position and the direction of the 'pendulum swing' between centralization and decentralization of business and support functions.

Centralized functions offer very different benefits than decentralized ones, and the balance between them changes over time. Devolved functions are less efficient, but more in touch with local business operations. They can also suffer from 'localitis', when the interest of the overall enterprise starts to become subordinate to the needs of the local business unit. Size also matters. Smaller functions have a more personal culture and a lower level of complexity.

Organization structures are short-term decisions. They rarely survive very long because of constant business restructuring exercises. But, on the positive side, this also presents opportunities for the career development of staff.

The shape of any organization design should also take account of professional development opportunities, as well as the skills and experience of the resources available.

It can be dangerous to place too much reliance on technical skills. Demands for these will come and go. Applied skills, such as project management, are longer-lasting. But behavioural and cognitive skills, such as problem solving, are more significant in the longer term. And every practitioner requires professional development. Luck won't do it, and ignorance can't. Education is the key to longer-term success, particularly in a world where there is a growing skill shortage for professionals.

Myers–Briggs indicators are a well-established measure and can provide a useful starting point for assigning people to roles. But they indicate nothing about whether people are actually any good at these roles or want to take them on. Job and function titles should not be designed around contemporary fashions, but rather to help the managers and staff to understand the function and role of practitioners.

Relationship management is a vital security skill. The key is to recognize that other people are more interested in themselves than they are in us. We have to take an interest in people and be pleasant and polite to make an impact. Exceeding their expectations is not difficult. The trick is not to promise too much. And should we be nasty or nice in carrying out security duties? It's a matter of taste. Fear and criticism will not get the best out of people. But many directors today prefer to take a hard line on security.

We also need to introduce new cues and motivators to alter people's perception. Security culture can only be changed by visible actions and rewards, not diktat or wishful thinking. A healthy security culture is one where people understand the risks and take sensible precautions to avoid incidents. In practice, the local environment and actions of nearby staff will have a contagious effect on security practices. We need to identify and focus on motivators that reward the right behaviour and create the right climate for security.

Organizations are very different when it comes to identifying sources of influence. Hierarchical ones respond well to champions, democratic ones to debate, and sophisticated ones to thought leaders. Understanding these differences can have a major impact on your change program. It's vital also to understand the key characteristics of different cultures, which can have very different priorities and values. In fact, it's best to assume that people from other cultures are different. You're quite likely to be right, and less likely to make an error. Language and cultural differences can easily result in misunderstandings. So it's essential to confirm that all instructions have been completely understood.

Here are seven learning points to help manage organization politics:

- Think objectively about your organization, perhaps as an outsider might view it
- A healthy security culture is one that's aware of risks and behaves intelligently
- Recruit security staff on their cognitive and applied skills, rather than their current technical knowledge

- Adopt a centralized approach if you're looking to cut costs or harmonize security practices
- Select a devolved approach if it's more important to influence the front-line business
- Never assume that people from different cultures think the same as you
- You can't avoid office politics if you want to make a real difference

CHAPTER 7

Designing effective awareness programs

Requirements for change

Staff awareness and understanding of security risks and requirements is a fundamental requirement for effective information security governance. It also reduces incidents, and leverages the effectiveness and influence of the security function. This chapter sets out proven tips and techniques for designing effective staff awareness programs.

Any major change program requires a clear strategy, starting with the identification of requirements and key problem areas, analysis of root causes and the development of programs of corrective actions. In any organization there is always tremendous scope for improvement in information security awareness. We simply can't do enough. Further investment in this area will most likely reduce incidents further, assure business continuity and safeguard company reputation.

In fact, threats, exposures and policies will never be fully understood by staff, partners or customers. They are generally too complex and sophisticated to convey effectively. Attitudes and visible behaviour will also vary, depending on whether the person in question is a career conscious manager, a risk-taker or a high flying executive. But generally they will all be far from ideal. And, increasingly, they will be based on the natural assumption that the overriding business interest is to cultivate greater trust, openness and sharing with the outside world, rather than lock away corporate secrets from prying eyes.

It's important to accept that there will always be much to improve, but we can't change everything, or everyone, at once. The best we can hope to achieve, in a single exercise, is a measurable improvement in a handful of areas. A good security awareness program should therefore aim to single out the highest priorities for

Managing the Human Factor in Information Security   David Lacey
© 2009 John Wiley & Sons, Ltd

change, and to set focused, measurable targets for improvement, before deciding and developing the nature of the change initiatives.

A clear distinction should also be made between the needs for changes to knowledge, attitude and actual behaviour. The reason for this is the nature of the solutions, which are very different. Conveying knowledge or awareness is a relatively easy fix, though it requires thoughtful consideration and planning. It's largely a matter of feeding the right information to the right people in the right form. And that can be done through presentations, e-mails, publications, web pages, newsletters, posters or any other form of corporate publication. We'll be covering this requirement in detail in the rest of this chapter.

Changing attitude is much harder. It generally involves a personal journey of some sort, a learning experience from an activity such as reading a book, watching a film or engaging in a creative discussion. At the outset the target audience might actually be skeptical and defensive, so it's important to adopt a patient approach that progressively introduces the problem and encourages people to temporarily suspend their disbelief until their journey has been completed. We'll cover the art of attitude change in more detail in the next chapter.

Achieving a change in behaviour is the hardest challenge of all. It requires a very clear understanding of the desired behaviour, as well as recognition of all the underpinning enablers and blockers. Understanding these will enable you to select motivators that can leverage the enablers and help overcome the blockers to the desired behaviour. We'll also cover that in the following chapter.

Understanding the problem

Many organizations take the wrong approach towards the design of security awareness programs. They start out by trying to dream up clever ideas for messages and slogans. That's not the right starting point. Before we can design any effective campaign, we have to find out what the people in our target audience actually know and think about the subject, as well as how they're likely to behave, especially when you're not watching them.

Making assumptions about your audience without adequate research can be dangerously misleading. You might focus on entirely the wrong messages, distracting as well as irritating your target staff. Using or copying educational material from other organizations' campaigns is equally flawed. The originators might not have done their research properly. They might also have developed ineffective messages or themes. And your own organization might have quite different needs.

We need to start by first establishing as much as we can about the current situation in the field: what people know, what they think and how they behave. This step is essential, both for identifying and for prioritizing the issues and messages that you will need to address. It's also valuable input for your own perception of how effective the existing or planned new security controls might be. In fact, without consulting people about their knowledge, attitudes and behaviour, you will have no real basis on which to judge that.

A consultation exercise is also highly useful for establishing an initial baseline, against which you can measure your future progress in educating staff and influencing their behaviour. The real key to any successful, ongoing, change initiative is to measure the impact of your interventions, to understand what is working, and what is not, and then, on this basis, to fine-tune your efforts.

The first challenge, of course, is working out how to go about this task. We can't read people's minds. And we haven't got the time to study large numbers of people at their work. But we can ask questions. And that's not that difficult. In fact, the questions are quite easy to identify. We just need to adopt a logical approach.

Asking the right questions

How can we best put together a questionnaire to measure people's awareness and behaviour? What sort of questions will we need to ask in order to determine how knowledgeable and effective our staff, or perhaps our customers, might be?

In fact, before we begin to brainstorm to identify suitable questions, it's important to recognize that there are major differences in the type of solutions needed to create changes in people, depending on whether it's their knowledge, attitude or behaviour that's the focus of the desired change. But we'll discuss the solutions later. For the time being, the important thing is to concentrate on the process for defining the requirements.

We should start by drawing up three sets of questions. Firstly, there are the questions that can measure people's knowledge and awareness of information security. Secondly, there are the questions to assess their perception and attitude regarding information security management. And thirdly, there are the questions that can help gauge actual staff or customer behaviour in carrying out information security responsibilities.

A further point worth noting at this stage is that it's much harder to make changes across a group of people, as opposed to at an individual level. We will need a much more ambitious initiative. So it's worth asking questions that can assess how well people perceive their own knowledge, attitudes and behaviour, as well as those of the rest of the target group.

This process of compiling questions is quite straightforward. Take knowledge and awareness. We can, for example, ask easily design questions that probe just how much people know about security objectives, policies and standards. For example, what do they really think we are actually trying to achieve? And how would they rank the priorities? Is it, for example, more important to lock away confidential documents, to maintain business continuity or to keep hackers out of systems? And how do they think we are going about information security? Are they aware of corporate policies, standards and incident levels? Do they understand the 'acceptable use' policy regarding social networking? Do they appreciate current levels and trends in information security incidents? Do we lose a handful or a hundred laptops a year? And do we experience a dozen or a thousand virus incidents a month?

Moving on to attitude, we can easily design plenty of questions to gauge what people really think about information security and how seriously they take it. Do they think, for example, that we've been exaggerating or understating its importance? Is it something they think should be left to experts, or is it something that they believe everyone has to do? Is it just common sense, or does it require a certain degree of technical expertise? Do they find the subject dull or exciting? And do they think we're spending far too much or too little, on the subject?

Information security behaviour is also relatively easy to measure. We can ask them questions about how they go about choosing passwords, whether they challenge strangers in the building and whether they lock away their papers at night. We can ask them whether they monitor the security of the contractors under their control, and perhaps how much risk they're prepared to take to meet a business objective. We can also find out whether or not they take regular back-up copies, and how well they're prepared for a potential disaster.

Questionnaires on these lines are easy to conceive. And they will produce valuable information to help shape security policies, controls and change management programs. Disappointingly, in practice, we see very few good examples of such intelligently structured surveys of people's knowledge, thoughts and practices. We often see surveys of security breaches, carried out through telephone surveys with security managers. There are also studies of major incidents, carried out by researchers such as the Ponemon Institute. And there are also plenty of consumer surveys carried out by vendors, primarily aimed at generating eye-catching media headlines. But we see very little in-depth surveys of what computer users and customers really know and think about the subject, and how they tend to behave. And that's the really useful stuff. Fortunately, it's not difficult to establish. I know that, because I've conducted many such surveys in the past and they have always delivered a host of useful information both to help shape my initiatives and to benchmark progress.

The art of questionnaire design

Designing a questionnaire is easy for an experienced practitioner but there are quite a few hazards for the novice. The challenge is not, in fact, in the creative process of dreaming up good ideas for the questions. That's actually quite straightforward. The tricky bit is deciding how to frame the questions and interpret the responses. If you get any of that wrong, you will have wasted your time, no matter how clever your ideas might have been.

Not all questions are neutral. Leading questions, the ones that prompt a particular answer, should be avoided, unless, of course, you wish to spin the results in some way. That actually happens a lot in practice. People with a vested interest often do this. Vendors usually aim to talk up the problems that their solutions alleviate. Political groups like to obtain answers that reinforce their claims. And even security managers might sometimes need a good result to enable them to hit their bonus targets.

Open questions, the ones that encourage open, variable answers, are quite good if you want to capture richer details. They're useful, for example, to review on a selective basis. But they're very difficult and time consuming to process on a larger scale. Closed questions, the ones which require a tick-the-box response, are much easier to process if you're looking for a more precise summary, especially across a large population.

All questions should be carefully tested in advance, to ensure that they're unambiguous and able to be interpreted correctly in all likely environments and circumstances. Questions designed with one context in mind, might not translate to others without misinterpretation. It's important also to allow the user to indicate 'not relevant' or 'I don't know' when that's appropriate, rather than simply leaving the answer blank. And blank scores should never be interpreted as 'zero' when calculating average scores of responses. They should be omitted or differentiated in some way. That might sound quite elementary, but it's a common fault in many widely used security questionnaires.

The key principle is to think about the questionnaire from a user perspective, which we rarely tend to do. I've found that a good acid test is the title of the questionnaire itself. If it says something on the lines of 'Employee survey' then it's probably not been designed from their perspective. Employees already know who they are. They don't need to be told. If it's entitled 'Information security survey' then it's likely to have been developed from a user perspective.

Processing the results of a questionnaire can be a major chore unless you use an automated system of some kind. I've done it manually on many occasions and, in every case, I've underestimated the level of effort. It's a good idea, therefore, to test the questionnaire from this perspective before you actually distribute it. Small changes to the layout of a question can often make big differences to the quality of the response, as well as the time required to process the results.

It's also a good idea to design any database that will be used to store questionnaire answers to enable the combination of results from multiple surveys. Again, this might sound obvious, but I've encountered many cases of survey results being processed by individual business units in an inconsistent way, requiring a large amount of manual effort to be expended in combining the results together in a single view to obtain a corporate perspective.

Maintaining a consistent benchmark over the years is also a major challenge. It's important to avoid the temptation to rush out a survey, on the assumption that you could always refine the questions at a later date. In fact, if you decide to change any questions at a later stage, it might undermine your future capability to measure progress by comparing successive survey results.

The overall, key learning point is that good questionnaire design demands careful design, objective testing and forward thinking. It should be seen as the first step in a long-term program, not a quick solution to a current problem. Security awareness is not a problem that will ever be completely solved. It's an ongoing requirement and a challenge that will continue to grow.

Hitting the spot

People today are bombarded with instructions and advice, both business and personal, asking them to either carry out actions, follow corporate policies or buy products or services. If we are to have any impact, we will need to differentiate our security awareness messages. And that means understanding what makes a good message, what makes it stand out, what helps to create an impact and what makes it stick.

It helps, for example, to match security messages to current business and personal issues. And whether it's a business theme you choose, or a personal issue this approach will pay dividends. People will be able to relate much better to the points that you make. People also need to compare and contrast what you are preaching against a well-understood frame of reference. It might be something from their day-to-day business life such as a corporate image or issue. Or it could be something from their personal life, such as a family activity or problem.

You can start by looking for strong business images that are likely to resonate in your organization, such as well-established corporate images. It's important, of course, to get permission for use of any brand images or any association of new slogans with them. Sometimes it's helpful to build on a brand image. Other times it can be quite inappropriate, and potentially damaging to the brand, by, for example, associating it with information security incidents.

One of the best examples I've seen of a business image was the use, many years ago, by Wells Fargo of the powerful image of Jack the dog for their internal information security campaigns. Jack was an established and highly popular Wells Fargo image, which conveyed faithfulness and fierce protection of assets. The campaign was well received. Employees were reminded that information security was an integral element of their traditional core values of safeguarding customer assets.

Many years ago, I commissioned a photograph of a broken pecten shell to convey the importance of information security for a management guide aimed at senior Shell executives. It was a powerful image that resonated with managers from all backgrounds. I could not have used the brand itself. That might have damaged its value. But a photograph of a similar object was close enough to make the association without compromising the brand itself.

Family themes are also useful to achieve messages that can resonate with users and customers. Everybody is concerned, for example, about the risks to children from networking with strangers or accessing inappropriate material. And they are similarly worried about identity theft or catching dangerous computer viruses. An education campaign that's designed to make families safer on the Internet, for example, is likely to be much more compelling, and attract greater interest and attention, than one aimed simply at safeguarding company records.

Campaigns that work

Understanding the types of messages that are required, and the style of message that is likely to have impact will give us a head start in launching an effective awareness campaign. But we also need to consider the number and frequency of these messages, as well as their individual format and content.

Awareness campaigns need to be ongoing, and based on a long-term structure and communications plan. We should aim to develop a forward-looking plan for our interventions, at least six to twelve months ahead, which aims to exploit a variety of coordinated channels, including, for example, e-mail, web pages, newsletters, journals, images, flyers, posters, competitions and presentations. As many channels as possible should be used to get our messages across. A campaign will only be as effective as the number of channels we can employ to communicate our messages.

Many distribution channels are outside of our direct control. A critical success factor will be our ability to charm, bribe or threaten the custodians of these channels to support our campaigns. Most managers today are overwhelmed with instructions and advice. In-house corporate communications functions have taken to protecting them from the excesses of corporate centre staff. They're unlikely to endorse a campaign without careful scrutiny and editing.

It's worth spending some time getting to know in-house communications staff. They will have a good understanding of the current themes that business units are keen to get across, and the style of message that's likely to have the most impact. And they will be the gatekeepers for controlling information feeds to business managers and staff. Exploiting ideas from, or links to, other current or previous themes for communications campaigns can also be useful. In Shell, for example, we often linked information security with safety, as this was the subject of long-running management campaigns.

Newsletters are a powerful means of getting information across on a regular basis. For any publication, it's generally much more effective to aim to generate 'executive pull' for news, rather than simply relying on blanket e-mail 'push'. This can be achieved, for example, by building an image with your target audience that it's an exclusive feed of privileged information. Start with an exclusive mail shot that goes only to top people, key stakeholders and selected, supportive managers. If the quality is good, it won't take long for other executives to realize that their bosses and colleagues have access to an exclusive source of corporate information. If you play this card correctly, you'll soon have a growing number of managers asking to sign up for this material.

Corporate newsletters have to be high quality to be effective. But that's not difficult to achieve, in today's riche world of newsfeeds and blogs. A quick, professional editing of external news feeds and features, combined with a few snippets of local information can deliver a surprisingly good choice of content. As we saw in Chapter 1, journalists are increasingly becoming 'DJs' for other people's material, rather than original writers.

You should also aim to harness the full capability of the information security function, as well as its related disciplines, to create regular articles or columns of general interest. Newsletters are easy, as long as you take the trouble to plan their production carefully in advance, and make sufficient effort to persuade enough of your colleagues to develop interesting contributions.

Adapting to the audience

There are many ways to present information to people. Some styles work better than others, depending, of course, on the type of individual you're trying to communicate with. But everybody is different. Clearly, we can't afford to personalize a campaign to each individual. We can, however, consider adapting the presentation of our information to suit a particular preference that's likely to be favoured by a sizeable section of our target audience.

As we saw in Chapter 4, people can be divided into a range of personality types, as Carl Jung first suggested. We can use similar criteria to shape communications styles. People of a particular personality type will relate better to certain presentations of information. For example, a 'sensing' person will generally have a greater preference for detail than an 'intuitive' type. Similarly, a 'thinking' person will probably have a stronger appreciation of process and structure than a 'feeling' person. By appreciating these differences, it's possible to improve the impact of a communication.

In fact, probably the best way to use this knowledge is to consider categories of jobs or roles that are likely to attract or perhaps encourage a particular personality type. Managing directors, for example, will clearly prefer a 'big picture' overview. Accountants and IT staff might favour a more detailed, logical presentation of information. Receptionists, and other staff who deal with people, are likely to prefer communications that focus on values. Marketing professionals often use these concepts to shape the design of their communications for particular target audiences. If you examine a range of advertisements in any newspaper or magazine, you'll find a large difference in the style and level of detail.

The main objective should be to try to understand, and take account of, the preferences of your audience. You might, for example, decide to appeal to their emotions and values, or, alternatively to present your message in a logical, objective way. Some people will wish to see more detail, but others will prefer to read something concise and simple. In fact, the most useful effective approach is to develop a range of contrasting messages that will appeal to each of the main personality types.

Memorable messages

At the heart of any awareness campaign is the creation of a small number of memorable, sticky messages. What makes a good message? Do you need creative people to help you, or can anyone do it?

The answer is that anyone can, as long as they take the trouble to understand the basic principles of effective communications. And there are, in fact, some fundamental tricks of the trade that can help you to craft compelling messages. A good, professional copywriter instinctively knows how to achieve this, so I would always advise you to draw on professional wordsmiths as much as you can. But everybody is capable of creating memorable messages, as long as they go about it in a logical way. You will also need to structure your own thoughts and requirements to brief any professionals you bring in to help you.

The starting point is to research and define your requirements as clearly as possible. What are the key points that you need to get across? Who is the audience? And what do they have in common? What themes might resonate with them? And can we learn from similar exercises that have been successful in the past? Understanding the context of each message is also important. Is it a local or global one? Is it short term or long term? Are you telling them something new or just reminding them of something they might have forgotten? And is it the first of many messages in a series?

Identifying potential images and themes is also a useful early step. A theme might suggest further ideas for the message content. And choosing an appropriate theme will be crucial to the success of your campaign. Not every theme will work well in every culture. But certain ones might go down well in a particular target community. I've always found, for example, that any association with dogs tends to go down very well in the UK and the Netherlands. Dogs are an appropriate image for security because they are loyal and fiercely protective of their territory. But this theme will not work in Eastern cultures. I've also found that a football theme works well in African countries. Football is all about teamwork, building for success and avoiding own goals, so again it's a useful metaphor for security. But soccer would be the wrong theme for the USA. It's a different ball game that's needed.

Drawing analogies with familiar objects and experiences is helpful for communicating abstract principles. The motoring one is the most popular one for security. It's interesting to consider, for example, how quickly we became programmed to using seat belts. It's instinctive to belt up when we enter a car. We feel unsafe without them. That's the instinct we need to develop for information security management. It's also useful to point out to business managers that the real purpose of brakes on cars is not to stop them, but to enable them to go faster. That can encourage them to see the purpose of security with new eyes. Professor Steven Furnell also uses the analogy of motoring for conveying the nature of information security management:

> *'Security management is rather like driving a ring-road; the overall route is more familiar the more times you do it, but that doesn't prevent unexpected hazards from popping up each time around, or the route ultimately changing as the road is developed over the years.'*

Combining messages together is also a useful way of getting more than one point across, as well as making people think for a bit longer about the connection. I've used this technique successfully in poster campaigns. One example for Shell used an image of an executive with a painted-out white space where his laptop should be, along with the caption:

> *'Is the information on your laptop worth more to you or the man who stole it?'*

This message gets across two key points at once, one about a loss of confidentiality of data, and the other about loss of availability. The combined messages create a stronger impression than two separate ones.

It's also very important to identify what seems to work best, and to keep refining your efforts. In fact, continuous improvement is the real secret of successful campaigns. One or two small tweaks can often make a huge difference in making a message more memorable.

So-called 'sticky' messages are often remarkably simple to create, though 'simple' is rarely that easy. *Made to Stick*, a book by Chip Heath, a Stanford Business

School professor, and his brother Dan, an education entrepreneur, examines the factors that appear to make ideas stick with people. Amongst other things, the authors discovered that the most memorable messages had common characteristics, particularly in way they were presented. In fact, stickiness is more to do with the showing, rather than the telling. Stories will work better than statements.

The Heath brothers claim that successful messages are simple, unexpected, concrete, credible, emotional and story-containing. This list conveniently almost spells 'success' so it's easily remembered. In fact, that's a sticky characteristic itself. But you should avoid editing a list of points too heavily just to create a memorable mnemonic. The authors also claim that the single biggest reason for failure is the 'curse of knowledge'. Once we understand something we find it very hard to imagine what it was like for us when we didn't know it. That's why it's hard for experts to share their knowledge. They can't easily recreate the audience's state of mind.

But nobody, including the advertising industry, has completely mastered the art of how to develop a memorable message. The old maxim in the advertising industry is that only half of advertising works, but we don't know which half. That's true. There's a surprising degree of trial and error, experimentation and luck, in creating memorable messages.

Let's play a game

One thing that will help to make messages stick is a degree of interaction with the audience. If you can engage them in a dialogue or game, you will gain far more of their attention. And they will also understand and remember it much better. Activity and engagement will beat passive listening every time.

One of the easiest and most powerful methods of engaging a large number of people's attention in this way is a competition. I experienced the power of this in the Royal Mail Group, several years ago, when we decided to mount a Christmas competition. We had been monitoring security incident levels for a few years, and we'd noticed a spike in incident levels in the build up to the Christmas holiday. It's a time when people are under pressure to hit end-of-year deadlines, and they're travelling more than usual, attending office lunches and celebrations.

The idea was to offer a small prize of a few hundred pounds worth of computer tokens to the staff who could best answer a series of carefully selected questions on information security. The questions were designed to test their knowledge of current corporate policy and responsibilities. To answer them properly, you had to go to the company intranet security web pages and read up on these items. We were staggered by the response. Within days we had experienced around 10,000 hits on these pages. It was an amazing response for a small outlay. And what was even more impressive was that the levels of security incidents dropped substantially. The concept had succeeded beyond our expectations.

In fact, the results were so successful that we decided to repeat the competition the following Easter, but this time with a smaller prize, of just a couple of luxury chocolate Easter eggs. We had the same response: a huge hit on the security web site followed by a significant drop in incident levels. Games work, and competitions with prizes work even better.

Creative, interactive communications channels are extremely powerful for getting points across. And their use often says more than the content of the message itself. As Marshall McLuhan famously put it:

'The medium is the message.'

The medium itself can help to convey important, subtle messages, including, for example, the suggestions that information security is fun or modern, that's it's targeted at me, that it takes priority over other messages and that it's important enough to warrant a corporate campaign of its own.

The power of three

An important device in helping to make an impact with your points is something I call 'the power of three'. I first learned this when I was preparing to take part in a debate at the London School of Economics in the early 1990s. I asked an experienced speaker for tips on how to make the most impact. He replied with one single piece of advice:

'Remember Winston Churchill's speeches. Make your points in threes.'

It certainly works extremely well. I don't know why it should, but there is something that is quite emphatic about points expressed in threes. They have a special ring. Other quantities don't work half as well. 'Blood, sweat and tears' comes across in a more powerful way than 'blood, sweat, bullets and tears'. Professional writers and analysts, such as Forrester Research, understand the impact of this phenomenon. You'll find that many of the points in Forrester's management guides are structured in threes to convey maximum impact.

That's also why the classic definition of information security as protecting the 'confidentiality, integrity and availability' of information works so well. It's the power of three. We should never be tempted to extend this any further. Donn Parker campaigned for many years to persuade professionals to broaden this definition to include three additional elements: authenticity, utility, and possession or control. But Donn's suggestion is purely academic. Information security management is a long way from being an exact science. Additional nuances don't add anything to the general shape and direction of the subject. They just detract from an otherwise clear, compelling sound bite.

In general, it's better to sacrifice completeness for impact, especially when aiming to get a message across to managers and staff. Structuring your points in threes creates an elegant and powerful communication. Forget what they teach you in school. Forget how academics write their research papers. Business communications are more about simplicity, style and stickiness.

Creating an impact

You can learn a lot by studying the style and format of management reports designed by professional publishers. They are often carefully constructed to make an instant, yet lasting, impact. There are numerous style guides to English and American English, at least a dozen, including Chicago, Oxford, New York Times and Economist style guides. They give lots of useful advice on how to structure paragraphs, whether to use capitals, how to use punctuation and abbreviations, and when to insert footnotes. But their objectives are quite different. Chicago style, for example, is more about accuracy for academic reports. Historians would follow it. Economist style is more about business communications.

You can also learn a lot from the style of communications used by the popular press. They aim to make an instant, hard-hitting impact and are severely minimalist in their choice of words. They will say 'get this' rather than 'consider the following situation'.

Personally, I've always tried to base my writing style on *The Economist* reporting style: short sentences in active English. I often start sentences, even paragraphs, with 'and' or 'but'. I probably overuse this feature. And many school teachers tell me I'm wrong. It's not how people are taught. It irritates many academics, including Professor Fred Piper who reviewed the manuscript.

I disagree with the teachers. Firstly, it's always best to write in the same way that you would speak. Secondly, placing a preposition at the start of a new paragraph can create a more powerful emphasis. And, thirdly, it's the teachers who are wrong. I checked with a professor of English, who assured me that it's perfectly correct to start a sentence with a conjunction. It's been used for centuries. The Bible is full of it.

Similarly, I don't mind using split infinitives. I like to boldly go where the English school teacher would never dare to venture. To me, if it sounds right, then it must be right. I think the teachers might have got this one wrong. Henry Fowler, an expert on English style, wrote in 1926 that:

> 'No other grammatical issue has so divided English speakers since the split infinitive was declared to be a solecism (a grammatical mistake) in the 19th Century.'

There is a marvellous story about Winston Churchill's attitude to English language pedants. In response to attempts by an overzealous editor to rearrange one of his sentences in order to avoid it ending in a preposition, the Prime Minister is reported to have scribbled a single sentence in reply:

> 'This is the sort of bloody nonsense up with which I will not put.'

We should never forget that the primary objective of our work is to communicate clearly, to get people to listen to what we say and to create an impact.

If you want to make a real impact and inject a lot of style into your communications, you could even consider hiring a professor of poetry from a leading university. I've seen that done by the Shell planners, and it certainly produces some excellent prose.

There are many tricks of the writing trade that can help us to make a better impact with communications. They're worth exploiting. A good technique for generating people's curiosity, for example, is to create or draw attention to gaps in people's knowledge. That will encourage people to think about the missing piece and to try to predict what it might be. It leaves them wondering about whether they were right. You could, for example, start out by raising a question or issue designed to trigger a question in your target audience's minds. Leave them to think about it for a few days, and then explain the solution.

Creating the right context for a message is also important, in order to ensure greater impact. I often find it helpful to prepare the ground for a particular message by using phrases that suggest that something important is coming. For example, try preceding your message with an introductory phrase such as:

'Pay attention, I'm about to tell you something important.'

That will not only help to grab the attention of your audience, it will also condition them to expect an important instruction.

The concept of 'priming' the audience is a psychological principle that's often used in marketing. Priming your subjects with a particular topic, for example, will actually set off an electrochemical reaction in their minds that will enable subsequent exposure to the same topic to be processed faster. Advertising campaigns often repeat key themes or messages to prime the audience, enabling faster assimilation of subsequent information to take place.

If you're making several points it will also help to use a memorable theme or device. Many checklists exploit mnemonics, such as the 'success' list used for remembering the elements of a sticky message. Another device for generating impact, and helping people to remember it, is to start each item in the list with the same letter.

A classic example of this is the '5Ws' of what, why, when, where and who. (We'll return to this particular list when we consider principles for architectures in Chapter 10.) There are many other examples of lists of words all starting with the same letter in the security world. The UK anti-terrorism strategy, for example, is based on '4 Ps' to contain the risks: prevent terrorism, pursue terrorists, protect the public and prepare for the consequences.

At a keynote session on social networking in London recently, I introduced my '6 Ps' to outline the key areas in which social networking will have a major impact: productivity, partnerships, politics, proxies, privacy and power. I originally wanted to include 'espionage' in this list, but it would have diluted the impact. Once you've covered the vast majority of issues with a consistent looking list, it's best to drop any further points that might detract from it. Information security is not an exact or complete science. Getting six out of seven points across is more than enough.

What's in a word?

Many sociologists believe that language influences thought. There is a theory, called the Sapir–Whorf hypothesis, which suggests that words influence the habitual thought of its speakers. Language can be imagined as a lens through which people understand the world. This is actually an old idea, which has been around for a couple of centuries. But it's only in the last 50 years that practical applications have been suggested.

It's certainly an interesting challenge to relate words to ideas. You can, for example, subconsciously relate time to money by use of expressions such as 'spend time' or suggest a connection between human rights and abortion arguments by employing phrases such as 'right to life' or 'right to choose'. Marketing people often aim to exploit such ideas.

But some words and expressions can be powerful on their own. They just sound right and compelling. It's worth paying attention to the choice of a word for promoting a particular issue. As we saw in the last chapter, job titles can have a significant impact on the perception of a role or function by other people in the organization. The same applies to other descriptions.

In the early 1990s at Shell, for example, we promoted the idea of 'baseline controls' as the minimum standard set of controls that everyone should implement. It was not a randomly selected term. Donn Parker originally conceived the term, but we consciously chose to use it as the term for our primary security standard because we believed it to be a strong phrase. It sounds solid, supportive, measurable and reasonable. In the same way, I much prefer the term 'information security' to 'information assurance'. It sounds much more compelling.

The most important thing when choosing a title for a new initiative is to put yourself in the shoes of your target audience. Ignore what teachers tell you about the perfect terminology. What counts is how ordinary business managers will perceive it. Which words sound best? What impressions do they convey? Which words will staff best relate to? What is likely to be the most memorable term?

One of my contributions to the English language was the word 'de-perimeterization', a term coined by Jon Measham, my head of security research at the Royal Mail Group. Everybody told me that it was a terrible word, far too long and technical sounding. It would never stick. And management would hate it. But I always thought the opposite, so I consciously promoted it. And it stuck. It might seem like an overlong word, but it certainly has a lot going for it.

Firstly, it's a single word that encapsulates both the problem and the solution space. The problem is easy to grasp. It's the disappearing corporate security perimeter. It sounds to the average manager like a difficult problem that's pervasive, messy and complex, without a simple, neat solution. It sounds like it's something we need to address with some urgency, and that it's likely to be expensive and take a long time to fix. When you present this concept to senior management, it sets them thinking about how on earth we could solve such a serious problem.

In other words, it's a highly effective, sticky and thought-provoking term. It's exactly what we need. The accepted wisdom, which I've always rejected, is that if a word is long, it will be a turn-off for business managers and they'll never get it. That's not necessarily true. Long words can also be sticky. We all remember 'Supercalifragilisticexpialidocious'. Incredibly, I was able to type it correctly, more than 40 years after hearing it. And I can still pronounce at least parts of it backwards. That's about as sticky as you can possibly get.

Benefits not features

One of the problems with any technical or specialist subject area is that practitioners tend to get carried away with details, such as the features, for example, of a security solution. It's the inevitable consequence of a software market in which old products become worthless, as open source versions overtake them, and new products have to be differentiated by including a set of features that you can't find in the free ones.

A further problem with security technologies is that they can often be used to solve several business problems. That makes the vendors greedy and over-ambitious. Their marketing people imagine that they might be able to sell it in many different types of market, for many applications, so they tend to be deliberately vague about the business benefits, not wanting to restrict themselves to a narrow set of opportunities.

But non-experts and customers are not interested in the details or the features of security products. They only want to know what it means for them. Unfortunately, that's not the way security technology salesmen operate. They describe all of the functions and features of a product, sometimes without even mentioning precisely what business problem the product actually solves. They have to change this approach, if they are ever to make a sale.

The most effective technique for achieving this change is something I've always remembered as the 'car salesman's trick' because that's the context in which I first heard it. It's something that any security professional explaining a new proposal to a business audience should learn to adopt. Car salesmen are notorious for describing every feature of a particular model in detail. They'll keep doing this until the customer manages to escape. Customers are rarely interested in mere lists or descriptions of features. They want to know what benefits they provide. The trick to overcome this failing is to always add the words 'which means that...' following any description of a feature. For example:

> 'This car has front wheel drive... which means that... it saves space and has better traction in slippery conditions.'

We should explain our security solutions in the same way, for example, when explaining to management the benefits of a new security infrastructure, we might say:

> 'This new security architecture enables greater agility in systems development...
> which means that... new business requirements can be accommodated quicker and
> cheaper.'

Quite a simple concept really, but, unfortunately, simple is rarely immediately
obvious.

Using professional support

Very few, if any, information security functions possess the range of skills that are
needed to develop effective security awareness material and campaigns. You might
know exactly what you want to achieve, but special skills will be needed to translate
your requirements into meaningful messages that will engage your audience.

Professional help will generally be needed. Otherwise, your efforts are likely
to achieve minimal impact. But specialist support in this area is not expensive. Journalists, copywriters, illustrators and other essential experts are all
generally a lot cheaper to hire than information security specialists. You can,
in fact, probably save money by using such expertise in place of your own
staff.

It's also important to cooperate with, and use to the full, all sources of professional support that exist within your organization. In-house communications
functions are the obvious starting point. But marketing, brand management and
media relations managers will also have relevant skills and influence, which
you can draw on to develop, support and maintain a successful education and
awareness campaign.

If you're planning to mount a sustained campaign, then you will certainly need
to consider sources and types of external professional support. Over the years,
I've used many different types of external expertise to help design and execute
security education and awareness initiatives. I've found them to be excellent value,
as long as you take the trouble to identify the correct skills you need, and to apply
them in the correct way. In fact, understanding the capabilities of the different
types of specialists that you will need, is a critical success factor for an effective
communications campaign. Knowing how to exploit professional support, at the
right time, and in the right place, is essential to help get your messages across to
your staff and customers.

The following paragraphs provide a few useful tips on some of the professional
skills that are available in the external marketplace, including what they can
achieve, and how best to use them. And, if nothing else, you will find it to be
interesting and educational to work with external professionals who can bring an
entirely different perspective and a complementary set of skills to your security
program.

The art of technical writing

Good technical writers are a rare breed of specialists. They operate largely behind the scenes, practicing the little-known, but much-needed, art of how to communicate complex information effectively and accurately.

I first encountered this world many years ago when the Shell Group CIO asked me to evaluate potential training opportunities in this area, as a vehicle for enhancing the communications ability of IT staff. I quickly discovered that technical writers have a different perspective on how to communicate information than you'll find in ordinary staff, or other specialists such as marketing or media experts.

There are, in fact, several varieties of technical writer. Some make a living by being knowledgeable about specialist standards or compliance demands. They add value by being skilled at writing accurate technical specifications and proposals. But the technical writers that I find to be most useful are the remarkable specialists who generally operate behind the scenes but know how to translate highly complex operating instructions, such as how to operate a DVD recorder, into plain English.

If you've never tried to write such an instruction guide then I'd recommend having a go, as an enlightening, learning exercise. It's much harder than you would expect. Such skills are, in fact, easy to teach and acquire, but surprisingly uncommon, as are the people who possess them. They are necessary skills for communicating complex information in the most simple and reliable manner. Unfortunately, not every company appreciates the need for such skills or would know where to find them. But the difference is quite obvious when you see it. You can instantly spot a good set of instructions. Apple's instruction manuals, for example, appear to have been put together by skilled technical writers. I can't say the same for Microsoft's.

The real art of technical writing is about putting yourself in the position of the user. Understanding what it feels like to carry out a complex set of operations, armed only with some outline explanatory text and a few diagrams. Good technical writing requires an appreciation of how to lay out text and diagrams to enable easier reading and understanding of essential information. Technical writers appreciate, for example, how to select the best fonts and column spacing, how best to use diagrams and symbols to convey procedures, and how to maximize the readability of text by using concise, active grammar.

For those who are not familiar with such concepts, it's worth pointing out a few of the basic principles. For example, large, lower case fonts with serifs are easier to read, though not generally fashionable. And text is much easier to read when arranged in columns to minimize eye movements. We see this style in magazines and newspapers. 'Active grammar' involves putting the subject before the verb. It's better, for example, to say that 'the security manager investigates the crime' rather than 'the crime is investigated by the security manager'. Unfortunately, many English teachers have failed to instil this style of prose into their pupils.

Technical writers also aim to understand and take account of the subtle differences in mindset, preferences and reading skills between different cultures. It's generally more effective, for example, to employ diagrams and symbols if you're writing for the benefit of Far Eastern readers.

These skills rarely exist inside organizations, but they can easily be brought in when required, and generally at reasonable costs. They will generally prove to be excellent value, certainly in comparison to the high day rates charged by experienced information security consultants, with lesser literary skills.

Marketing experts

I have to admit that I'm not a marketing expert myself. But I know a man who is. When I needed marketing advice, I employed an ex-professor of marketing. I drew on his expertise to teach myself and my fellow information security colleagues about how to go about developing services that would be better aligned with what business managers and customers actually needed and wanted. It made a big difference to our outlook and effectiveness. Marketing is the art of achieving that by helping to define, develop and deliver value to customers.

Marketing is a fascinating subject and an interesting skill that's constantly changing and evolving. Each year, sales and marketing people uncover entirely new dimensions that can significantly influence the sale of their products. Practitioners are well used to discovering that it's hard to anticipate what will emerge in future years to influence future promotions of their offering. The concepts of marketing are very simple, but its execution is far from easy. As the distinguished marketing expert Professor Philip Kotler once put it:

'Marketing takes a day to learn and a lifetime to master.'

It's also no exaggeration to suggest that marketing is currently in a crisis. They are challenged by an explosion in the number of customer touch points, the breakdown of traditional models of consumer classification and the failure of many marketing functions to demonstrate any significant increase in productivity. In fact, the impact of digital networks is a major factor behind this crisis.

Marketing is not a set formula. It's constantly evolving. There are logical steps that need to be carried out, and methodologies to be followed, much of it logical and common sense, but it will certainly pay dividends if you can afford to hire a professional expert, perhaps for a day or two, to help you to set off in the right direction. We can learn a lot from marketing professionals, about how to better understand the business that we're in, how to go about shaping a portfolio of services that will delight our customers, as well as how to best communicate these facts to them.

Such skills are extremely useful to any security awareness campaign. Marketing consultants challenge our perception of our function, role, objectives and services portfolio. They will ask simple, but powerful questions about our objectives, aspirations, customers, strengths and weaknesses, and the benefits of our initiatives.

Alternatively, you might consider aiming to beg, steal or borrow a marketing professional from one of your retail business units. That might even be your best starting point. Not only would you gain a useful source of expertise, you might also gain a valuable business ally, and an agent who can champion the benefits of security in developing and selling business products, as well as safeguarding the company's brand value.

Brand managers

One special ally that you should always try to cultivate is the person that manages your company brands. And if you approach them and explain that you're here to help safeguard the reputation and value of corporate brands and products by reducing incidents, they will almost certainly give you a very warm welcome.

Brand management and information security have all the makings of a beautiful friendship. In fact, we have a lot in common. Both functions can be unpopular with business mangers, because of the restrictions we place on them. Both functions will claim to deliver large amounts of indirect value, which is hard to demonstrate, and even harder to measure. And, at the end of the day, both will often have to call on Executive Board support to ensure their existence and their budgets.

Information security can also deliver tremendous value to corporate brands, by assuring customers that they're buying a product or service from an organization that has a secure, compliant and reliable infrastructure. And that message is even more powerful if the brand supports an intellectual product, such as software, information or an IT service. Large customers are increasingly demanding evidence from their major suppliers that products and services are secure and compliant. Information security is now a routine criterion for purchasers. Not only does it enable the customer to demonstrate that they are managing their supply chain effectively, it also enables deeper sharing of critical information, systems and infrastructure.

Brand managers can also teach information security managers a great deal about how to leverage support for a particular service through thoughtful, focused presentation of the perceived image and benefits. They are also aware of the need for periodic re-branding of tired, failed brands that no longer perform. Many brands follow an inevitable, relentless life-cycle of brand loyalty, where the perceived reality of the claimed benefits rapidly ascend and then decline in popularity as customers progressively lose confidence in the sales pitch. And once the user perception has gone, we can no longer reverse the inevitable decline. The only solution is a re-invention of the brand.

Information security follows the same pattern. Requirements change continuously. New challenges emerge. And old solutions become less effective. Trends, fashions and images come and go. Every now and then, we have to accept that an older image is outdated or dying, and that we need to re-launch information security as a fresh initiative, with a new, modern image.

Creative teams

Behind every successful advertising campaign is a two-person creative team, comprising a copywriter who contributes the words and an art director who contributes the images. They are a powerful combination.

Creative teams are responsible for all of the major advertising content that we experience. They're the backroom boys. Even the client has limited contact with them. Supporting every campaign might be a large network of specialists: business development executives, account managers, media specialists and slick presenters who can deliver the compelling pitch to clients. But it's the creative teams that contribute the real content.

Creative teams are the people who translate your requirements for a security message into a real, compelling set of words and images. They add the most artistic content. Throughout the 1990s, I used an ex-Saatchi and Saatchi professional creative team, to develop educational material for Shell information security campaigns. They were excellent value, helping to deliver compelling material that created a powerful impact.

It was also interesting and instructional to observe them at work. They changed many of my pre-conceptions about creativity, a subject we'll cover in more detail in the final chapter. I used to think it was all about sitting back and waiting for inspiration. But professional creative teams operate in a more disciplined, logical way. They have to, of course, in order to meet their deadlines.

Creativity is a disciplined process, starting with a clear definition of your requirements, followed by a logical assessment of potential solutions. Anybody can do this. But the advantage of using a creative team is that they generally have a lot more sources of ideas than we could ever identify. And they are faster at evaluating them. That's what makes a good creative team. And that's why they're great value.

The power of the external perspective

Gaining and maintaining business support for major campaigns or proposed changes in security behaviour is vital, so it pays to seek out as much leverage as possible for your proposals. Many business executives have a tendency to believe outside experts in preference to their own specialists. Personally, I'd rather seek out the opinion of an experienced insider myself. But it's common for senior management to look externally for inspiration or a second opinion.

Often this is because there's a lack of trust in internal functions. That might, for example, be the result of poor internal communications. Perhaps the presentation of messages, or their content or timing was poorly conceived. The nature of the service that we might be aiming to deliver to a business unit can also be a negative factor in business relationships. We can't, for example, easily sell a partnership style approach to a business unit that just wants a basic set of services. Neither can we market a low-cost services model to a business unit that wants to innovative through new technology.

In some organizations there can also be a deep-seated, negative perception of an in-house function. It happens a lot with IT functions. I've often heard business managers remark that 'IT people don't understand out business' or that 'IT people don't know how to run projects'. In most cases, the criticism is wrong. Many IT managers have an excellent perspective of business. And they're generally quite experienced in project management. But IT projects involve a more complex set of risks than other projects, such as construction projects. And the consequences of these risks can often produce a negative perception.

Political grudges can also be a factor that works against an in-house function. I once asked the CIO of a top UK company what motivated his organization to carry out such a radical outsourcing of IT services. 'Business revenge' was his answer. It's a lesson for many IT functions. Office politics can become surprisingly aggressive. But, whatever the state of politics in your organization, maintaining an external perspective, and being able to demonstrate a second opinion to other managers is often essential.

There are several ways to achieve external leverage for a campaign or proposal. The most expensive approach is to employ expensive outside consultants or analysts with a well-known brand name. That will provide a veneer of credibility to your recommendations. I've often asked colleagues in other companies why, for example, they persist in buying expensive research services from top analysts, when they appeared to have better insight and skills within their own teams. 'We don't need their expertise,' they often reply, 'but the business likes to ask what they think about our proposals.'

A cheaper and better strategy is to build on successful case studies from other well-known companies. Security clubs, user groups and societies are good sources for these. Vendors are also a useful source, as case studies help to sell their products. I've regularly used examples from Fortune 100 companies to help sell new ideas. They're a powerful source of influence, especially if they're from a respected competitor or an important customer.

But probably the best source of outside influence is a leading business school. If you can persuade a Harvard professor to promote your ideas then you'll find it an excellent long-term investment. Even better is to connect with a business school that has a good relationship with your managing directors. I've used that trick quite successfully myself. Such research pays dividends for your credibility and influence.

Managing the media

I once asked a senior Shell IT manager how we could best get a key security message across to top business executives. 'Simple,' he said, 'Just get it published in the Financial Times.' He was right. Most executives read the FT. It has a lot more clout with business directors than any internal corporate briefing paper.

There's nothing more effective than to having your views supported by journalists in a quality newspaper or journal. Getting something in the *Financial Times* or *The Economist* will have much more impact on the perception of senior directors, than any briefing or message you could possibly deliver yourself. For that reason,

I never turn down an opportunity to contribute opinions to serious journalists, especially the ones that write for broadsheet newspapers or quality business magazines.

Journalists can also help you when you have a major incident, by providing a sympathetic ear or a source of external intelligence. Most journalists are reasonably well informed, and they do not report everything they know. And, if they trust you, they might be prepared to share some of their knowledge with you. Many external relations functions discourage executives from talking to the press, but some can help you achieve a good relationship with them.

It's important to be selective about the journalists you talk to. Some are uninformed and unreliable. Others are reasonably trustworthy and tactful. And a few are world-class investigators. The most important thing when dealing with journalists is to understand what they're really looking for. Contrary to many opinions, it's not just bad news. Some professional journalists and broadcasters in the UK use a mental checklist of key trigger words. They look for stories that are topical, relevant, unusual, trouble and of human interest. Appropriately this list of words spells 'truth'.

If you're likely to conduct regular interviews with journalists, I'd recommend attending a media training course. They are extremely enlightening and generally very good value. You can learn a lot from a single one-day course, not just about how best to manage the media, but also about how to pitch your presentations more professionally. For most press purposes you will need to master the art of delivering a three to four minute summary of your views, as well as a 25 second sound bite. This is also ideal preparation for Executive Board presentations.

One important lesson I've learned from media interviews, is that if the interview is pre-recorded, you should never be reluctant to stop and try again if you haven't got your response 100% right. You will generally have more than enough time to get it right. And it's in the interests of your interviewer to capture the best possible response. Good journalists can be trusted to maintain small confidences and provide helpful reporting in the interests of building a long-term relationship in which they can get regular briefings and information. They also make excellent role players for crisis exercises. But it's important to appreciate that there really is no such thing as 'off the record'. Most of the time, journalists will aim to retain your trust. But for a good journalist, the story will always come first. A big exclusive is what they're really aiming for. And who could blame them?

Behavioural psychologists

Behavioural psychologists are rarely employed by information security functions, thought they are increasingly being drawn into academic research on the subject. It's a shame because they have a lot to offer. The state-of-the-art in the psychology of information security might be relatively immature and unproven, but there is a large body of academic theory and research that can help with designing and conducting effective security awareness and behaviour change programs.

I first used such expertise in the early 1990s, when I was working for Shell International. We had decided to run a major security awareness program across the Shell Group, but we had very little experience of the skills required. So we brought in a specialist team of consultants, with previous expertise in changing corporate security behaviour. Some of the detailed findings from that exercise are covered in more detail in the next chapter. But the key learning point is that there are many useful techniques that have been developed by psychologists for subjects such as industrial safety, which work extremely well in the security field.

How can psychologists help you? The answer is in three ways. Firstly, they are considerably more perceptive in interviewing managers or staff and understanding what makes them tick, how their culture operates, what influences them and how they arrive at decisions. Interviews by psychologists will uncover more interesting findings than can be achieved by a normal security manger or consultant.

Secondly, psychologists can provide invaluable advice on how to design and structure an enterprise change program for maximum impact on managers and staff. They will have a much better insight of the critical success factors for such a campaign, and how these are likely to influence opinions and events on the ground.

And, thirdly, psychologists can help you to assess the effectiveness of your interventions, helping to pinpoint the reasons for successes and failures. The real secret of successful campaigns is to monitor what works, what doesn't and establish why. In particular, behavioural psychologists can help you to identity the root causes of failures, which is probably the most important input for future information security campaign planning.

Blogging for security

No chapter on communication would be complete without a reference to blogs and bloggers. It's something I've been doing for a couple of years. And I've found it to be a useful exercise, which motivates me to keep up-to-date with current events, and encourages me to form opinions and structure my thoughts, as well as providing a channel to a global audience that provides valuable feedback and networking.

My own security blog for *Computer Weekly*, a leading weekly UK publication, is a combination of news, personal commentary and short essays on subjects. Blogging is very different from journalism, because it's more of a personal commentary, rather than an objective reporting of events.

Internet blogs offer the potential to reach and influence customers, as well as staff. They're a powerful channel if you are aiming to get particular messages across in a less formal and more sincere fashion. Blogging is a convenient real-time channel for connecting with colleagues and staff. It can be a refreshing change from traditional channels of corporate governance. Blogs are concise, informal, personal and up-to-the-minute. They are also very useful for pointing readers to other interesting articles, news items or educational items of relevance.

Many blogs come and go, according to the evolving aspirations of professionals, and the time they have available to maintain them. Because of this, it might be a good idea to share blogging space with the rest of your team. Corporate blogs have the advantage that they're virtually free to maintain, as long as your security colleagues are happy to volunteer their contributions. And the only skills required are a few items of useful knowledge, a touch of creativity and a writing style that's understandable. All these things can be acquired with determination and practice.

Blogs are a powerful method for enhancing the public perception of a product or service. They provide an impression of openness and honesty. And at the same time, they can help to communicate key messages to citizens. A good example of this is the blog established by the US Transportation Security Administration, to encourage dialogue on innovations in security, technology and screening processes. This blog provides interesting, up-to-date information on new developments in transport security, as well as helping to explain and justify many of the security measures being taken.

Blogs are the channel of choice for promulgating and debating information on issues that are immediate and affect many staff or customers. They can also be used to float and gain feedback on controversial new ideas. No security campaign is complete without one.

Measuring your success

Early in this chapter we discussed the importance of creating a baseline against which progress can be measured. There are many ways to go about this, but the most important principle is to plan carefully and think ahead. A key underpinning consideration is that we should aim to maintain consistency in our questions and measurement systems across all surveys.

It's important, therefore to get the first set of questions and measurement criteria absolutely right. Subsequent modifications to questions will invalidate comparisons with older material. A forward-looking approach is essential. Your measures will need to be as timeless as you can make them. Here are some tips for achieving that.

Firstly, avoid short-term terminology such as current organizational roles or technology descriptions. Use general terms that are longer lasting. Business unit names, job titles, service descriptions and computer platform descriptions should be avoided as far as possible.

Secondly, adopt a structure that can accommodate changes without a major restructuring. It will pay dividends to invest some time up front in order to develop a flexible data structure that can enable and accommodate future change.

Thirdly, make sure that you consider the audience carefully. A good technique, for example, is to conduct a survey of a representative sample of people both before and after a campaign. Clearly you can't really use the same people, so you will need to identify a second group of people to complete your questionnaires after the campaign.

And, finally, when conducting any form of awareness campaign, it's useful to take samples of other relevant metrics associated with your target audience, before and after the campaign. Noting items such as, for example, the number of incidents, of various types, and perhaps the number of hits on relevant, in-house web pages, such as those that provide essential advice on policy, will provide an extremely useful set of information to help judge the success of the campaign.

Learning to conduct campaigns

Ensuring that staff, and customers, are fully aware of information security risks and requirements is an essential requirement of good corporate governance. Awareness campaigns also help to reduce incident levels, and increase the overall effectiveness and impact of the information security function. We set out in this chapter to identify proven tips and techniques for designing effective awareness programs. What have we learned?

The starting point is to accept that a major change program requires a clear strategy, an understanding of current requirements and key problem areas, an analysis of root causes of incidents and an appropriate program of corrective actions. In any organization, there will always be plenty of scope for improvement in security awareness. Staff rarely understand all of the relevant threats, exposures and policies. It's a complex and constantly changing landscape. Employee attitudes and security behaviour will vary depending on the position and background of employees. But we can't change everything and everyone at once. A good security awareness program will need to focus, therefore, on the highest priorities for change

Clear distinctions should be made between knowledge, attitude and behaviour. The interventions required are very different. Conveying knowledge is an easy fix. Changing attitude is much harder. It requires a personal journey. Changing behaviour, however, is the hardest challenge of all. It requires identification of, and attention to, the underpinning enablers and blockers.

But before we can design an effective campaign, we need to find out what people know and think about the subject, as well as how they behave. Questionnaires are, in fact, quite easy to develop, and they can provide a mine of valuable information to help shape policies and controls, as well as set priorities for change management programs.

People today are bombarded with instructions and advice. It's important to be able to differentiate your security awareness messages. It helps to match security messages to business and personal issues, and to choose images that will resonate with people in your organization. It also pays to find out how best to communicate with employees in business units, and to understand how to develop memorable messages that will stick with your target audience. Engagement with people will help, through interactive methods such as games and competitions. We can also learn a lot about the art of good communications by studying the style and format of management reports designed by professional publishers. There are many 'tricks of the trade' that can help us make a much better impact with the presentation and content of your material.

Professional support also helps. Copywriters, technical writers, marketing experts, behavioural psychologists and other experts can make a substantial difference to the impact of your campaign. Such skills rarely exist inside information security functions, but can be brought in when required. And they are generally a lot cheaper to hire than information security consultants. But a useful starting point is to identify the skills that exist within your organization, in the marketing or communications functions, for example.

Modern channels, such as blogs, are now becoming essential channels for disseminating information in a real-time, interactive fashion. And you don't have to be a natural writer to contribute. As we saw in Chapter 1, the journalists of the future will be more like DJs, assembling items from numerous sources, rather than drafters of original prose. One day, in fact, everyone will be capable of becoming a first-rate journalist.

Here are seven learning points to help manage security awareness campaigns:

- Prioritize your efforts; you can't fix everything at once
- Find out what people think and how they behave, before setting out your security awareness campaign
- Surveys will help to better understand user requirements, as well as to benchmark your progress
- Design security messages that are 'sticky', and will resonate with staff
- Use professional support to leverage your campaign
- Make maximum use of in-house communications experts
- Use modern communications channels, such as blogs and social networks, to the full

Transforming organization attitudes and behaviour

Changing mindsets

We've seen that there is both an art and a science in raising people's awareness. That's quite a challenge for the average information security professional, aiming to launch a new awareness-raising campaign. But it's only half the story. Changing people's level of knowledge and awareness is major challenge. Transforming people's attitudes and behaviour, however, is a much more complex task, especially across a large, conservative organization.

This chapter examines some of the motivators for human behaviour, some of the theory about how we should go about changing it, and a few of the methods that I've employed successfully for changing attitudes and behaviour.

We saw in the last chapter that in order to raise people's awareness, we have to present the right information to them, in the right way and through the right channels. But it's a different ball game if you wish to change their attitudes. That can't be achieved through a simple one-way communication process. It requires a degree of self-discovery on the part of the target audience. In fact, the only reliable method for changing attitudes is to persuade people to engage in a learning process. We need to get them involved in a game or story that will capture their attention, allowing them to draw lessons from it, which will help to shape their future attitudes.

Even harder than transforming people's attitudes, is the daunting task of changing their day-to-day security behaviour, especially the collective behaviour of a large, conservative group of people. But there are some logical starting points. We can start with 'activators' of behaviour, such as rules, instructions, commands,

Managing the Human Factor in Information Security   David Lacey
© 2009 John Wiley & Sons, Ltd

orders and policies. They will have a certain amount of impact, but, unfortunately, it will be nowhere near enough.

Direct orders are rarely effective outside of a military environment, which will have conditioned people to react instinctively, unquestioningly, to commands. We can see this, for example, when we're trying to get a large group of people to cross a busy street, with traffic coming from several directions. Some will always be busy in conversation and start to step out into the traffic. We can try shouting 'Stop!' but most people will happily ignore our command, even though we're trying to save their life, except for those with a military background, who will instinctively respond to an authoritative sounding order.

If people won't pay attention to you when you're trying to save their lives, what chance have you got when you're trying to get them to safeguard information? The answer is that, in most cases, you have to go far beyond activators, such as instructions and commands, and focus instead on the perceived consequences of actions.

Consequences are much more compelling. If people expect something good or bad to happen as a direct result of an individual action, it will shape their behaviour. But not every consequence is equally effective. Some are more compelling than others. And the most powerful ones are those that are personal, immediate and certain.

We've all experienced the power of consequences as a motivator for behaviour change. Tell a child not to put his hand in the fire, and he might pay some attention to your suggestion, but probably not enough. He'll be completely convinced, however, once he tries it and gets his hand burned. Then he will know for sure never to do this again, for the rest of his life. His behaviour with fire will have been completely transformed. We need to establish how to do this for information security.

Reward beats punishment

Psychologists have argued for years about whether reward or punishment is more effective. There's often a moral element behind these views. And, as we saw in Chapter 6, managers can have fundamentally different perspectives, either favouring an authoritarian management style or a more participative approach. There are also arguments against the use of rewards and punishments. For example, you could argue that they don't necessarily have the right long-term effect. And, in some cases, they will encourage rebellion or discourage individual responsibility. Punishment can also be an ineffective strategy in competitive business situations, as it can serve to discourage collaboration.

But, in practice, there's no doubt that both rewards and punishments have a significant effect on behaviour. As the poet W.H. Auden once put it:

> *'Of course behaviorism works. So does torture. Give me a no-nonsense, down-to-earth behaviorist, a few drugs, and simple electrical appliances, and in six months I will have him reciting the Athanasian creed in public.'*

Every motivator has its limitations of course. Punishment is only effective if people are afraid of it. And rewards are only motivating if people value them. But most people will respond to them, especially if they follow quickly and consistently. They will help to reinforce or discourage particular behaviours.

The effectiveness of rewards or punishments will, of course, depend on the nature of the incentive, and the perception of the staff. It's important, for example, that people judge them to be fair, reasonable and consistent. And that they come across as sensible, realistic measures, rather than ones that are worthless or foolish. We certainly can't persuade people to perform for rewards they don't value. The presentation also matters. It's far better, for example, to say 'great job' rather than the more condescending 'good boy'. And it's important also to avoid conveying the impression that we're surprised that a person can actually do something right.

But the impact of incentives will vary according to the person, and it will also change over time. As Maslow and Herzberg, the pioneers of motivation theory, pointed out, motivators fall into a hierarchy. As people's basic needs are satisfied, they look to higher-level ones, progressing from essential ones such as safety and security towards more complex ones such as self-esteem and self-actualization.

But reward is certainly a more pleasant and positive motivator. As Catherine the Great put it:

'I praise loudly. I blame softly.'

And she was not alone in believing that it's best to avoid apportioning blame. Abraham Lincoln also sought to avoid criticizing people. In fact, it's a good strategy for a politician or manager, as it will help to make you more popular and avoid creating enemies.

Punishments definitely have a downside. They involve a loss of face, which is not always immediately apparent. People might stay calm and quiet when you criticize or punish them, but they will rarely accept it deep down. Many will justify their actions to themselves, and anyone else that listens to their complaints. They can become de-motivated. They might even hold a long-term grudge. None of that is pleasant or helpful.

Reward, on the other hand, is an uplifting response that can inspire and motivate people. Dale Carnegie, in his book *How to Win Friends and Influence People* gives numerous examples of the benefits of keeping staff on your side by not criticizing them. In practice, however, to achieve a major change in behaviour, we will have to draw on a lot of different motivators. We will probably need to eradicate a number of undesirable behaviours, as well as encourage the development of several good ones. We will therefore have to identify a wide range of incentives. And it might well be that we can't identify enough rewards, but we have plenty of punishments available. Unfortunately, that's often the way it often turns out.

Changing attitudes

Before moving on to the more challenging task of changing people's behaviour, let's start by considering techniques for changing people's attitudes, which is a little easier in practice. As we've discussed, we can't change attitudes through a one-way communication process. We need to persuade people to embark on a journey of self-discovery, during which they might explore new ideas or situations which they might not normally consider in depth. And, hopefully, in the process they will absorb new facts, concepts and learning points.

Stories and games are useful for this. I've tried out most variants of this theme on executives and staff at various levels. I've conducted scenario planning sessions, sponsored the production of videos and even persuaded executives to create fairy tales based on a particular theme. They're all equally effective techniques. It just depends on your taste, your nerve and the facilities, materials and budget available.

There are also other influences on attitudes, besides personal experiences. We also take many cues from our role. And it's not just the role that our management intended. It's how we perceive or imagine it. Let's take an example. If I'm a security manager working for a public sector organization, for example, I could envisage that I'm there to defend its secrets from sinister, hostile intelligence agencies, to protect its executives from the dangers of organized crime, to safeguard its staff from terrorist threats and to maintain essential citizen services against attacks on critical national infrastructure. I could, in fact, become quite excited about the role and how I could best fulfil it.

On the other hand I could also imagine that it's just another low paid, public sector job. I'm just an unappreciated bureaucrat and I'd be a fool to carry out any more than the minimum duties, especially when there are so many obstacles placed in my path whenever I try to do anything remotely innovative. I could complain about the salary they pay me and the inadequate budgets and resources that are available to me.

Clearly the former perspective approach is much more likely to motivate me to go the extra mile. But would my colleagues regard me as patriotic and inspiring, or perhaps an eccentric individual, living in a Walter Mitty style fantasy? What is a responsible, motivated image for a role? In Chapter 3 we considered the dangers of placing people in dominant roles, as shown by the results of the Stanford University research experiments with college students acting as guards and prisoners. Roles can have a significant impact on people.

Role models also make a big difference, especially on younger people. As we saw in Chapter 3, many young people are influenced by their peers, particularly the ones they perceive as 'cool'. Kids don't smoke because smoking is cool. They do it because smokers are cool. If we want to make security cool, we need to find cool, fashionable people that practice good security.

Then there is the environment. We take quite a few cues from that as well. If you're working in an environment where people leave cupboards open and leave confidential papers out at night, then you're unlikely to develop good habits. And in many offices today, the level of local security is not good. People in nearby functions often share laser printers and fax machines. Open plan offices encourage visitors and staff from other departments to roam freely. People read confidential papers and e-mails openly on trains and planes. Company laptops are taken home for children to play with.

And few people bother to challenge visitors in the office. Receptionists are generally more concerned about creating a pleasant experience for their visitors, rather than keeping bad people out. And security guards are generally more interested in making sure that you have the right paperwork, rather than sizing you up. You, yourself, might be a sensible, safe executive that sets out to behave securely. But that behaviour might not last long in a sloppy environment. You'll give up, feeling that there's no point in banging your head against a brick wall.

To change these attitudes, and to encourage the good behaviour that might ensue, we need to work not only on the personal perspective of what information security might mean, but also the nature of the role we wish to encourage, and the state of the environment that people inhabit. And we need to find some appropriate, selected allies that can help us to influence our target audience. We'll return to the subject of roles, fashion and environmental influences in Chapter 11.

Scenario planning

Scenarios are imaginary stories about possible futures. They can help us to identify and understand significant events, trends, paradigms, players and markets. That's valuable in itself. But, more importantly, they can help to alter the perceptions of people, and even enterprises.

Scenarios help people and organizations to learn and adapt. People can experiment with hypothetical challenges and absorb learning points by participating in games, imaginary situations, fairy tales, stories or visions of the future. Scenarios encourage people to suspend disbelief, and to put objections and defensive arguments to one side, whilst contemplating the scenario. They can help managers, for example, to explore alternative future business environments, without having to accept the likelihood and risk of the situation actually arising.

Scenarios provide alternative views of the future. They help us to explore what the future might look like and, in particular, what the personal and business implications might be. As Ged Davis, a pioneer of scenario planning, puts it:

> 'At times, the world can look so complex and unpredictable that it becomes hard to make decisions. Scenario building is a discipline for breaking through this barrier.'

Scenarios help executives and teams to prepare for change, especially ones that are unexpected, outside of their experience, or perhaps beyond their comfort zone. They help us explore what is possible, not just what is probable, enabling management to consider left-field interventions and unexpected developments, which they might otherwise have dismissed as unlikely. Scenarios encourage managers to think the unthinkable, to prepare themselves for the unexpected.

Good scenarios must be possible and achievable to be convincing. But they do not have to be likely. Exploring the characteristics of alternative outcomes, extremes never before encountered, can provide an insight into the limits of current business strategies. And they can help identify ones that might also work in other possible future worlds. But the objective should always be better decisions today rather than a prediction of the future.

Shell, for example, uses alternative, long-range scenarios as a tool for reviewing business strategy and evaluating new investment decisions. It provides a useful indication of how their business operations might be affected by an unexpected turn of events. The same approach can also be used to explore the impact of unlikely, but possible, high-impact events of security interest, such as a global pandemic, a stock market meltdown or a future information war.

How many scenarios are necessary? Shell used two opposing extremes for many years. The danger with this approach is that the two approaches are so extreme that they become too unlikely. It's like pushing a pendulum to the extreme left and right positions, when the most natural position is dead-centre. More recently, Shell switched to three scenarios, each of which represents the intersection of two out of three opposing forces, a set of situations that is more realistic.

You might also decide to try four scenarios, which offers the advantage of being represented by the familiar two-by-two matrix. But for my taste that's beginning to border on being too many scenarios for the average manager to cope with, especially if he has to consider a strategy for each separate scenario.

Successful uses of scenarios

Shell was the first major company to discover the potential of such mental models in shaping business strategy. In the turbulent early 1970s, Shell's traditional approach of consensus management had been stretched to breaking point by massive, rapid expansive growth. Yet they faced dangerous discontinuities in the marketplace. Historical smooth growth in oil demand and supply was threatened by chronic shortfalls and excessive demand.

Shell's planners could see the potential impact of these changes in the market-place, but lacked a mechanism to impress this thinking on Shell managers around the world. They pioneered the technique of scenario planning as a technique for stretching the mental models of their managers, rather than a predictive technique for guessing the future oil price.

The scenarios that Shell developed in 1973 forced managers around the world to consider the impact of an oil crisis. It was spectacularly successful. It prepared Shell management for the real crisis that followed. By the end of the decade, they had overtaken most of their competitors and propelled themselves from being the weakest oil major to becoming the strongest. Since then, Shell has had less spectacular commercial success from its scenario planning, but it's delivered deep insights, as well as a fair degree of attitude shaping.

A different success story for scenario planning can be seen from the use of the technique by the South African Government in the early 1990s. Faced with mounting international pressure and growing internal strife, South Africa began to contemplate a possible future without apartheid. The De Klerk government announced that it would end apartheid and have open elections in 1994. They wanted to encourage a country-wide debate and agree a plan with all stakeholders for a stable, peaceful transition. Scenario planning was a key enabling tool for this.

The government organized a series of workshops at a conference centre near Cape Town, called Mont Fleur. The aim was to use scenario planning to enable strategic thinking and debate amongst South African leaders about the future of their country. The Mont Fleur scenario team included politicians, activists, trade unionists, economists and business executives from across South Africa. The conference used four alternative scenarios to provoke debate. Each was based on a characteristic bird, which helped to provide the appropriate 'stickiness' factor.

The 'Ostrich' scenario represented the idea of a non-negotiated resolution that was not sustainable, a situation in which no change would occur as the parties dealt only with their allies, not their opponents. The 'Lame Duck' scenario represented a situation of a transition that was slow and indecisive. The 'Icarus' scenario represented a transition that was rapid, but short-lived, as government pursued an unsustainable, populist agenda. The 'Flight of the Flamingos' scenario was the preferred scenario, in which government policies were sustainable and the country took a path of inclusive democracy and growth. These scenarios provided a common language and a clear set of options, with powerful associated images. They steered many of the crucial discussions and thinking that underpinned the subsequent transition from minority to majority rule.

The Royal Mail Group has also made interesting use of scenarios, creating videos of imaginary, future interviews with different types of customers. These videos helped retail managers to better understand the potential changes in customer needs and perspective that might take place over a long-term period.

I've also use scenarios myself to stretch the strategic thinking of my security research team. I selected three scenarios to represent alternative future states for security technology. 'Order' represented the triumph of the security standards community in creating an electronic business world, underpinned by consistent interfaces and trusted services. 'Chaos' represented a marketplace dominated by pervasive proprietary solutions that could not inter-operate securely. 'Silver bullet' represented the compelling, proprietary solution that might emerge and progressively capture the market. Each of these three scenarios suggested adjustments that would be needed to the focus and priorities of the research team, changing the balance of effort applied to standards, inter-operability or horizon scanning of emerging products. As with all scenario planning exercises, the most realistic future outcome is never one or another of the scenarios but a mixture of all three.

Dangers of scenario planning

Scenario planning is not without its dangers, especially when applied to business strategy. It can encourage a risk-averse approach to innovative proposals. It might, for example, put you off entering a lucrative new market because of the worst case risks highlighted by an unlikely future scenario.

Scenarios put extreme alternatives at the forefront of your mind. As we saw in Chapter 4, many people have a perspective of risk that's distorted by ease of recall, recent attention or over-familiarity. It's often the case that a business might view routine business risks as acceptable, because they are familiar, yet view remote risks, highlighted by scenario planning, as unacceptable because they are unusual and dramatic. But scenarios can also polarize people's thinking, making it hard to focus on the more likely, middle path.

We could argue, on the one hand, that banks might have been put off leveraged, sub-prime investments if they had spent time exploring the downside of the scenarios. But they would also have then missed out on the huge profits made in the preceding years.

Scenario planning is a superb tool for exploring the impact of dangerous, unlikely options, ones that a regular business manager would never address, situations such as the Black Swan events we discussed in Chapter 3. We might even encounter one of these scenarios. But the challenge is to be prepared for potential Black Swan events, without wasting undue time and effort concerning ourselves about events that are highly unlikely to happen.

Images speak louder

Videos are an excellent and entertaining way of changing perception. I've seen them used successfully in several organizations and I've also helped create several films myself.

Videos first became a viable option in the early 1990s. At that time, the making of a short five-minute video might have cost $80,000 to $100,000. But that was affordable for a large organization when compared with the cost of developing, printing and distributing paper documents, and the savings obtained in the costs of conducting remote presentations or training courses. Today, of course, all of these costs and savings are much lower, especially with the availability of low-cost, high-quality equipment and the increasing capability of ordinary staff to shoot professional quality videos.

We developed two videos in the early 1990s for Shell companies, which were designed to promote a major attitude change. Both were well received. The second of the two, entitled *Who Knows*, was a classic of its kind, distinguished by the fact that a commentary on information security threats was combined with visual images of an ordinary household, without a single image of a computer shown. Hackers were illustrated by vandals, viruses by a plague of rats, espionage by a cleaner looking through personal drawers and availability by a house fire.

This is a powerful trick to gain 'stickiness': combining key security messages with everyday household images. Other videos that I've seen produced by other companies have been less memorable, generally relying on images of computers and IT users. But one useful idea for a video that's both compelling and easy to film, and has been used successfully by companies such as Boeing, is to shoot short interviews with senior directors or Executive Board members, enabling them to communicate what they really think about the subject and why it's important for enterprise staff to pay attention to it.

A novel approach

One of the most interesting and imaginative initiatives I've ever encountered for encouraging an attitude change to security was the commissioning of a paperback novel, for internal use, by a leading television screenplay writer.

The company, a leading international manufacturer, decided to adopt this novel approach following an industrial espionage incident in 1990. They needed to explain the nature of the threat and the learning points from the incident to their executives. It was a rich and fascinating story. What more compelling way could there be than explaining the events through a short paperback novel penned by a professional writer?

It might seem to be an ambitious, expensive approach. But the costs of such an initiative are not prohibitive. Hiring a professional copywriter to draft the text is not expensive. And there are plenty of cheap services available for printing paperback books. The downside is that it's unlikely to be as popular a read as a best-selling novel. And the shelves of most home and office libraries are filled with dozens of unread books. I started to read this book myself but I never finished it. It was good but not quite 'unputdownable'.

This type of approach would work much better when combined with an incentive to actually read the book, perhaps by running some form of game or competition about text or events that are buried in the book. But commissioning a book about an interesting incident is a relatively fast and easy method for a security manager with limited time and resources to produce a quality, eye-catching source of relevant, educational and attitude-changing material.

The balance of consequences

The 'balance of consequences' is a technique developed back in the 1970s by behavioural psychologists. I first encountered this technique when we employed a team of Dutch psychologists in the early 1990s to help with a Shell security awareness campaign. I've since successfully employed it on several occasions. With sufficient imagination, it can be surprisingly powerful.

The idea is to identify all of the potential enablers and blockers that might act either for or against the desired behaviour. This type of analysis not only helps us to understand why people are not behaving in the way we would like, it also helps us to identify the measures that we need to create, change or remove, in order to encourage the desired behaviour.

The balance of consequences is a simple process that's essentially a practical technique, rather than an academic theory. It's a similar approach to 'force field analysis', which aims to identify and analyse the forces at work that might help or hinder change or a desired outcome. But the balance of consequences is different, in that it focuses exclusively on the identified motivators for people's behaviour.

The assumption is that to change people's behaviour, we should focus on the perceived consequences of people's actions, the perceived outcomes that are expected to flow from the behaviour, rather than the things that activate it, such as policies, rules and commands. As we discussed earlier in this chapter, the consequences that are the most powerful motivators are the ones that are personal, immediate and certain. These motivators, which we'll call 'PIC' for short, will need to be highlighted in some way.

The starting point is to define the desirable behaviour that you wish to encourage, as well as the corresponding, undesirable behaviour that you also wish to discourage. They might at first sight appear to be two versions of the same thing, such as doing something or not doing it. But it's useful to be able to view the problem from two different perspectives. For example, in the security field, we might choose 'keeping laptops secure' as a desired behaviour, and 'loss or theft of a laptop' as a behaviour to be removed.

The next step is to draw up four separate lists, as indicated in Figure 8.1. These lists represent the four sets of consequences that work either for or against the desirable behaviour, as well as the undesirable behaviour. There will be some inevitable duplication in drawing up these lists. But that does no harm. At this stage, a good imagination is the critical success factor. In fact, the exercise is best done as a team 'brainstorming' exercise.

Let's consider the type of factors we might identify. For example, considering the example of 'keeping laptops secure', we might identify consequences that encourage the desired behaviour such as it 'safeguards enterprise data' or it 'ensures the laptop and data are always available'.

The latter consequence is a powerful one as it is personal, immediate and certain. It has a lot of PIC, as we might put it. But the former factor has none of these attributes, so by itself it will have little or no impact on people.

CONSEQUENCES THAT ENCOURAGE THE DESIRED BEHAVIOUR	CONSEQUENCES THAT DISCOURAGE THE DESIRABLE BEHAVIOUR
A list of factors to be reinforced	A list of factors to be removed
CONSEQUENCES THAT DISCOURAGE THE UNDESIRABLE BEHAVIOUR	CONSEQUENCES THAT ENCOURAGE THE UNDESIRABLE BEHAVIOUR
A list of factors to be reinforced	A list of factors to be removed

Figure 8.1 Assessing the balance of consequences for behaviour change

We can then imagine adding additional factors to strengthen the motivation for this behaviour such as being 'rewarded for securing my laptop'. That would have a strong PIC factor, though it will require some creative thinking to determine an appropriate measure and a suitable reward.

Thinking of factors that *discourage* the desired behaviour of 'keeping laptops secure', we might identify consequences such as the 'time gained in not bothering to take security precautions'. That's also very PIC, and will therefore be very powerful. But it discourages the behaviour we want, so we should aim to eliminate or minimize this factor, for example by introducing automation or a better design of security features.

Now let's turn our attention to the factors that might encourage the *undesired* behaviour of 'loss or theft of a laptop'. We might identify perceived consequences such as 'we get the latest new model as a replacement'. This is certainly a real motivator for losing or damaging smaller items of equipment. I know a few executives who dropped their old mobile phones from a great height in order to qualify for a new latest model.

Finally, let's look at the factors that might discourage staff from losing their laptop. In fact there are quite a few. They might include consequences such as 'an inability to work' or 'the loss of personal data' or 'the hassle of replacement', all of which are very strong PIC consequences. We could also add 'loss of enterprise data' but that doesn't have much of a PIC factor, unless we introduce a further factor such as 'disciplinary action' which is very PIC, as long as we ensure it's communicated and consistently applied.

So what would be the conclusions of this exercise? And how might it have changed our existing thinking? The answer is that it will have almost certainly made a substantial impact on the strategy for the change campaign.

Before this exercise, we might well have chosen a rather typical but ineffective message such as: 'Look after your laptop because it's a valuable asset and its loss might cause serious damage to the long-term interests of the organization'. But that would have no PIC factor and absolutely no impact.

After the exercise, the messages to staff might include the following, more powerful PIC-oriented messages:

- 'If you lose your laptop, you will be unable to work and you will lose your personal data'

- 'It will be a major hassle for you to replace your lost laptop'

- 'You will have let your colleagues down'

- 'You will lose out on any rewards and will face disciplinary action'

We might also communicate the fact that we will be aiming to introduce new systems that will eliminate or reduce the time it takes to apply security safeguards.

All of these messages will serve to encourage the right behaviour and help to eliminate the bad behaviour. This type of exercise might throw up a large number of fairly small considerations. But that's the nature of effective behaviour change. It's all down to careful analysis of the problem areas, identification of many small ideas, followed by fine adjustments to a set of factors that might have otherwise seemed unimportant to less enlightened observers.

The power of attribution

We saw in Chapter 4 that criminals seek to rationalize their behaviour and justify their actions by blaming it on someone else, convincing themselves that 'they had it coming' or 'he made me do it'. In social psychology circles, this phenomenon is called 'attribution theory', because it's concerned with the way people attribute the causes of actions or events.

And such attributions are made not just towards other people, objects or events. Sometimes the blame, or more likely the credit, is also aimed squarely at themselves. We see this all the time. If a fisherman lands a great fish, for example, he's likely to claim that it was skill rather than luck. There is, in fact, a strong bias towards over-attributing causes to people, rather than to circumstances.

When people make an attribution for their actions, they will also adjust their attitudes and beliefs about themselves. This presents an opportunity for changing behaviour. If we get can people to accept that their actions are directly responsible for a good outcome, one that we desire, we might actually encourage them to maintain the behaviour that delivers this outcome. It does not matter so much whether they actually had much to do with it, as long as there's a credible connection that they accept.

For example, we might tell our staff that the level of computer virus outbreaks has been reduced directly because of their good behaviour in not opening attachments in unsolicited e-mails. This will have more impact than just advising them not to open attachments, because they will note a direct connection between their behaviour and the level of virus outbreaks in the enterprise. People are more likely to try harder at doing something if they believe it's likely to get a result. And attribution theory suggests that they're more inclined to believe that an outcome is the result of their actions, rather than just the circumstances at the time.

Applying such interventions will work best when people are actually thinking about what causes the event in question. It will help, therefore, to create such a climate, by, for example, preceding your message with a question to set them thinking. Start, for example, by asking a question such as 'What do you think caused the recent drop in virus outbreaks?' Then you can go on to suggest that 'The answer is you and your smart behaviour'.

Encouraging staff to develop attributions to their own behaviour for desired outcomes can be much more effective than applying external controls, such as supervision or monitoring. If people believe that it's up to others to stop something happening, they'll take a less responsible approach. That's a limitation of external factors, such as monitoring, or ad hoc rewards and punishments. They have to be continuously applied to be effective. In contrast, a few well-timed suggestions to staff can help to build the internal motivators that encourage the right future behaviour.

Environments shape behaviour

I've always been fascinated by the phenomenon that the same group of people will behave very differently in rooms of different shapes or sizes. As we discussed in Chapter 3, the size and shape of a crisis room will have a significant influence on crisis team behaviour. I've experienced this myself on many occasions. When you're in a big conference room, you just can't help yourself from standing up alongside a white board and setting down your ideas to get things moving. Yet in a small room it seems so much more natural, and more comfortable, to sit down with your colleagues and work on paper. In fact this phenomenon extends to all types of group and all sizes of room.

The Royal Mail Group began to experiment with environments when they built their Innovation Lab in Rugby in the late 1990s. Initially it was a showcase for technology as well as an environment to stimulate innovation. Progressively it's become primarily the latter. Amongst other things, the facilitators discovered that teams operate and interact very differently according to the shape, size and style of the room, as well as the height and arrangement of seating or standing areas.

We see this phenomenon in many other environments. Consider the Houses of Parliament, for example, an arrangement of two directly opposed sets of tiered seating, clearly designed to provoke confrontation and argument between two opposing sides. In contrast, an auditorium is designed to encourage a large audience to train their view onto a single central stage, enabling the announcement of important messages. A more formal variant of this can be seen in old-fashioned classrooms, which have carefully aligned rows of listeners arranged in neat rows to encourage attention to a teacher or lecturer.

Different again, is the arrangement of seating we usually see in an executive boardroom, with a chairman facing down a table, his vision at right angles to the line of sight of the other board members. Such an arrangement discourages challenge and therefore facilitates endorsement. A healthier alternative to this is a round table which encourages a more democratic discussion amongst equals. And for a crisis room, you might consider a semicircle or horseshoe arrangement of seats around a central screen to enable collaboration to resolve a shared problem.

The style of the fixtures, fittings and furniture also makes a difference. The Royal Mail Lab contains a variety of environments, including stand-up and sit-down areas equipped with high-tech furniture, children's furniture, settees and armchairs, and a variety of toys, games, puzzles and creative tools. The Lab has been successful in providing an effective environment for executives that encourages them to shed their normal persona and enter a more creative world to help brainstorm and develop roadmaps and strategies. Researchers at the University of East Anglia have also built on the experiences of the Lab to develop improved designs for school classrooms.

The learning point for information security is that, by attention to the design and state of the physical environment, we can encourage people to behave in a consistent, disciplined way or in an argumentative, disruptive manner. We can persuade people to sit quietly, stand up, argue or behave in a creative, individual manner. Physical surroundings will have a major influence on staff perception and organizational culture. We should take much greater care when we design them.

Enforcing the rules of the network

The above findings are based on real-life experiences with physical environments. But similar concepts can also apply to digital networks. All networks require rules and protocols. In public networks some form of self-regulation will generally emerge. Critical comments from peers will quickly establish a baseline of acceptable behaviour, which will become the norm for a network.

We're all familiar, for example, with the basic e-mail netiquette, which discourages use of block capitals, as it conveys shouting, and encourages smiley faces in order to suggest to recipients whether a comment should be taken as a criticism or a harmless joke. All organizations need to implement netiquette rules for e-mail because staff e-mails convey an image to the outside world. Education on the finer points of e-mail communication is important for efficiency in communications, as well as for avoiding legal liabilities through careless criticism, unintended contract acceptance or casual remarks that might be used against the organization to support a legal claim.

In business today the first, and often the only contact with business partners, colleagues and customers will be through e-mail. It's very different from face-to-face communication, where most of what you convey is through physical appearance, style and body language. E-mail has an informal feel, which can lead to more casual, perhaps over-familiar remarks. We tend to say 'Hi Fred' rather than 'Dear Mr Smith' to people we've never met, even if we're discussing a serious matter or negotiating a large commercial contract.

It's even more important to set down the rules when it comes to surfing the Internet, or engaging in social networks. Downloading of inappropriate material or posting of confidential information on public websites can have serious implications. Yet most companies do little more than establish a simple corporate policy and conduct a degree of automated monitoring for inappropriate material.

Much more than that is needed to maintain a disciplined, acceptable level of 'acceptable use' of corporate networks and Internet communications. Ignoring bad habits suggests that the organization doesn't care, that nobody enforces corporate policy, and that it's quite acceptable to break company rules. These are dangerous signals to send out. Visible toleration of minor bad practices can progressively lead on to more serious abuses.

In a public network, someone will eventually step forward and take a lead in defining and promoting desirable behaviour. For an enterprise network, that will generally be left to the corporate centre. Bad practice needs to be challenged. Inappropriate behaviour needs to be tackled with disciplinary action. Insecure communications need to be strongly discouraged. We need to apply much greater attention to our network behaviour, and apply the electronic equivalent of the 'broken window theory' that helped to reduce crime in New York City, an initiative we might perhaps think of as 'the bad e-mail theory'. We'll return to the 'broken window' theory in the final chapter when we discuss the power of 'tipping points'.

Encouraging business ethics

In its broadest sense, ethics is a branch of philosophy, about correct or inappropriate conduct, right or wrong decisions and good or bad lifestyles. In business practice, it's implemented as a set of rules and principles that encourage prudent decision-making.

But life is full of contradictions, and so is business. Managers have responsibilities and incentives to maximize profit for their shareholders, not just a desire to make the world a better place. Sometimes these objectives coincide. When they do it's down to serendipity, a happy coincidence that's rarely encountered in everyday business practice.

People do like to work for and buy products from a company that has good business ethics. In the right business climate, for example an industry with a shortfall in skills that operates within a growing market, adopting an ethical approach to business can deliver a significant competitive edge. In such cases, it makes sense to encourage ethical practices.

Unfortunately, managers are not just influenced by logic. They are also driven by targets, peer competition, politics, ambition and greed. But in competitive situations, codes of practice and business principles can make a difference by serving as the 'rules of the game', a means of differentiating good business practice, as well as a reason to find fault with the performance of other businesses or executives.

We should never ignore the power of this latter factor. There is no easy way for us to monitor and enforce the right behaviour across a team of empowered, competitive executives. But if we set a minimum standard we will find that, especially in competitive situations, our peers will implement it for us. Like many techniques for leveraging intellectual assets, the real trick is to get others to do the work for us. We have to think more like a shepherd, someone who sets and reinforces the direction of group behaviour, rather than a sergeant major, who simply barks direct orders at individuals.

The art of on-line persuasion

Professor B. J. Fogg has coined the term 'captology' to describe his work at Stanford University's Persuasive Technology Lab into how computing products, ranging from websites to mobile phone software, can be designed to change people's beliefs and behaviours.

Recent themes at the lab have included mobile persuasion: how to influence people over mobile phones; the psychology of Facebook: what makes it compelling and what persuades people to install new applications; as well as the more idealistic concept of 'peace technology': how technology can help change attitudes and behaviours in ways that bring about global harmony.

This work is still in its infancy, but there are many emerging ideas and principles that will be valuable to anyone aiming to gain influence and cooperation across digital networks.

One motivating factor, for example, that's believed to encourage people to post their photograph on Facebook, is the use of a question mark as a default image. Few people are comfortable seeing their personal image presented in this way. It's a simple but highly effective trick.

Learning to change behaviour

This chapter set out to examine some of the motivators for human behaviour, as well as how we might go about changing it. What did we learn in this process?

Firstly we learned that there is both an art and a science in changing people's attitudes and behaviour. And it's especially hard to influence a group of people. Activators, such as rules and policies, will have some impact, but it will be very limited. We need to encourage self-discovery of new attitudes, through games or stories, and to concentrate on motivators such as the perceived consequences of people's actions. But not all motivators are the same. The ones that count are those that are personal, immediate and certain.

When it comes to incentives, rewards will always beat punishments, but in practice we might not have that choice available. Both should therefore be explored and exploited.

There are many techniques for changing attitudes, including scenario planning, videos, games, novels or fairy tales. The choice is a matter of taste, imagination, facilities and budget. We also take many cues from our role and our immediate environment. And it's not just how they were intended and designed, but, more importantly, how they're perceived or imagined. To change people's behaviour, we have to focus on these important influences.

Scenario planning is a powerful method for changing mental models. It's a rich subject area with many different examples of how to encourage executives to consider ideas they would previously never have imagined. Good scenarios enable managers to think the unthinkable, to prepare for the unexpected.

Changing behaviour is much harder than changing attitudes. There is a useful practical technique called the 'balance of consequences', which helps to identify the key enablers and blockers to a desired behaviour, based on an analysis of perceived consequences, especially those that are personal, immediate and certain.

There are also other factors that shape people's attitudes and behaviours, such as the 'power of attribution', which encourages people to attribute outcomes to people, things or events, rather than circumstances.

And environments also shape behaviour. Groups will behave completely differently depending of the shape, size and cues of their physical environment. It's not just physical environments that matter. Netiquette and other on-line protocols have a major impact on behaviour.

Existing corporate 'acceptable use' policies are rarely effective. They need to be richer, more personalized and enforced, less by central policy or compliance units, and more by the members of the network. But we are only at the beginning of this new science of on-line persuasion.

These are the ten things that most influence people's attitudes and behavior:

- Stories that they read, and games that they play
- Their perceived organizational role
- The influence and authority of their management
- Accepted corporate rules and procedures
- The nature of the local office or cyberspace environment
- The actions of their immediate colleagues
- The cues and controls in the systems they use
- The personal consequences of their actions
- Things that are personal, immediate and certain
- Their most recent experiences

Gaining executive board and business buy-in

Gaining buy-in to enterprise programs requires more than good ideas and content. Style, presentation, and alignment with investment appraisal, coupled with pro-active relationship management, are the keys to achieving support and funding. This chapter examines pragmatic strategies and tactics for selling new ideas to the organization. In particular, it addresses the psychological factors associated with preparing, selling and presenting proposals for information security expenditure.

Countering security fatigue

One of the more unfortunate aspects of security is that the better we become at preventing incidents, the more likely it is that we will lose credibility. In other words, 'security fatigue' will set in. The result is that management will challenge budgets and staff will become complacent. As a Dutch colleague of mine used to put it, 'We're in danger of drowning in our own success'. It's important therefore to be aware of this phenomenon, to anticipate security fatigue, and to adapt your strategy to compensate for it.

There are many things that can be done to overcome security fatigue. Firstly, it's essential to keep your management up-to-date about changes in the risk landscape. You won't, for example, be able to justify support for an increase in your budget, unless you can point to something new that demands it. Fortunately, there's always plenty of independent evidence around to suggest that new risks are emerging, and existing risks increasing.

Secondly, don't cry wolf, or if you do, do it once and make it last. Back in 1999, for example, I forecast that we would probably not witness an 'electronic Pearl Harbor' until around 2006 to 2008. The logic behind that statement was the conclusions of a long-range, information security road mapping exercise, which

Managing the Human Factor in Information Security   David Lacey
© 2009 John Wiley & Sons, Ltd

indicated a peak in general risk profiles at that point. A forecast such as this will keep people alert for several years, despite no major incidents occurring. And if they did, I could still have claimed, 'I told you it was coming'.

Thirdly, it helps to place a realistic quantification on your projections. For example, if you assess the risk of a major incident in the coming year as, say, one in five, there's a very good chance that it won't happen at all. You should therefore point out that the organization was lucky this year, but that this luck will run out in future years. And if you point out that the risk is much higher than that, say four out of five, then you will also have a good chance of justifying immediate expenditure, in order to reduce the risk to an acceptable level.

Fourthly, when bidding for budgets, adopt a richer vocabulary for individual countermeasures. Don't lump them all together in a single, general category, such as 'network security' or 'identity and access control'. New technologies in the same solution space are appearing all the time. Any accountant worth his salt will notice that you already have a product that sounds very similar. So why should they support further expenditure on the same thing? It's hard, for example, to explain why you might need an extra million for 'intrusion prevention' when you already have a sizeable budget for expenditure on 'network security'.

Fifthly, explain that the enterprise needs to move to a 'defense-in-depth' approach, a Swiss cheese or onion skin model. Most managers will understand the concept, and it makes absolutely perfect sense. It also implies that you need more than one level of countermeasure, so your management and accountants will naturally anticipate several tranches of spending to be forthcoming.

Money isn't everything

Many security managers claim that a major problem in making a business case is proving that it will deliver a positive financial return on investment. But making or saving money is not the only way to demonstrate value.

The real requirement is to be able to demonstrate that the expenditure in question is a sensible one. That's quite simple in a small, informal business. You just need to put together a convincing argument. But in a medium or large organization you will have to do a lot more. There will be approval processes and pre-defined hurdles to overcome. In fact, in many organizations today, it's becoming more important to present a business case that passes the enterprise's investment appraisal criteria, than it is to make a convincing pitch to the executive board.

To meet investment appraisal criteria, however, you don't always have to present hard evidence of a financial payback within a particular time period. There will also be other criteria for justifying investments, such as regulatory compliance requirements for instance, or the need for urgent action to prevent the imminent collapse of an essential service. There might also be the possibility that business communications might collapse if preventative action is not taken immediately to block a rising tide of spam.

In fact, metrics are always helpful in making business case, though not everything in life is knowable or measurable, especially in the dark, hidden and fast-changing world of information security. But if your figures don't meet the necessary financial criteria, you might still have an outside chance of succeeding through a brilliant pitch to the board. It's rare, but I've seen it happen. I recall a case where the chairman of a large organization responded to a forceful presentation by a colleague with the words, 'I don't care about the business case, I'm backing that person'.

What makes a good business case?

Business cases are the primary vehicle for gaining approval to spend money, so it's important to know how to put a compelling one together. Making the case for any expenditure on security can be a challenge, especially if it's an investment in enterprise infrastructure, which individual business units would prefer not to pay for, as it's expensive and rarely delivers immediate benefits.

Business managers expect their investments to deliver enhanced revenues or profits. And IT managers look for enhanced performance and functionality. Unfortunately, most of the benefits delivered by information security are invisible, uncertain and often impossible to measure. People who engage in espionage or fraud don't advertise their activities. And we might not be aware of failed attempts or successful attacks that have no immediate business impact. Many of the benefits associated with security investments are also long-term ones, impossible to guarantee, and often benefiting someone other than the manager who pays the bill.

Many experienced business managers will also be unconvinced about the effectiveness of new security technology. They might have had previous encounters with ambitious schemes that failed to deliver benefits, expensive solutions such as PKI schemes and intrusion detection systems. With hindsight we can see why many such solutions failed. They were not proven as complete, practical business solutions, for example, and did not take sufficient account of commercial or operational constraints. In fact, many enterprise security solutions are a leap of faith, from an investment perspective, and few deliver clear, measurable benefits. We can only get away with that sort of investment once within the memory of our management team or investment appraisal function.

And, as we've already seen in earlier chapters, most managers have a poor grasp of security threats and exposures. They are likely, therefore, to underestimate the risks to their own organizations. Their starting assumption might be, 'Why should anyone want to attack us?' So you will have to lobby strongly to convince them otherwise. A good business case, however, can overcome these negative perceptions by presenting compelling evidence of the need for change and by explaining how the benefits generated align with current business strategy and objectives.

Aligning with investment appraisal criteria

Most organizations have an appraisal process for determining whether a project or investment meets a set of minimum investment criteria, and, in particular, how the investment compares to other projects that might be competing for the same money. In a perfect security world, we should be able to set out the case for a security investment by simply explaining the benefits that it brings. Unfortunately, if every project took such an approach it would be impossible to compare and rank them when they compete for funding. For this reason, enterprises need to maintain a standard set of categories and criteria to support investment appraisal decisions. You will have to present your case in this standard format in order to get it approved.

Investment appraisal processes are generally based on a set of criteria with a strong focus on the speed and rate of the projected return on investment. But, as mentioned earlier, financial return is not the only factor. Expenditure can also be justified because it's needed to either satisfy regulatory compliance demands, or to support essential maintenance purposes, or to enable an expansion of sales, or perhaps to deliver 'softer' benefits such as staff satisfaction, innovation or business agility.

A key consideration will also be the contribution to current business goals, corporate strategies or enterprise programs. Many organizations will sort competing capital expenditure proposals into categories reflecting key business drivers, such as expansion or enhanced profitability. But expenditure on security often delivers multiple benefits and can often impact each of these categories in a number of distinct ways.

When times are hard, many executive boards will suspend less essential categories of expenditure, so it's important to find out which categories are currently in favour and which are not. In fact, the most effective approach is to seek out your investment appraisal function, and ask them what they look for in a good business case. They will usually be delighted to put you right. It makes their own job much easier, and it gives them advance intelligence of a new proposal that's coming their way.

Translating benefits into financial terms

The aim of a return on investment (ROI) model is to establish the value of a project by calculating the value of the benefits, minus the associated costs, and expressing the resulting value as a percentage of the overall costs. The benefits can include intangible as well as tangible benefits, as far as they can be assessed and measured in financial terms.

Calculating ROI is best done as an iterative process, starting with the obvious tangible benefits and then progressively including the difficult-to-calculate, intangible ones, if any further financial justification is necessary to meet the investment criteria. For a phased deployment, this process will need to be done in conjunction with the development of the project plan, to ensure that the timing of costs and benefits can be adjusted where necessary to fit the investment criteria.

There are a number of financial methods that are commonly used to calculate and express financial returns of projects, ranging from simple calculations of the average rate of return per year, to more sophisticated discounted cash flow and internal rate of return calculations of the 'net present value' of the project, which take account of the reducing value of expenditure that will occur in future years.

One of the most widely used yardsticks for comparing projects is the 'payback' method, which measures the time required for the cash inflows to equal the cash outflows associated with the project. A detailed analysis of such financial methods is outside of the scope of this book, but a basic appreciation of the methods used to calculate and compare the financial implications of projects is essential for understanding how to put together a compelling, professional business case.

Aligning with IT strategy

In many organizations, information security investments are either embedded in, or aligned with, the governance process for managing IT expenditure. In a sophisticated IT function, there will be a structured approach for managing the IT portfolio of systems and projects. IT portfolio managers generally apply four main criteria when examining the business value delivered by investments in applications and services:

- **Alignment with strategic goals:** How investments meet the objectives of the business, and the metrics used to assess whether they have been achieved

- **Financial benefits, costs and metrics:** The return on investment expected and how will it be measured

- **Inhibitors and risks:** The actions that need to be taken to overcome obstacles and risks to delivering value

- **Timeliness:** The time imperatives and constraints, including dependencies between different investments

Information security initiatives should be translated into such terms, in order to ensure understanding, comparison and acceptance by IT portfolio managers.

A major benefit of this approach is that alignment with IT strategy and portfolio management processes will encourage IT managers to regard security expenditure as an integral, visible component of IT budgets and expenditure, rather than just an optional extra, requiring exceptional treatment.

Achieving a decisive result

As we've seen in previous chapters, organizations have very different cultures, risk appetites and compliance requirements. Security threats, and their potential business impact, can vary considerably. A business case that works well in one organization, might not necessarily translate to another.

Decision-making processes can also be quite different. At one extreme is a rigid, decisive type of approach, where decisions are taken once and for all, and rarely revisited. If you try to argue against them later, you'll be criticized yourself, for not speaking up at the time the decision was made. At the other extreme, is a more volatile approach, where decisions are constantly challenged, and can be overturned in response to changing business parameters and drivers, or by appealing to a more senior authority. One of my colleagues used to refer to the consequences of that governance model as 'The Court of Infinite Appeals'.

Understanding where to aim your briefings and lobbying is important. Sometimes it pays to focus your efforts on perfecting your pitch to a particular business committee. In other cases, it might be necessary to obtain buy-in from multiple stakeholders across an organization. But, as far as possible, the presentation of your business case and arguments should be tailored to suit the preferences and language of the individual stakeholders that can influence the investment decision. If all else fails, there is always the potential of an appeal to the executive board, or perhaps beyond that, the audit committee. And that's when it will really pay to get your presentation of the business case perfectly pitched.

Evidence of wider organizational support will always add a powerful dimension to any business case. But the most important aspect of any business case is that the reason for change is both compelling and easy to grasp, and that it focuses on the ends rather than the means, i.e. it spells out what benefits will actually be delivered, rather than just explaining how it will be done.

Key elements of a good business case

Regardless of the particular investment appraisal standards and formats of an organization, there are certain key elements that are common to all business cases. These are:

- **Setting out the business need for change:**   Why the investment is needed, and why it's needed now
- **Options:**   What other action can be taken, including the 'do nothing' option
- **Costs and benefits:**   The full costs and benefits over the life of the project, and when they will occur
- **Managing the risks:**   The risks of failure, or success, and how they will be managed
- **Your recommendation:**   A clear recommendation, taking account of all of the options, costs and risks

Some organizations have set templates for presenting business cases or executive board papers. They will generally be similar to the above structure. And, like all corporate rules, they need to be strictly obeyed if you are to succeed in any authorization process. Sometimes you can get lucky, and drive through a business case by the seat of your pants. But the professional practitioner should not set out to gamble. It's better to have all of the bases covered before you submit your case. The last thing you need is to have your case rejected on a technicality.

Assembling the business case

The starting point in assembling a business case is to identify the reason for the change, and to establish the timing for the change. It's important to identify and set out clearly why a change is needed, and why it's needed now. Key arguments that could be used to make the case for an immediate investment might include the following:

- The need to secure an identified and unacceptable high risk
- The need to add further security to an existing system to enable it to operate in a higher risk environment
- The need to meet legal, contractual or regulatory compliance requirements

The benefits and costs associated with the change should then be identified and quantified, as far as possible. Some benefits are likely to be tangible, measurable savings, such as operational efficiencies that will deliver cost savings or headcount reductions. Others might be powerful, but less tangible and more uncertain, benefits, such as enhanced business agility, or a projected reduction in incident levels.

The tangible, measurable benefits should always be considered first. If they outweigh the projected costs and meet the organization's investment appraisal criteria, then the business case can be made purely on these savings alone. That reduces the amount of work you will need to do. But, if not, then the next step will be to address and try, as best as you can, to quantify the intangible benefits.

Identifying and assessing benefits

A short brainstorming session is the best way of identifying and assessing the full range of benefits associated with a security investment. A useful technique for comparing benefits is to plot them on a 2 × 2 matrix, similar to the one we used in Chapter 4 for risk identification and ranking. In this case we will be aiming to identify the relative business value, and the probability of its realization, for each of the identified benefits. This is illustrated in Figure 9.1.

Identifying and illustrating the likelihood of realization of each of the benefits is a useful dimension, as it demonstrates to management that you are aiming to ensure that the claimed benefits will be realized. Many investments fail to deliver the promised benefits in practice. And some benefits are illusory, such as the prospect that a saving of five minutes of every employee's time might actually deliver a tangible cost saving. It won't. In fact no experienced manager would regard this as a real cost saving, but it's still a useful 'soft' benefit to include, in order to enhance the attractiveness of the business case.

Comparing and ranking benefits in this way helps to establish quick, order-of-magnitude estimates of the business value of non-tangible benefits. Potential benefits might include, for example:

- Operational risk reduction
- Incident prevention

- Reputation or brand protection or enhancement
- Operational improvements such as savings in administration
- Legacy system enhancement or extension
- Enabling business agility
- Meeting regulatory compliance requirements
- Increased visibility of attempted or accidental breaches
- Leveraging sales to customers who demand secure products or vendors
- Contribution to strategic business initiatives

The most valuable benefits tend to be business improvements, rather than operational savings. Unfortunately they're often impossible to guarantee. Enhancing the attractiveness of a corporate brand or business product, for example, would clearly represent a significant gain. But it's one that's indirect, uncertain and difficult to measure. Such benefits should therefore be regarded as the icing on the cake, rather than the fundamental basis of the business case.

In fact, all changes present opportunities for improvements in efficiency and ergonomics. Every proposal should therefore aim to save money, improve the user experience and reduce operational risks, regardless of the primary purpose of the investment.

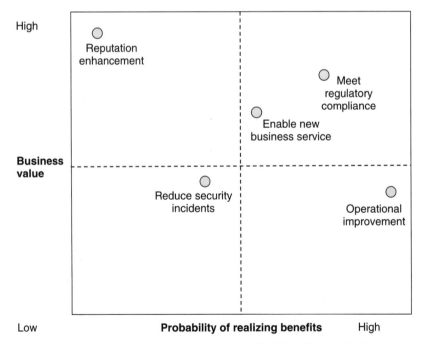

Figure 9.1   Assessing benefits and the likelihood of realization

Something from nothing

No business case should be submitted without options, no matter how unlikely they might seem. Options should include cheaper and more expensive options, where they can be identified. And they must always include the implications of the 'do nothing option', which is, in fact, the most important option, as it represents the essential argument for change. Examples of the implications of doing nothing might include one or more of the following negative consequences:

- An unacceptable level of risk is presented
- Inability to meet pressing business requirements, such as the provision of direct connections to external business partners
- The need for immediate, expensive upgrades to legacy systems, in order to enable unacceptable, inherent security vulnerabilities to be reduced to an acceptable level
- Inability to respond to a security incident when it occurs, with a consequential serious impact on business operations

A good business case will clearly set out the potential risks and costs of not proceeding with the recommended expenditure. It helps to play your very best cards. You should always aim to present the most unattractive, unacceptable 'do nothing' option. Otherwise there is a danger that your management might accept your arguments, but consign your proposal to the back burner, perhaps never to see the light of day again.

If your management likes to compromise, then present at least three options of varying costs and benefits, with your preferred solution firmly in the middle. That way they will believe they have achieved the prudent compromise of limiting your spending ambitions, without major security risks being presented. On the other hand, if your management is set on ruthlessly minimizing all expenditure, then make sure your preferred solution is the lowest cost of at least three options.

Never think that such tactics are devious or unprofessional. All's fair in love and war. And when it comes to competing business cases it's most definitely a state of war.

Reducing project risks

The risks associated with each option in any business case should always be clearly identified, assessed and set out, together with proposed measures to reduce these risks to an acceptable level. Typical risks would include items such as:

- The risk of failure of the project, which can be reduced by good project management

- The possibility of a technical, operational or security failure of the proposed solution, which can be mitigated through product evaluation, testing and use of reference sites

- The residual security risks associated with the various options

It's important to remember that risks are events, rather than issues, and each one should have a calculated probability of occurrence and an estimated business impact. Demonstrating that the risks associated with an investment have been properly identified, evaluated and addressed delivers confidence that the project has been well thought through and that it's being professionally managed.

Framing your recommendations

Every business case must have a clear and compelling set of recommendations, which should be as prominent as possible in order to enable the reader to immediately grasp the size of the investment, as well as the nature of the product, service or resource that's being sought.

Some organizations will have standardized formats for business cases. These will need to be followed as closely as possible. An important point to note is that if the format requires the recommendations to be presented towards the end of the document, then they should also be summarized at the beginning, or in a brief executive overview. This is important, as it's the first thing that any authorizing executive will wish to establish. They will be irritated if they have to search through the document to find the recommended actions. And they are more likely to warm to your arguments if they are presented in a natural, logical sequence.

Recommendations should always be expressed in a clear, compelling and authoritative style, with a short, confident summary of the arguments as to why a particular option is the best choice. Most executives tend to instinctively favour the lowest cost option, so key deciding factors such as the impact on compliance, operational risk and business agility need to be clearly brought out.

In particular, one of the most powerful deciding factors for any business case is the support of other parts of the organization. So it will be a good investment of your time to seek out and collect as many independent endorsements as possible for the recommendations set out in the business case. Even if you can only get these from an individual member, rather than a designated representative, of a business unit it will carry weight. And, in the absence of any objections, business endorsements will often be the deciding factor as far as the recipients of your proposals are concerned.

Mastering the pitch

If you have to present to an executive board, it's worth considering the style of presentation you will need before gathering together any of the content. That means getting into the minds of executive directors and appreciating their perspective, which is likely to be very different from your own.

Firstly, it's important to understand that directors are bright, busy people. They didn't get there by being slow on the uptake. And their job will demand that they have to deal with many different issues in a very short time. That means a number of things. You will have a very limited time to make your pitch. And you cannot assume that they will have had sufficient time to study your briefing papers. They might have had more pressing items to consider. There will also be a danger that the time available for your slot will be curtailed when it comes up. You should therefore plan to be as brief as possible in your introduction, and be ready to summarize your recommendations rapidly if your session is cut short.

Directors will quickly grasp points. Their patience will be limited, and they will be annoyed if you talk down to them. Your presentation will need to be slick, and to the point. They are likely to absorb information faster than you can actually explain it to them. They will become irritated if you labour a particular point. They can also read, so it's best not to read out each bullet point on a presentation slide. In fact, pictures will work better than text to convey complex points.

You should keep an eye on each director's body language. If they look uncomfortable it's worth moving on. If they look confused, there's a danger you might have lost them, so ask them 'Are you with me so far?' Conveying complex arguments or subtle points is much harder. There is always a danger with senior directors that they will jump to a conclusion before you've presenting your full argument. So it's useful to convey a high-level overview of the full scope of the issue before exploring any of the detail.

It's vital also to be confident, compelling and authoritative. Board members are unlikely to be familiar with your own background or achievements. They won't know if you're an expert or a charlatan, though they will have to decide quickly whether to accept your advice or not. If you appear confident, they will be reassured. If you seem clumsy or unsure, they are more likely to challenge your advice. And first impressions count. People will judge you as soon as you walk into the room. Malcolm Gladwell's book *Blink: The Power of Thinking Without Thinking* illustrates how much we tend to rely on split second, intuitive decisions, judgments made without really thinking about them. He calls it 'thin slicing'.

Thin slicing can present serious problems when arguing a business case. If you are too slow at presenting the most important facts, there is a real danger that board members will have already mentally decided before you get a chance to argue these points. And once a director has formed an opinion, it's an extremely difficult task to change it, especially in a very limited time slot. You will probably have lost your chance. So it's vital to convey, or at least hint at, the most important arguments in the opening minutes. Never keep them to the end. They will be wasted.

Some people have suggested to me that whatever you do, it's important to be remembered by your audience, no matter what the reason might have been, or whether it was good or bad. The logic is that busy people are more likely to remember you, rather than what you presented. I'm not too sure about that, but I do believe it's helpful to make a positive impact. And I can suggest a few tricks for ensuring this, if you have the confidence to employ them.

Adding a touch of drama, for example, is one way to make an impact. It can bring a presentation to life. Try throwing a thick bundle of confidential papers on the desk and adding 'We're losing the equivalent of this much sensitive data every hour through bad security'. That will certainly make an impact on your audience. And it will also help convey the impact of the risk on business interests.

Statistics are less useful. You can try quoting as many of them as you like. But in my experience most directors prefer to base their decisions on an opinion from an expert that they can look in the eye, and hold accountable, rather than a set of statistics that might have been heavily massaged. They are also more inclined to 'thin slice' rather than consider the real facts.

Security should always, of course, be linked to business aims. But it can also be sold on its own merits. All managing directors instinctively support security. It would appear irresponsible for them not to do so. But they also tend to challenge the level of spend. This is understandable, as the nature of any modern information security program will be far outside of their experience. They might be able to judge what should be an appropriate level of spend should be for a new product launch or new office accommodation. But they will have absolutely no idea how much money should be spent on an intrusion detection technology, a laptop encryption system, or a security education campaign.

Learning how to make the business case

In this chapter we set out to understand how to gain executive board and business buy-in to expenditure on enterprise programs, through analysis and mastery of the psychological factors associated with the design, marketing and presentation of business cases. What have we learned?

Style, presentation, alignment with investment appraisal and good relationship management, are the keys to achieving support and funding. In particular, it's important to get into the mind of your audience, appreciating their particular perspective which will be very different from your own.

One of the challenges is to overcome the inevitable problem of 'security fatigue'. All successful organizations face this. And the better we become at preventing incidents, the more likely it is that security will appear less necessary, and progressively lose authority and credibility. It's important to anticipate this problem, and to adapt your strategy accordingly.

It helps to deliver a positive financial return on investment. But saving money is not the only way to demonstrate value. The real requirement is to demonstrate that the expenditure you seek is a sensible investment. It's important also to meet your organization's investment appraisal criteria. Metrics can help, but not everything in information security is knowable or measurable.

A good business case presents compelling evidence of the need for change, together with a clear set of benefits that are aligned with business objectives and IT strategy. Many organizations have a common template for setting out the business case. An important principle to adopt is that no business case should be submitted without options, no matter how unlikely they might seem. And it's especially important to include the 'do nothing' option, which should, of course, be clearly unattractive and unacceptable, if we are to achieve an immediate, positive result.

One of the most powerful deciding factors for any business case is the support of other parts of the organization. It will certainly pay to collect as many endorsements as possible for your recommendations. This helps to de-risk the decision in the minds of the decision-makers. Again, it's the human factor, rather than the economic case, that's likely to prove to be the deciding factor.

When presenting to executive boards, it's important to remember that directors are generally very bright, busy people. You will have to be brief and be able to quickly summarize your recommendations. It's also vital to be confident, compelling and authoritative. Board members have to decide quickly whether to accept your advice or not. They will form an instant judgment, which will be extremely hard to overcome. Most directors will also prefer to base their decisions on an opinion from a convincing expert, with a neck on the block, than a set of statistics that they can't so easily blame.

These are the ten things that make a good business case:

- A compelling argument for immediate change
- A clear argument as to why things cannot continue as they are
- A positive financial return on investment
- Evidence that the costs and benefits have been well thought through
- Support from other stakeholders, especially from the sharp end of the business
- An excellent, well-rehearsed pitch to management
- A format that meets the requirements of investment appraisal managers
- Alignment with business and IT objectives and strategies
- An indication of how risks will be managed
- Evidence of a road map to realize the business benefits

CHAPTER 10

Designing security systems that work

Why systems fail

Many information security management systems and programs fail to deliver on promises. They often start out with highly ambitious aspirations, but for one reason or another they seem to lose momentum as they encounter problems or security fatigue, and they progressively fizzle out. There are many reasons for this. Some strategies are far too ambitious. They don't take account, for example, of the difficulty of introducing radical changes across legacy infrastructure and conservative cultures. And they don't anticipate the raft of changes demanded by an evolving risk landscape or the new problems presented by emerging technologies.

Other strategies are simply badly executed. And it's not just the planning that goes wrong. Many management frameworks are flawed in their structure. They're not built to accommodate change or the wide range of exceptional circumstances you can encounter out in the field. A system that works in one area might not be universally viable.

And all of these failures are not entirely unexpected, because many security managers are self-taught, or have unconsciously absorbed expensive practices designed by management consultants primarily to maximize their revenue, rather than solve business problems. Not enough security managers take the trouble to look outside, to compare and contrast different approaches, and identify the key learning points from user organizations who have managed to get it right, or who have learned from their mistakes.

Good design and execution are crucial to the success of any major enterprise program. Many fail at the first hurdle because strategies are not appropriate,

---

Managing the Human Factor in Information Security   David Lacey
© 2009 John Wiley & Sons, Ltd

or architectures incomprehensible, or theoretical security methods far too difficult to apply. Some people blame the system for not delivering what they expected. But as the late Stafford Beer, a pioneer of operational research, put it, 'Systems do what they do'. They take inputs and deliver outputs, according to how they've evolved. They don't necessarily do what you'd like them to do.

This chapter explores the art of designing and deploying effective, usable information security systems that take account of the human factor. It covers the whole range of tools that you will need, ranging from the soundness of your vision right through to the usability of your systems. In the process we'll consider principles and techniques for designing compelling, effective and long-lasting management frameworks and security architectures.

Setting the vision

Establishing a mature information security management system across an organization is a long-term aspiration. It can take years. You might never get there. There will be obstacles in your way, such as budget cuts and skill shortages. And there will be regular setbacks from changes such as restructures, mergers and acquisitions. You need a vision of where you want to get to. And it should be a simple one that you can easily communicate to your management, colleagues and staff. That way at least you'll have a fighting chance of herding everyone in the same direction.

A vision statement is a short, compelling and inspiring statement of what your organization intends to do or become. It can hint at past weaknesses, but it primarily needs to convey an impression of the new attitude, strength or capability you are aiming to build. It is your desired future state: the end goal rather than the path towards it. At the same time it also has to be relevant to business today, in order to ensure that people can relate to it.

Some visions are designed to be achievable, perhaps over a three or four year period. They define a clear goal with realistic but challenging targets. Such a vision would help set the scene for a strategic long-term program.

Other visions are more of an aspiration, ones that you can never really expect to fulfil within your lifetime in the job. This style of vision would help serve as a continuous motivator and direction for an evolving, maturing security function. I once, for example, heard Allan Leighton, Chairman of Royal Mail Group, comment that, in his view, a vision is something you never really achieve. It's like saying:

> *'That's what I want to be when I grow up.'*

What makes a good vision?

It has to be said that, in practice, most corporate visions have little impact. That's because few people take the trouble to translate them into action.

They're often there because developing a vision is a typical starting point when applying business school planning methods. You're expected to have one.

Information security visions have to be more ambitious and practical than that. Few business managers would, in fact expect us to have one. But, in practice, we will need one to help guide the organization in the new direction that we need to send it: one that anticipates and is aligned with the changing business and technology landscapes. In fact, a good security vision will set the direction for the evolution of a new style of security for the information age: a style of security that enables new business methods, that inspires confidence in new technology, that supports a mobile, networked enterprise, and that focuses on people and dynamic formation flows.

And if the vision is a good one then it might even inspire or energize your staff. Emotional engagement is a powerful motivator. Many years ago when Shell decided that their true purpose in life should be to 'make the world a better place', I was pleasantly surprised to find that this vision really did inspire many ordinary managers and staff across the world.

We don't encounter many examples of security visions in practice, but there are a few that are worth drawing to your attention. The Jericho Forum vision, for example, sets a clear aspiration for both business and security in an extended enterprise environment:

'To enable business confidence beyond the constraint of the corporate perimeter through:

-   *Cross-organizational security process*
-   *Shared security services*
-   *Products that conform to open security standards*
-   *Assurance processes that when used in one organization can be trusted by others'*

Another useful approach is to split the vision into an inward-looking aspiration, as well as an outward-looking one. And there's no reason why you can't, in fact, have more than one vision. I used this approach for the Post Office Group, for example, when setting the vision in 1999 for a new information security program and function. I had initially set the following outward-looking vision to emphasize the importance of ensuring that our achievements were visible to clients:

'We are admired by our major clients and business partners for excellence in information security management'

I showed this to several managing directors, who looked at this and said, 'It's a fine statement, but we'd also like to see some emphasis on the internal perception.' I thought that was an excellent point, so I added the following, complementary, internal vision:

> *'Our managers and staff have full confidence in the confidentiality, integrity and availability of our information services and infrastructure'*

Five years later, things had moved on, and a major accredited certification program had addressed many of the earlier issues. It was time to set a fresh, forward-looking vision, with more emphasis on mobility and information flows.

> *'Secure access to electronic information and services from anyplace, anytime, anywhere'*

And as we were replacing two visions, I decided to add a further one that combined the previous two, but within the context of a broader technology environment.

> *'Trusted by colleagues and customers to deliver reliable services and to safeguard personal and business data across any channel'*

Vision statements might seem pretentious to some people. But they help to communicate a clear sense of direction and priorities across the organization. And they are absolutely essential when managing a decentralized security community. They serve to channel individual efforts in a common future direction.

Visions are also valuable in helping to convey to senior management the business value that security can deliver to the enterprise. In the absence of any clear statements of intent, management will tend to make assumptions about the aim of security. That can be dangerous. Management might see security as a cost and assume that the objective is to reduce or remove it, or they might see it as a problem to be kept hidden from the view of customers and investors. It's unlikely they'd see it as something positive that might enable new forms of business operations.

The critical success factors for a good vision statement are that it's quick to grasp, credible, realistic, compelling, memorable and relevant to the business. It should also be tailored to the organization's specific needs, rather than just promoting the need for better security.

The classic acid test for a *corporate* vision statement is that if you can replace your company's name with any other, then it's far too general. Now that's not absolutely critical for an information security vision. But it's an exercise worth carrying out. Because, after all, the last thing you want is just another bland, general, motherhood statement.

Defining your mission

From a general management perspective, the word 'mission' can mean different things to different people. It can be a purpose, a strategy, a project or a destination.

But what everyone seems to agree on, is that it's very much about *what* needs to be done, rather than *why* it needs to be done. It's about action rather than aspiration.

I tend to use the term mission as a means of encapsulating the true purpose of an organizational function, initiative or program. It's the real reason why it exists, the whole point of it all, and the value that we're intended to add. In practice, we have expectations but they don't always coincide with what our management really expects us to do, or what our own people really want to do, or what we will all eventually decide to do. People and systems do what they do, not what we'd like them to do. If a system or function has survived for many years, but doesn't produce outputs that we like, then it's not necessarily failed in any way. It's more likely that it's simply been, programmed to deliver a different set of results than the ones we currently need.

A mission statement can help refocus systems, efforts and priorities. It should be a brief, concise statement of our goals and priorities. The Jericho Forum mission statement, for example, sets out how this group intends to deliver its vision:

'Act as a catalyst to accelerate the achievement of the vision by:

- *Defining the problem space*
- *Communicating the collective Vision*
- *Challenging constraints and creating an environment for innovation*
- *Demonstrating the market*
- *Influencing future products and standards'*

Mission statements are very useful for providing a ready-made, succinct explanation of the purpose of an information security function to both senior management and staff. The mission statement I developed for the Royal Mail Group, for example, sets out the essential purpose, priorities and modus operandi of the information security function:

'We safeguard the information assets of The Royal Mail Group, especially the trusted reputation of The Royal Mail and the value of its brands and products. We do this by preventing and minimizing the business impact of security breaches, operational incidents and project failures, and by delivering assurances to Royal Mail stakeholders.'

Executive boards like to see simple statements such as these, which indicate, at a glance, the role of the information security function.

Simplicity is important. A classic example of this is Google's motto which came out of an exercise to elucidate the company's core values. Having brainstormed a list of aspirational clichés such as 'Treat everyone with respect', one of the engineers suggested that all of them could be covered by the single statement 'Don't be evil'.

Google's logic was that one all-embracing motherhood statement is just as effective as several. Of course, we can all be cynical and dismiss such a virtuous statement as a hostage to fortune in a fiercely competitive business world, perhaps something that might trip them up if they're subsequently found to be wanting. But we should never underestimate the motivating power of a statement of good intent. No matter how corny or hypocritical it might seem to some individuals, it will also inspire many well-meaning staff.

And good intent is important in the security world, because it has both a good side, involved with protecting assets and promoting good behaviour and integrity, as well as a darker side, involved with snooping, crime, investigations and discipline. Sometimes the dark side takes over, and we begin to focus too much on the bad things that people might do, rather than the good things we'd like to achieve. Mission statements are valuable in helping to emphasize and communicate our key objectives and working methods. And they are also especially useful when we are trying to drive through a major change in purpose, focus or strategy.

Building the strategy

Information security management is a never-ending task. There will always be a lot that needs to done, much more than we can ever hope to achieve. It's the nature of the subject. In fact, the only thing that is absolutely certain about information security is that you can never do enough. We can't address all of the most urgent activities in one fell swoop. Information security always lags behind the discovery of new vulnerabilities, as well as the emergence of new threats. It's about catching up as best we can, closing the gap as smartly and efficiently as possible.

Ignore what many consultants and pundits say about the need to avoid excessive security measures. In practice, we rarely see such a phenomenon. Very few systems and infrastructures have been built with too much security. There were some examples in the national security area several decades ago. But today we simply cannot do enough to secure our valuable information assets. The problem, in fact, is not getting the right level of security, it's deciding where best to focus our limited resources.

And it's worth noting that security requirements are always increasing. The bar is constantly being raised by new flaws and risks. Legacy systems, infrastructure and practices constantly need to be refreshed across the enterprise. At the same time, we need to prepare the organization for new security challenges. That means we need forward-looking strategies and architectures to help secure our future business operations in a more hostile, open network environment.

Strategy is all about how we aim to get to where we want to be, and how we actually intend to achieve our vision. It's about doing things in the right sequence, and preparing the ground for the bigger future changes that we will need to deliver. A strategy should aim to translate our mission statement into a series of achievable goals or initiatives over a reasonable period of time, perhaps 3–5 years.

As Sun Tzu, the ancient Chinese military strategist, once put it:

'Strategy is the great work of the organization. In situations of life and death, it is the Tao of survival or extinction. Its study cannot be neglected.'

We might think that information security is far from being a matter of life and death. But a major breach can put an unprepared company out of business. And the quality of our strategy will also influence the life or death of the information security function.

Developing an effective, appropriate strategy, one that will resonate with both management and staff, is a challenging objective. Key factors to consider will, for example, include the following:

- The attitude of the Board and business unit managers

- Whether a long-term or short-term focus is more appropriate

- Current business plans, strategy and initiatives

- Current IT strategy, programs and plans

- The level of maturity of information security processes

- The capability of information security function

- The budget and resources that are available, or might be possible

- Planned major upgrades to systems or infrastructure

- The organization's investment appraisal criteria

Critical success factors for effective governance

Every information security professional has their own views on what constitutes the critical success factors for effective information security governance across an organization. Here's a list based on my experience, drawn up a few years ago, as part of the development work for a *Capability Maturity Model for Information Risk Management*, commissioned by Chronicle Solutions, a vendor of security monitoring technology:

- **Top management commitment** – the level of understanding, engagement and visible support for the information risk management process

- **Understanding of information risks** – the amount of reliable information available to management on the nature, probability and impact of information risks across the enterprise

- **Professional competence** – the degree of professional knowledge, skill and experience supporting risk assessments and specialist technical decisions on IT security

- **Benchmarking of costs** – how well the organization understands the costs associated with the information risk management process, and how this compares to the value of the benefits delivered and the spending levels of other similar organizations

- **Visibility of incidents and events** – the availability of current and historical incident data in order to highlight problem areas, prioritize and shape risk reduction initiatives, and better understand the costs of incidents and the value of information risk measures

Critical success factors are the quintessential factors that underpin the likelihood of success for a mission or strategy. They need to be singled out for special treatment, priority and management attention. Information security management encompasses a very broad, complex set of requirements. We can't immediately address and monitor everything that needs to be done. Some things will need to be put on the back burner. The above items can't.

The smart approach to governance

The smart approach to information security governance is to learn from the successes of others, rather than your own mistakes. Many of the problems and practices associated with corporate governance are well established, though they're often outside the personal experience of the people who have to design and operate governance schemes.

There are many important learning points and principles that have been developed over the years to enable enterprises to design, implement and manage governance processes of all shapes and sizes. Applying these learning points and principles will enable you to establish efficient, adaptive and long-lasting management frameworks. Here are some key learning points that I've identified over the years, and used to develop successful, large-scale, governance processes, covering many hundreds of systems and company sites. They should be at the front of the minds of all security and compliance managers.

Don't reinvent the wheel

Firstly, don't invent a completely new way of approaching security governance. No matter how clever you are, it's bound to be sub-optimal. Designing, implementing and auditing complex control structures is not a new science. Information security and compliance might appear, in many ways, to be relatively new fields. But the science of designing and auditing management control structures has been practiced by auditors, certification bodies and security managers for many years. We should build on that existing body of experience.

That doesn't mean that we can't improve on the state of the art. I'd be disappointed if we couldn't. Many of the methods and systems used in the field have plenty of scope for enhancement. However, we shouldn't aim to develop new methods from scratch. All of the principles and most of the tools needed for designing and implementing efficient information security management frameworks are already available. But we need to be selective. We first need to establish what works well, and what doesn't. Otherwise there's a possibility that we might copy and further extend the use of a bad practice from another organization. And there are certainly plenty of sub-optimal practices out in the field.

The starting point is to recognize the underpinning principles of effective corporate governance. And, in particular, to learn from those authorities who've done it successfully before. '*Experto credite*', as they say in classical circles: put your trust in an expert who's done it before.

Look for precedents from other fields

Often the best sources of expertise are not where you'd initially expect to find them. You can find great ideas and principles for effective solutions from fields other than security. In fact, it's the first thing I do when tackling a new challenge. I instinctively ask myself: 'Who else might have tackled this type of problem?' and 'What approach did they take?'

For example, when designing a global security certification framework for the Shell Group in the late 1990s, we looked outside the security field for solutions, employing a Dutch management consultant with excellent knowledge and experience of designing certification schemes. He helped us solve many problems associated with standards and audit processes, by pointing out how designers of other types of certification scheme had gone about solving them.

Lessons from long-established schemes, such as those that govern driving tests, vehicle inspections or electrical safety, can be surprisingly useful sources of ideas for tackling information security governance. The designers of these schemes will already have resolved many of the practical issues associated with defining, implementing and auditing policies and standards across large communities of people and assets.

Take a top down approach

Many security and compliance managers struggle with the complexity of determining the exact scope and interfaces of the wide variety of individual units, systems and infrastructures that need to be compliant with policies and standards. It's a major challenge in a large, modern enterprise where systems operate across overlapping boundaries and supply chains, and where in-house staff and external contractors share accommodation, networks and services.

The initial dilemma is deciding where to start, especially when conducting enterprise-wide risk assessments or compliance reviews. Reviews need to be carried out with the support of the management who are responsible for the business activities. If we select an office to review, we'll often find that many of business units, services, systems and contractors operating within the building are under different management authorities, some of whom might be outside the scope of our responsibility. If we pick a system or a network, it's even harder. We'll usually find that it operates across numerous locations, and is accessed by many people reporting to different authorities. Even if we take a business process, such as manufacturing, we will encounter the same set of problems.

The answer is not to start with an individual business process, or an asset, such as a building, system or network, but to establish a top-down, cascading set of demands through the corporate management structure, with each unit defining the scope and requirements for its individual departments and support services. It's a surprisingly simple approach. And it works. But it's not always obvious in practice. The learning point is that governance needs to follow corporate lines of responsibility. And that starts at the top.

Start small, then extend

Before launching any enterprise program, it's important to pilot the systems and methods to be used. This provides an opportunity, not just to prove the concept, but also to develop the necessary supporting guidance, tools and expertise. Everything will go much smoother the second time a new system is tried out.

The ideal starting point is a large, well-defined business unit or service with a relatively mature information security profile. New systems are best piloted in an environment in which managers have a good understanding and sound experience of security, and in which systems have a reasonably high degree of compliance.

It's important, however, not to be tempted to continue or expand in a piecemeal or bottom-up fashion. That will result in gaps and overlaps in the scope and interfaces between units, systems and services. The scheme should be extended progressively, in controlled phases, accompanied by a steady refinement in guidance and support systems. But the scope of definition of each target of evaluation should be decided on a top-down basis, as this is the most effective, efficient and appropriate approach.

Take a strategic approach

There are several reasons, in fact, for avoiding an ad hoc or piecemeal approach to information security governance. Firstly, it's expensive to introduce major changes, although all new systems offer some opportunities for process improvements, which can at least partly offset the cost of change. It's important, therefore, to carefully plan and schedule changes for optimum effect.

Secondly, it takes time to build effective governance processes. Few business units and budgets can accommodate a radical, overnight change to a new way of managing information security. It's much better to introduce controls progressively, slowly enhancing the range, reach and maturity of the control framework, while at the same time gaining business cooperation at each step of the process.

Thirdly, the problem and solution spaces are constantly changing. Quick fixes and instant solutions are unlikely to be the best answer for the medium and longer term. It's better to take a step back, and plan for a longer-term, strategic change, than to react to immediate problems in a less efficient and effective manner.

And, fourthly, we simply don't have all of the solutions, nor do we have the skilled resources to solve all of the problems we face. It will take time to develop all of the sound, proven enterprise systems we need, and to build an effective team and set of services to deliver them.

Management will usually press you to implement a quick fix. It's important to resist that approach. Tactical, short term solutions are wasteful of resources and ineffective. The pressure of individual regulatory compliance demands might sometimes demand an immediate response. But if we take a step back, we'll generally find that many of these demands cover much of the same ground. It's more efficient and effective to adopt a single, strategic approach to risk management and compliance. Maintaining separate schemes, initiatives or checklists for each compliance requirement, for example, will result in expensive duplication and distraction for managers and staff.

A strategic approach to regulatory compliance is absolutely essential. The important principle is not to become obsessive about the fine detail of individual requirements, but to establish a general set of responsible good practices that address the underlying issues.

Implementing a strategic solution, however, is far from easy. It requires consistency in corporate processes, methods, standards and management frameworks. That's a substantial challenge, but it's far better than the alternative of a regime with widespread duplication and uncertainty, resulting from a proliferation of uncoordinated solutions.

Ask the bigger question

The business environment is full of apparent contradictions and seemingly insolvable problems. We come across many these when we tackle a large organizational problem for the first time. Our general instinct is to break the problem down into smaller ones, and then try to solve each one in isolation. But every so often, we'll hit a brick wall, a problem that appears to have no solution, because, for example, the costs or timescales are prohibitively high.

When this happens, the best strategy is not to abandon the initiative, but to take a step back, and rethink the approach to the overall objective. Sometimes the solution to our problem is right there in front of us, perhaps in the minds of our colleagues, consultants or advisers. We just have to ask the right question: not a specific, narrow one, but a broader one that engages their thought processes in a free ranging, problem-solving mode.

Back in the mid 1990s, for example, my team faced a seemingly impossible governance problem. One of our operating companies had outsourced a wide range of business activities to several different contractors. Numerous contracts had been negotiated at various times, each with varying levels of security requirement. We then introduced a revised portfolio of security policies and standards. But they could not be implemented without changes to the contracts.

We asked our legal advisers for an idea of the cost of changing all the contracts, and they informed us that it would be prohibitively expensive to renegotiate them. That presented a major problem. If we didn't change the contracts, many critical processes and systems would be non-compliant.

It seemed as though we'd hit an insolvable legacy problem, until we decided to take a step back, and change the question to our legal advisers from 'How much will it cost to change these contracts?' to 'How would you go about solving our problem?' That did the trick. Our legal adviser devised a simple, new agreement that covered all past and future contracts. The problem was solved. The contractors signed up without any major objections. In fact, most of them found the new arrangement preferable.

Solving this problem required two things. Firstly, we required some lateral thinking. We needed to view the problem from 'outside the box'. And, secondly, we needed an expert who knew that a different approach was feasible. But the real key was to change our question, from a narrow specific one, to a much broader request for creative assistance. Open questions, which encourage rich responses are much better for encouraging creative problem-solving.

Identify and assess options

We all know that there's more than one way to skin a cat. But, in practice, when designing enterprise frameworks, we rarely take enough trouble to identify the full range of alternative approaches that are available, or to evaluate their strengths and weaknesses. Often it's the first well-articulated design that comes to our attention that gets implemented.

Yet there are always alternative options available. And, for any organization, at any one time, there will be one that's clearly more efficient or effective than the others, though one size does not fit all situations, and circumstances will change, as organizations merge, split, restructure or adopt new ways of working.

Alternative options for managing information security should always be carefully considered. Unfortunately, there's generally pressure to make a fast decision when choosing or designing a new system, than there is when we operate them. As a result, we often adopt the first promising solution that we encounter. It's a false economy. The result is that the organization might be saddled for years with unsatisfactory processes and systems.

On many occasions, I've had to persuade managers to bite the bullet and abandon inefficient management frameworks. In all cases, they were subsequently grateful. Nobody, in fact, is comfortable with inefficient systems and methods. But most managers generally assume that the problem is caused by the security requirements, rather than the quality of the solutions.

Arriving at the best solution requires an insight into alternative approaches, and an appreciation of their respective strengths and weaknesses. There are often diametrically opposed options to choose from.

A classic example of this is the dilemma of how to determine the security controls a business unit requires. Should it be on the basis of a series of individual, detailed risk assessments? Or is it better to apply a more prescriptive approach based on standard control descriptions?

Risk assessment or prescriptive controls?

Let's take a step back and examine the ongoing debate of risk assessment versus prescriptive controls for the selection of security countermeasures. In practice, most organizations apply a combination of these two classic approaches.

At one extreme is an approach based on carrying out an individual risk assessment for each new system. This is time consuming, but it's generally more popular with business units, as it supports a business focused approach to information security.

At the other extreme is the approach of applying a set of universal security controls across all systems. This is faster and generally more popular with corporate centres and enterprise service providers, because it enables economies of scale and simplifies compliance.

In fact, neither approach is superior. They are complementary. We actually need a mixture of both, but the optimum balance will be different for each organization. In determining how best to use these techniques, it's important to understand the full range of associated costs, benefits and limitations.

Every information security professional should be aware of the arguments for and against each approach. Many consultants, trainers and lecturers advocate a single approach. They're wrong. We need to arrive at our own, unique conclusion on what's best for our organization. Table 10.1 illustrates the key arguments for each method. It should be noted that their significance will change over time, with changes in the threat landscape, the business environment, and the technical infrastructure, occasionally tipping the balance towards one particular approach or the other.

The methods used in practice for determining controls have evolved slowly over the years. The use of risk assessment as a basis for selecting controls was developed in the days before the growth of networks. At that time, risk assessment was the preferred approach because system security requirements were different, security solutions were more expensive, and security threats and risks were largely focused on individual, isolated systems.

The introduction of networks provided a compelling need to eliminate 'weak links', promoting the use of baseline controls as a minimum standard during the 1990s. The nature of attacks also changed at that time from targeted attacks to general ones, such as computer viruses. And the initiatives of large companies to globalize their business operations and support services also favoured a move towards a more standardized approach.

Table 10.1   Arguments for risk assessment or prescriptive controls

RISK ASSESSMENT	PRESCRIPTIVE CONTROLS
Slow and expensive to determine the required controls	Fast and cheap analysis, but less than perfect match of controls
Encourages diversity of controls across systems and services	Promotes consistency of controls and enables common services
Takes account of individual threats and attacks	Does not address specific threats and attacks
Controls might be less adaptable for use in less secure environments	Controls are designed to suit a range of environments
Harder to check or benchmark the choice of controls	Easy to specify, audit and benchmark the choice of controls
Appropriate for systems that might attract bespoke attacks	Suited to everyday systems exposed to a general range of security threats
Helpful for prioritizing the implementation of controls	Provides no guidance on priorities for implementation
Enables a selective approach to be taken	Eliminates weak links

A further change has taken place in the last decade: the growth in targeted attacks on specific information assets. These threats are of such a level of sophistication that they cannot be easily defended using baseline controls. That means, amongst other things, that the pendulum is swinging back to greater use of risk assessment as the primary basis for determining controls for sensitive or critical systems.

Today, we need a combination of prescriptive controls and risk assessment to meet all possible or likely needs. We need baseline controls to protect the weakest link in networks, and to demonstrate a system of controls is in place for compliance purposes. And we need risk assessment to prioritize our efforts, to harden the systems that are most at risk, and to demonstrate to our external stakeholders that we understand and are managing the risks to our information assets.

In a class of their own

For many decades, sensitive information has been highlighted for special protection using important sounding classification labels, such as Restricted, Confidential or Secret. Some security managers have also been inspired to design similar schemes to cover data integrity, availability and business criticality. But ensuring confidentiality of information remains the primary purpose of classification schemes.

It's not clear, however, that we're making the best use of classifications to safeguard our intellectual assets. As Soren Kierkegaard, an existentialist philosopher, once put it:

'Once you label me, you negate me.'

Judging by the way we use labels in information security, he was right. Security classifications are generally used to stop people accessing sensitive data, rather than to enable trusted users to exploit intellectual property for business value. In fact, huge amounts of useful knowledge and intelligence have been negated in the interests of national or corporate security.

Classifications are a crude, but powerful, differentiator. In an ideal world, it would be reassuring to treat everyone and everything as a unique entity. Unfortunately, that would be both unmanageable and expensive. Classifications are needed to simplify complex decision processes. Their disadvantage is that, when we label any data with a classification, we freeze its perceived value and the rules that determine its handling. But the utility of information is not static. It changes with use and over time. Labels, in fact, need to be handled with caution.

Security classifications are one of the most traditional approaches to specifying and selecting security controls. They provide a level of gravitas to the security field. Labels such as Secret and Confidential are used widely across industry. Unfortunately their usage is inconsistent: one company's Confidential might equate to another's Secret. And their military origins convey a distinctly old-fashioned feel, one that's out of step with modern business, more appropriate to a bygone era in which 'loose lips sink ships'.

There's also an unfortunate aura of self-importance associated with being granted access to Top Secret material. It can even be slightly comical, bringing to mind John Steed in the *Avengers* and his 'Top Hush' and 'Button Lip' labels, or Toby Esterhaus in *Tinker, Tailor, Soldier, Spy*, and his 'Ultra, Ultra Sensitive' source.

Security classifications have long been used in government and defense circles. The range of labels used for that purpose is quite staggering. In addition to the well known ones of Restricted, Confidential and Secret, there are protective labels, such as 'Commercial in Confidence', warning caveats such as 'UK Eyes Only', and code words such as ULTRA to protect individual sources of intelligence. In practice, it's not unusual to encounter government documents with several different classification or privacy labels. And each one is underpinned by specific rules, procedures and legislation. Government classification systems are, in fact, quite an achievement in attention to detail. The question is whether the average public servant can actually keep track of it all.

It's not therefore surprising to find that many people now regard classifications as an outdated concept. That's an understandable conclusion, but the sentiment is wrong. In fact, few contemporary practitioners appreciate the real reasons for their use. Classifications have long been misunderstood and misused in practice. There are quite different drivers behind the use of classifications, and they constantly change.

Classification schemes need regular adjustment, to fine tune the number of levels, the labels and the definitions associated with them. They often lag behind the times, but their use will grow in importance in the future, because they are a powerful tool for reducing diversity, especially the kind we find across a modern, extended enterprise environment.

Not all labels are the same

National security is not a major driver for most organizations. Outside the defence and intelligence fields, the primary reason why companies first adopted classification schemes was, in fact, to safeguard trade secrets, and in particular to be able to defend them in a court of law. That's why we tend to find classification systems in technology companies, rather than in banks. Unfortunately, the designers of these schemes might not have actually grasped this fact, because most are based on national security schemes, using similar standards and labels.

Yet the requirements for protecting trade secrets are very different from those for national security. As IBM discovered more than a decade ago, when they revisited the requirements of their classification scheme, we only need a single classification label to achieve this. And we don't need a complex system of pre-defined, security measures to protect our trade secrets in court.

Despite the fundamental differences, the designs of government and industry classification systems have been progressively converging, though the labels in use remain different. Conventional practice for classification systems has tended to be based on a two or three level classification system, using similar sounding labels, though with the government standard generally operating one notch higher than the industry ones, perhaps not a very sensible idea.

But the classification needs of the private sector are becoming richer and evolving rapidly. Classifications are a powerful mechanism for defining and communicating a set of options for implementing controls to company staff, business partners or customers. They can also help control the dissemination of information of varying sensitivity across enterprise, extended enterprise and public domains. This latter objective was, in fact, a primary driver behind the revision of long standing classification schemes at Shell and the Royal Mail Group.

Unfortunately the use of classifications labels and their meanings are far from standardized, though they look very similar. And close is not enough. In fact, it's positively dangerous. Labels such as Confidential and Secret can mean entirely different things to different people. Some, such as Restricted, present a particular problem because they are low level classifications in some companies, and quite high level ones in others.

Attempts have been made to rectify this problem but they've all failed. When we drafted the original Code of Practice that became the basis of the BS7799 security standard, we considered recommending a common set of labels. But organizations at that time were not keen to consider changes to their classification systems. Eventually we came up with the idea of encouraging a 'neutral' set of labels such as SEC1 or SEC2. But this system was not well conceived or marketed, and it completely failed to achieve any impact. Perhaps we should have adopted more eye-catching classifications, such as Top Hush or Button Lip?

Guidance for technology and people

It's tempting to develop a single set of guidance for a particular governance or compliance requirement. However, one style of guidance will not suit all of the assets, processes and people within its scope. The needs of technology and people are very different.

Information systems and computer platforms, for example, require precise, unambiguous, technical instructions. But people require clear, non-technical explanations of the control objectives for which they're responsible. They also want to know why they are doing it: the precise law, regulation or corporate policy that demands it, as well as what might happen if, for example, they fail to deliver. Technical detail does not impress them.

The ideal information security portfolio would incorporate individual guides with different styles of presentations and varying levels of detail and explanatory background, each tailored to the specific characteristics and needs of a particular type of person or asset. But there also needs to be an overall means for users to find their way around the growing mass of guidance that is typical of a modern portfolio. Unstructured content is difficult to navigate, and maintain, without a clear mapping of relationships between compliance requirements, policies and controls.

It's tempting, but short-sighted, to develop individual policies, standards, control requirements and audit checklists as free-standing sources of guidance, designed to satisfy a specific purpose, at a particular time. Today's regulatory compliance requirements are not ad hoc demands; they are part of a developing landscape that's here to stay, and will progressively become more complex and demanding. We need to develop a more structured approach, one that's less of an alphabet soup of assorted demands, and more of a patchwork quilt of complementary requirements.

And designing guidance around a structured framework enables it to be more easily and consistently tailored to specific target people or objects. It also enables it to accommodate mappings of high-level requirements to more detailed controls. And not only will this streamline implementation and compliance, it will also simplify future content management.

Designing long-lasting frameworks

A key learning point in information security management is to understand the underlying principles for designing frameworks that can stand the test of time. Over the years, in designing and managing control frameworks for large enterprises, I've identified a number of key principles for designing long-lasting, low maintenance frameworks. It's no exaggeration to say that applying these principles can mean the difference between a management framework that is abandoned within months, and one that lasts for more than a decade.

The structure of the framework is the key to easy navigation by users, as well as efficient maintenance by security managers. The high level appearance of the framework is actually less important than most people realize. It can be based on cosmetic or political considerations. And the latter point should not be overlooked, because the surface presentation often generally conveys an impression of the relative importance of each subject area covered. What really counts in any architecture, however, is the underlying structure, the grouping and the presentation of the detailed content for the users.

A tiered approach to all documentation is essential for efficient development, management and use. And the content of each level should be selected on the basis of the expected length of the life of the content. Long-lasting content should never be mixed with fast-changing text. That will increase the maintenance burden substantially. General policy statements that rarely change should not, for example, be mixed with organizational detail that requires frequent revision.

My recommended approach is to structure all documentation on the following lines (Figure 10.1):

- **Top-level:** The overall vision, scope, objectives and architecture of the governance scheme itself. This should be designed for a lifetime of around ten years

- **Second level:** General corporate policies and high-level standards. These require periodic updating, but should be good for around five years, which is the length of the cycle for revising national or international standards

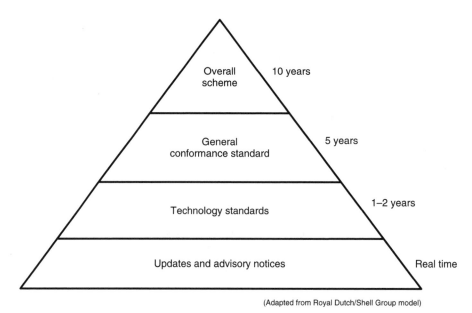

(Adapted from Royal Dutch/Shell Group model)

Figure 10.1 A framework for long-lasting documentation (adapted from Royal Dutch/Shell Group model)

- **Third level:**   The technical standards and guidance required to apply controls at the platform level. These require updating for each major release of software, so should be good for at least one or two years
- **Fourth level:**   Advisory information and updates on recently discovered vulnerabilities, which must be addressed in real-time and applied at least weekly or monthly

By separating these layers of documentation, the content becomes much easier and faster to manage. Frequent updates will generally be restricted to the lower levels. A tiered approach also makes it feasible to develop appropriate templates for each layer, speeding the development time for new security guidance.

Applying the fourth dimension

The above approach to designing long-lasting frameworks is a good example of the benefits of considering the 'fourth dimension' when designing new solutions. Time should be a key factor in the design of all policies, frameworks and architectures. Developing a four-dimensional approach might seem ambitious, but it's highly practical and is a major consideration in architectures developed by leading practitioners.

Matthew West, Shell's former top information architect and a visiting professor at Leeds University, has pioneered techniques for developing four-dimensional data architectures. It makes sense to consider the past and future state of an entity or relationship. People don't carry out the same role for life, for example. If you say you once met the President of the United States, it might be one of several people that you're referring to. Similarly a company or business unit might not have a permanent owner. It could have been acquired, or it might be sold off in the future. Systems and models should be designed to survive such changes.

Many solutions implemented for identity management do not stand the test of time. People change identifiers, job titles, jobs and roles many times throughout their career. The impact of future events is also a major consideration. And systems should be designed with features to take account of the potential need to recover from catastrophic events, such as a large-scale compromise of identity information.

It's essential for any system, model or architecture to consider the time dimension, whether from the perspective of structure, functionality or maintenance. Considering this also provides an entirely different perspective on the value of information. This characteristic of information is far from static. Not only is it constantly changing, it also varies with the context, as well as the perception of the users. But information has no absolute value. It's no more than a means to an end for its users.

In fact, it's often better to think of information in terms of its utility rather its value. Many of us have encountered information that becomes less sensitive or useful with time. Sometimes it's quite an abrupt change, such as accounting information that's sensitive until announced. But, if you dig deeper, the subject becomes much richer than we generally appreciate.

The most advanced thinking about the impact of time on information is done by the custodians of national archives, who have to think many years ahead. Ian Byant, Information Assurance Adviser to the UK National Archives, has considered the impact of long-term changes in the utility of several specific characteristics of public sector information over several decades.

These characteristics include not just confidentiality, integrity and availability, but also aspects such as usability and privacy. Over time, each aspect will change in different ways and at varying rates. The importance of the confidentiality integrity and availability aspects of information, for example, will drop off relatively quickly, but at different rates. Other characteristics, such as privacy, however, might stay high indefinitely.

In fact, the real learning point to note is that you will discover an entirely new perspective by incorporating the fourth dimension into your thinking.

Do we have to do that?

Security guidance can be either mandatory or just desirable. Experience shows that, if it's the latter, it won't be consistently followed. Many central security functions, however, simply don't have the authority to impose demands on their business units. In those cases we have to consider imaginative ideas to obtain broader business buy-in, for example by getting business units to sign up to an agreed scheme or standard. In Shell, for example, we were able to implement an accredited certification scheme across 200 sites by gaining the agreement of each of the global business sectors.

League tables of performance and awards can also help to motivate individual business units to raise their game. And even on an ad hoc basis, you can always apply some psychology or politics to persuade managers to implement security measures. As a colleague of mine used to say whenever a manager asked whether his advice could be ignored: 'Yes, it's only advice, but if you don't do it we'll advise your management that you're not paying attention.'

Guidance varies in style. It can be highly prescriptive: required to be done in a particular way. Or flexible: open to interpretation to suit your circumstances. And it can be highly detailed, with lengthy descriptions of what should be done, or just a high-level set of guiding principles or control objectives.

Often it's left to the author of a policy or standard to set the tone, by deciding the length of the guidance and the choice of words, especially for example the use of words such as 'must', 'should' or 'shall'. But these choices should not be left to chance. They are important governance decisions. They should be carefully considered, and consciously taken.

Establishing the most appropriate leadership style is the starting point. Does the organization, for example, prefer to impose a prescriptive approach across all business units? Does it wish to issue detailed, central guidance on how to do things? Or does it prefer more of a 'light hand on the rudder'. Determining these choices requires a dialogue with top management. I've successfully used the diagram in Figure 10.2, for example, to illustrate the four main options available for security guidance: guiding principles, big rules, code of practice or conformance standard.

A code of practice is a special form of standard that's designed to allow a more flexible interpretation. ISO270001 is one, for example. It's deliberately designed to be adaptable to many different environments. These types of standard are very different in style from the prescriptive standards that are used to specify communications protocols or electrical safety standards.

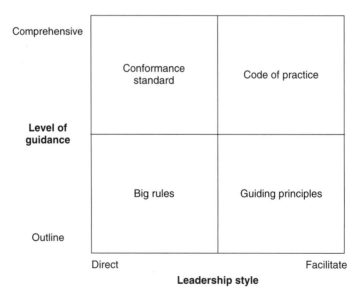

Figure 10.2   Different styles of security guidance

There is, in fact, no reason why we cannot apply a combination of all four of these options, as long as we don't mix these styles within the same document. A set of rules is a set of rules. It's confusing to include optional items. But there is no reason, in fact, why we can't complement a set of big rules with a more flexible code of practice.

In fact, the most appropriate choice changes as we move downwards through the levels of advice and control, generally becoming more mandatory and more specific as we move from high-level principles to low-level standards. It's common, for example, for compliance requirements to be highly general, but applied through a flexible code of practice, which in turn might be translated into a more rigid technical standard.

But it's also important to understand the needs, and to anticipate the behaviour, of the individuals who will use the guidance. Give a business manager a choice of options, for example, and he'll generally select the fastest or cheapest option, not the most appropriate one. Present a busy IT service manager with a flexible code of practice and he'll be confused as to what's required. Operational managers have little time for creative interpretation. Generally, they'd prefer to be told precisely what they have to do.

The most satisfactory approach is to maintain a clear, consistent 'nudge' towards the preferred choice when decisions are required. Suggestions such as 'If in doubt, do this' can help. Maintaining a consistent language also helps. With experience, a manager will learn to interpret the degree of latitude associated with a particular turn of phrase.

Steal with caution

No matter how tempting it might seem, it's a mistake to import a complete controls framework from another organization. But it's often done in practice. Newly recruited managers often import familiar methods from a previous organization. Big consultancies often push common solutions onto their clients. But every enterprise is different, and there's no guarantee that a system that works well in one environment will be successful in another.

We should also, however, avoid the opposite extreme of handcrafting a complete new controls structure from scratch. Many organizations choose to do this. I know one or two that are doing this at present. But it's a dangerous gamble. It takes a lot of time and resources, perhaps a couple of years, to complete, and the results will be unproven.

The ideal is somewhere in between. Smart organizations look for solutions that are fast, cheap and proven. I know one company, for example that adopted the slogan 'We'll steal with pride'. They developed an outline, bespoke management framework and then set out to fill it in with carefully selected, and suitably adapted, best practices from outside. That approach was successful.

The most important considerations when developing a successful security framework are to understand what's best to develop yourself and what's best to adapt from outside. It helps also to know where to look for suitable sources and how to assess the quality of imported guidance.

Items that don't vary a great deal across organizations, and can be safely based on external best practices might, for example, include the following:

- Descriptions of external compliance requirements, and their translation into more specific control descriptions

- High-level, generalized control descriptions, such as those contained in standards such as ISO27001, which are designed to be applied across a wide-range of environments

- General guidance on how to translate higher-level controls into technical standards for specific platforms

Items that vary considerably across organizations, and are best tailored to the enterprise would include the following:

- The specific wording of corporate policy statements, which needs to reflect the values, culture and governance style of the organization

- The implementation of technical standards for a particular information system or service, which requires testing and adaptation to take account of local application systems and management practices

The golden triangle

In the early 1990s, my Shell colleague Richard Mapleston, an expert on business process reengineering, introduced me to the 'golden triangle' of people, processes and technology, illustrated in Figure 10.3. This is a useful device for encouraging managers of change programs to ensure that their proposals are appropriately balanced and aligned.

The golden triangle can serve as an excellent mental check to ensure that your proposals, frameworks or documents are adequately balanced. It can also help to

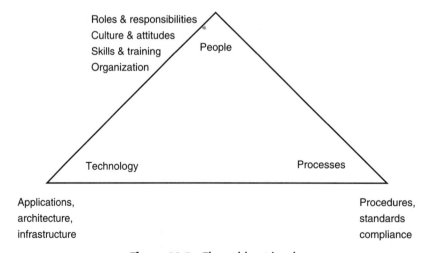

Figure 10.3   The golden triangle

identify potential gaps in proposed measures. You can use it in many ways: as a creative space, for example, to identify new requirements by plotting ideas around each part of the triangle. I used it in Shell, for example, to check that published guidance, including standards such as BS7799, were suitably balanced in their emphasis on these three areas. A simple count of paragraphs that address each area can, for example, provide a quick indication.

The BS7799 standard was surprisingly well balanced for the time, perhaps reflecting the more process-based approach to information security that existed in the UK, at that time, compared to the stronger technology focus in the USA, where thought leadership had been more influenced by the academic, military and vendor sectors. But in general if we try to map security standards and initiatives against the golden triangle, we often find that the outcome is far from balanced.

There are some good reasons for that. Firstly, as with any new or developing problem space, the focus is not static but constantly shifting. Over the last decade, for example, the most effective source of security solutions has evolved from technology, to process, to human factors.

Ten years ago, for example, if you'd asked me where the biggest bang for the buck could be found, I would probably have pointed to 'platform security'. Attention to that would generally have made the biggest improvement to the overall security risk profile of the infrastructure. Five years ago, I would have suggested that it was 'security management processes' that delivered the best return on investment. Today, it's the 'human factor' that perhaps makes the biggest difference.

And the balance will continue to change. Over the next decade, we can expect to see the emergence of new security technologies that will deliver unprecedented capabilities to see and control security events across the enterprise, through a single dashboard. The primary focus will begin to move away from the human dimension towards investment in more reliable automated security processes.

Managing risks across outsourced supply chains

Managing risks and controls across complex, outsourced supply chains is a major challenge. It's perhaps, in fact, the most difficult area of information security management, because the control of change is in the hands of the outsourcer, whereas the consequences of failure remain firmly with the user.

The key to successful management of risks across outsourced services is a combination of careful planning and good contract schedules, coupled with exceptional relationship management. But the latter is the most important. If you have a bad contract, a good relationship will improve it. If, however, you have a bad relationship, the contract alone will not guarantee a satisfactory service.

Policies and standards need to be understood and accepted by all parties, including sub-contractors. In particular, it's important to ensure that the policies are appropriate for both you and your service providers. At the outset, you will need to establish that they are comfortable with your security requirements, and competent to carry them out. Never assume you can enforce a management framework on a supplier. You have to establish what is actually possible from their perspective.

And when defining your security requirements it's important to be specific, but flexible. You can't be specific enough, but it should be designed to accommodate change. Write down and agree everything you can. Define policies and standards at every level. Otherwise you can never guarantee that everything you expect will be done. This is especially important for offshore contracts, where your specification will generally be followed to the letter and no more. But requirements change, and you will need to ensure that changes can be incorporated without incurring excessive charges.

Establishing the right relationships at the right levels is crucial. It's also important to avoid playing a zero-sum game. There should be no winners or losers. Managing relationships goes beyond mere diplomacy. It also requires that both sets of management processes, including those for risk and incident management, are fully aligned and working.

Never assume that everything that's written down in a contract will be done, or that anything that's not included cannot be done. Everything is possible if good will exists on both sides. Good diplomacy and excellent relationship management are the keys to managing events outside of your direct control.

And visibility is everything in security. In the absence of compelling evidence of conformance with policies and standards then you have to assume that nothing is in place. Accredited certification is the easiest and most effective option. Otherwise you will need to implement a framework of independent audits.

You will also need to agree schedules, codes of practice and agreed interfaces for audits, risk assessments and other governance processes that require access to your supplier's staff. Unscheduled visits and interruptions could have an impact on service performance, and be used as an excuse for failure to meet contracted service levels. Managing enterprise-wide processes such as risk management, incident response and compliance management is difficult enough. But managing these processes across a virtual supply chain is infinitely harder.

Models, frameworks and architectures

When I was a student at a business school in the 1970s, I recall one of my tutors quoting a famous person who said:

'Give me a framework and I'm free.'

I've never since been able to track down the source of that quote. But it's absolutely correct. Frameworks serve as the powerful foundation we need to enable people to contribute and build creative ideas and content to help solve business problems.

But what exactly is a framework? Is it any different from the other terms that are often used interchangeably, such as model, architecture, strategy or solution?

And does it matter which term we choose? The answer to the last question is 'no'. The key objective is to use these tools to solve business problems. The terminology is unimportant from that perspective.

But it's worth appreciating the subtle nuances between different terms. So, for what it's worth, here's my best shot at defining them:

- A framework is a simple conceptual structure to help address complex problems by breaking them down into components and illustrating their relationships

- A model is an abstraction of reality, a simplified representation of a real life that is used to highlight certain important characteristics for a particular purpose, ignoring other things, judged to be less relevant

- An architecture is a framework or model that is used as a basis for constructing a more specific solution, whether it be a building, a system or anything else

- A strategy is a plan to achieve a set of objectives, generally long-term, rather than short-term, ones

- A solution can operate at any level as an individual feature or control, or a set of them that collectively address a business problem

All models and abstractions are no more than a means to an end. Frameworks break down problems into manageable chunks. Models help us to focus on the most important features of a problem or solution. Architectures provide the foundation for taking us to the next level of detail in solving a problem.

As something artificially introduced into a problem-solving process, these constructs can also be a major distraction to the primary goal. But they are the essential first step in building the sophisticated solutions we need to address today's complex business problems.

Why we need architecture

Architecture is a powerful concept in the technology field. Not every IT manager actually understands what such constructs really are, why they are needed, what they look like, or what they can deliver. Most people, however, seem to accept that business architectures, IT architectures and data architectures are needed to enable the design, development and implementation of enterprise systems.

But very few people seem to understand the purpose or requirements of a security architecture. Security architectures are very different from the architectures we use to construct buildings or systems. The latter are complete and they guide the detailed design, while the former are often incomplete, sometimes providing little more than a general sense of direction.

There are, however, many good reasons why it's important to develop architectures, especially in the field of information technology. Grand designs require architecture. Complex systems have to be developed in manageable chunks, just like the old adage suggests: 'How do you eat an elephant?' Answer: 'One bite at a time.'

Modularity also builds greater agility into systems and frameworks. Amongst other things it enables changes to be more easily accommodated. I've seen many monolithic programs thrown away because they were designed without replaceable interfaces. Architecture delivers agility by enabling such changes to be quickly applied.

A further benefit of modularity is that it enables re-use of components for other purposes. From the security perspective, there is always the danger that changes in context might introduce security exposures. For that reason alone, it's important to ensure that components can respond to changes in environment, and, as the Jericho Forum design principle suggests, can maintain their security and integrity in even the most hostile of physical or network environments.

The folly of enterprise security architectures

Enterprise security architectures are an excellent idea in principle, though their implementation is often flawed in practice. Many organizations set out to develop ambitious enterprise security architectures completely from scratch. This task takes a lengthy period of time, around two years perhaps.

Some see it as a potential long-lasting investment for the enterprise. But, in many cases, it's a wasted effort. Most enterprise security architectures run to hundreds of pages. Some turn out to be unusable in practice, far too long to absorb or maintain, and yet, at the same time, not sufficiently specific to be useful. Many are abandoned before completion. And others are ignored in practice.

Security architects often start by designing a multi-dimensional matrix, setting out all permutations of a range of security attributes and requirements. The greater the number of dimensions or the degree of granularity in an architecture, the more ambitious the task will be. Filling in the cells of the matrix is a slow, laborious process. By the time it's finished it will be out-of-date. But, more importantly, it will often be long, complex and unwieldy, and impossible to sell to the business managers and security practitioners who are expected to use it.

It's a folly to aim to develop enterprise architectures, without building on existing, proven constructs and obtaining continuous feedback at every step of the way from the practitioners who have to use it. Good security architectures can be built, but they need to be designed from the bottom up. They are not like governance systems, which, as we discussed earlier, need to be developed in a top-down fashion to reflect the lines of management accountability.

Security architectures are a means to an end. They can serve a useful purpose, by, for example, providing a blueprint for the security of a system, platform, service or network. Security architectures should therefore be focused on assets, rather than people.

There is also a misconception that security architectures are part of a natural family of enterprise architectures, based on an assumption that business architecture drives IT architecture, which in turn drives security architecture. That's not realistic for several reasons.

Firstly, the target of business architectures is different from security architecture. The former is focused on processes, whereas the latter, if it is to be useful, needs to be focused primarily on systems or platforms.

Secondly, business processes are complete and defined. Otherwise it would not be possible to run the business properly. Business architectures simply have to provide an abstraction of this reality. But security architectures are a collection of solutions to numerous requirements assembled from multiple sources.

Thirdly, many security requirements cannot be derived from business or IT architectures, and will not follow an identical structure. Most security requirements are derived from external demands, perceived vulnerabilities, risk assessments and security management considerations. These do not map neatly onto business process models.

Security architectures are a means to end, in fact, many ends. They can serve as a means to document or communicate the design of the security features for a new information system, a blueprint for developing a set of enterprise security services, or a set of standards for collaborative working across shared infrastructures. But security architectures need to be shaped around individual services, platforms and information systems, not around enterprise business models.

In fact, every major, strategic platform should be supported by a comprehensive security architecture, which should set out the full range of policies, compliance requirements, management processes and control specifications. Without that, it's unlikely the services supported would ever be fully secure and compliant.

Real-world security architecture

When colleagues ask me what a good security architecture should look like, I generally shock them by saying:

> *'A good, modern security architecture is ragged around the edges, full of holes and exists largely in the minds of practitioners.'*

To many people hearing that statement for the first time, it comes across as no less than heresy. But I mean every word of it, so let's examine it in more detail.

Firstly, when I say security architecture should be ragged around the edges, I'm suggesting it should be continually pushing the boundaries of its scope, even before it's been completed. As we've just discussed, the target scope of any architecture will need to start small: bounded and finite, perhaps associated with a single platform, system or infrastructure. But, throughout development, there will be increasing pressure to extend elements of the security architecture beyond the original boundaries, to reach out and connect or deliver services to platforms and parties outside of the original scope.

Secondly, when I say security architecture should be full of holes, I'm referring to the reality that, if you're addressing today's latest challenges, we simply won't have a full set of solutions. There are always new security services that have yet to be specified; secure platforms and protocols that have yet to be developed; and security technologies that have yet to be fully evaluated. Intrusion detection systems were a good example of this. They were incorporated into many security architectures well before they became viable to implement.

Thirdly, when I say security architecture should exist largely in the minds of practitioners, I mean that, like all security documentation, it will have no practical impact unless it's understood and at the forefront of every practitioners' mind. A lengthy document, of several hundred pages, that remains unviewed on the shelf, or on a server, has no value. It's better to have a series of simple, memorable rules or principles that business and IT staff can quickly absorb and apply.

The 5 Ws (and one H)

Whenever we set out to build a framework of any kind, it's worth taking a step back and asking ourselves the key questions of what we're aiming to achieve, why it's needed, who it is that needs it, and when, where and how it will be used.

This type of analysis is an old, but extremely powerful technique, long used by journalists, investigators and researchers. It's one that's also essential for architects and designers. This checklist is generally referred to as the 5 Ws (and one H). It was famously expressed by Rudyard Kipling in one of his *Just So Stories*:

> *'I keep six honest serving-men; (They taught me all I knew); Their names are What and Why and When And How and Where and Who.'*

These six questions can also be used as the basis of any high-level structure or contents list for an architectural framework. A classic example of this is John Zachman's Framework for Enterprise Architecture, one of the most famous and influential frameworks for developing enterprise architectures, whether for business processes, information systems, data management or IT.

Essentially it's a framework based on a 6 × 6 matrix of individual models. Each of the columns of the matrix is based on an element of the 5Ws and one H: What, How, Where, Who, When and Why. And each of the rows represents a stakeholder: Planner, Owner, Designer, Builder, Sub-contractor and Functioning Enterprise.

The weakness of the Zachmann approach is that, for presentation reasons, it provides equal emphasis to each of the 5Ws and one H, and to each of the stakeholder perspectives. That structure might be very useful to an architect, to serve as a framework and a useful two-dimensional checklist, to brainstorm ideas, requirements and content. But it's the wrong approach for a user, who wants to see more relevant headings and a minimum amount of unnecessary padding.

A good architecture should focus on bringing out the most important aspects at the expense of the least critical ones. That's the whole point of models: they serve as an abstraction of reality, to enable the user to focus on the most essential elements, while filtering out the less relevant ones. Architectures should aim to generate a sparser matrix, rather than one that is complete. In fact, we should be

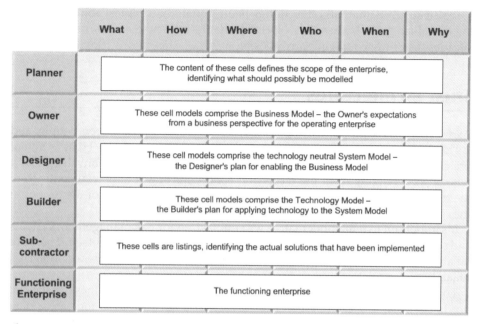

	What	How	Where	Who	When	Why
Planner	The content of these cells defines the scope of the enterprise, identifying what should possibly be modelled					
Owner	These cell models comprise the Business Model – the Owner's expectations from a business perspective for the operating enterprise					
Designer	These cell models comprise the technology neutral System Model – the Designer's plan for enabling the Business Model					
Builder	These cell models comprise the Technology Model – the Builder's plan for applying technology to the System Model					
Sub-contractor	These cells are listings, identifying the actual solutions that have been implemented					
Functioning Enterprise	The functioning enterprise					

Figure 10.4 An outline of the Zachmann Framework (reproduced from http://en. wikipedia.org/wiki/Image:ZachmanFramework6.png)

suspicious of any matrix that looks perfectly balanced and complete, because real life is simply not like that.

Occam's Razor

There is always a real and present danger of over-engineering architectures, adding unnecessary layers, dimensions or features, which not only confuse the user, but also reduce the efficiency of the systems delivered.

Standards committees are frequently guilty of this. The X.400 e-mail address standard is a classic example. If implemented universally, it would have required us to key in around five times the current amount of data for an e-mail address. The seven layer OSI communication model is another example of unnecessary complexity, with excessive layers, padding and protocols. Fortunately, the Internet, and its more pragmatic protocols, turned up just in time to save us from the excesses of the international standards community, though it also introduced security problems and limitations.

Over-engineering of protocols and architecture is a classic example of an area that is in need of what's known as 'Occam's Razor'. This is a principle named after William of Ockham, a 14th century logician and a Franciscan friar. Essentially, Occam's Razor encourages the reduction of unnecessary assumptions, eliminating those that make no impact on the observable predictions of a hypothesis.

It also suggests that, all other things being equal, the simplest solution will be the best. Standards bodies, in particular, should take note of this principle. For decades they've encouraged the opposite.

Trust architectures

As we saw in Chapter 4, trust is the basis of relationships between people, and it's at the heart of decisions to grant access to people or objects. Trust is a vital pre-condition for any successful collaboration. It operates at many levels in a relationship, ranging from the terms and conditions of a commercial contract, to the response process for a breach of security committed by either of the parties to the contract.

It's important to remember that, as we emphasized for risk management systems and security architectures, trust is a means to an end, not an end in itself. There are no absolute measures of trust, whether based on honesty, competence, integrity, reliability or reputation.

Trust levels are relative, and appropriate to the context of a business or societal need. They can, for example, be expressed as a binary value to indicate a pass or failure for a particular action; or as a range of levels, such as a high, medium or low, to indicate a permitted access level; or as a numerical scale to indicate a particular measure of creditworthiness.

Real-world models for managing trust across complex business applications require a range of measures, and a capability to transfer judgments and permissions securely across different environments. This can also be a major problem, of course, as the factors indicating a person or entity's trustworthiness for a particular role might not be quite so relevant in an entirely different context. Standards can help, of course, to ensure inter-operability but, unfortunately, we can't standardize the problem space. We need rich solutions that can address multiple business requirements.

There is also a growing spectrum of mechanisms, of varying degrees of reliability, to support trust measures, ranging from independently signed digital certificates, to self-signed certificates. Unfortunately, trust architectures that can bring all of these elements together in a complete model, are still in their infancy. We need to accelerate our efforts in this area. And it's a large, challenging problem space. The typical elements of a trust architecture, for example, would include:

- Trust establishment processes to define levels of trust between partners
- Trust specification services to specify the authorized actions of each party
- Trust evaluation services to gather and assess the evidence for a trust relationship
- Trust monitoring services to update and re-evaluate trust specifications based on experience
- Trust analysis services to identify unwanted, implicit relationships or possible conflicts of relationships

Such trust management models require a rich set of protocols and algorithms. They are developing rapidly, but remain a long way from universal application in everyday business. Trust architectures are the long-term key to enabling collaboration across extended-enterprise environments.

To achieve practical implementations, however, we need to develop a better understanding of the business requirements for implementing such models. We also need to encourage greater alignment of security management processes across corporate processes. Technology and theory will not be enough. People and practices are the real enablers of trust architectures.

Secure by design

One of the weakest areas in the systems development life cycle is the lack of universal, established, design principles for information systems and software products. This is surprising as the concept of design principles is a very old one.

Many classic, long-lasting systems are based on a simple set of sound design principles. Gordon Bell, the designer of the Digital VAX and Microsoft NT operating systems once showed me his original design principles for the VAX range. It was a perfect example of concise specification, less than two sides of paper but incorporating all of the key design elements.

Security architectures should be based on sound security design principles that recognize the fundamental strengths and weaknesses of security features such as logical access control, authentication mechanisms and cryptographic key management.

We should aim to collect and apply good design principles. I encounter many that are rarely specified in systems design life cycles. Examples of good design principles might be, for example, the need to design information systems on modular principles, based on components that can be readily adapted to new environments. Or the need to employ open, intrinsically secure protocols, to enable secure connectivity between any environments.

These are all worthy principles that underpin the design of intrinsically secure systems. We should apply them to all system developments.

Jericho Forum principles

The Jericho Forum principles are a good example of the type of principles that we need to ensure that information systems are designed with optimal security features and maximum business agility.

The principles set out key security design considerations that should be embedded in the thinking and judgment of all system designers in order to ensure that systems are developed in a form that can be implemented in a de-perimeterized environment. They are simple but powerful enablers for achieving system designs that are capable of operation across a wide range of network environments:

1. The scope and level of protection should be specific and appropriate to the asset at risk

2. Security mechanisms must be pervasive, simple, scalable and easy to manage

3. Assume context at your peril

4. Devices and applications must communicate using open, secure protocols

5. All devices must be capable of maintaining the security policy on an untrusted network

6. All people, processes, technology must have declared and transparent levels of trust for any transaction to take place

7. Mutual trust assurance levels must be determinable

8. Authentication, authorization and accountability must inter-operate/exchange outside of your locus/area of control

9. Access to data should be controlled by security attributes of the data itself

10. Data privacy (and security of any asset of sufficiently high value) requires a segregation of duties/privileges

11. By default, data must be appropriately secured when stored, in transit and in use

Each of these principles is accompanied by further explanatory text. There are also a range of position papers setting out further advice on specific aspects associated with these principles. These principles are constantly evolving, so practitioners are advised to keep up-to-date with Jericho Forum publications which are published as open standards on the Internet.

These principles do not cover the full spectrum of security requirements but define the rules and considerations that must be observed when planning for a de-perimeterized future. There is, in fact, a need for a broader collection of security design principles that can be incorporated into information system development life cycles.

Collaboration-oriented architecture

Collaboration-oriented architecture (COA) is an emerging form of information architecture, pioneered by the Jericho Forum, that enables business processes to operate in a secure and reliable manner across multiple organizations.

Implementing a COA requires adoption of many of the Jericho Forum principles for operating in a hostile environment. COA allows business aspirations to be met by positioning appropriate security processes and controls at more effective levels in the infrastructure.

The COA framework defines the key components within which inter-operable, secure solutions can be provided to meet the needs of collaborating enterprises. Systems, networks and architectures can be considered to be compliant with the COA framework if all of these components are present.

A COA enables provision of secure systems in a global networked environment, able to keep pace with the growing threats and the business need for faster and more flexible collaborative business arrangements, ranging from outsourcing to joint ventures, from merger today to divestment tomorrow, all within a global working, global manufacturing and global procurement environment.

Forwards not backwards

I've often wondered at the strange phenomenon of security that encourages us to address security issues from the end point of a process, rather than its starting point. I first noticed this rather illogical approach when we were designing the original BS7799 Code of Practice.

The thinnest and least developed area turned out to be the chapter on security in systems development. The most mature and best documented areas were those covering operational security aspects. That largely reflects the inevitable priority for short-term priorities over longer-term interests.

Most security initiatives start from the operational perspective. We find shortcomings in systems, so we focus on testing. When we find that testing is not enough, we address the need for secure coding standards. Eventually we realize that the most important issues need to be addressed much earlier in the systems development cycle. But few security managers ever get to grips with reengineering this process.

In fact we can go a long way backwards in the cycle to find major opportunities for improvement. Start with education at schools, then computer science courses, then training courses for systems designers and programmers. That will ensure that we fix the problems properly. But, unfortunately, the further back we go, the longer it takes to get a result and the less compelling it becomes for a security manager with a set of short-term performance targets.

That's where professionalism kicks in. We need to get more of a contribution from security practitioners towards solving general industry problems. Each security professional and corporate security function should devote a small amount of their time to addressing the longer-term issues facing the security industry and society. That way we will get increasing recognition of the requirements for building security earlier into the processes, and the development of better methods to enhance the security of our information systems.

Capability maturity models

Not all business or functional processes are equal. Some are better designed and executed than others. In fact, processes can be differentiated by three important differentiators: their effectiveness, their performance and their maturity. And these three characteristics are closely correlated. Experience in measuring process effectiveness for complex processes such as software engineering has demonstrated that there are big gains to be made in process improvement.

Process maturity is a criterion for categorizing processes according to the sophistication of their management. Mature processes are ones that are well defined, managed, measured and controlled. That makes them effective, efficient and capable of continuous improvement. Mature processes will tend to have lower operating costs and faster completion times, and they will produce higher-quality deliverables. They are also likely to have more predictable costs and schedules, based on objective historical data.

In contrast, immature processes tend to be characterized by a tactical, fire-fighting approach, with inconsistent quality of outputs, and cost and schedule overruns. Successful execution relies more on heroic efforts by talented individuals than on the effectiveness of management systems. Policy is likely to be poorly communicated and enforced. Improvisation will be widely applied. That makes the outcome of these processes uncertain, inefficient and with a high risk of failure.

Capability maturity models are a useful, though potentially bureaucratic, management tool for benchmarking the effectiveness of processes and identifying process improvements. The first model of this kind was developed by Watts Humphrey in the 1980s at the Carnegie Mellon Software Engineering Institute. At the time it was a major breakthrough for measuring the effectiveness of software development processes. It drew on earlier work by experts in the field of quality management.

The original model was based on the recognition that complex processes require sophisticated management systems, able to anticipate potential problem areas and manage identified risks. We can't implement such systems overnight. That requires time and experience. But we can define and measure their progress on a process maturity scale. Capability maturity models draw on observed best practices. They define degrees of process maturity that are measurable, which provides both a starting point and a common language for benchmarking and process improvement targets.

The original Carnegie Mellon used a five-level scale, with each maturity level reflecting a typical plateau of achievement in process improvement. The lower levels reflect organizations that recognize the need for better management, but have yet to implement the necessary measures. The middle level reflects an organization that has defined the necessary controls, but has yet to deploy them. And the higher levels reflect the best practices of organizations that have achieved an effective management system and are beginning to harness the benefits. At the very highest level, organizations should exhibit continuous improvement and optimization of management processes.

Maturity models for information risk and security are not new. Many examples have been developed in the past by institutes and consultancies. But few have been more widely adopted, as they tend to be over-engineered, prescriptive and focused on the presence or absence of controls, rather than on the effectiveness of the governance processes.

The power of metrics

'You can't manage what you can't measure' is a phrase that's commonly quoted by consultants. Some people attribute it to W. Edwards Deming. But he didn't actually say that and it's not completely true. There are lots of things we have to manage that are unknown or not measurable. The point Deming actually made was that it was a deadly sin of management to manage an organization on visible information alone. He understood that you have to dig a little deeper to get your hands on the essential data you need to manage a process properly.

Visibility and metrics are the foundation of security risk management. If we can't see what's happening we can't manage risks. But metrics have other additional uses and benefits. They help to satisfy regulatory compliance requirements. They provide a basis for mature process management. They can contribute to balanced scorecards and other corporate targets. They demonstrate achievements. They underpin business cases. And they help focus and prioritize security effort.

Organizations that use metrics to shape their security initiatives are likely to have fewer incidents, less risk of compliance failure and lower cost operations. Metrics enable security managers to 'close the loop' on their policies and standards, to check both that controls have been implemented and that they are actually working.

So how do you go about developing an effective metrics system? What are the key requirements and principles? The starting point is to recognize that security is a support function to the business, not a business in itself. We need to consider metrics that can support business objectives, and the IT processes that enable them.

Firstly, we should consider corporate goals and the metrics that indicate whether they're being met. Typical goals might include objectives such as reducing costs, improving service levels or safeguarding revenue. Security metrics can easily be identified to support these targets. They prevent incidents, for example.

Secondly, we can identify security metrics that support or demonstrate regulatory compliance, for example the level of compliance of units, systems or platforms against security policies and standards.

Thirdly, we should aim to support IT strategy, which might, for example, include objectives such as improving service levels or IT portfolio management. Metrics, such as the security profiles of individual systems, or the levels of incidents affecting service quality, can contribute to this.

Fourthly, we can use metrics to prioritize our security efforts. In fact that's what we aim to do with risk assessments. By measuring the criticality of business processes and information systems, as well as their relative vulnerability to breaches, we can identify the most appropriate places to target our resources.

Fifthly, and perhaps most importantly, metrics can help prevent security incidents. As we saw in Chapter 3, monitoring of bad practices, near misses and minor incidents are the keys to avoiding major incidents. If we continue to turn a blind eye to our smaller failings, we will eventually be punished by a major incident.

In addition to all of these benefits, metrics can also support process improvement. We can measure items such as the cost and time taken to carry out security activities such as risk assessments, investigations, vulnerability management, or security reviews and audits. For mature security functions, that is the key to continuous improvement and optimized operations.

Closing the loop

Achieving a high level of process maturity requires a cycle of continuous improvement, such as the classic Deming cycle, illustrated in Figure 10.5. The key point

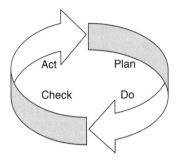

Figure 10.5   The Deming cycle of 'Plan, Do, Check, Act'

is that plans and actions are not enough. We also have to check the effectiveness of our initiatives and take appropriate corrective action. There are many ways to 'close the loop'. But, in my experience, the most effective means is through the use of accredited certification.

I've always been a strong advocate of accredited certification. The reasons are simple. It's the only process that meets the key requirements of any monitoring process. For me, that means that it's executed independently and regularly, against an objective standard, using a disciplined, predictable process, by accredited auditors with minimum qualifications and operating to a code of practice. And, if you pass, you get a formal certificate, which helps to impress and motive the business unit and its stakeholders.

These are all essential requirements. You can't leave it to your internal auditors. They will have other, potentially higher priority tasks which will, from time to time, take precedence. It's also highly extravagant to bring in expensive consultants, operating on a free-ranging basis to evaluate your security. They will be delighted, no doubt, to get bogged down in any detailed problem or opportunity that catches their eye for promoting future business.

Accredited certification is the quickest, cheapest and most satisfactory process for 'closing the loop'. Many people imagine it's an expensive process. It's not. It's like testing a car for road worthiness or a plane for air worthiness. It should be fast, focused, objective and indicate precisely where things are not right.

Accredited certification also provides a helpful certificate to business units, and that's an important motivator. Often the motivation of winning a certificate, coupled with the fear of failure, will be the tipping point to make a business manager go the extra mile, encouraging it to fix those small but vital items that are generally difficult to get to the top of the agenda. There's an understandable perception with most business managers that when you have 80–90% of your requirements in place, you can leave off and move on to other, more pressing problem areas. That strategy might work for many other things in business, but, unfortunately, a single security vulnerability can expose and entire enterprise infrastructure. That's why thoroughness counts in closing the loop.

If you are wondering what gives me the confidence to assert the benefits of accredited certification, I can assure you that it's based on real experience in two large, but very different, organizations.

For the Shell Group, my team achieved the world's first ever BS7799 accredited certification, through KPMG for Shell IT services across Europe. For the Royal Mail Group, my team held one of the largest scope certifications ever achieved, covering 8000 user areas across 500 buildings and including three large outsourced contracts for CSC, BT and Xansa. And all of that was relatively straightforward, requiring no more than a modest budget, a large dose of common sense and an appetite for hard work.

The importance of ergonomics

Ergonomics is the field that studies the design of products, systems, processes or environments from a human user perspective. It's often referred to as 'human factors' in the USA. And it's essential that any designer who wishes to ensure the correct or best use of their designs, understands the principles developed from this field. Unfortunately, not every product or system designer aspires to this goal.

In most cases, products are designed to be cheap to manufacture, or to contain features that will help to sell the product. We've all experienced this with electrical goods, such as DVD recorders that subsequently prove to be fiendishly difficult to operate. But we might not have appreciated this fact when we actually bought the product. We generally pick items, not for ease of use, but primarily on price, appearance and features. And in the software field, it's the features that differentiate proprietary products from free, open source ones.

But in the field of information security we cannot afford to be complacent about the ease of use of our processes, systems or guidance. If users cannot make sense of a policy or procedure, or if they cannot operate the security features associated with a system, then the security controls will fail. And the business and consumer worlds are littered with failed security systems. So it's vital that security professionals pay attention to ergonomics.

Steven Furnell, a professor at the University of Plymouth, has conducted an evaluation of how the usability of security-related features has evolved within new releases of Microsoft's Internet Explorer and Word. He concluded that, although there are improvements over earlier versions, there are many aspects that represent new or existing problems for users. In particular, the use of technical terminology and a lack of accompanying help were amongst the most frequent failings.

Ease of use of features is becoming a growing problem with many products and systems because of commercial business pressures. It's not serious if we can't operate an advanced feature on a DVD recorder. But it's a major problem if it leads to a failure in operating security features.

It's more than ease of use

It's generally agreed that there are five aspects of ergonomics: safety, comfort, ease of use, productivity (or performance) and aesthetics. I thought for a while that there was a missed trick here, as the initial letters don't appear to spell anything vaguely memorable, which might have enhanced the 'stickiness' factor. But on reviewing the draft of the book, Steven Furnell suggested that, by including the word 'ergonomics' itself at the start as the keyword, we can reshuffle the list to spell the word 'ESCAPE', a good mnemonic, perhaps to indicate how we can help users to 'escape from difficulty'.

For information security purposes, we can easily substitute 'security' requirements for 'safety' in this list. The same principles apply. For example, security can be improved by clearer menus and documentation, by features that are easy to find and operate, and through defaults and prompts that help the user to make the right decision.

Comfort is also important in the design of security features. Users who become irritated by security warnings, prompts or actions, will tend to ignore them or switch them off. Many users of Microsoft Vista tell me that they're irritated by excessive prompts. Some anti-virus software products will also prompt the user every few minutes to remind them that the signatures are out of date. It might be acceptable to remind them once, but not repeatedly, especially when the PC is being used off-line and there is no capability to update the signatures. Well-designed programs should consider these points.

Ease of use is also essential, for similar reasons, and because it's vital that security features are properly operated. Mistakes in security administration can have long-lasting and far-reaching security consequences. It can be dangerous to accidentally disable a security feature, grant privileged access to the wrong person or close down an important business transaction. The more powerful the security feature, the more critical its design becomes. The same logic, of course, applies to security policy and guidance. If a user can't make sense of it, then it's ineffective.

Productivity and performance are also important. In practice, users and administration staff will only commit a finite amount of their time to carrying out a security-related activity. If a security task is not fast and slick to execute, it will be ignored, put on the back-burner or accumulate a back-log that will most likely be discarded at some point in the future.

Aesthetics might seem at first sight to be an optional extra, perhaps the icing on the cake. But in many areas of security it's crucial. Security warning signs for example need to be eye-catching to gain attention. They also need to be attractive, rather than garish, as otherwise they might not be placed in the most suitable positions in an office or on a display.

Unfortunately, very few people in product development roles are aware of the principles of good design. We should all aim to improve this situation, because good design holds the key to building useable systems, ones that are better able to reduce the risks of people committing security breaches.

The failure of designs

Understanding the impact of the human factor is not an instinctive skill. It's based on experience, and an objective observation of how people go about their tasks. We don't do enough of this. That's probably why the state-of-the-art in man–machine computer interfaces is so poor. Most personal computers are designed, for example, to make it easier for users to write, rather than read information. Yet we read a lot more than we write. The interface is based on the wrong assumptions.

And there are many flaws in basic tasks. When we 'save' documents, for example, we destroy our previous work. And when we wish to close down our computers (at least those using older versions of software), we click 'start'. None of this makes sense. The designers have clearly failed to understand human requirements and cater for human nature.

Neil Stephenson, a writer and journalist, suggests in his entertaining book *In the Beginning was the Command Line* that analogue media and graphical user interfaces are effectively dumbing down communications. They serve as a popular interface to the real world, but without the precision of text. That might be true. But there are also huge advantages in analogue, graphical user interfaces. They can help overcome the limitations of traditional, linear presentations of information. Much better data visualization techniques are becoming available that can provide far superior presentation of information to enable users to make sense of multiple, parallel data streams, a demand that will continue to grow with the information age.

Researchers at Xerox PARC and MIT Media Lab, two of the leading technology research labs, have been aiming to develop more effective methods of reading and writing information for many years. Unfortunately, they've made very limited impact with the technology companies that are building new IT and security products. But there's certainly no shortage of research. The problem seems to be that the commercial business models of technology vendors simply don't focus on ease of use. It's the features, rather than the usability, that sells their products.

We need a better approach. Perhaps we need to find a way of incentivizing vendors to go back to first principles and develop better solutions. Because in practice, each new release of a technology product tends to be based on a selection of relatively small upgrades to existing products, rather than the revolutionary changes we need to cater for real customer needs.

Ergonomic methods

The starting point with ergonomics is to talk to users, to discover and define their culture, requirements, likes, dislikes and expectations. You can watch users at work, see how they use existing systems and security features, and also observe what they don't use. Observing users is, in fact, both an educational and a diplomatic task. People like to be consulted. And they often have strong views on what's wrong with products and systems. Information security managers need to get out more and talk to users about what they really think about security policies and systems.

It's useful, for example, to exploit focus groups, assemblies of users that use your systems or follow your policies. In a focus group, you can explain and discuss new ideas, ahead of their planned deployment. This makes sense, because the earlier you can identify problems, the easier and cheaper it will be to fix them.

You can also use so-called 'cognitive walkthroughs' to advantage, in which users imagine a new system, by stepping through all of the key stages and actions with the interviewer. Usability tests of prototype designs for new systems and processes using actual users, performing realistic tasks and scenarios, is also both effective and simple to execute.

Interactive screen designs can also be significantly improved by exploiting technology that monitors user eye-movements, identifying hot spots for eye gazes on the screen, as well as plotting their tracks across the screen. This type of analysis is useful when researching why security features have failed to work as affectively as envisaged.

A nudge in the right direction

University of Chicago professors, Richard Thaler and Cass Sunstein's book *Nudge: Improving Decisions about Health, Wealth, and Happiness* explores the little, unnoticed factors that often influence our choices. It's about those small things that make a difference, such as the school cafeteria that nudges kids toward good diets by putting the healthiest foods at the front.

They call it 'choice architecture'. But the technique is nothing new to retail marketing consultants. Supermarkets have been calling it 'shelf space management' for years. But the important point that the authors make is that we should also be applying these techniques to public policy. In fact, we should also consider their potential for information security.

In the IT world, defaults are the nudges for users. When faced with any technology, most users will avoid reading manuals at all costs and simply switch on and hope for the best. If an upgrade to a higher security level involves extra work, uses unfamiliar words or requires reference to an instruction manual, it will not happen.

It's always been the case. In the early 1990s, when I first explored why IT systems managers were failing to apply the recommended standards, I discovered that the reason was that in the first few paragraphs of our instructions, they encountered no less than three terms they were unfamiliar with. That nudged many of them to give up immediately.

Switching to an approach that assumes a higher level of security as the default is a safer bet. If there is no significant business overhead in operating at a higher standard, then risk-based approaches that allow options should not be used. Often it's easier and cheaper to operate the entire infrastructure at higher-level security, than offer options to a user. In the past, this level of operation, called 'system high' was expensive. But today, it's more likely to be diversity and exceptions that drive up cost. Secure by default is the strategy we should be aiming towards.

Learning to design systems that work

Many information security management systems and programs fail to deliver on promises. This chapter set out to explore the art of designing and deploying effective, usable information security systems. What did we learn?

The starting point for any long-term program of change is to develop a vision of where we wish to get to, and a mission statement of how we will operate in order to get there. These need to be simple statements that are easy to communicate, both to management and staff.

In the field of information security, there will always be more to be done than we have the resources to deliver. Strategy is important. It translates our vision and mission into a series of achievable goals and initiatives over a reasonable period of time. Our vision, mission and strategy statements should be designed to resonate with management and staff.

Critical success factors for a successful information security program include top management commitment, a good understanding of risks by management, professional competence, good visibility of threats, incidents and events, and benchmarking of best practice. The 'Golden Triangle' of people, process and technology considerations is always a useful starting point in designing an appropriately balanced and aligned program or framework.

Good management frameworks draw on a combination of prescriptive controls, risk assessments and classification schemes. In fact, there is no single solution that will fit all organizations. Frameworks should be designed to be long-lasting, which is not difficult, as long as they're carefully planned. Future maintainability is one of the major considerations for the design of any architecture. Standards are also central to any information security framework. New ones should not be developed if suitable ones already exist.

We all need a structure for our work, whether it's called a model, a framework or an architecture. But such structures are a means to an end, not an end in themselves. Architectures enable re-use of components and promote business agility. It's important, however, to avoid being distracted by the architecture design itself.

It's not unreasonable to say that a good modern security architecture is 'ragged around the edges, full of holes and exists largely in the minds of practitioners'. That's a sharp contrast to architectural models such as the Zachmann Framework, which promotes structures that follow a rigid, formal and complete design. But security architectures are rarely up-to-date and complete. The solution space always lags behind the problem space.

Clear design principles can help to ensure secure systems designs. The Jericho Forum principles are a good starting point for contemporary designers. Managing risks and controls across business partnerships and complex virtual supply chains is a growing security issue. We need to look beyond our own infrastructure, and to focus on the requirements of the broader security community. The emerging Jericho Forum 'collaboration-oriented architecture' is an important step forward in developing extended-enterprise security models. But much further work is needed to translate this into reality.

Metrics are a useful tool for shaping security initiatives and helping to 'close the loop' on policies and standards. Achieving a high level of process maturity requires a cycle of continuous improvement, the type suggested by the classic Deming Cycle of 'Plan, Do, Check, Act'. In fact, accredited certification delivers a range of benefits, not all of which are immediately obvious to most business managers.

Ergonomics is also a field of growing importance, as we rely increasingly on the actions and interactions of staff and their networks. There are five major aspects of ergonomics: safety, comfort, ease of use, performance and aesthetics. Unfortunately the state of the art in man–machine computer interfaces is generally poor. But the starting point with good design is to talk to users, to discover and define their culture, requirements, likes, dislikes and expectations. It's often small things that make a difference. Once identified, these cues and catalysts can be exploited to 'nudge' people's behaviour in the desired direction. In the IT world, defaults are the nudges for users. We need to ensure that user behaviour and the systems they use are secure by default.

Here are six critical success factors for successful information security management frameworks:

- A compelling security objective that makes business sense
- A balanced, and aligned, program that addresses people, processes and technology
- A framework that's long lasting and easy to maintain
- An architecture that can guide real world designs and decisions
- Maximum use of accepted, established public standards
- Cautious use of other people's work

CHAPTER 11

Harnessing the power
of the organization

The power of networks

Networks are eroding the power of central policy-makers. But they also provide the leverage to harness the power of the organization. This chapter explores how to turn a threat into an opportunity, how to exploit networks to leverage the power of central initiatives and encourage security innovation across the organization.

Exploiting the latent power of networks is the key to gaining the resource needed to manage the growing complexity of systems and infrastructure, as well as the increasing sophistication of network-based security threats.

Networks offer almost unlimited power to amplify our skills, resources, speed of response and defensive capability. We need to develop our capability to exploit them to our advantage. As Margaret Thatcher once said 'There is no alternative'. The new competitive edge, the key to wealth and the focus of the next arms race will be the ability to operate across networks and harness network effects.

Surviving in a hostile world

Networks are as dangerous as they are useful. We need a survival strategy that will enable us to safeguard, as well as leverage, our interests in a networked world that is full of opportunities and hazards.

There are many different survival strategies. In the face of a dangerous threat we can, for example, act like a hedgehog, an animal that rolls into a tight ball for protection, or we can behave like a strawberry plant, which places its key, genetic material securely on the outside and sends out suckers to extend its domain.

Managing the Human Factor in Information Security   David Lacey
© 2009 John Wiley & Sons, Ltd

Reaching out is a better bet than putting up a defensive wall. And it's particularly appropriate if the threats are coming from networks, because we can only effectively fight a network with another network. And that's increasingly being recognized in business, where collaborations are necessary to deliver the growing and changing set of skills and resources that are needed in today's global, competitive business environment.

Today's security manager needs to change the focus of security from maintaining a secure physical and network perimeter around the enterprise to enabling secure information flows and relationships across corporate boundaries. We need less attention to securing our own private back yards, and more focus on building collaborative security architectures to enable extended enterprise working with our industry colleagues.

Clearly, our strategies need to be more aligned with strawberry plants than hedgehogs. But the starting point is to focus on the internal organization, because that's where the extended enterprise begins.

Mobilizing the workforce

'People are our greatest asset' is a common mantra of executive boards. Unfortunately, this claim is often little more than an empty slogan. People are not fools. They can see, every day, the way their management actually treats staff, rather than how it aspires or claims to treat them. Employees will not be taken in.

But it's clear that people are generally the corporate asset with the greatest untapped potential. That's because other major assets, such as money, property, systems or trade secrets are relatively fixed or steady things. You can't do much more to increase their value, at last not without introducing a degree of downside risk. But given the right direction and leadership, you can achieve remarkable results from people with quite modest skills.

If a team is failing to deliver on targets, the usual management response is to condemn or replace the members. That rarely fixes the problem. It's more likely that the root cause will lie in a deep-seated flaw in the structure of the processes, rather than a lack of effort by the workforce. And if it's the latter then it will probably be the result of a failure by the leadership team to exploit the potential of the resources at their disposal.

Good leadership skills are hard to find. In fact, leadership is more about behaviour than skills. Few managers have sufficient charisma, or can walk their talk enough, to inspire their staff. Most are autocratic rather than democratic, much more focused on the task rather than the people. But modern leaders need to be much more like a shepherd than a sergeant major. The complexity and distractions of day-to-day business make it virtually impossible for a contemporary leader to keep track of detail. And organizations today are much less formal, and much more likely to respond to a shared direction rather than a set of orders.

Every organization is different, however, and different leadership styles will be required at different times. Managing a growing enterprise is different from managing a shrinking one, and it calls for a different style of leadership. Sometimes it's necessary to take tough decisions, to cut costs, shed staff or close plants or offices. That's when the hard, sociopathic leader excels. Tough leaders are also needed to drive hard bargains and stamp out corruption. They will, however, become progressively unpopular, especially in a socially networked world.

One useful tactic is to alternate a nice leader, who inspires staff and builds good community relations, with a nasty one who tackles underperformance and negotiates better terms with suppliers and customers. But a brutal leader will rarely last the distance. They will inevitably create enemies, and in a socially networked environment, opposition is very easy to muster.

Work smarter, not harder

The key to business success in an accelerating, competitive business world is not to work harder but to work smarter. In the absence of innovation and creative improvements, productivity and performance quickly tail off. Excessive hard work can also reduce valuable thinking time that could be spent improving systems and structures.

Any manager can reduce costs and push staff to their limits. But it takes a special one to understand and respond to the true potential of the workforce, as well as the intrinsic flaws and inefficiencies in the structure of systems.

There are many guidelines on working smarter. It's long been a booming industry. But most of them miss the point. It's not about better time management or other immediate efficiencies. The real art is about doing everything the easy way, and getting others to help you, especially the key influential networkers who can help get others on board. It's also about designing systems and methods that will naturally create and exploit positive feedback loops.

It's often said that lazy people are the most creative workers. They find the short cuts, the easiest approach to getting the work done. And that leads to greater productivity. Lazy people have a desire to perform work at minimum effort. We need more of them.

Finding a lever

Archimedes is reported to have said:

> *'Give me a lever long enough and a fulcrum on which to place it and I shall move the world.'*

Archimedes clearly understood the power of leverage.

Unfortunately, not everyone takes the trouble to find a lever. Many people naturally dive in to a task without adequate resources. In the field of security, good intentions and conscientious hard work are rarely enough. Many managers tell me things like 'I've only got a small shovel but I'm making progress'. The answer is to give them diggers. In fact, the most useful thing a chief information security officer can do is equip his staff with the best possible power tools available.

Leverage is the real key to successful security campaigns, especially those across large populations, carried out by small functions. A security manager cannot make enough impact without finding a lever to amplify his efforts. The reality is that there will never be enough budget and staff to deliver the program that's needed. But it's better to design or discover new levers to enhance our efforts, rather than cut our cloth to suit our budget.

Levers come in all shapes and sizes: networks, technology, fashion, company staff, customers, communities and the media are all potential levers. Getting the right structure and design for your security architecture is the starting point. Clever use of technology to automate your processes might be the next obvious step. But the smartest way of all is to get other people to do the work for you, especially when it's free.

The art of systems thinking

Understanding how to get the best out of systems is also important for harnessing your efforts. 'Systems thinking' is a structured, holistic approach to problem-solving. It looks at the inputs, outputs and linkages between individual system components and processes, in order to ensure that particular outcomes are avoided or optimized.

It's important to consider how systems are inter-related. Too often, we accept the individual performance of management systems based on silos of responsibility, without examining how they collectively meet the overall needs of the organization. Sometimes there is absolutely nothing you can do about this. It's a result of established contracts and working methods that can't easily be changed. But the starting point in escaping from these constraints is to recognize the source of the problems and, at the very least, aim to work around or compensate for these intrinsic shortcomings.

Key concepts in systems thinking are to focus on the behaviour of the whole, rather the individual components of the system, to examine the relationships between components, rather than the objects themselves, and to assess the impact of patterns, rather than the mere content.

Four-dimensional thinking is also important because components of systems can be separated by distance and time, which can produce surprisingly unintended effects in behaviour, as managers respond to out-of-date information by, for example, applying system corrections that are far too large or too late.

There might also be occasional 'butterfly effects' where small changes in systems input are greatly amplified to produce huge swings in systems behaviour, similar to the impact of a butterfly flapping its wings in Brazil that sets off a tornado in Texas. These are the type of changes that we should aim to harness to leverage our influence across large organizations or network populations.

Creating virtuous circles

We're all familiar with 'vicious circles', the positive feedback loops that amplify undesirable behaviour. We see them all the time in business. A company cuts its costs in response to falling sales. The quality of its product falls. Sales go down further. So they're forced to take out more costs. The company spirals downwards and eventually becomes bankrupt. Hyperinflation is another classic example of a vicious circle. Prices increase rapidly as a currency loses its value. A positive feedback cycle is created which further accelerates the rate of price increases.

Less familiar to us are the 'virtuous circles', the positive feedback loops that amplify desirable behaviour. We make a great product, for example, which sells well. We increase production, and gain economies of scale. That enables us to reduce prices further, and gain more sales. The process continues until we saturate the market. Virtuous circles are the waves of successful business performance that we all seek to emulate.

The one thing both have in common is a feedback loop that feeds changes associated with a system output back into a system input. But feedback loops can be very different. Most are negative ones, serving to correct deviations in system outputs by adjusting system inputs to reduce the size of the deviations.

In contrast, vicious and virtuous circles are based on positive feedback loops that adjust input values, in a way that amplifies the effect of any deviations in the system outputs. Such outcomes can be for better or worse. They can energize or destroy a security program. Security managers need to consider how to prevent damaging vicious circles, as well as how to create virtuous circles to leverage the effectiveness of their efforts.

An example of a vicious circle in security might be a situation in which a delay in applying critical patches results in a higher level of security incidents, the handling of which results in further delays to the patch management process, resulting in a growing level of incidents. The solution requires the application of more resources, better processes or new technology. But the cycle has to be broken in order to stem the levels of incidents.

An example of a virtuous circle in security might be a situation where a small increase in time spent by helpdesk staff in advising users on good security practices results in lower incident levels. That in turn enables even more time to be spent on this advice, progressively lowering the incident rates.

But in all cases, there are limits to how far a positive feedback loop can be sustained before it hits either an enforced brake or natural ceiling, or perhaps triggers a response that corrects the growth. Vicious and virtuous circles might be short-lived, but during their brief period of existence they can transform a problem area or solution space.

Triggering a tipping point

Malcolm Gladwell, a journalist for *New Yorker* magazine, has developed an interesting and important theory about 'tipping points', the threshold or time when the momentum for a change becomes unstoppable. Every security professional should read his book on the subject.

The key theme is that ideas spread quickly across large populations, especially networked ones. And they are often unplanned and unexpected. Typical examples of tipping points range from the sudden fashion for wearing Hush Puppies, which began with a handful of trend setters in Greenwich Village, and quickly spread across America, to the unexpected, dramatic drop in crime in New York in the late 1990s.

What causes this to happen? Malcolm Gladwell compares such large scale changes in behaviour with epidemics. In his book, *The Tipping Point: How Little Things Can Make a Big Difference*, he sets out three key rules for such epidemics.

Firstly, there is the 'law of the few', the surprising power of the actions of a small number of key people with particular, rare social skills, people who are widely networked or knowledgeable people that collect information, spot trends and pass them on.

Secondly, there is the 'stickiness factor', the ability to craft a memorable message that has impact on your target audience. Interestingly, experience shows that this owes a lot more to careful research and fine-tuning, rather than left-field, creative inspiration.

And, thirdly, there is the 'power of context': the conditions and circumstances of the time and place in which events occur that determine the ultimate success of an idea or campaign. Amongst other things, research and experience suggest that environments play a big role in influencing responses. Even relatively small details can act as cues to stimulate particular behaviour. And this, in fact, is consistent with my own experience with experimental environments for innovation and crisis management.

It's worth reflecting on these conditions, because they are the key enablers for generating the type of simultaneous, widespread behaviour change that we seek to achieve across our organizations.

Many of the examples that Malcolm Gladwell gives in his book were largely unplanned, unexpected phenomena, things that occurred by chance rather than design. But we should seek to exploit these observations to create planned changes to people's perception, attitudes and behaviour. We'll examine the potential of some of these ideas in the following sections of this chapter.

Identifying key influencers

For any major change program it's vital to identify and engage the key movers and shakers within an organization, the people who actually influence staff attitudes and behaviour, the people who can best help you to make a bigger impact.

We saw in Chapter 5 that there are different structures in organizations that influence attitude. Sometimes it will be the CEO or senior management, sometimes an individual thought leader. There are also different types of individual within an organization, with different levels of capability to influence attitudes and behaviour.

Certain individuals are well known and well respected across their community. Others might be connected through deep friendships, so-called 'strong ties', perhaps with a small, private circle of important senior executives. And then there are those who are proficient in building large numbers of casual relationships, so-called 'weak ties', across a range of communities.

The latter types are the rare individuals that Malcolm Gladwell would call the 'connectors', the ones that seem to know everybody, the types that strike up conversations with fellow passengers on a plane. They are one of the key components needed to achieve the 'tipping point', that point of critical mass when a new idea starts to take off in a big way. I'm one of these types, for example. I like to join and bridge different communities, so many people ask for my help in promoting new ideas.

Another type of person that can help to create a tipping point is the know-all, the expert who likes to research, trade and share information with anyone they encounter. They are the people you go to when you want advice on buying a washing machine or DVD recorder. They have an encyclopaedic knowledge of many kinds of things. And they will be the first ones to pick up on any new trends and pass it on to their colleagues. Sociologists call them 'mavens', a Yiddish word, and they are often the key to the propagation of knowledge across networks. These are the people we all hope to find. I always use my good friend, Andrew Yeomans, for example, to keep up to date with new developments in security technology. He's one of the leading security mavens.

We can use all these types of individuals to leverage our initiatives. We just have to identify them and enlist their help. Good connectors are useful in helping to cascade an idea or message across multiple communities. Mavens are the ones who are most likely to pick up the idea and pass it on to their colleagues. Respected individuals are the ones who will help those ideas become accepted within a community. And people with strong ties to senior executives are the ones who can help you obtain the backing and influence of senior management.

It's a smart and highly effective technique to exploit the influence of individuals with strong ties to senior executives, especially for subtle messages that are hard to convey in a brief elevator speech. In my early years at Royal Mail Group, for example, I hired a retired company director with high standing and strong ties to company directors specifically to help promote new concepts in strategic crisis management. It was a subject area in which corporate executives were already highly experienced, and would have resisted advice from a relatively new executive from outside. This strategy worked very well.

The concept of strong and weak ties is also a very interesting one from a security intelligence or investigation perspective. Surprisingly, each type provides very different insights when, for example, examining records of communications between known or suspected criminals or terrorists.

Heavy communications patterns, for example, might indicate close collaborators. Occasional but regular communications might suggest a professional associate, for example the use of an outside expert for a particular job, or perhaps indicate an attempt to limit communications to keep below the radar of investigators who might be examining traffic patterns of known or suspected associates.

In search of charisma

In the case of the sudden popularity of Hush Puppies, it was a handful of stylish, charismatic individuals that triggered the trend. Then it was spread by the phenomenon of fashion which takes a cue from acknowledged thought leaders and creates a bandwagon effect to copy the trend.

But who are these rare people that have the ability to trigger major trends across a large population? One thing they all seem to have is the rather enigmatic characteristic that we term charisma. It's worth examining this rather exclusive but powerful phenomenon.

Charisma is a seemingly magical, magnetic quality that helps enormously to promote leadership and influence. Those that have it can do no wrong. It's long been an elusive trait that is difficult to pin down. It encompasses many indefinable qualities, including charm, inspiration and persuasion, perhaps the three essential qualities for making an impact with people and obtaining buy in and support for ideas and actions.

The idea of charisma was first suggested by Max Weber, the German sociologist. He believed it was one of three forms of authority (the other two being traditional authority and legal authority). Weber believed that charismatic individuals were endowed with a special gift that set them apart from ordinary people. In other words they were natural leaders.

Clearly it helps enormously if you are clever, good-looking, well-spoken and gregarious. But I don't completely buy the idea that people are born with the magical qualities that result in charisma. To me, knowledge, determination and practice are more important factors than circumstances.

And charisma can, in fact, be influenced by conscious behaviour, body language and expression. Politicians and presenters often use hand movements, for example, to help make points. Smiling and enthusiasm help. As do expressions of empathy and support. People will warm to you if they believe that you genuinely like them. Surprise is also a useful device, as it conveys an impression that the audience is special.

Good salesmen are instinctively proficient in exploiting non-verbal cues, the tiny, micro-movements that influence communications between individuals. Research shows that there is, in fact, a mass of small, unconscious interactions that take place when we connect with other people. We communicate emotions and empathy, and we synchronize our speech rates and physical movements. Non-verbal cues will also have a substantial impact on how people perceive you, as well as how your messages are received, especially on first encounters, when 'thin slicing' can determine whether people like you or not.

Understanding fashion

Fashion is a further powerful phenomenon. And it's not just for younger people. Today fashion affects all age groups and social sectors. Fashion is driven by several factors. One is the natural, competitive instinct of people to stay one step ahead of their peers. Another is the desire for many people to identify themselves with a particular group.

In the fashion world, analysts aim to identify specific existing or emerging tribes, understand their taste and preferences, and then advise manufacturers on what styles to build into their products to appeal to particular markets.

In my youth, we had a fairly limited choice, initially between being a mod or rocker, and then later on, a hippy or skinhead. Since then, the number of fashion tribes has been slowly increasing, though surprisingly slowly. Around the turn of the century, leading trend analysts, such as Cay Bond, were identifying a much richer set of fashion tribes, including luxury goods enthusiasts, back-to-nature green types, sadomasochistic types who liked gothic fashions and the 'space trash' tribe who liked the comical juxtaposition of high-tech and old trash, as epitomized by the style of the Mir spacecraft.

Since then, we've seen a slow 'long tail' growth in styles. In 2008, for example, social experts in the UK identified 26 different young tribes, including emos, scenesters, grungers, skaters, trendies, blingers and many others. The fashion world is progressively fragmenting into a growing range of very different, but highly specific tastes.

Understanding the key likes and dislikes associated with such trends is important for designers of products and managers of change initiatives. It will help you to appreciate the potential appeal and impact of new images and messages for security awareness campaigns, especially those aimed at younger staff or customers.

Another interesting aspect of fashion is the impact on both the value of, and the threats to intellectual assets. In fast-moving markets, such as clothes for example, there's much less emphasis on the enforcement of intellectual property rights, compared to, say, the entertainment industry, where products continue to sell for longer periods.

Counterfeit goods are a major nuisance to fashion retailers. But there is a greater emphasis on creating and leading new trends, rather than milking profits from existing products. Clothes, for example, are at their highest value at the time of their creation, and they progressively lose their value over time.

This type of fast-decaying intellectual value is typical of many emerging intellectual assets. With faster product cycles and increasing networking potential, companies need to refresh and exploit their ideas and products at a faster and faster pace. That's one reason, for example, why security managers need to focus more attention on maintaining and securing flows of information, rather than firewalling old, static stocks of data.

The power of context

The third rule identified by Malcolm Gladwell for creating a tipping point in a network is the power of context. This rule suggests that the precise conditions and circumstances, during the time and place of any campaign, are pivotal in determining its success.

There is some evidence to support this theory. There is the 'broken window' theory of preventing crime by paying attention to small details that serve as cues for good or bad behaviour. Criminals, for example, are encouraged by environments that suggest that nobody takes the trouble to stop or fix damage to local assets. It's also much easier to fix a small problem, such as a broken window, than a much larger problem such as the street crime that begins to develop in a run-down area.

The broken window theory was originally developed by James Wilson and George Kelling in the early 1980s. Kelling was subsequently hired as a consultant to the New York City Transit Authority, who actually put these ideas in action, targeting relatively minor, but highly visible problems, such as graffiti and fare-dodging. This eventually led to the 'zero tolerance' strategy of Mayor Rudy Giuliani to combat crime across New York City. The results were astounding. Violent crime dropped by 75%.

There are many critics of this theory who point out that other factors, such as demographic changes, the decline in crack usage and the legalization of abortions were the real causes of the improvement. All these factors would have contributed to the overall drop on crime. But something very special happened at that time, and the techniques applied were based on the broken window theory.

This theory also makes perfect sense. We've discussed the impact that authority, peer pressure, perceived consequences and environments have on people. This fits that pattern. People are heavily influenced by the circumstances around them. Exploiting this, amongst other things, is the key to large-scale culture change.

The bigger me

Some people like to operate as empowered individuals. Others prefer the safety and leverage of working within a collective group. Both strategies can deliver effective value across networks. Entrepreneurs are a powerful catalyst for innovation. And large networked communities can harness a tremendous power for change.

Often it's a cultural influence that determines how people operate. Some environments tolerate mavericks. Other cultures encourage people to build a consensus with their peers. One interesting study by Shell, for example, examined the longer-term implications of these approaches on the energy industry.

Every three years, Shell develops a set of long-range scenarios to challenge the mindsets of its executives. Traditionally these were based on rather extreme, opposite outcomes, such as a world dominated by free trade or a market constrained by trade barriers. In 1995 the Shell planners adopted a slightly different approach and assumed that the powerful forces of liberalization, globalization and technology were unstoppable and would lead to a single market outcome. The scenarios then became focused on opposite strategies for adaptation to this brave, new world.

The Shell planners selected two distinct strategies for their scenario planning exercise. These scenarios are worth reflecting on because they illustrate different approaches to harnessing the power of networks.

The first one was called 'Just Do It!' and described a world characterized by the strengths of the Western culture for quick, flexible, decisive reactions by empowered individuals to fast-moving threats and opportunities. This approach sacrifices consensus for speed and tolerates creative anarchy. It is a self-organizing world that values freedom, autonomy and empowerment, and encourages innovation.

The second scenario was called 'Da Wo', an Eastern term which translates as 'the big me'. In this world, countries and companies discover that success and strategic advantage is based on long-term trusted relationships that can be harnessed across networks. This scenario can be characterized by a Chinese proverb:

> *'Xi Sheng Xiao Wo Wan Cheng Da Wo.'*
> *(Sacrifice 'small me' to benefit 'big me'.)*

In practice, the world will always be based on a mixture of the two approaches. Some cultures favour entrepreneurs, others prefer collaboration. But there are strengths and weaknesses in each approach. One strategy offers the prospects of inventiveness and agility, while the other promotes cohesion and inclusiveness.

Not all networks are the same, of course. A network of anonymous strangers cannot be approached in the same way as a community of networked colleagues sharing a mutual interest. Good networkers need time to build a reputation. Established networks can always be influenced by such individuals. But new networks are built on compelling ideas.

The power of the herd

Some industries tend to operate as a herd. The big banks, for example, often do. They rarely differentiate themselves in any substantial way. Certainly many of their systems and products are very similar. And their security standards and methods are largely the same.

Herds are different from fashions, bandwagons and tipping points. They are a group of people or organizations who consciously choose to stick together, rather than simply picking up a fashionable idea to keep up with the rest of the pack.

We see symptoms of herd behaviour in financial market bubbles and stock market crashes. It's an effective defence strategy in response to a common threat. In nature, when faced by a predator, many animals will instinctively position themselves as close as possible to the centre of a group. In security, we sometimes observe similar behaviour in response to a common regulatory or legal threat.

Interestingly, herd behaviour, even in animals, does not occur as a result of any central planning or coordination. It happens because each member chooses to act in a way that corresponds with that of the majority of other members. They imitate others, consciously or unconsciously. That means it's hard to influence the direction of the herd. You can't simply focus your efforts on a handful of leaders. You will need a much larger bandwidth of influence.

Herds are networks that often exhibit some of the more negative aspects of collaboration. They stifle innovation. Decisions are unpredictable or bureaucratic. Progress is slow. The lowest common denominator might become the only point of consensus. Herds present problems for vendors and innovators. Companies that behave like this are conservative, perhaps defensive, when presented with fresh ideas or new technology. Gaining acceptance for a new security standard or technology is difficult.

That's one reason why new approaches to security are often slow to become accepted in communities that operate this way. Cryptography is a particular case in point. Few organizations will take a chance on a new system or product. Most prefer to copy what others do. New approaches or algorithms need to be around and available for peer review for many years before they will be taken seriously by the community.

Maverick products are not welcome in the cryptographic space. A classic example of this was Tristrata, a novel encryption system, backed by leading venture capitalists and endorsed by Price Waterhouse. Tristrata developed a new approach to encryption in the late 1990s. But it burned all of its investment capital long before it made a single sale. Tristrata was a classic case study of the pitfalls in attempting to introduce new security technology into a herd environment.

When you have to operate in an environment dominated by herds, you need to adapt your tactics. It's important to keep sight of the big picture, but big initiatives will take a long time to be accepted. It's better to aim for easy, progressive improvements that present no major threats to any stakeholders. And you will need to aim to build consensus at each stage. That means identifying and addressing potential blocking influences at the earliest possible stage, and building contingency, resilience and agility into your strategy.

The wisdom of crowds

James Surowiecki's book *The Wisdom of Crowds* suggests that collective group behaviour is smarter, wiser and more innovative than individual efforts. What can we learn from this? Can it be possible to improve decision-making by exploiting the collective views of networked individuals?

Firstly, it's important to realize that not all crowds are wise. Many come up with dumb recommendations. In fact there are several effects at play in arriving at any group decision, such as diversity of opinion within the group, the independence of its action and the degree of specialization and local knowledge.

Surowiecki believes the advantages of collective decisions are in obtaining market judgment, establishing common understandings, and encouraging free market forces. Bad judgments are caused by members being too conscious of the opinions of others, and not being prepared to think differently. Failures in group decisions can be caused by a lack of diversity within the crowd, a hierarchical management bureaucracy, or a divided, imitative or emotional population. These ideas are, in fact, largely consistent with everything we've discussed in the book. They are typical human weaknesses.

But the learning point is that diversity underpins good collective decision-making and bureaucracy, obedience and politics kills it. We should not expect a rigid, hierarchical network to develop sensible recommendations. And the more people associated with a decision, the better. As long, of course, as they are free to express their opinions.

Unlimited resources – the power of open source

Open source software development harnesses the free time of huge numbers of keen designers and programmers. And it's growing bigger all the time. In the early days, there were many doubters and misconceptions. In the 1990s, Robert Metcalfe, a pioneering technologist, predicted its death. He was wrong. It's since gone from strength to strength.

It was also initially assumed that the use of open source products would be inappropriate from a security point of view. That's not so. There are just as many advantages as drawbacks. Even more radical was the idea that you actually could develop new security technologies using this method. But several successful cryptographic products have been developed this way. And the most successful and widely used intrusion detection system, Snort, is an open source product.

In fact, not only can you build excellent, free security technologies using open source methods, you can also make serious money from selling further products and services that add further value to the basic technology. Marty Roesch, the founder and CTO of Sourcefire and the founder of Snort, has built a business worth hundreds of millions of dollars on the back of his intrusion detection engine. Gartner Group rates his Sourcefire product range as the most visionary in the solution space.

Marty has been successful because he knows what his customers want, he has a vision for his products that's clearly aligned with the marketplace, and he understands the strengths and weaknesses of open source development methods. He's also a very smart person and a really nice guy. These things help too.

Open source is neither better nor worse than proprietary developments. It's just different. And that applies to its security aspects as much as its functionality and performance. If you're worried, for example, about a trap door being planted in the code, then home-grown software will clearly present a lower risk. But few organizations build their own systems. And purchasing proprietary products of unknown provenance can present an even higher risk.

The characteristics of open source developments vary, of course, according to the nature of the community and the business model. But open source has some typical characteristics.

Fit-and-finish, for example, as well as support and training are generally weaker. Few programmers enjoy documentation. And not everyone is overly concerned about the look and feel of user features. Feature sets can also be thinner, as products are designed more for utility than sales appeal. And there might not be a reliable road map for longer future development though proprietary product plans are rarely fully revealed to customers. Release cycles are also different, as they are largely constrained by development resources, rather than corporate targets.

Open source provides a powerful, alternative approach to in-house development or bought-in products. It can be a powerful lever for your own resources and budget. But it requires a different customer mindset. You have to align your requirements with those of the general user community. And, of course, you can't solve all of your problems with open source products alone. It's about achieving the right mix of products, as well as the correct architecture and interfaces to solve your security problems.

But, one day, no doubt, we will be able to build complete, collaborative security solutions around open source products. And that's a powerful thought to make us revisit our views on security architecture.

Unlimited purchasing power

Interestingly, if you can harness a large network of similar thinking individuals, you can not only establish an open source development community, you can also raise serious money.

In April 2007, a website called MyFootballClub was established with the goal of raising enough money from soccer fans to buy the controlling interest in a football club. By the end of July more than 50,000 people had registered their e-mail addresses. In the first ten days of August they raised £500,000. Three months later they paid £700,000 to take over Ebbsfleet United Football Club. Six months later Ebbsfleet won the FA Trophy on their first ever trip to Wembley. It sounds more like a plot for a feature film. But it was real.

This unlikely success story demonstrates just how easy it now is to raise money through the power of the Internet. And it's just the tip of the iceberg. For practical purposes there is no limit to the purchasing power of the Internet. It's only constrained by the amount that citizens are compelled to invest. A popular cause can raise a substantial amount of money.

Barack Obama's presidential campaign, for example, used a social networking site to raise hundreds of millions of dollars from relatively small donations. In fact, this method of fund raising has no limits other than our imagination.

What would be the impact if this style of funding became commonplace for other serious investments, such as the takeover of a bank, or energy company? All we need is a web site and we're away. We don't need to be established venture capitalists. We don't need bank loans. We can now raise money for any purpose, instantly, as long as we can capture the imagination of the public.

Of course, you might argue that there's nothing novel about the idea of raising money for ventures through networks of individuals. Banks have been arranging this for their clients for centuries. What's new is the use of social networks to exploit the same concept. And, more importantly, the altruistic motive, engagement and behaviour of such shareholders. If it catches on, it will introduce a powerful new dimension to corporate governance. Companies will be at the mercy of the wisdom or madness of the crowd, rather that merely responding to the whim of the chief executive. Now that would be something.

Let the network to do the work

Clay Shirky's book *Here Comes Everybody* begins with the tale of a woman named Ivanna who accidentally left her phone in the backseat of a New York City cab in May 2006. Ivanna bought a replacement phone, and found she was able to access some of the details of a woman who had taken possession of her missing phone. She contacted this person, but the finder refused to return it.

Ivanna therefore decided to publish the story of her stolen phone on the web. Within days, millions of people were reading about it. Bulletin boards were set up, but crashed under the weight of demand. Within a few weeks the police had arrested the person and recovered the phone.

The power of networks to leverage such efforts is quite remarkable. Guaranteeing to harness it is another matter. Not every cry for help will receive as much immediate, widespread attention. But some will. And if you don't ask, you don't get. So it's certainly worth trying.

What is it that makes a call for help compelling? We can copy professional journalists and try to ensure that our request fits as much as possible of the criteria they use. As we saw in Chapter 7, they look for stories that are: topical, relevant, unusual, trouble and of human interest.

We can also try to inject some of the characteristics of a memorable message that we identified in Chapter 7. Many small things make a difference. It helps to understand the community you're addressing, and to identify themes that will resonate with them. Context, presentation and timing can also be pivotal. And of course monitoring which techniques work best, even if you can't work out why they do, is essential in order to learn and improve.

An increasing number of people now have the same idea. Web sites are springing up to enable citizens to report incidents of concern to the community and of interest to local councils. 'Community Fix', for example, is a UK website that lets local people report anything unsightly or anti-social, such as graffiti, abandoned cars or 'fly tipping'.

In the same way, we can encourage staff, partners and customers to report information security incidents, suspicious behaviour or bad practice. Incident reporting needs to be much more than a help desk telephone number. It demands an interactive web site. And it shouldn't be that hard to encourage people to take a closer interest in information security, especially if you've already convinced them it's a team game, for which everyone's responsible.

Why is everything getting more complex?

Wherever you look things seem to be getter more complex. Most people fear complexity and seek to avoid it. Personally I like it. It means that our products and systems are becoming richer. Unnecessary complexity should always be avoided, of course. But a lot of complexity is inevitable, the result of good things, such as greater collaboration of effort, increasing functionality of products, greater outreach of services, more centralization of control, and growing combinations of systems.

Complexity is neither good nor bad. It offers as many opportunities as challenges. And it's both here to stay and set to grow, so we have to understand it and come to terms with it.

I've always been fascinated by the challenge of managing complexity, ever since I was introduced to the world of cybernetics and control theory at City University Business School in London in the late 1970s. In those days it was largely a theoretical concern of the operational research community. Since then it's become a major problem and priority for virtually every IT and security professionals, because we are all now experiencing the difficulty of trying to manage highly complex infrastructures and systems.

The starting point in managing complexity is to accept that it's not just a case of 'keep it simple, stupid'. Simplicity can either help or hinder, depending on how you go about it. In fact, there are several dimensions to the problem. Some of them are related. But all of them are a direct result of the nature of computers and networks themselves.

Firstly, there is the problem of scale, caused by the power of networks. Big government programmes are classic examples of that. We keep attempting to build bigger systems, simply because it can be done.

Secondly, there is the problem of increased variety, i.e. the number of states a system can be in. This is caused by the variety-amplification effect of computers: they enable many more states to be achieved. You can read Stafford Beer's books for more thoughts on that.

Thirdly, there is the slow but sure change from a deterministic to a probabilistic model for our information systems, brought about by the introduction of networks. Let's stop and consider that for a moment, because it's a very significant paradigm shift. In the past we built information systems based on algorithms that generated a pre-determined output for a given input. (Of course that's assuming the software was reliable and it never can be absolutely correct in practice. But that's a separate point.)

Once we begin to connect networks to information systems, however, then this deterministic model breaks down. The output will vary according to the state of the network and the responses generated by other connected users and systems. Repeat a transaction a minute later and it might well give you a completely different result. David Tennenhouse, Intel's Research Director, was the first to draw attention to this change. He's compared it to the paradigm shift that occurred in physics when quantum mechanics appeared on the scene. Amongst other things it necessitated a change in perspective, attitude and problem-solving skills.

Fourthly, business networks are becoming more complex as we move from old fashioned point-to-point networks towards more efficient hub-and-spoke networks. Initially that's a surprise. You'd expect hub-and-spoke networks to be simpler to manage, as they require fewer connections. In fact they might look simple, but the mathematics needed to calculate the impact of risks and failures is much more complex. Hub-and-spoke networks are part of a class of networks called scale-free networks. Scale-free networks exhibit very different topological (and other) characteristics, with implications for quality, risk, reliability and vulnerability management.

Fifthly, on top of all this there is a trend towards less prescriptive, fuzzier methods of decision-making caused by shorter business cycles and higher degrees of freedom and personalization.

The end result of all this is that our infrastructures and systems are getting bigger, more varied, more adaptive, less predictable and much harder to measure and control. And these trends are unstoppable unless we elect to halt the progress of technology and business.

Getting to grips with complexity

What can be done to about all this complexity? In fact, the best course of action when it comes to addressing any form of permanent change is generally to embrace it rather than fight it. But there are arguments for both options.

Many professionals will instinctively react by attempting to simplify the situation. And there are many techniques for achieving this. We can introduce limits, filters, standards, classifications and rules to reduce the number of states a system can be in, though this will, of course, reduce the richness of systems we operate.

It's also possible to break down complicated problems and solutions into smaller pieces to make some aspects of them more manageable. But it's important to realize that the overall system will still have a comparable level of complexity. For example, you can break software into modules to make testing easier. But it doesn't reduce the size of the input and output space, or the number of permutations of paths through modules. It does however enable re-use of modules, and it also enables an architecture to be developed with standardized interfaces, which reduces complexity at the overall management level.

A good architecture also helps to manage and maintain a system. At the very least you can avoid having to ditch a system when only one part needs to be changed. But there is also a real danger that an over-engineered architecture might itself add to the complexity of developing or managing the system. We encountered this in the last chapter when we considered the excesses of standards committees who have produced models exhibiting unnecessary complexity, classic examples being the X.400 e-mail standard and the seven layer OSI communication model.

Over-engineering of architecture can be avoided by the application of Occam's Razor, as mentioned in the last chapter. The objective should be to eliminate all things that make no real impact on the overall results. Simplicity is more than a characteristic of a system or framework. It's a fundamental design objective that needs to be addressed at all levels in the design process.

Simple can't control complex

Henry Louis Mencken, a journalist, is alleged to have once said:

> *'For every complex problem there is an answer that is simple, neat and wrong.'*

He was right. There is an old law of control theory that few managers and process designers understand. It points out that there must be the same number of states in your controlling system as the system you're aiming to control. This law is called Ashby's Law of Requisite Variety, after the eminent British operational researcher Ross Ashby:

> *'If a system is to be stable the number of states of its control mechanism must be greater than or equal to the number of states in the system being controlled.'*

In Ross Ashby's terminology, variety is a measure of the number of states a system can be in. It makes perfect sense when you think about it. A traffic light, for example, requires an equal number of states in the controlling mechanism to match the number of required permutations of lights. Otherwise the system will not be completely under our control.

In practice, we tend to reduce the number of states in the systems we wish to control by a range of measures: we place limits on the behaviour of people and systems; we use filters to reduce the scope of incoming or outgoing information; we classify items into a smaller number of categories to minimize the range of possibilities; we impose structure on items to minimize their context and we impose standards to reduce the variety of states to a manageable number. Using all these devices, often sub-consciously, we somehow manage to muddle through.

But the world is getting more complex. And networks will ensure that this trend continues indefinitely. So, if we can't reduce the number of states within our information systems to a controllable level, what else can be done? This is a fundamental challenge that we all need to address. But there are, in fact, several techniques that might be considered.

Data visualization techniques, for example, can improve the monitoring capability of human users by enabling them to monitor parallel streams of events simultaneously.

A more powerful technique is to increase the number of states in the controlling mechanism, through some form of 'variety amplifier' that allows us to monitor a much higher number of states than we can manage with the resources at hand. In fact, this is surprisingly easy to achieve through the application of technology.

Computers and networks are, in fact, natural variety amplifiers. They enable control mechanisms to be scaled up to whatever level we require. In theory, a computer can assume an almost infinite number of states. Time, memory and processing power are the only constraints. And those can be extended far beyond our own resources, if we wish, by the use of networks, grid computing and virtual storage. We can also exploit the leverage of networks, to create positive feedback loops that increase the variety in our controlling mechanism, in the same way that viruses spread and mutate.

A more ambitious approach might be to change the nature of the controlling mechanisms themselves, to build complex, adaptive governance systems that can evolve to meet the changing nature of our networked systems. Certainly we need to move away from static, deterministic approaches to the management of information systems. But much further research and experimentation will be needed to develop these ideas further. They are, perhaps, more than a decade away from realization. But they will come.

Designing freedom

Experiments in building more sophisticated control systems have, in fact, been taking place for more than 50 years. Unfortunately they've had little impact on everyday business.

The classic attempt at using computers in the controlling mechanism for a complex set of systems was Stafford Beer's heroic efforts in the early 1970s to build a cybernetic control system for the Chilean Government. Beer was a leading pioneer of management science, and the founder of SIGMA, the world's first management consultancy. In 1971 he was invited by President Salvador Allende to design and implement a real-time computer system to control the Chilean economy. The resulting 'Cybersyn' project was a visionary concept built on cybernetic principles.

Beer designed and embedded an 'electronic nervous system' into the Chilean economy. The vision was that voters, workplaces and the government would be linked together by an interactive, national communications network, which carried daily information about the output of factories, the flow of raw materials and other economic information. It was, in fact, a concept for electronic government that was at least three decades ahead of its time.

The underlying concept was that the best way to manage the variety in the economy was to use a computer system, which is better equipped than humans to monitor a large number of possible states and respond with a richer set of policies. It was intended to overcome the traditional constraints in management systems arising from Ashby's Law of Requisite Variety.

This was in contrast to the generally applied alternative of reducing the number of states in the system by applying crude, across-the-board economic policies and maintaining a small number of simple bands and thresholds. Beer's idea was that a computer could deliver a richer, more fine-tuned controlling mechanism.

Although essentially a Big Brother concept, Beer called it 'designing freedom' because he believed it would free companies from the restrictions of crude, blanket economic policies. He built a classic 1960s style operations control room, complete with white and orange swivel chairs with inbuilt controls. The design, in fact, had more in keeping with the bridge of the USS Enterprise than the traditional corridors of national power. Linked to the control room was a national network of 500 telex machines and a central computer centre.

Unfortunately Stafford Beer was never able to fully prove the concept. His client was assassinated in the 1973 coup d'état.

Fast forward to 2008 and we can still find attempts to build on Stafford Beer's ideas. David Goldsworth, a UK technology entrepreneur, has designed and built a new type of computing technology modelled on Beer's ideas that aims to match, rather to reduce, the problem space. He aims to solve problems in real-time that would take a conventional computer technology the age of the universe to solve.

A process-free world

Processes have been a fashionable business topic over the last two decades, ever since Michael Hammer, a former MIT professor, unleashed waves of radical downsizing on a comfortable, but overmanned business world with the introduction of business process re-engineering.

The business environment has never been the same since. And it never will be the same again, because of the relentless trend of ever-greater cost-cutting, speed and productivity. But there has also been a huge impact on the quality of life. Employees are working too long, too hard and too fast. Many secretly yearn for the halcyon days of big offices, fixed working hours, slow processes, large budgets and long lunches. But they're long gone.

The problem is that our work methods have not kept pace with the changes. If we continue to accelerate traditional working processes we are on a certain course towards a burned-out workforce. We need to work smarter, travel less, exploit automation and free ourselves from processes, in order to reclaim our leisure time.

Processes have been around for centuries, as they're the fundamental basis of the industrial age. They underpin mass production. And that will continue to be needed for the rest of time, though it's not in keeping with the spirit and structure of the new information age. Computers and networks enable variety and personalization on a massive scale. We don't need standard, scripted solutions, though there will always be a place for them, especially where they might enable network effects through common standards.

A process-driven approach is not the best way forward for a forward-looking organization. Repeatable processes and prescriptive solutions only serve to maintain static ways of doing business. Scripted approaches restrict operational business agility. They also limit creativity, lower esteem and generally dumb down people's real capabilities.

Processes cannot deliver cutting-edge goods in a fast-changing business world. We would be better equipping our staff with an up-to-date electronic tool kit, streetwise training, and a clear set of objectives and standards. Allowed to improvise, employees can exceed customer expectations by continuously transforming the quality of our services. There will be risks and mistakes, of course. But that's inevitable whenever you allow any level of experimentation.

It's important to be aware of a number of qualifications regarding process-based design. Automation is a good example. It's instinctive for engineers to design and build fixed, deterministic manufacturing processes. And we will naturally tend to shape our business processes around these. But it's also possible to design process-free information systems using expressive system techniques. We'll cover that in the next section.

Some products, like pharmaceutical products, also demand a carefully controlled manufacturing process. Otherwise people might be harmed. They are perhaps exceptions. And liability is also a major concern for many companies that might consider encouraging empowered, process-free experimentation. But we shouldn't allow these constraints to inhibit creative innovation, and the use of tool-kits, rather than scripts. Many business services are repetitive, but that's largely by design rather than customer requirements. All workers can improvise and add greater value if empowered, but our governance structures would also have to be revolutionized.

Though, to promote radical changes to long-standing institutions is akin to heresy. The world is not yet ready for the change. As Pope Pius XII was once heard to say:

'One Galileo in two thousand years is enough.'

The power of expressive systems

In fact, it's perfectly possible to design entirely script-free business processes and information systems. The only barrier is that we don't know how, so we therefore never try. But it can be done, if only we would believe it, and convince our masters that such an achievement is possible.

Unfortunately the business world is far from ready for such a radical departure from their comfort zone. For some time to come, process will continue to be 'king' in the business, IT and security worlds.

It need not be so. Richard Pawson, a brilliant ex-CSC researcher, solved the problem many years ago. He developed a set of principles, and a methodology, called 'naked objects'. It's no less than a blueprint for designing operationally agile systems: systems that can accommodate changes, not only in their functionality, but in how a user interacts with them. Unfortunately it's not caught on, and it's unlikely to, at least in the short term.

Richard gives a couple of examples to explain how existing approaches to information systems design lack the agility to adapt to individual customer requirements.

The first one is based on an occasion when he was attempting to book an airport limousine from a New York hotel. In this example he's asked repeated questions about his name, account number, hotel address, flight number contact details and other identifying information, only to be informed at the end of the dialogue that that all cars were booked for that day. This example shows the weakness of scripts. A single question and database check at the start of the dialogue could have established the situation. But the system was designed around an inflexible script.

The second example is more interesting. It's about the difficulty of arranging a business tour of several European countries. The traveller might have some flexibility around the departure and return dates and times but he might wish to be in specific cities on certain dates, or have a preference for certain hotels and airlines. The problem is how to optimize the arrangements for such a trip over the Internet. The answer is that you can't. All travel booking systems are based on the assumption that you have a clear idea when you wish to start the trip and how you wish to proceed, step by step. They are not designed to cope with journeys that have flexibility and gaps in the schedule.

Richard has developed an approach that gets around these limitations. It's a very simple, but powerful approach based on established IT practices, but with a different design perspective. The first key principle is to follow best practices for object-oriented design, for example, rules such as 'nouns first, verbs second'. (Interestingly, you need the opposite approach for process models.) The second key point is to present the main objects to the user in a simple interface that enables relationships between objects to be created through dragging and dropping links. In practice, that means just presenting the 'naked' objects on a screen, without the need for a user interface or input script. This approach not only enables operational agility, it also saves development time.

The key learning point is that deterministic processes are part of the management problem. The smart solution lies in the design of operationally agile information systems. But it's doubtful that the business world is ready for such advanced concepts.

Emergent behaviour

Emergence refers to the way seemingly complex systems and patterns of behaviour can arise from a large number of simple interactions across a networked system. It's a fascinating subject area, demonstrating that it's possible to build networks where the whole might be much more than simply the sum of the parts.

Nature is full of emergent phenomena. We often see swarms of bees, colonies of ants or flocks of birds behaving in a magical, seemingly orchestrated way, though in reality they have little more than a few simple rules to guide their behaviour. In fact, the emergent structures we observe are not created by a single event or rule. The key is in the interaction of each part with its immediate surroundings.

Emergence has several points of interest to security managers. Firstly, it helps us to understand how large networks of simple components might behave collectively. And that can help us to understand, anticipate, and perhaps manage, emergent patterns of behaviour.

Secondly we might consider whether we can actually create useful behavioural patterns across large networks, based on simple sets of rules for relatively dumb network elements. Research in these areas is in a very early stage but it will become increasingly important with the relentless fragmentation of technology into larger and larger networks of smaller components.

Over the past 50 years, for example, we've gone from single mainframes to networks of minicomputers, then microcomputers, laptops, PDAs and personal area networks. The future offers large-scale networks of miniature components based on nanotechnology. Managing 'smart dust' might well be the challenge for the future security manager.

Why innovation is important

Information security is a constantly changing challenge, reflecting a business environment characterized by new threats, new technologies, exposures and increasing business dependency. Existing security countermeasures have a limited shelf life, demanding continuous improvement and innovation.

As Bruce Schneier commented in a recent interview with me:

> *'Somehow we seem to muddle through.'*

And that's certainly been the case so far. We've managed to survive through new threats such as computer viruses, network worms, phishing, and denial-of-service attacks. Some enterprises and individuals have been hit hard by these threats, and many are not coping as effectively as they should. But we've not yet experienced a real, global crisis. Such good fortune might not last indefinitely, however. Sooner or later, there is a good chance that we will face a level of security threat that we are unable to counter with the tools at our disposal.

Creativity and innovation are the keys to our long-term survival. Without it we might have to scale back our ambitions for greater external connectivity and mobility. And the answers are not something we can leave to governments, academia or vendors, because their response cycles to new problems are generally far too long. Industry will have to address new problems in real time. That means, amongst other things, developing a good antenna for emerging risks and becoming sufficiently agile, responsive and innovative to conceive and build imaginative new defences when old solutions begin to break down.

What is innovation?

Many organizations aspire to be innovative, but few manage to achieve it. Part of the problem is that most people have the wrong ideas about innovation. They think it's some form of secret sauce, a magic recipe that involves special people working in a novel way within a different environment. Nothing could be further from the truth. Innovation is a simple, teachable skill, coupled with a straightforward process that's easy to implement in any situation.

The other part of the problem is that organizations rarely make a serious effort to implement innovation. It's often little more than a token gesture, such as setting up a small function, an innovation lab, an ad hoc program, or a special budget set aside for the purpose. But that's not the best way to go about innovation. To be successful it needs to be embedded in mainstream business activities.

So what is innovation? Innovation is concerned with conceiving and introducing improvements to business products and processes. But it's more than just a quality circle that constantly seeks to find slightly better ways of doing things that might delight customers. Innovation suggests a more radical, creative type of change, one that makes a much bigger difference.

Innovation demands creativity and invention, but it's more than that. It's also about applying the breakthroughs that arise from such thinking, and realizing the business benefits. Innovation is about applied creativity.

Many people have aimed to identify the secret of creativity and innovation. Some believe it's about recruiting a special kind of person, one who's perhaps a little bit quirky, who appears to think, dress and act differently. A creative person, who dresses in black, wears an earring and uses an Apple computer.

Others believe it's about developing a new form of process, one that's not constrained by existing culture, that's allowed to operate outside the normal rules, perhaps bypassing project management standards, procurement policy or investment criteria.

Another viewpoint is that it's about a change in culture or attitude: getting people to be more imaginative or experimental in their day jobs. I've heard many senior directors suggest, for example, that they'd like to persuade their staff to be more innovative. But they don't know how to go about it.

Environments are another popular solution. The Royal Mail Group Innovation Lab is perhaps the most mature example. Many others have come and gone, as management fashions change. There used to be an interesting one at IBM in London, but it's long gone. I've also just visited a nice one at Atkins Group. At the height of the dot com boom, many start-up technology businesses introduced pool tables and other games into the work environment to create a different mood. But few experiments have stood the test of time. Creative environments, however, certainly do help to shape team behaviour and they can encourage people to be more adventurous.

Some people also believe that it's more about management, having, for example, a demanding managing director who constantly challenges his managers to come up with something better. The classic example of this was famous story of the Sony chief, who when ever he was presented with a new prototype product in his office, was reported to bring out a hammer, smash it into pieces, pick up one of the pieces and then demand:

'Bring it back to me when it's that size.'

A further claim is that it's all down to making money available to fund new ideas and projects. Innovation funds are an excellent idea, of course. They ensure that a certain amount of money is set aside for new ideas. The problem is demonstrating their value. Not every good idea can be translated into business value, and the more adventurous the idea, the less likely it is to come off.

But none of these things are either necessary or sufficient to achieve innovation. As I often point out to my colleagues:

'Innovation is no more than two very simple things:

(a) encouraging people to look at things from a fresh perspective, and
(b) establishing a process to collect and address the ideas generated.'

And these two things are very easy to implement, though in practice they are rarely grasped by managers. Perhaps they are expecting to discover a more complex, colourful or sophisticated solution?

What inspires people to create?

I'm very privileged to have a wonderful friend and music tutor, Michael Moore, who is an exceptional jazz musician. For many years he's been playing with Dave Brubeck, a wonderful composer who has never ceased to produce brilliant, original ideas.

I once asked Michael how it was that Dave could be so productive, when so many others with equal or better knowledge of music, seem so stuck for ideas. Michael replied:

> *'He just has something inside him that wants to come out. The rest of us don't have that.'*

Everybody is different. Some people have lots of ideas waiting to come out. Others prefer simply to listen and observe. And some people experience 'writer's block' whenever they sit in front of keyboard.

In the security field we often see a similar phenomenon with risk management enthusiasts. Some will spend many years designing, programming and refining multi-dimensional structures that set out every permutation of security threats, impacts and controls. Such people are valuable assets in the right role. They'd be ideal, for example, working for a vendor of security products. But they can be dangerous in a user organization. They might spend too much time and budget developing an original, bespoke framework, when existing solutions are already available. Worse, they may move on to a new job, leaving less enthusiastic colleagues the task of maintaining their legacy. Sometimes creativity can work for you, but it can also work against you.

Just one idea is enough

You don't need to be a prolific, creative composer to think of a better way of doing something. Just one simple good idea, once in a while, is all that is needed to fuel the process of innovation. Anybody and everybody can do that. And the more people that try, the greater the odds of success.

At Eli Lilly's UK research centre in Surrey, there is a transparent container filled with hundreds of white balls and a solitary coloured one. 'What's that all about?' I enquired when I saw this. 'That represents the single breakthrough idea that we strive for in the pharmaceutical industry,' was the reply.

In some industries a single idea or discovery can be the difference between success and failure. And this might be increasingly so for new intellectual products in a global, networked consumer market, where production costs are insignificant, distribution instantaneous and free, and the market size only limited by your ambition.

Creativity can sometimes be a percentage game. The more lines you follow, the greater your chance of a breakthrough product. The ultimate leverage is to open up your search to other Internet users. Interestingly, Eli Lilly are already doing that. They are moving from being a fully integrated pharmaceutical company to a fully integrated pharmaceutical network, advertising research topics on the Internet.

Increasing the numbers of researchers is one way of improving your chances. But it's clear that some people are better than others at generating a new idea. What is their secret? Can we identify a formula that can be harnessed by others?

The art of creative thinking

Surprisingly, there is no agreed definition of creativity. Dozens of them can be found in psychological literature. It seems likely therefore that there might be more than one type of creativity.

Arthur Koestler, the author and polymath, believed there were three types of creative individual: the artist, the sage and the jester. We can recognize these profiles in many people within our organization. They add different types of value. Koestler also developed the concept of bisociation, the concept that creativity arises as a result of the intersection of two quite different frames of reference. I've certainly experienced that.

Behind every successful advertising campaign, for example, is a two-person creative team consisting of two individuals, an artist, who creates the images, and a copywriter, who composes the messages. It's often the combination of entirely different perspectives that does the trick.

For several years I drew on the services of a professional creative team to help me design security awareness campaigns for Shell. They were excellent value. It was fascinating to watch them at work. They didn't sit back and wait for inspiration to hit them. They followed a simple, logical methodology, the same as any good systems developer would employ.

The starting point was to establish the message that needs to be put across, and to define the audience that needs to receive it. The next step was then to consider every possible means of conveying this message. The creative team would spend a day or two methodically trawling through books, images and subjects, short-listing possible ideas and refining them until they had a shortlist of good ideas. Then they would draw up a selection of proposals for the client to inspect.

They never failed to deliver imaginative, original concepts. But what was most striking for me was the logical, methodical approach employed: disciplined and thorough, rather than haphazard and inspirational.

It's a process that all of us can apply. But in practice we simply don't devote enough of our own time to such disciplined exercises. That's why we're so impressed with the work of the professionals.

Yes, you can

Professor Denis Sherwood, a Sloan Fellow of the London Business School, is an expert on innovation. He's highly critical of the so-called experts that suggest that creativity is something you're born with and can be tested with simple questions such as 'How many uses can you think of for a brick?'

The reason most of us can't do this exercise well is not because of any innate lack of creativity, but because our thinking is constrained by imagining the conventional, physical uses of a brick. And that's a reasonable starting assumption. It might well be the case that the people who can rattle off dozens of uses of bricks are those that have encountered the exercise before, rather than the ones that are naturally creative.

There is, in fact, a simple technique to generating more ideas for how to use an everyday object such as a brick. The trick is to think about the features of the object: its size, shape, texture, weight, and so on. And then think of alternative uses for each feature. If it's heavy, you can use it as paperweight. If it's rough you can use it as a loofah. If it's a consistent size you can use it as a measure.

Many of us also have a mental barrier when it comes to drawing. Given a pencil and paper, few of us can produce a decent drawing of a person, object or scene. But it's not because we don't possess the dexterity. Anyone who can sign their name in joined-up handwriting has the necessary skill.

It's because of the way we perceive things. The left-hand side of our brain has a tendency to take over the operation. It seems to prefer to work on symbols. So it decides to replace the object we see with one of its symbols. It's a natural reaction. That's why children always draw little rays around the sun when there aren't any. That's why they draw symmetrical, square houses with triangular roofs when few houses actually look like that. They are drawing the symbol in their mind, rather than the view that they see.

Again, there is a simple technique to overcome the problem. The trick is to try not to recognize the object. You might, for example, turn your view of the object upside down. Try that with a photograph for example. It works a treat. Alternatively you might imagine a frame around the outside of the scene and focus on the spaces and shapes between the object and the frame. It's counter-intuitive, but the fact is that's much easier to draw things that you don't recognize. In fact, using techniques like the ones described we can all begin to draw like Michelangelo.

Creativity is always much simpler than we'd expect to find. In fact, simplicity should be its goal. As Charlie Mingus, a great jazz musician, once put it:

> *'Anyone can make the simple complicated. Creativity is making the complicated simple.'*

Outside the box

Innovation is about seeing things differently, from a fresh perspective. And it's not that difficult. We all have the basic skills to think of new ideas. They're essential for our survival. We just need to overcome our natural constraint to see and think strictly on familiar lines.

Figure 11.1   Join all of the dots using four straight lines

Denis Sherwood has a simple puzzle for illustrating this point. Many of you will be familiar with this but will have probably forgotten the solution. The challenge is to imagine a square formed from a three-by-three matrix of dots, as illustrated in Figure 11.1. What you have to do is work out how to connect the dots using four connected straight lines, without the pen leaving the paper.

Few people can get the answer without some help. But it's very easy when you've seen the answer.

The trick is to draw lines that extend beyond the constraints of the square. In this case, you draw a line that runs south east from the top left hand dot to the bottom right hand dot. Then you switch direction, drawing a line that runs due north, joining the right hand side dots and extending slightly beyond the box. Then you switch direction south west drawing a line that joins the dot in the middle of the top row to the dot in the middle of the right hand side column. Again you need to extend the line outside the box, until it is level with the bottom row of dots. The final line is due east joining the bottom row of dots.

'Of course!' we immediately respond when we're shown that solution, 'We need to think outside the box'.

But we can take this puzzle much further than that. The next challenge is to find as many possible different solutions as possible. It seems hard until you spot that there are at least four ways of drawing the lines for the standard solution.

Then there are the more radical options. There are numerous ways of joining the dots with four lines if you cut, fold or bend the paper. It might seem like cheating. But nobody said you couldn't do it.

And the really interesting challenge is to imagine how it could be done with three, rather than four straight lines. 'Impossible' many would say. But it's quite easy if you draw thick dots and stretch the lines a long way outside the box. You can do it with three near-horizontal, angled lines that just touch the top of the dots at one side of the square and the bottom of the other side of the square.

It's all very simple once you've seen it done. And hopefully a good illustration that you can come up with a lot more alternatives than you might imagine by looking at the solutions from a fresh perspective. Think of solutions that extend outside of the box. Think of ways of changing the basic structure of the problem definition. Think of solutions on a different scale to the problem space. Creative solutions are not that difficult.

Innovation environments

We saw in Chapter 8 that environments can help shape behaviour. Can they help us to achieve the innovation we seek?

Certainly, they are helpful. That's been the experience of organizations such as the Royal Mail Group, who've maintained a professionally staffed, innovation lab for more than a decade. But innovative labs are much more than a vehicle for creativity and innovation. They're also an excellent environment for any business meeting or workshop, where people need to come together to discuss, agree and plan a collective program of action.

Creative environments are different from normal day-to-day office surroundings. They are informal, with a sense of fun and play, encouraging experimentation and discovery. They encourage people to take a different perspective. Innovation labs also serve as a vehicle for providing people with the time and space needed to think through new business ideas, and the tools and facilitators to capture and structure ideas in the most efficient way. Creativity is a chaotic process. To turn raw ideas into business initiatives requires a structured approach, and professional facilitation.

Innovation environments are highly effective for developing strategies and plans. But they're neither essential nor sufficient to guarantee innovation. People can think of a great idea sitting alone on the top of a mountain, when having a shower, or when driving a car. A creative environment, however, provides the cues for adopting a different, less formal style of behaviour. It also removes the conformity of the normal environment that might act as a blocker to alternative styles of thinking and acting.

Turning ideas into action

It's surprisingly straightforward to turn ideas into action. The problem is that most organizations don't bother to do this, or if they do, they tend to go about it the wrong way.

The starting point is to encourage staff to look at things from a fresh perspective and get them to communicate their ideas in a form that can easily be collected and assessed. But it's important to respond consistently to ideas from staff. Many organizations discourage innovation by ignoring suggestions from staff. And once a person has been ignored two or three times when promoting a good idea, they're unlikely to suggest any further ideas.

Quality circles are a useful process for this, but they tend to focus on incremental improvements, rather than the innovative ideas we need to meet the inescapable challenges of the future. Jotting down ideas on cards is an excellent, simple method that can be encouraged at team meetings. It's been used successfully by large companies such as Exxon to stimulate the creative process. But the most important consideration is to allow people to generate ideas in the way that suits them the best.

Assuming we are able to generate sufficient good ideas, the next challenge is to identify the best ones and do something with them. This requires a new, but very simple process to scan all suggestions, assess if they're useful and feasible, and then turn them into initiatives. The original idea might not itself be viable but it might prompt one that is. This is often the case for some of the better ideas, so it will pay to apply some imagination during the sifting process.

Taking a radical idea forward is often a difficult challenge for an organization that is risk averse or has strict investment appraisal criteria. You need to think like an early-stage venture capitalist to get such ideas off the ground. Innovations that offer very high returns often include very high risks. Similarly a high-risk proposal should not be taken forward unless it can deliver a high return. It's a percentage play. Perhaps only one in five such innovations will succeed. You should therefore be looking for a return that is an order of magnitude higher than the investment cost.

It's also important to manage high-risk proposals with the ruthless approach of a venture capitalist. Share the risks with other stakeholders. Assign good management. Provide the necessary infrastructure. Monitor performance carefully. And don't be afraid to pull the plug if it's not working out.

Steps to innovation heaven

Introducing innovation is not a difficult process but, as with anything that involves people, it's often better to introduce the process in simple steps. We applied the same consideration in Chapter 10 when we considered levels of process maturity.

Rolf Smith, a former Colonel in the United States Air Force and the founder of their first innovation centre, recommends seven levels of change, of increasing ambition, moving progressively from effective and efficient thinking towards lateral and imaginative thinking:

- Do the right things
- Do things right
- Do things better
- Do away with things
- Do things other people are doing
- Do things that haven't been done
- Do things that can't be done

This approach has the benefit of enabling quick wins from simple, easy actions, and then providing a new dimension at each new stage to keep some novelty and interest in the innovation process. His book *The 7 Levels of Change* is an excellent source of practical tips that can be applied at each stage.

Howard Wright, former Head of Innovation at the Royal Mail Group and Director of Futures Strategy at Pitney Bowes, has also developed a practical, 10-step framework for planning and implementing successful innovation projects. His book *Ten Steps to Innovation Heaven* provides a step-by-step guide based on the experience of an expert with more than a decade of professional experience.

The road ahead

In the security world, one thing is absolutely certain: the future will bring bigger risks, greater business dependency and substantial changes to the way we manage security. Tomorrow's business, technology and security landscapes will be more challenging, with faster product cycles, volatile business partnerships, more complex supply chains and new technologies that will introduce new sources of risk.

Increasingly, we will have to learn to look forwards and understand the future better to manage today's challenges. This needs to form part of our corporate consciousness. We need more than just a perspective of the past. Just as the White Queen says to Alice, in Lewis Carroll's *Through the Looking-Glass*:

'It's a poor sort of memory that only works backwards.'

All organizations need to build an awareness of future trends and risks because many of today's security solutions are simply not scalable or appropriate for a future landscape of highly networked, mobile business operations across organizational boundaries. We need to extrapolate our appreciation of the business environment into the future, in order to prepare for these emerging challenges.

But can we predict the future? The answer is 'yes', we can, but only to a certain extent. We can, for example, anticipate many of the emerging trends, technologies and issues that are coming our way, though we can't always foresee precisely how or when they will unfold. In fact, the only thing that's truly guaranteed is that the future will be different. As the author Jorge Luis Borges put it:

'We know only one thing about the future or, rather, the futures: it will not look like the present.'

But we can already see many emerging trends. The impact of the Information Age has been extensively researched by authors such as Alvin Toffler. We can also gain some insight into the potential impact of the Internet from studying the impact of previous infrastructure changes, such as electricity or railways. We can conduct road-mapping and scenario planning exercises to explore the impact of key drivers, trends and events. And most of the technology products that are likely to emerge over the next decade will be sitting somewhere in today's research labs. That's because it takes a decade to develop, fund, productize and market any new technology.

But trends often take longer to emerge than you think. As Bill Gates correctly put it in his 1995 book *The Road Ahead*:

> *'People often overestimate what will happen in the next two years and underestimate what will happen in ten.'*

There are many factors at play that affect our judgments about the future. Vendor hype about a new product tends to grow much faster than the real-life uptake. Gartner Group's famous 'hype curve' plots the ups and downs in the visibility of a new product or solution, as its passes through the 'peak of inflated expectations' followed by the 'trough of disillusionment' before we see the slow rise in the 'slope of enlightenment' followed by the steady 'plateau of productivity'. In fact many technology trends do not follow straight lines. Network effects can cause dramatic changes, perhaps following exponential curves that take off slowly at first, but then accelerate very rapidly.

There are also many relative certainties for trends over the next 10 to 15 years. For example, the US National Intelligence Council's global scenarios for 2020 set out in their publication *Mapping the Global Future* contains a list of 'given assumptions', such as the world economy becoming substantially larger, the rise of China, increased environmental awareness, an aging population in the West and several other trends. Over the next two decades we can also anticipate the development of quantum computers, as well as the occurrence of a global pandemic.

Even better, of course, is for us to take some action ourselves to shape trends and events in the way we desire. As the technologist Alan Kay once put it:

> *'The best way to predict the future is to invent it.'*

But to do that we first need to gain a better insight into how trends and technologies might unfold. The best starting point for that is to assemble a group of experts and take a dump of their brains. That's a process we call 'technology road mapping'.

Mapping the future

As the author William Gibson once put it:

> *'The future is already here, it's just not evenly distributed.'*

That's generally correct. It can take many years for new ideas to spread. We can say the same thing about our knowledge of the future. Everyone has a few pieces of the jigsaw. We just need to assemble them, understand the implications of bringing them together and fill in the gaps with some educated guesswork.

As Donald Rumsfield once put it:

> *'There are known knowns. These are things we know that we know. There are known unknowns. That is to say, there are things that we know we don't know. But there are also unknown unknowns. There are things we don't know we don't know.'*

We can't do much about the 'unknown unknowns'. But we can do something about the 'unknown knowns', the things we'd like to know, but don't actually know that we know. By bringing people together in a creative planning exercise we can capture knowledge that has been hidden away in people's heads. The most effective method for this is technology road mapping.

It's a process that varies with each application. You can shape the process and the tools to fit the problem. The power of technology road mapping is in the assembly of numerous individual judgments and pieces of information, the analysis of the connections and dependencies between them, and the establishment of a consensus view of the resulting events, trends and timelines.

Figure 11.2 shows an example of the structure of a technology road map. The key is to develop each layer in turn, starting from the top with the process of identifying and agreeing the time line for major drivers and events, perhaps based on a PESTLE analysis, as suggested in Chapter 4 as a technique for categorizing risks. The middle section can then be developed by considering the impacts and the capabilities needed to respond to these drivers. The final, bottom row of the map will be the research, the developments and the potential solutions that we will need to deliver the identified response.

In practice, every technology road map is different in presentation, tailored to meet the particular requirements of the users. I've conducted many exercises with teams of information security professionals from all over the world,

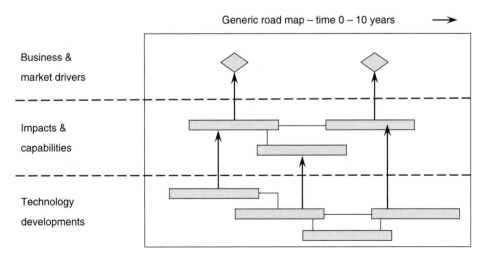

Figure 11.2   Example of a technology road map framework

including the UK Information Assurance Advisory Council, the International Information Integrity Institute and the Jericho Forum. Each provides a unique insight. But the most striking discovery is just how much consensus there is amongst professional security managers about the future of information security.

Learning to harness the power of the organization

So what have we learned in this chapter? We set out to explore how to exploit the power of networks to leverage the power of our central initiatives and encourage security innovation across the organization.

We found that networks are as dangerous as they are useful, and they offer almost unlimited power to amplify our skills, resources, speed of response and defensive capability. When faced with threats, there are many different survival strategies, but it's generally better to reach out, rather than retreat inside a shell.

We noted that people are the greatest asset to security. The key to greater effectiveness is to work smarter, not harder, by getting others to help you. Leverage is the key to successful security campaigns across large populations, especially ones carried out by small functions. Levers come in all shapes and sizes: networks, technology, fashion, company staff, customers, communities and the media are all potential levers.

Systems thinking is an essential tool for gaining a perspective of the whole of a system rather than its individual components. We should also aim to create and harness virtuous circles, positive feedback loops that amplify desirable behaviour.

Tipping points, the point at which an idea rapidly spreads and becomes unstoppable, are often caused by small things, the actions of a small number of key people, the small details that make an idea stick, and the context created by the environment and circumstances. Small details can act as cues to stimulate and propagate a particular behaviour.

To encourage a tipping point for a security message, we need to pay close attention to the fine details of the message and its context, and identify key players in the community who can act as connectors, advisers or salesmen. We can learn a lot from examples of large-scale change, such as the role and impact of the 'broken window' theory in reducing crime in New York City.

Networks are equally useful for leveraging the ideas of a single, empowered individual or for leveraging the common goal of a networked community. Collective group behaviour can sometime beat the judgment of individuals, but not every time. Diversity often underpins good collective decision-making.

Open source software development illustrates the power of social networks to construct powerful systems and products. It can be a powerful lever for your own resources, but it requires you to align their requirements with those of a larger community. In fact, social networks can solve just about any problem if they can be harnessed in the right way.

Complexity is an inevitable consequence of networks, the result of good things such as greater collaboration, increasing functionality, further outreach and centralization. It offers as many opportunities as challenges. Simplicity is not necessarily the answer. It can help or hinder, depending on how you go about it. The best course of action is to embrace complexity rather than fight it. There are several techniques to tackle complexity, ranging from the use of data visualization techniques to the development of richer controlling mechanisms based on automation and networks.

We are slowly moving towards a more process-free world. Repeatable processes are an industrial age concept. Scripted approaches restrict business agility and they dumb down people's capabilities. They cannot deliver cutting-edge goods in a fast-changing business world. But the business world is a long way from being ready to accept and exploit process-free operations.

Innovation is vital in information security to meet the constantly changing challenges, presented by a business environment characterized by new threats, technologies, exposures and increasing business dependency. Security countermeasures have a limited shelf life, demanding continuous improvement and innovation.

Creativity and innovation are the keys to our long-term survival. Innovation is a simple, teachable skill and a straightforward process that's easy to implement. It's essentially about encouraging people to look at things from a fresh perspective, and establishing a process to collect and address the ideas generated. Just one idea is enough to set off a revolution. Anybody and everybody can do it, and the more people that try, the greater the odds of success.

Innovation environments can help by shaping behaviour and providing a focus to think through new ideas, supported by appropriate processes, tools and facilitation. But they're neither essential nor sufficient to guarantee innovation. In fact, it's easy to turn ideas into action if you put your mind to it. But innovations that offer high returns will also include high risks. That might demand a projected return that is an order of magnitude higher than the investment cost. Innovation is best introduced in stages, moving progressively from more effective and efficient thinking towards more lateral and imaginative thinking.

The future will bring greater risks, dependency and changes. Tomorrow's business, technology and security landscapes will be challenging, faster, volatile and complex. Many of today's solutions are not scalable or appropriate. We must therefore extend our understanding of the business environment into the future, to prepare for these challenges.

We can't accurately predict the future, but we can anticipate many of the emerging trends, technologies and issues. Technology road-mapping and scenario planning exercises can help us to identify and explore the impact of key drivers, trends and events. And we can see the future more clearly, and operate as a more powerful unit, if we take the trouble to bring people together in creative planning exercises. Each exercise delivers a unique insight, but they all enable professional security managers to share a common perspective about the future of information security.

Here are seven ways to harness the power of networks to leverage your information security efforts:

- Reach out for help and cooperation, rather than retreating inside your shell
- Always look for levers to amplify your efforts; otherwise they will never be enough
- Practice makes perfect: small enhancements can build tipping points
- The context for your actions will determine its impact
- Scale, not simplicity is the answer to complexity
- Innovation is easy; it's more about effort than cleverness
- The starting point is to harness the efforts of your own team

In conclusion

I hope you found this book interesting, educational and fun. I certainly enjoyed writing it. I intended it to be a practical book, a collection of many small pearls of wisdom, rather than a popular book that sets out to promote a single idea. In fact, we've addressed an immense subject area. Your mind will probably be spinning from the mass of theories, ideas and opinions that we've covered. I think it's helpful, therefore, to summarize some of the key points that we've covered and, hopefully, learned from.

We started out with the premise that networks are eroding our traditional approaches to security, cutting through boundaries, including those between personal and business lifestyles. Business and home life will never be the same again. Even politics will be transformed by the power of networks, which are no less than the new engine of wealth and power for this millennium.

But networks also provide a powerful lever for promoting ideas, policies and initiatives. And we need fresh inspiration and collaborative approaches to security, because the problem space is moving outside the corporate boundary. Networks will help us to build the new community solutions that we need to manage the challenges of the future.

The future will be much riskier than it is today. Knowledge bases and information flows will be under threat from more sophisticated spies and fraudsters, who might aim not only to trash them or steal them, but also to manipulate the contents to their advantage.

To meet this challenge, we need to harness the efforts of everyone in the corporation, as well as many people outside it, including our customers and business partners. Everybody counts in security, but in different ways. We therefore

Managing the Human Factor in Information Security   David Lacey
© 2009 John Wiley & Sons, Ltd

need rich, tailored security campaigns that are compelling to different types of people, working in very different contexts.

A good starting point is to understand the nature and root causes of the mass of security events, near misses and incidents that surround us. Visibility, of events, risks and operating practices, and an appreciation of their context, is the key to the prevention of future incidents. But looking backwards at historical incidents and trends is not always the most reliable portent of future events.

Mistakes can be lessened, but they can never be eliminated. Systems should therefore be designed with an appropriate margin for human error. We will also need to improve our incident response capability. Incidents today are more complex than they used to be. They demand a greater degree of improvisation. The process of incident response has become more important than the plan.

Crisis management is hard. It demands exceptional analysis, problem-solving and communication skills, and these skills need to be applied across corporate boundaries and networks. But major incidents, handled well, can present opportunities for business improvement, for example by creating a climate for change and generating free publicity. Companies who manage a crisis in the full glare of the media can actually boost their share price.

Risk management will always be a major challenge. It's an unusual blend of logic and feeling, with the latter dominating the former. And most people are bad at assessing risks. They have different perceptions, shaped by their personality, experience, culture and other influences. Risks can also trigger powerful emotions, even outrage.

Even the most sophisticated risk management system will not stop executives from gambling their assets away. Big stakes create vested interests and they can intimidate cautious people. It takes time to coach executives to manage risks. But ornate management frameworks rarely capture their imagination. It's much better to aim for a progressive increase in sophistication and process maturity.

Risk management is a decision support tool, not a decision-making process. It's a vast oversimplification of reality. You'd be unwise to base an important business decision on such a narrow set of data. And risks are not the only source of information security requirements. Other drivers include functional requirements, commercial considerations, corporate policy and legal requirements.

We also have to accept that not everybody is honest. Many people will cheat if they can avoid getting caught. Employees who commit fraud and espionage tend to fit a particular profile. But it's also one that coincides with that of highly effective managers. We can detect warning signs of insider threats. But experience has shown that identifying and acting on them is far from easy.

In fact, catching crooks after the event is not the only option. It's far better to design systems that are intrinsically secure. We can also vet new staff, monitor their actions and reduce incentives for corruption. But from an attacker's perspective, the human factor will always be the soft underbelly of business operations. People are easily fooled. And we are a long way from establishing foolproof identity management systems.

Understanding organization culture is not easy, especially if you're part of it. Much of it is the invisible madness that surrounds us: the unique perspective and peculiar habits to which we've become acclimatized. Recognizing this is the first step in developing a better security culture. We can build a security culture based on either fear or inspiration. But the latter is more effective. Fear and criticism will not get the best out of people. A healthy security culture is one where people understand the risks and take sensible precautions to avoid incidents.

To build an effective information security function, we need to take account of the skills available, the needs of the business, and the politics of the day. There is no single structure that will work best in all circumstances. And new structures rarely survive for long, because of frequent business restructuring. We also need to take account of the periodic 'pendulum swing' between centralization and devolution of political power.

Demands for technical skills come and go. Applied skills, such as project management are more enduring. But behavioural and cognitive skills are the most significant in the long term. And all practitioners require professional development. Luck won't do it, and ignorance can't. Unless we can buy or attract the best staff, we will need to invest in training and career development for our information security practitioners.

Relationship management is also a vital political skill. It's needed to gain support for security campaigns and business cases, as well as to maintain smooth business and security operations across a complex supply chain. To be successful, we need to take an interest in people, and to be pleasant and polite. Diplomacy, presentation, alignment with business aims and meeting investment appraisal criteria are the keys to achieving support.

We must also be aware of our limitations. We can't change everything or everyone at once. A good security campaign will focus on the highest priorities. People are bombarded with instructions and advice. We have to ensure that our security messages stand out by matching them to current business and personal issues, and by choosing images that will resonate. Professional support will help, and communications specialists are cheaper than information security consultants.

Changing people's attitude involves a personal journey. There are many techniques available, such as scenario planning, films, games and stories. Changing their behaviour is more complex. It requires manipulation of key enablers and blockers. The most powerful ones are the consequences that people expect from their actions, especially those that are personal, immediate and certain. But we also take many cues from the role we are given and the environment in which we work. Changing these will also have a significant impact.

To make a good business case, we need to present a compelling argument for change, and to align the benefits with business objectives and IT strategy. Saving money is important. But it's not the only way to demonstrate value. Metrics can sometimes help, but not everything is knowable or measurable. A more powerful deciding factor is the support of other parts of the organization. It will pay to collect such endorsements. But success in information security will also lead to 'security fatigue' from a lack of incidents. We need to anticipate this problem and adapt our arguments and forecasts accordingly.

Information security is a long-term journey. The starting point is to develop a clear vision of what needs to be achieved, and a strategy setting out how we intend to get there. Everybody needs a structure for their work, but it's important not to become distracted and lose sight of our real objectives. Frameworks and architectures are a means to an end, not an end themselves.

Good frameworks should be designed for future ease of maintenance. They can draw on a combination of prescriptive controls, risk assessments and classification schemes. There is no single, complete solution that fits all situations. But they cannot be both up-to-date and complete. The solution space always lags behind the problem space. My definition of a good, modern, security architecture is one that's 'ragged around the edges, full of holes and exists largely in the minds of practitioners'. It's much better that it's up-to-date and communicated, rather than complete.

Clear design principles help to ensure secure systems designs. The Jericho Forum principles are a good starting point. We also need to look beyond our own infrastructure, and focus on the requirements of the community, to adopt 'collaboration-oriented architectures'. Good, ergonomic design is also increasingly important as we rely more and more on the actions of individuals. We should talk a lot more to our users to better understand their culture, requirements, likes, dislikes and expectations. It's often small things that make the most difference. Small cues can be exploited to nudge people in the desired direction. In the IT world, default settings are the primary cues and nudges for users.

Social networks present many security risks. But they also offer huge potential power to amplify our skills, resources, speed of response and defensive capability. People are our greatest security asset and they can be reached through networks. We need to work smarter, not harder, by getting others to help us. Leverage is the key to successful security campaigns, whether through exploiting networks, technology, fashion, people or the media. We should aim to create virtuous circles to promote desirable behaviour. Tipping points can be triggered by relatively small changes, such as the actions of a few key people, an adjustment to people's roles and circumstances, or a small detail that helps to make an idea stick.

Networks can leverage the ideas of a single individual or the common goal of a networked community. The collective decisions of groups are sometimes, but not always, wiser than those of individuals. And diversity underpins good collective decision-making. Open source software illustrates the real power of social networks to build complex business solutions. It can be a powerful lever for your own resources, but it will require you to align your requirements with those of a larger community.

Complexity is an inevitable consequence of modern networks. It's not something that's all bad, as it's generally the result of many desirable goals, such as greater collaboration, functionality and outreach. Simplicity is not necessarily the answer. And it's generally better to embrace complexity, rather than fight it. Richer controlling mechanisms are the most effective solution.

Scripted, repeatable processes are an industrial age concept. They restrict business agility and they dumb down people's capabilities. But the business world is far from ready to exploit process-free operations, though we could build them if we wish.

Innovation is vital in information security, to meet new threats, technologies, exposures and the consequences of increasing business dependency on IT. Creativity and innovation are, in fact, based on quite simple skills and processes.

We just need to get our people to look at things from a fresh perspective, and to establish a simple process to collect and address their ideas

We can't predict the future, but we can anticipate many emerging trends, technologies and issues. Technology road mapping and scenario planning exercises can help us to identify and explore the impact of key drivers, trends and events. Such planning exercises also enable practitioners to pool knowledge and develop a common perspective of the future.

And however pessimistic you might be, it's worth remembering that the future is always a better place. In the long run we will be healthier, we'll live longer and most of us will be financially richer. We will also have a lot less privacy, and we'll be much less secure, unless we decide to do something about it by working together to develop and implement the ideas contained in this book. These trends are inevitable and irreversible. They are the way of the new information age.

Bibliography

Adams, Douglas, *The Hitchhikers Guide to the Galaxy*, Pan Books, 1979.

Adelson, Edward H., Lightness perception and lightness illusions, Chapter 24, in M. Gazzaniga (ed.), *The New Coognitive Neurosciences*, 2nd edn, MIT Press, 2000.

Allport, Gordon and Leo Joseph Postman, *The Psychology of Rumor*, Henry Holt, 1947.

Anderson, Chris, The long tail, *WIRED* Magazine, October 2004.

Anderson, Geraint, *Cityboy: Beer and Loathing in the Square Mile*, Headline Publishing, 2008.

Asch, Solomon E., Effects of group pressure upon the modification and distortion of judgment in H. Guetzkow (ed.), *Groups, Leadership and Men*, Carnegie Press, 1951.

Ashby, W. Ross, *An Introduction to Cybernetics*, Chapman & Hall, 1956.

Ashenden, Debi and Professor Angela Sasseon, *From Corporate Bully to Security Cheerleader: Transforming the Identity of the CISO*, submitted for New Security Paradigms Workshop, 2008.

Axelrod, Robert, *The Evolution of Cooperation*, Basic Books, 1984.

Beer, Stafford, *Platform for Change*, John Wiley & Sons, Inc., 1975.

Berners-Lee, Tim, *Web Architecture from 50,000 Feet*, 2002. URL: http://www.w3.org/DesignIssues/Architecture.html

Bernstein, Peter, *Against the Gods: The Remarkable Story of Risk*, John Wiley & Sons, Inc. 1996.

Bianconi, Ginestra and Albert-Lazlo Barabasi, Bose–Einstein condensation in complex networks, *Physical Review Letters*, June 11, 2001.

Borges, Jorge Luis Borges put it: We know only one thing about the future or, rather, the futures: it will not look like the present

Managing the Human Factor in Information Security   David Lacey
© 2009 John Wiley & Sons, Ltd

Cameron, Kit, *The Laws of Identity*. URL: http://www.identityblog.com

Carnegie, Dale, *How to Win Friends and Influence People*, Simon and Schuster, 1937.

Carroll, Lewis, *Through the Looking-Glass and What Alice Found There*, MacMillan, 1871.

Chatham, Robina and Keith, *Patching Corporate Politics for IT Managers*, Butterworth-Heinemann, 2000.

Clancy, Tom, *Clear and Present Danger*, Putnam, 1989.

Clarke, Arthur C., *Profiles of the Future: An Inquiry into the limits of the Possible* (rev. edn), Harper & Row, 1973.

Cornwall, Hugo, *The Hacker's Handbook*, E.A. Brown Co., 1986.

Crosby, Colin, *Data Handling Procedures in Government: Initial Report*, UK Cabinet Office, June 2008.

Deming, W. Edwards, *Out of the Crisis*, MIT Press, 1982.

Feynman, Richard, *What Do You Care What Other People Think?*, W.W. Norton, 1988.

Fogg, B.J., *Persuasive Technology*, Morgan Kaufmann, 2002.

Furnell, Steven M., Magklaras G.B. and Brooke P. J., *Towards an Insider Threat Prediction Specification Language Information Management & Computer Security*, Vol. **14**, no.4, 2006.

Furnell, Steven M., Making security usable: are things improving? *Computers and Security*, **26** (6), 2007.

Gates, Bill with Nathan Myhrvold and Peter Rinearson, *The Road Ahead*, Viking, 1995.

Gladwell, Malcolm, *The Tipping Point: How Little Things Can Make a Big Difference*, Little Brown, 2000.

Gladwell, Malcolm, *Blink: The Power of Thinking Without Thinking*, Back Bay Books, Little Brown, 2005.

Heath, Chip and Dan, *Made to Stick*, Random House, 2007.

Heinrich, Herbert William, *Industrial Accident Prevention, A Scientific Approach*, McGraw Hill, 1932.

Howe, Jeff, The rise of crowdsourcing, *WIRED* Magazine, June 2006.

Humphrey, Watts, *Managing the Software Process*, Addison-Wesley Professional, 1989.

ISO/IEC 27000 Series of Information Security Management Systems (ISMS) Family of Standards

Jung, Carl, *Psychological Types Collected Works of C.G. Jung*, Vol. **6**, Princeton University Press, 1971.

Kahneman, Daniel and Amos Tversky, Prospect theory: an analysis of decision under risk, *Econometrica*, **XLVII**, 1979.

Knight, Frank H., *Risk, Uncertainty and Profit*, Houghton Mifflin, 1921.

Knight, Rory F. and Deborah J. Pretty, *Reputation and Value: The Case of Corporate Catastrophes*, Oxford Metrica Press, 2001.

Koestler, Arthur, *The Act of Creation*, Hutchinson, 1964.

Kotler, Philip, *According to Koetler*, AMACOM, 2005.

KPMG, *Profile of a Fraudster Survey*, 2007. URL: http://www.kpmg.co.uk/pubs/ProfileofaFraudsterSurvey(web).pdf

Levy, Steven, *Hackers: Heroes of the Computer Revolution*, Doubleday, 1984.

Mackay, Charles, *Extraordinary Popular Delusions and the Madness of Crowds*, 1841.

Maslow, A.H., A theory of human motivation, *Psychology Review*, **50**, 1943.

Herzberg, Frederick I., One more time, how do you motivate employees? *Harvard Business Review*, **65** (5), Sep/Oct, 1987.

Kirsner, Scott, The legend of Bob Metcalfe, *WIRED* Magazine, Nov 1998.

Kahane, Adam, The Mont Fleur scenarios: What will South Africa be like in the year 2002? *Deeper News*, **7** (1), Global Business Network URL: http://www.generonconsulting.com/publications/papers/pdfs/Mont%20Fleur.pdf

McAfee, Andrew P., Enterprise 2.0: The dawn of emergent collaboration, *MITSloan Management Review*, **47** (3), Spring, 2006.

Macgregor, Douglas, *The Human Side of Enterprise*, McGraw-Hill, 1960.

Measham, Jon, *Value-Less Security*, Consignia. URL http://www.opengroup.org/projects/jericho/uploads/40/5368/Value-Less_Security_v3.pdf

Milgram, Stanley, *Obedience to Authority: An Experimental View*, Harper & Row, 1974.

Milgram, Stanley, The small world problem, *Psychology Today*, **2**, 1967.

Miniter, Richard, *Disinformation: 22 Media Myths That Undermine the War on Terror*, Regnery Publishing, 2006.

Mitchell, Professor William, *e-topia*, MIT Press, 1999.

Myers, Isabel Briggs, McCaulley, Mary H., Quenk, Naomi L. and Hammer, Allen L., *MBTI Manual (A guide to the development and use of the Myers Briggs type indicator)*, Consulting Psychologists Press, 1998.

Parker, Donn B., *Fighting Computer Crime*, John Wiley & Sons, Inc., 1998.

Pawson, Richard, *Naked Objects*, John Wiley & Sons, Inc., 2002.

Pirsig, Robert, *Zen and the Art of Motorcycle Maintenance*, William Morrow, 1974.

Pretty, Deborah, *Catastrophes, Reputation and Shareholder Value*, IMC Seminars September 2000, URL: http://www.imc-seminars.com/uploads/papers/Deborah%20Pretty.ppt#400,1,Catastrophes, Reputation and Shareholder Value.

Reason, James T., *Human Error*, Cambridge University Press, 1990.

Reed, David P., *That Sneaky Exponential – Beyond Metcalfe's Law to the Power of Community Building*, URL: http://www.reed.com/gfn/docs/reedslaw.html

Ropeik, David and Gray, George, *Risk: A Practical Guide for Deciding What's Really Safe and What's Really Dangerous in the World Around You*, Houghton Miffin, 2002.

Sandman, Peter M., *Responding to Community Outrage: Strategies for Effective Risk Communication*, American Industrial Hygiene Association, 1993.

Schneier, Bruce, *Beyond Fear*, Copernicus Books, 2003.

Schumacher, E.F., *Small is Beautiful: A Study of Economics as if People Mattered*, Abacus, 1974.

Sherwood, Dennis, *Smart Things to Know About Innovation and Creativity*, Capstone Publishing, 2001.

Shirky, Clay, *Here Comes Everybody: The Power of Organizing Without Organizations*, Allen Lane, 2008.

Sloan, Robin and Matt Thompson, *EPIC 2014*, 2004. URL http://www.robinsloan.com/epic/

Smith, Rolf, *The 7 Levels of Change*, The Summit Publishing Group, 1997.

Suler, John, *The Psychology of Cyberspace*. URL: http://www-usr.rider.edu/~suler/psycyber/psycyber.html

Surowiecki, James, *The Wisdom of Crowds: Why the Many are Smarter Than the Few and How Collective Wisdom Shapes Businesses, Economies, Societies and Nations*, Little Brown, 2004.

Taleb, Nassim Nicholas, *The Black Swan: The Impact of the Highly Improbable*, Random House, 2007.

Tapscott, Don and Anthony Williams, *Wikinomics: How Mass Collaboration Changes Everything*, Atlantic Books, 2007.

Thaler, Richard and Cass Sunstein, *Nudge: Improving Decisions about Health, Wealth, and Happiness*, Yale University Press, 2008.

The Jericho Forum, *Commandments and Collaboration-Oriented Architectures*. URL: http://www.opengroup.org/jericho/

Toffler, Alvin, *The Third Wave*, Bantam Books, 1980.

Toffler, Alvin and Heidi, *Creating a New Civilization*, Turner Publishing. 1995.

US National Intelligence Council, *Mapping the Global Future: Report of the National Intelligence Council's 2020 Project*. URL: http://www.dni.gov/nic/NIC_2020_project.html

West, Matthew, *An Introduction to 4 Dimensionalism in Data Modelling*, Presented to the School of Computing, Leeds University, 2007. URL: http://www.matthew-west.org.uk/Documents/AnIntroductionTo4DimensionalismInData-Models.pdf

Wilson, James Q. and George L. Kelling, Broken windows, *The Atlantic Monthly*, March 1982.

Wright, Howard, *Ten Steps to Innovation Heaven*, Cyan Communications, 2007.

Zachman, John, A framework for information systems architecture, *IBM Systems Journal*, **26** (3), 1987.

Zimbardo, Philip G., *Stanford Prison Experiment: A Simulation Study of the Psychology of Imprisonment*, Stanford University, 1972.

Index

3Com 10
3G mobile phones 95
5Ws (and one H) 223, 296–7
6Ps, social networks 223–4
9/11 terrorist attacks 87, 102, 109–10
42 answer 103
Abagnale, Frank, Jr 160
access control systems 16, 145, 150–1
accidents waiting to happen 48–51
    see also incidents
accounting aspects, information
        security 42
accredited certification schemes 287–8,
        304–5, 309–10
action plans, ideas 339–40
actuarial science 115
    see also insurance
Adams, Douglas 103
address books, hijacks 12
Adelson's Illusion 103–4
advertising
    beneficial aspects of incidents 48, 72
    maxims 220
age factors, risk appetites 95, 193
alcohol effects 95–6, 145
Allport, Gordon 26
Amazon 5, 9
Amdahl, Gene 28
Ames, Aldrich 134, 152
Anderson, Chris 3

Anderson, Geraint 184
anti-social personality disorder 157–8
anticipation benefits
    incidents 73–5, 83–4, 109–10, 150–1,
        243–4
    opportunities 74–5
Apple 17, 141, 227
Archimedes 313–14
architectures 20–1, 223, 290, 292–310, 327,
        350–1
    see also frameworks; IT...
Arthur, Brian 8–9
artificial trust 173
Ash, Solomon 136
Ashby' Law of Requisite Variety 327–9
Ashenden, Debi 202
Asians, diversity considerations 206–7
ASIS 139
assets
    see also intellectual...; staff
    irreplaceable assets 63
Atkins Group 334
attacks 25, 36–7, 50–1, 60–1, 121–5, 214,
        348–51
    see also incidents; risk...
attitudes 71–5, 78, 82–4, 183–210, 211–36,
        237–53, 316–18, 320–1
    see also cultures
attribution theory 248
Auden, W.H. 238

Managing the Human Factor in Information Security   David Lacey
© 2009 John Wiley & Sons, Ltd

Indexed by Terry Halliday.